Arne Hintz

Civil Society Media and Global Governance

Medien & Politik

herausgegeben von

Hans J. Kleinsteuber

in Zusammenarbeit mit der

Arbeitsstelle Medien und Politik

an der Universität Hamburg

Band 37

LIT

Arne Hintz

Civil Society Media and Global Governance

Intervening into the World Summit on the Information Society

LIT

Cover pictures:
Top right: Tilos Radio, Budapest, by Laura Ranca
Top Left: Street Blockade in Buenos Aires, by Arne Hintz and Stefania Milan
Bottom Left: Prometheus Radio Project Barnraising, courtesy of Jacques-Jean Tiziou/www.jjtiziou.net
Bottom Right and background: Preparatory Committee of the World Summit on the Information Society (WSIS), by Arne Hintz

Bibliographic information published by the Deutsche Nationalbibliothek
The Deutsche Nationalbibliothek lists this publication in the Deutsche Nationalbibliografie; detailed bibliographic data are available in the Internet at http://dnb.d-nb.de.

ISBN 978-3-8258-1806-7

A catalogue record for this book is available from the British Library

Fresnostr. 2 D-48159 Münster
Tel. +49 (0) 2 51-620 32 22 Fax +49 (0) 2 51-922 60 99
e-Mail: lit@lit-verlag.de http://www.lit-verlag.de

Distribution:
In Germany: LIT Verlag Fresnostr. 2, D-48159 Münster
Tel. +49 (0) 2 51-620 32 22, Fax +49 (0) 2 51-922 60 99, e-Mail: vertrieb@lit-verlag.de

In Austria: Medienlogistik Pichler-ÖBZ GmbH & Co KG
IZ-NÖ, Süd, Straße 1, Objekt 34, A-2355 Wiener Neudorf
Tel. +43 (0) 22 36-63 53 52 90, Fax +43 (0) 22 36-63 53 52 43, e-Mail: mlo@medien-logistik.at

In Switzerland: B + M Buch- und Medienvertriebs AG
Hochstr. 357, CH-8200 Schaffhausen
Tel. +41 (0) 52-643 54 85, Fax +41 (0) 52-643 54 35, e-Mail: order@buch-medien.ch

Distributed in the UK by: Global Book Marketing, 99B Wallis Rd, London, E9 5LN
Phone: +44 (0) 20 8533 5800 – Fax: +44 (0) 1600 775 663
http://www.centralbooks.co.uk/html

Distributed in North America by:

Transaction Publishers
New Brunswick (U.S.A.) and London (U.K.)

Transaction Publishers
Rutgers University
35 Berrue Circle
Piscataway, NJ 08854

Phone: +1 (732) 445 - 2280
Fax: + 1 (732) 445 - 3138
for orders (U. S. only):
toll free (888) 999 - 6778
e-mail: orders@transactionpub.com

Table of Contents

Preface

With the beginning of the new Millennium, new interest in community, alternative and citizens media has emerged. Media scholars have increasingly asked questions on what lies beyond the traditional dual (public service and commercial) media system and have studied a variety of self-organised grassroots media located in both 'new' and 'old' technological environments. Academic networks, such as OURMedia, have been created to advance knowledge and scientific discussion on these media, and established associations, such as the International Association for Media and Communication Research (IAMCR), have recognised the research field and offer spaces for debate.

Slowly the new media type is also emerging on the policy radar. A number of studies have been commissioned by regional policy bodies such as the Council of Europe, leading to declarations on the positive role of community, alternative and local media for social development. A growing number of countries provide legal recognition to these media. Advocacy coalitions by and for community media have been established and are increasingly making their voices heard in policy debate.

All this calls for a more detailed analysis on the connection between community, alternative and citizens media and the policy level. How do these media intervene in policy processes, what are their agendas and strategies? Do policy fora and institutions recognise their concerns and offer them a place in policy decision-making? With these questions in mind I embarked on my doctoral research between 2003 and 2006, looking particularly at the World Summit on the Information Society (WSIS) which was being prepared and finally taking place during that period. My PhD thesis "Civil Society Media as a Global Political Actor" was submitted to University of Hamburg, Germany, in January 2007. This book is based on that thesis and summarises the results of my research on and at WSIS.

The book would not have been possible without the support by Prof. Dr. Hans J. Kleinsteuber who was my PhD superviser in Hamburg and who is also the editor of this book series at LIT. I would like to thank him for his help and for the inspiration he provided as someone who has contributed significant scholarly work on community media, media governance and information society. I also thank all the nice people at the Research Center Media and Politics in Hamburg where I was based during my doctoral research for being great colleagues and friends. Crucial support in form of both a scholarship and scholarly advice was provided by the Heinrich Böll Foundation and its political think tank, the Green Academy. The New Media department of the foundation, and particularly its head Olga Drossou, helped me to attend a large part of the WSIS preparatory process and to gain deep insights into a transnational policy process at United Nations level. Olga Drossou also created the web platform www.worldsummit2003.org which allowed Ralf Bendrath and me, as web editors and reporters, to follow the summit process in detail.

Stefania Milan has contributed important comments and helped uncover linkages between this particular piece of research and the field of social movement studies. I am grateful for her advice, moral support, and for her immense help in pursuing and finalising this project. Several other colleagues and friends helped at different stages of the thesis and provided valuable comments. I would like to thank Tony Credland, Julia Leifeld, Jordi Blanchar, Magnus Kutz and Gabi Hadl. Hella and Jörg Hintz have consistently supported both the PhD and this book, and I am very grateful to them.

This research has been inspired by the incredible wealth of community and alternative media worldwide. I should mention the London-based directmedia collective and Indymedia UK as examples that allowed me a more thorough insight into self-organised media-making. I am grateful to all the media activists who agreed to be interviewed at WSIS and who included me in their debates. Particularly I want to thank Steve Buckley, President of the World Association of Community Broadcasters (AMARC).

A number of scholars have inspired this research because of their work on community and alternative media. Many of them are part of the global network OURMedia and/or of the Community Communications and Participatory Communication sections at IAMCR. After my PhD, I was lucky enough to move to a research centre which has a strong focus on these themes and which has advanced research on activist and community media – the Center for Media and Communication Studies (CMCS) at Central European University (CEU) in Budapest. I thank all my colleagues there for the opportunity to dig deeper into this fascinating subject.

1 Introduction

Media in the global political system

Control over and access to symbols, norms and interpretations of current events play a vital role in the societies of the 21st century. Actors who produce and distribute information – such as the mass media – hold an increasingly important position in contemporary social orders. With regards to the structural framework of the production and distribution of this information, we are witnessing two opposing trends: a rapid concentration of established media power in the hands of large transnational media corporations, on the one hand, and an increasing number of local and alternative media projects as well as growing pressure by campaigns promoting the democratisation of, and public access to, media, on the other.

Even though the large and powerful actors – media corporations, big broadcasters, communications empires – still represent the core object of media studies, research has increasingly recognised the 'other side' – small media initiatives, community and alternative media, activist projects and other citizen- and civil society-based communication systems. A growing body of case studies has analysed the practices of community radios, activist websites, and alternative news agencies, to name just a few examples, and the understanding of concepts such as alternative, radical, and citizens media has been enhanced substantially (see, e.g., Downing 2001, Rodriguez 2001, Atton 2002, Carpentier et al. 2003, Couldry/Curran 2003, Bailey et al. 2007, Coyer et al. 2008).

However, their specific roles in international political economy and in global governance have received less attention. Usually conceived as small media and as local alternatives, occupying fringe positions around the edges of big media and in the corners that the latter do not reach, their connection with global policy and regulation processes has largely been neglected. Yet with interdependence between states, regions, and social actors increasing, global political processes are no longer the exclusive domain of governments. In the age of global governance, channels are opening to include business and civil society in global decision-making. A growing number of civil society actors have recognised the increasing possibilities of intervening into policy processes and have started to make their voices heard on the global political level.

The aim of this book is to find out whether civil society-based media activists/groups/organisations – those defining themselves as alternative, community, or citizens media – are using such new channels to interact with global political processes and are becoming a participant in global governance. It seeks to draw a connection between a supposedly local and often marginalised actor who usually operates outside the institutional level, and global policy-making arenas.

World Summit on the Information Society

The case study for examining the involvement of these media in a major event of global communication governance will be the World Summit on the Information Society (WSIS). The WSIS was a United Nations (UN) world conference, which took place in two halves: the first in Geneva, 10-12 December 2003, the second in Tunis, 16-18 November 2005. Within the recent series of UN summits on issues such as environment, development and food security, WSIS was the first to focus on information and communication, and it was the first major forum of debate on media issues since the conflictual negotiations within the UN Educational, Scientific and Cultural Organization (UNESCO) over a New World Information and Communication Order (NWICO) in the 1970s and 80s. It thus opened a space for discussion as well as a platform for struggles on the future of the global communication system, and a potentially interesting opportunity for media actors to influence communication governance. For the most part, it did not have a major decision-making role, but it was crucial in setting agendas and discourses around global communication. WSIS provided a prominent platform for civil society actors to develop critical thinking on communication governance, create transnational coalitions, discuss policy alternatives and test their proposals in a global political forum.

As a substantial event in communication governance, which spanned over a period of four years (including the extensive preparation process and a plethora of related conferences and meetings), WSIS was closely observed by communication scholars worldwide. Already during the summit process, and then directly afterwards, academic publications analysed aspects such as the civil society participation and Internet governance (see, e.g., Cammaerts/Carpentier 2006; Dany 2006; Frau-Meigs 2006; Hamelink 2004; Kleinwächter 2004; Ludwig 2003; MacLean 2004; Ó Siochrú 2004a/b; Padovani 2004; Padovani/Tuzzi 2004; Peyer 2005a; Raboy 2004a/b; Raboy/Landry 2005). However the media-related debates and negotiations at the summit, particularly with regards to community, alternative or citizens' media, and the interventions of media actors into the summit process, received less attention.[1]

---

[1] Thomaß (2005; 2006) has provided an exception by discussing connections between the WSIS outcomes and public service broadcasting, but her analysis does not focus on the participation in, and the contributions to, the summit process by media actors, and it does not refer to the types of media which are at the centre of this book. Her major concern is "the role

Objectives of this book

The prime objectives are thus a) to deliver a detailed account of the interrelations between community/alternative/citizens media and the WSIS summit process, and b) to extract general findings about the characteristic approaches of these media to global communication governance. I will analyse their emerging practices of intervening in a policy process, the strategies they use, the objectives they seek to achieve, the challenges they face, and the results of their efforts.

The case study of media interventions into the WSIS process will, furthermore, expand existing knowledge on both community/alternative/citizens media and global governance. With regards to the former, I will develop the model of 'Civil Society Media' as an umbrella for these actors and as a conceptual tool for understanding their interventions into global policy processes. The concept seeks to clarify commonalities as well as fragmentations within this sector, carving out the distinct perspective of 'Civil Society Media' on both media practices and communication policy. With regards to global political processes, the detailed tracing of WSIS negotiations and of the development of WSIS outcomes (in the sub-field of media) will shed light on the dynamics and the constraints of a UN summit process, on the preferences of different actors and on their capacities to influence the debate. I will look at the strategies, motivations, and successes of civil society actors (i.e. the 'new' participants) in global governance, discuss the openness of the current global governance system and contribute to the understanding (and further development) of recent 'multi-stakeholder' policy processes.

This book is thus to explore five different areas:

1. Civil Society Media: What are they, what are their characteristics, com monalities and fragmentations, and why do we need such a concept?

2. What are their policy objectives? What would a favourable regulatory environment look like?

3. Which strategies do they choose to influence policy processes, how do they mobilise and advocate?

Public Service Broadcasters can play (…) to become an instrument in WSIS aims" (Thomaß 2006: 195) – not how media actors, particularly community/alternative/citizens media, have influenced these aims.

4. What were the outcomes of WSIS for Civil Society Media? Did WSIS create important foundations for the practices of these media, or was it an overrated talk-shop?

5. What are the current trends in global governance, and do Civil Society Media point to necessary changes in governance mechanisms?

A question that cuts across all these areas is the relation towards other (i.e. public service and commercial) media. How far do the differences between the media sectors go? Is there a common 'media interest' and a common strategic approach by media actors?

Normative objectives

In addition to providing a contribution to the academic field, this book may offer insights to the actors that it examines. From the research results, it seeks to extract guidelines which may be useful for media actors in future policy interventions, and to point to issue areas which require increased attention. In this sense, it tries to

- Develop outlines of an alternative policy programme
- Provide recommendations for effective strategies for policy interventions
- Propose ideas for enhancing participation in global governance

This book cannot and should not be an advisory paper for community and alternative media. However, as most research, it is based on a certain political and motivational vantage point. Following Hackett and Carroll (2006: 16; quote adapted by the author), "my analysis is informed, but I hope not trapped, by my own political and social location." This location is one of a media researcher / media activist who has been working with several community and alternative media projects. I "broadly share the commitment of most of the activists" (ibid.) who I met, interviewed and accompanied during my research. For that reason, I hope to provide findings which may be useful for these media in their efforts to influence policy-making.

Theoretical background

This book is situated at the boundaries between several academic disciplines. From media studies, it draws from work dealing with the conceptualisation of different types of media, particularly 'non-mainstream' media, and it refers to an increasing body of literature on community and alternative media. From political science, international studies and public policy it takes a perspective on policy-making processes, international regulation and global governance. Thirdly it relates to both research findings and ongoing debates on civil society, social movements and collective action, which are usually located in sociology as well as political science.

My interest in the role of actors, their objectives and their capacities in shaping the global political and economic system is equally reflected in the literature on International Political Economy[2]. The basic question of the discipline – "Who gets what?" (Strange 1994: 18) – serves as an underlying motivation for analysing the participation of media actors in a global summit. An emerging research body of a Political Economy of Communication looks at actors and structures in the field of media, information and communication (e.g., Comor 1994; McChesney 1998; Chakravartty/Zhao 2008). This disciplinary perspective does not imply an exclusive focus on the material conditions of power and on the interests of dominant actors. From Neo-Gramscian understandings of hegemony and counter-hegemony (e.g., Cox 1983) to the analysis of contentious politics and collective action (e.g., Keck/Sikkink 1998; Tilly/Tarrow 2006), several academic strands have highlighted the role of supposedly 'weak' actors in political processes and their capacities to influence these processes by lending or withdrawing legitimacy and by working towards norm change.

The relation with International Political Economy may explain my use of the term 'media'. The term, as it is applied here, refers not to objects but subjects. Rather than at the technical means of communication, I look at the individuals, groups, networks, and organisations which are developing and making available both the content and the technological channels of information. 'Media', in this respect, equals 'media organisation' in the widest sense. Such an 'organisation' will share some sort of common structure and objectives, however it need not be a formally and legally established body, but it may also be a temporary and spontaneously created project or network. Furthermore, the understanding of 'media', as it is used here, does not refer to their journalist function as 'observers' but to their engagement as actors and as protagonists in the international political realm.[3] Even more so, their self-generated image as 'neutral observers' will be abandoned here and will be replaced with a focus on the interests and objectives of particular

2 … or, rather, the "British School" of that discipline. According to Cohen (2006), this school is more interdisciplinary, more actor-oriented, more historical, more normative and often more critical than its US-American counterpart. The author of this book holds a Master of Arts degree in International Political Economy from the University of Warwick, UK.

3 Accordingly, this book will not include classical media analysis. I will not look at media texts, i.e. newspaper, radio, TV or web publications, but at explicit political texts, i.e. statements directly addressing political and institutional actors.

organisations as well as the individuals that belong to them. This preliminary clarification of the term 'media' may suffice at this stage. Other relevant terms, particularly civil society media, the information society and global governance, will be clarified in the following chapters.

Methodology

In accordance with its broad approach and multi-faceted research object, the research for this book was based on methodological triangulation, combining different techniques of data collection and analysis. It is based on three pillars:

(1) Participatory observation in the summit processes. I participated in the lobby coalitions of mainstream and community media; the German civil society coalition ('Zivilgesellschaftlicher Koordinationskreis'); and in preparatory meetings for the alternative event WSIS?WeSeize!. I attended both WSIS summits; four official meetings of the Preparatory Committee (PrepCom); civil society plenary sessions at PrepCom meetings and at the summit; parallel events around the Geneva and Tunis summits (World Forum on Communication Rights, Community Media Forum, World Electronic Media Forum, Citizens Summit); and WSIS-related meetings at the European Social Fora 2003 and 2004. Researching through participatory observation provides in-depth access to processes and actors, even though it entails the risk of compromising both an analytical perspective and the ability to contextualise research findings. Keeping these potential pitfalls in mind, a participatory approach was essential for grasping the complex nature of the summit process, the interactions amongst participants and the underlying dynamics which led to a mixed and often contradictory set of outcomes on a variety of levels.

(2) Document analysis. I analysed the official summit documents – the 'Declaration of Principles', the ''Plan of Action', the 'Tunis Commitment' and the 'Tunis Agenda' – in their various versions, from the very first drafts to the final outcomes; declarations adopted at regional and preparatory conferences; statements and contributions by a variety of actors; and press statements. Sources of research-related information included Email listserves which facilitated discussions amongst summit participants, the official WSIS website http://www.itu.int/wsis as well as website for civil society and alternative events.

(3) Expert interviews. Complementing extensive participatory observation and the wide variety of informal talks with participants during the summit process, I conducted longer interviews with 13 media activists and represen-

tatives of media organisations. Several of these were email interviews.[4] The selection of interview partners was to represent the diversity of media actors involved in WSIS processes (from loose activist projects to well-established organisations), the diversity of approaches to such involvement (from active lobbyists to those rejecting the summit and acting outside), different intensities of involvement (from core members of civil society structures inside the WSIS to those observing from abroad) and different geographical backgrounds (Africa, Asia, North and South America, Europe). Interview partners included the chairs of the lobby coalitions for media and community media; representatives of major community media associations, such as Asociacion Latinoamericana de Educacion Radiofonica (ALER) and World Association of Community Broadcasters (AMARC); members of other civil society networks, such as Association for Progressive Communication (APC); the chief editor of the news agency Inter Press Service (IPS); activists from the Indymedia network, and the minute-taker of the closed governmental negotiation group on media issues at WSIS.

The research was, furthermore, grounded in the debates and discourses around civil society-based media which have taken place during the past two decades, and it reflected my own experience as a practitioner and activist within a variety of alternative and community media between 1999 and 2005, as well as several years of work in more 'mainstream'-oriented media.

Structure of the book

Mapping the terrain of an heterogeneous and conflictive media sector, I will start by defining the 'subject' of this analysis. I will develop the umbrella concept of 'Civil Society Media' as an analytical framework for non-commercial and non-governmental media and will discuss their main practices and characteristics.

Chapter 3 will give an overview over the political background of the WSIS process. It will outline the main aspects of global governance, highlight current trends in global communication policy and take a look back at the NWICO debates as the main precedent for WSIS on the global level. Chapter 4 will change perspective from the systemic to the actor level and focus on the 'new' players in global governance. I will discuss the role of civil society actors, present findings from social movements research regarding strategic interventions in policy fora, and outline the perspectives and agenda proposals by civil society groups and media activists on communication policy.

---

4 Information from these interviews informed my judgement of WSIS processes and will therefore be incorporated continuously throughout the text. In some chapters I will refer more extensively to the opinions expressed in interviews and highlight these sections specifically.

Chapter 5 will provide background to the debates around the WSIS summit by introducing discourses which have emerged on the concept of 'information society'. I will look at several lines of conflict which have persisted in debates on information technology and information-induced social change, focusing on those which show connections with the practices of Civil Society Media and which are relevant for the latter's involvement with the WSIS summit.

Introducing the institutional arena and thus the structural and thematic context of the interventions by Civil Society Media, chapter 6 will give an overview over the WSIS process, the debates and conflicts that dominated it and will focus particularly on the involvement of civil society actors. Chapter 7 will give a detailed account of the activities of media actors at and around the summit process, illustrating the structures and spaces which these media have used to participate and intervene in summit processes, and looking at the policy proposals they have submitted to the thematic debates as well as the strategies they have applied to achieve their objectives.

Changing the focus back from the actors to the institutional level, chapter 8 will scrutinise all relevant summit documents, including regional declarations and the various draft versions of the summit outcomes, and will trace all sections of these documents which refer to Civil Society Media or affect their operations in either positive or negative ways. This content analysis will be complemented with a detailed account of the negotiation process and an examination of the major forces acting as allies and adversaries, respectively, of these media.

Chapter 9 will combine the findings of the previous two chapters and will draw a wide range of conclusions regarding the extent, the strategies, the challenges, successes and failures, the policy proposals, and the future perspectives of the involvement of Civil Society Media in global governance. Underpinned by summaries of the interviews, it will compare the different approaches by CS Media to a policy arena such as WSIS, identify commonalities and differences and thereby discuss the value of the conceptual model introduced before. Chapter 10, finally, will summarise the main threads towards a brief set of core results and provide an outlook on future governance interventions by Civil Society Media.

2 Civil Society Media

Let us begin with a look at the actors. In this chapter I will develop the concept of Civil Society Media, present its main characteristics, and place it in the context of the wider media sector.[1] I will first discuss the concept of 'civil society' and highlight a few contours of the background from which Civil Society Media emerge. Based on the understanding of the term 'civil society' laid out there, I will then explain what I mean by Civil Society Media and present characteristics for defining this type of media. As a third step, I will confront these characteristics with dominant aspects of the current media mainstream.

2.1 Civil Society – a definition

States, business, and civil society

The term "civil society" is a frame which has been filled with different meanings by different people at different times. With no generally agreed definition, its characteristics as well as its borders often remain ambiguous and blurred, while, on the other hand, this vagueness enhances its attraction as a common platform for ideas, projects and policy proposals to be shared by a variety of actors. Interpretations of civil society as an open space of communication and exchange have been quite prominent in the common usage of the term, and so have been traditional understandings which have highlighted distinctions between 'civil' and 'uncivil' societies – in which 'civil' has often described the democratic or republican 'civilised' West. Normative concepts related to this interpretation remain an important part of civil society research, for example the focus on minimising violence in social relations, or on 'civilised' rational discourse (Kaldor 2003). Anheier et al. (in their introduction to the Global Civil Society Yearbook) take these perspectives into account as they suggest the simple working definition of a "realm of non-coercive collective action around shared interests and values" (Anheier et al. 2004: v).

---

[1] The term "Civil Society Media" appeared publicly for the first time in the paper "Media Actors at the Dividing Lines of Information Society: Civil Society Media at the World Summit on the Information Society", which I presented at the Euricom Colloquium "Information Society Visions and Governance: The World Summit on the Information Society and Beyond" in Venice, 6 May 2003. It has since then been used by colleagues, particularly Gabriele Hadl (Ritsumeikan University, Kyoto, Japan) and Stefania Milan (European University Institute, Florence, Italy) and has been developed and applied in conference papers and publications (see Hadl 2004; Milan 2004a; Hintz/Milan 2006a; Hadl/Hintz 2009) and in a doctoral dissertation (Hadl 2006).

The interpretation of 'civil society' which I want to use as the background for the following conceptualisation of 'civil society media' takes a slightly different route by focusing on structures and actors. According to this approach, civil society represents a certain sector of society: the non-state and non-business realm. It entails forms of social interaction that are distinct from both the state and the market – from neighbourhood associations to transnational non-governmental organisations (NGOs), from grassroots activist groups to trade unions.

Thus I follow a growing common understanding of the term during the second half of the 20th century which is distinct from earlier interpretations of civil society. The legacy of mercantilism and enlightenment had originally led to a binary view of two overlapping social spheres – state and civil society. Liberal thinkers, such as John Locke and Adam Smith, focused on a non-state social sphere that was structured by private property and self-interest and were thus primarily occupied "with the well-being of the bourgeois, not the citoyen" (Calabrese 2004: 318). Understood in this way, the concept of civil society "was a foundation for the articulation of the economic interests of the emerging bourgeoisie, which had begun to assert its independence from the state" (ibid.). Marx, equally (yet, normatively, with a different perspective), included the private sector and market actors into the civil society realm and criticised the latter for being dominated by the interests of capital and the bourgeoisie.

The rise of powerful business actors in the 20th century, many of whom aggregated more economic power than nation-states, challenged this two-sector division. While a new type of influential player emerged beside the state, civil society became viewed as a space of oppositional citizens groups and social movements which seek to assert their interests vice versa the dominant players of both state and business. A 'three-sector' model emerged, suggesting three interdependent but distinct spheres: state, market, and civil society.[2]

---

2 However these two models are still in struggle. For example, the Commission on Global Governance in 1995 highlighted the role of NGOs, citizens groups, womens groups, neighbourhood associations and other strictly non-state/non-business actors in the civil society chapter of its report *Our Global Neighbourhood*, but it did not draw clear boundaries to the business sector (Commission on Global Governance 1995). The Cardoso commission for outlining relationships between the United Nations (UN) and civil society, in the first draft of its report, adopted a "broad, inclusive definition of civil society" which included the private sector and all forms of media, while at the same time recognising that incorporating business actors is problematic and may cause objections (http://www.un.org/reform/pdfs/cardosopaper13june.htm).

The Cardoso Commission for outlining relationships between the United Nations (UN) and civil society has defined civil society as "associations of citizens (outside their families, friends and businesses) entered into voluntarily to advance their interests, ideas and ideologies. The term does not include profit-making activity (the private sector) or governing (the public sector)" (Cardoso et al. 2004: 13). The rules of the UN Economic and Social Committee (ECOSOC), which regulate the consultative status of NGOs at the UN, equally exclude for-profit entities (Ó Siochrú 2004a: 331). The WSIS Secretariat has adopted a notion of civil society which "covers the entities of the third sector (distinct from the State and from the private sector) that are engaged in non-profit activities" (WSIS Executive Secretariat 2003a: 2).

Still, such a structural definition leaves room for interpretation. It excludes for-profit business actors, such as companies, but it is unclear about non-profit organisations which are established to further business interests. Hamelink calls these BINGOs – business interest NGOs (Hamelink 1994). An example for a particularly influential BINGO is the International Chamber of Commerce (ICC), and there is a large variety of (often thematic) associations and organisations which are founded by coalitions of companies to engage in pro-business lobbying. So we need a further level of characteristics for defining civil society actors: the level of 'purpose', which includes interests, objectives, and constituencies. Two aspects can be identified here: First, civil society actors advocate a collective good (Mueller 2004). Whereas business associations seek to achieve economic benefits for a specific constituency, civil society groups are typically 'public interest groups' in that their activities are believed to benefit wider social groups or even society as a whole. Secondly, their prime characteristic and motivation is a "search for meaning" and the "application of principled beliefs" (Khagram et al. 2002: 11), rather than the use of authority (state) or the drive for profit (business).

'Activist' and 'neo-liberal' civil society

Civil society, understood as non-state/non-business associations and initiatives, appears in a variety of forms, with diverse motivations, and sometimes even opposing objectives. It may exert a counter-balance to the power of the state and of major institutions from both the political and the economic realm. Yet at the same time it may become a substitute for the state and the market and take over parts of their former functions. Different parts of civil society focus on different objectives and practices – change or stability, advocacy or service provision, struggle or consent generation. The concept of civil society, which I apply, takes into account these different approaches. It has a strong base in what Mary Kaldor (2003) calls the "activist" or "Post-Marxist" version of civil society, which aims at a redistribution of power, a radicalisation of democracy, an extension of participation and autonomy, and which is based on active citizenship and social movements. Yet it also incorporates what she calls the "neo-liberal" version of civil society – a non-profit voluntary "third sector" which provides a substitute for many former state functions, particularly in the field of welfare and public services. In accordance with these two different perspectives on the state and society are different approaches towards international institutions. While the 'activist' sector of civil society typically challenges the legitimacy of these institutions, points out their responsibility for global problems (such as environmental degradation and poverty), seeks to abolish them or limit their influence, and thus to fundamentally change the political environment in which global problems have emerged, the rather 'reformist' or 'neo-liberal' sector interacts constructively to achieve individual limited change, such as concrete (even if marginal) changes to an institution's practices, individual monetary support for relief initiatives, or a focus on individual rights abuses. These differences in approaches will re-appear throughout this book.

The 'neo-liberal' aspect remains one of the most widespread points of criticism towards the concept of civil society. As "de facto instruments of extended states" (Zehle 2003: 3) NGOs represent a response to (and an integral part of the changes towards) downsized governments, post-fordist restructuring and outsourcing. In many cases, their dependence on corporate funding and on support from state agencies puts their 'third sector' position into question. Focusing on isolated 'projects' and decontextualising social struggles, they may "stabilise and normalise conditions that are seen as threats or disturbances to the welfare of human populations" (Lipschutz 2005: 28). Lipschutz argues that civil society, in this respect, is an essential element of "global governmentality" (ibid.), i.e. a force that integrates the subversive activities and aspirations of people into "an expanding liberal regime of power" (ibid.). Similarly, neo-Gramscian approaches have pointed to the crucial role of civil society for legitimising power structures, and to the need for dominant (state and business) actors to include civil society representatives and agendas in international regulatory institutions (Cox 1981).

With material resources, fundraising opportunities, and organisational capacities concentrated in the Global North[3], asymmetries persist between a

[3] Throughout this book, I will use the terminology of the 'Global North' and the 'Global South' instead of the more traditional terms 'developed' and 'developing' countries, or 'First' and 'Third world'. The 'Global North' embraces the richer part of the world, typically the liberal-capitalist countries in North America and Europe, but also including countries in the Southern hemisphere such as Australia and New Zealand. The 'Global South' is the

small group of large, influential (and mostly Northern) NGOs and a wide range of marginalised (and mostly Southern) NGOs. While the latter tend to focus on collective economic, social, and cultural aspects, Northern NGOs are criticised of being more interested in individual political and civil rights and thereby revealing an individualist bias which reflects a Western capitalist ethos (Sikkink 2002). Participation of these NGOs in development programmes which require 'governance conditionalities' in social, economic, or human rights areas increases the power of donors in domestic governance, and may thereby lead to "new forms of colonisation" (Abugre 2006). Adopting the concept of civil society as a foundation for the main theoretical framework of this book, I do not suggest that civil society as such has been dominated by regressive approaches, yet it is important to note that civil society is a pluralist category which may embrace contested activities and actors.

Normative commonalities

Thus the structure- and actor-oriented model of civil society which I use here – although drawing clear boundaries to state and business actors – integrates different perspectives and objectives and cannot be condensed into a monolithic block. However, despite these differences, there is a set of normative aspects common to most actors embraced by this understanding of civil society. Most of these organisations, associations and movements have their roots in discontent with state paternalism and in an opposition to the overwhelming power (and power abuses) of large institutions. They therefore share a tendency towards autonomy, self-organisation, empowerment, emancipation, pluralism, voluntary association and horizontal networks – even if their own organisational structures may have evolved in very different ways over time. Common to these values is a social model that is based on the decentralisation of control. Civil society advocacy "puts at risk, however slightly, the advantages of those who currently enjoy [...] power" (Tilly/Tarrow 2006: 4). Accordingly, civil society groups tend to agree on the need for increasing and deepening democracy on all levels of governance, often including a commitment to participatory democracy and increased engagement of local communities. With freedom of speech, freedom of movement and freedom of association representing vital conditions for a lively civil society, such human and civil rights and freedoms are often at the core of civil society demands. Common campaigns by civil society

---

poorer and often marginalised part of the world, typically situated in the Southern hemisphere, such as Africa, Latin America and South Asia. This rather crude division is used for practical purposes, yet keeping in mind that it is increasingly difficult to carve up the world into distinct territories. Castells, for example, has spoken of a "Fourth World" (Castells 1998: 164) which is not territorially confined but is distributed around the globe and "present in literally every country, and every city" (ibid.).

groups, and civil society gatherings such as the World Social Forum, have converged civil society agendas and formed a rough set of shared objectives which include the protection of collective 'common goods', human, social, and labour rights, peace, the fight against environmental degradation, and the eradication of poverty, racism and sexism (Dawkins 2003). Oppositional political activity in the new millennium is rarely state-centred and intent on 'taking the power' to change social and economic arrangements from above through state hierarchies, but is more often conceived as a democratising force from below and from within.

So is civil society necessarily a political actor? Not in an immediate and open way. It encompasses radical social movements as well as groups which are set up to fulfil people's hobbies and past-times. Yet its roots of self-organising, active citizenship, and direct action have political implications and are in themselves political. Civil society is "the setting from which social movements and political activism originate" (Lipschutz 2005: 20). It is usually "making claims" in some way or another (Tilly/Tarrow 2006: 3), and often these claims amount to "political contention" (ibid.).

Global Civil Society

Considering the current globalisation of civil society identities and practices, many observers have assumed the notion of a 'global civil society' as an interpretative category for the expanding networks of non-state/non-business actors. Some claim that these networks are gradually becoming a transnational political actor, aggregating many 'civil societies' towards a global force with similar sets of values and with a collective power that allows them to viably confront the equally globalised business and political elites (Anheier et al. 2001). Others are more cautious about a concept that suggests global civil society as a unitary actor, and highlight instead the persistent differences in histories, identities, tactics and interests between a diversity of movements, groups and organisations (Halperin/Laxer 2003). The scale on which the unity of a global civil society is suggested or refuted varies, yet the increasing connections between, and the expanding scope of, transnational NGO networks and social movements are widely recognised (Keck/Sikkink 1998). Civil society networks have been transcending national borders and converging previously isolated struggles.

The 'intergalactic gathering' held by the Zapatista movement in the jungle of Chiapas in Southern Mexico in 1996 constituted one of the main starting-points for weaving and intensifying transnational webs between civil society actors from a variety of localities, struggles, and ideological backgrounds. It led to the establishment of the People's Global Action Network (PGA) in February 1998, to several 'global days of action' against the institutions of global political and business elites from 1998 onwards[4] and thus to what came to be known as the 'anti-globalisation'[5] or 'social justice' movement. The annual World Social Forum (WSF) which started in 2001 developed into a major gathering, regularly drawing around 100,000 people. Networks such as the WSF and PGA have linked environmental activists with indigenous farmers, anti-war campaigners with consumer advocates, trade unionists with media activists. Connections have been intensified through common campaigns, such as the resistance against the Multilateral Agreement on Investment (MAI) – a business-friendly set of investment regulations which was negotiated in 1997/98 within the Organization for Economic Co-operation and Development (OECD) and which would have represented, in the words of then-Director General of the WTO, Renato Ruggiero, "the constitution of a single global economy" (quoted in Dawkins 2003: 97). A campaign by more than 560 NGOs opposed this new 'constitution' and led to its demise.

'The media'

A major gap of civil society and social movements research concerns the role of media actors. Many scholars unquestioningly include 'the media' in the civil society realm (as an example, see Keck/Sikkink 1998). Media is usually seen as a black box, without differentiating between different media organisations, approaches, interests, objectives. The result is a seemingly homogenous construct – 'the media' – which cannot be subsumed under either state or business and is therefore aligned with civil society. Only few scholars ask the question "Where do media fit in?" (de Jong et al. 2005) and cast doubt on its wholesale inclusion in civil society. The following sections will deconstruct 'the media' into the different groups of actors – state, private sector, and civil society – and ask which types of media can be regarded as 'civil society media'.

2.2 Civil Society Media

A synthesis of Civil Society Media

The concept of Civil Society (CS) Media encompasses media organisations, groups, and projects, which fit into the basic non-state/non-commercial model and which share the structural and thematic tendencies of civil soci-

---

4 The most well-known being the 'Battle of Seattle' against a meeting of the World Trade Organisation (WTO) in November 1999 and the protests against the G8 meeting in Genoa in July 2001.

5 The term is a media invention and has been rejected by most participants in this movement who have preferred the term 'alter-globalisation' or 'critical globalisation' movement.

ety. Generally it comprises all 'third sector' media and therefore excludes the two biggest sectors, namely commercial and public service media. While commercial media are core members of the business sector and their exclusion can therefore easily be justified, the role of public service media is not so obvious. However, as I will argue below, their organisational structures, their journalist principles, and their fundamental links with the objectives of the nation state put them firmly outside the realm of CS Media.

CS Media have been described in different names and forms. Here I will point to some of the most widely used terms.

Community Media constitute media based in and operated by and for a community (which can be a community of interest, a geographical or a cultural community). Ownership, accountability and programme content are directly tied (or linked) to that community. Content may focus on news from the village, programmes in migrant or traditional languages, educational programmes, or issue areas marginalised by the mainstream media. Community media may be a response to pressures of cultural homogenisation, political and social marginalisation, threats to traditional languages, or they may just show the ability of 'non-professionals' to organise media production themselves. They are often characterised by a high degree of openness and possibilities for participation.[6] A possible limitation is caused by the explicit focus on particular sections and niches of society, which may lead to self-marginalisation vis-à-vis other forms of media.

Despite their bias towards the local, community media projects and organisations have achieved a high level of international networking and exchange, particularly through organisations such as the World Association of Community Broadcasters (AMARC) and the Community Media Forum Europe (CMFE). For that reason, community media has been the most outspoken amongst the CS Media presented here in asserting itself as a "third tier" of media[7], in addition to (and with the same legitimacy as) commercial and public service media. This third tier has specific characteristics which distinguish it thoroughly from the other two media types: It is "driven by social objectives rather than private profit, bottom up rather than top down, empowering people rather than treating them as passive consumers, nurtur-

---

6 However, the increasing popularity of the concept, particularly in development discourses, has also led to the top-down establishment of so-called 'community media' which are not initiated, owned and controlled by local communities but which respond to the needs and requests of donors and international institutions (see the excerpts from an interview with Frieda Werden in chapter 9).

7 UK Community Media Association http://www.commedia.org.uk; CMFE http://www.cmfe.net

ing local knowledge rather than replacing it with standard solutions" (Community Media Initiative 2003).

Alternative Media are 'alternative' in a structural sense, focusing on collective production, economic independence from both state and market, and a non-hierarchical organisational model, but especially they are 'alternative' in terms of content. Counter-information is their main objective. They seek to break hegemonic discourses, as transported through the mainstream media, uncover and criticise power and domination, highlight social struggles and the activities of social movements, and have a strong base within those movements. They openly and directly support social change. Politically and intellectually, the concept is connected to Marxism, socialist anarchism (Downing 2001; Atton 2002), feminism (Downing 1984) and radical democracy (Rodriguez 2001).

The "alternative vs. mainstream" dichotomy has been both the distinguishing feature of this approach and the main point of criticism launched against it. It has been called limiting (Rodriguez 2001), self-marginalising (Carpentier et al. 2003) and theoretically weak (Atton 2002, Downing 2001), yet its clarity has contributed to its continuing popularity. Related categories (which depart from this dichotomy) are Radical Media (Downing 2001) and Citizens Media (Rodriguez 2001).

Tactical Media are leaving the bipolar world of counter-information behind and seek to break out of sub-cultural ghettoes. A "repertoire of dirty little practices" (Garcia/Lovink 1999; also Lovink 2003), they encompass critical media actions, campaigns and interventions, which are often ad-hoc, temporary, pragmatic and flexible. They do not wage open opposition against hegemonic media systems and do not create sustained 'alternatives' but seek to infiltrate, appropriate and pervert their messages and technologies, obstructing and sabotaging the forces of neo-liberal capitalism from inside their own parameters. They are often based on the innovative activities by smaller groups or individuals, rather than wider social movements or stable communities. With a strong 'new technology' focus, their proponents also consider issues beyond the usual 'media' horizon, such as intellectual property rights, open source software, surveillance and biotechnology.

As is the case with the above-mentioned concept of Alternative Media, Tactical Media's main achievement is also its main limitation. Deeply rooted in post-modern thought and in current socio-political analysis, it responds to recent changes in the global political-economic system, but as ad-hoc and flexible mode of intervention, it "has an affinity with that which it seeks to oppose" (Lovink/Rossiter 2005) – post-fordist capitalism.

Independent Media is a concept highlighted by the recent rise of Independent Media Centres ("Indymedia") since 1999. It re-appropriates the term 'independent' used by commercial media and thereby refutes the latter's claims of constituting truly independent (i.e. not state-connected) media, instead pointing to their strong links with business and with related political interests. Independent from capital interests and choosing to work with as little financial resources as possible, these media often operate as voluntary activist projects. Activist Media is thus a related umbrella term.

Autonomous Media (Langlois/Dubois 2005) complement the strong focus on independence from hegemonic media/political/economic systems with an emphasis on self-organisation and do-it-yourself culture. Independent, Activist and Autonomous Media share with Alternative Media the wish to generate alternative infrastructures to mainstream journalism (rather than just complementing the latter as a 'third tier'), and with Tactical Media a deep scepticism towards established institutions and forms of organisation.

These categories highlight different aspects of CS Media. Each category only represents a certain section of the vast range of non-state non-commercial media, and each model comes with certain limitations. For example, the concept of Radical Media deals with characteristic types of media content and, to a lesser extent, organisational structures, but does not focus on public participation as a determining factor of many non-state/non-commercial media, whereas Community and Autonomous Media emphasize exactly the latter. The notion of Alternative Media allows for straightforward categorisation but neglects the many hybrid forms of media as well as the interconnections between hegemonic and underground cultures. Tactical Media have filled these gaps, but they may as well be understood as a particular historic formation of media alternatives, based in the context of the post-cold-war hegemony of a neo-liberal 'end of ideology' (see chapter 5) but increasingly changing their tone back towards more straightforward alternative information with the revival of anti-capitalist discourses and the assertion that 'another world is possible', leading to renewed interest in 'alternative' media (Bailey/Cammaerts/Carpentier 2007, Coyer/Dowmunt/Fountain 2008).

Furthermore, each of these concepts carries its own set of discourses, with specific histories and ideological, geographical and political contexts. While in many regions of the world, the term Community Media implies a dissident political stance and thus has substantial overlaps with Alternative Media[8], in countries such as Japan it embraces all 'local' (including locally-

[8] See the explicitly political statements of the Community Media Forum Europe and AMARC, www.cmfe.net and www.amarc.org.

based commercial) media (Kanayama 2006). And whereas the term Citizens Media has radical connotations in Latin America, its German translation – *Bürgermedien* – has a rather bourgeois and non-political undertone.

Thus what we need for the further analysis is a category which combines the different aspects highlighted by the different existing models and which, at the same time, draws a clear line of distinction to other media forms – an umbrella term which is open to a diversity of similar media types, yet reduces the blurring of boundaries.

The concept of **CS Media** seeks to do exactly that. It creates a common frame of reference for a wide range of media actors, from small grassroots media projects to large media organisations, from a photocopied newsletter, to an activist website, to satellite distribution of film material, to a global news agency – provided they are non-state and non-commercial actors. This common frame picks up the established category of 'civil society', which makes it particularly usable in the area of global policy and governance and thus in the field of concern for this particular research.

However, the 'non-state/non-commercial' characteristic can only serve as a general basis and does not yet suffice for defining a media sector. It is necessary to identify a wider set of common features of its members, as well as aspects of distinction towards its non-members. From the concepts mentioned above, we can aggregate these features and thus build the framework of characteristics and values which connects different CS Media actors.

Characteristics of Civil Society Media[9]

Using the terms 'non-governmental and non-commercial' as a first rough framework for approaching the concept of CS Media suggests that questions of **ownership and control** are at the heart of what divides and defines different media forms. Hadl (2004) suggests as a basic definition "a media organization owned/controlled by members of civil society", and adds other layers by further defining them as "media for and by members of civil society, with 'civic' content" (Hadl 2004: 10). Ownership is thus at the centre of what constitutes CS Media. Control is not exerted by a business entity or by representatives of the state or the state/party system, but is ultimately in the hands of self-organised and independent citizens' groups, associations, or organisations.

---

[9] These characteristics have been aggregated from literature on community, alternative, etc. media, in particular Atton 2002, Couldry/Curran 2003, Downing 2001, Garcia/Lovink 1999, Hintz 2000, Langlois/Dubois 2005, Rodriguez 2001, and the additional sources mentioned in the text.

Closely related to issues of ownership and control is the organisational structure of CS Media. These media are **non-profit** or not-for-profit entities, and they are typically designed with an emphasis on **democratic structures**, allowing all members/workers/activists a highest-possible participation in steering the organisation, favouring collective decision-making over hierarchical command structures, and relying to a larger extent (or entirely) on voluntary work. This does not mean that CS Media are necessarily 'small media'. However, while there are CS Media which have adopted certain hierarchies in their organisation and have employed professional media workers, the general tendency is that CS Media offer a distinct counter-model to large-scale and highly-professionalised mainstream media organisations.

CS Media offer low-level access for media non-professionals to **participate** in media production and for communities and social groups to take media operations into their own hands. They break the boundaries between active producers and passive consumers and thus refute the "vertical communication model evident in most (particularly mainstream) media organisations" (Meadows et al. 2005: 7).[10] Audiences are not merely conceived as receivers of information but as participants in a dialogue between the organisation and its environment. Sometimes the traditional roles of producers and audiences are even turned upside-down – the most explicit example being the open publishing system of Indymedia (http://www.indymedia.org), which allows the public to determine the content in its entirety and reduces the role of the editors to one of moderators arranging the public's reports. So whereas traditional commercial and public service media are operating according to a one-way flow of information from sender to receiver, CS Media are based in a model of **communication** as a two-way interactive process.[11]

This process also applies to those participating directly in media production. **Sharing skills and know-how** constitute integral parts of many CS Media

---

[10] … and thus they put into practice what Bertolt Brecht demanded in his radio theory in the late 1920s: "Aufstand des Hörers, seine Aktivierung und seine Wiedereinsetzung als Produzent" (Brecht 1967: 130) – the rising up of the listeners, their activation and their re-establishment as producers. Brecht called for the transformation of the radio from a distribution channel to a communication mechanism.

[11] Interactivity is often reduced to a feature of technical media systems. For example, Lipschutz (2005) calls television a "one-way medium" which delivers "processed and commodified information to consumers", whereas the Internet is a "two-way medium" which permits "both the production and consumption of information, and its transformation into knowledge and action". However, while some media platforms certainly offer better preconditions than others, CS Media show that interactivity is primarily a choice – an objective which some media organisations try to achieve while others choose to deliver a product to audiences.

practices. The use of technology is emancipatory and interactive, and it values popular involvement higher than the professionalised production of perfectly-polished products. Experimenting with media technology develops capacities and empowers people. The public may find out that their capacities are far more developed than elite forces may want to make them believe.

CS Media thus re-interpret the notion of media **access** by embracing in this term both the ability to receive information and to participate in its construction. Yet even in terms of information provision they offer original services as the main access channels to news and other information for large parts of the world population. Particularly in rural areas of the Global South, community radios offer the prime means to receive news. For many marginalised communities, CS Media constitute the only channel to hear about their culture and their realities. Reaching beyond the territories of mass media distribution, catering for tastes, interests, and orientations neglected in the mainstream media, and giving voice to groups, ideas, and cultures otherwise not heard, CS Media support the participation of marginalised communities in political, social and cultural processes (Sreberny-Mohammadi 1997; Kidd et al. 2005). Some CS Media explicitly address **development** needs (Gumucio-Dagron/Tufte 2006).

Critique of mainstream media content, provision of **alternative views**, articulation of 'subaltern' experiences and expressing oppositional strands within popular cultures represent a general tendency in the content of CS Media. By addressing trends like poverty, inequality and environmental degradation, they confront people with the disruptions and cleavages in modern societies and motivate them to address such issues themselves. Expressing "an alternative vision to hegemonic policies, priorities, and perspectives" (Downing 2001: v) represents the key characteristic of those CS Media coming from the tradition of 'alternative' or 'radical' media, but is equally a widespread rationale for CS Media based in other traditions. Often content emphasizes the context of an event and the processes leading to it, rather than reducing it to a piece of spot-news. Thus even a civil society news agency "focuses on a different type of information" (Interview MG) than do big commercial agencies.

Many CS Media explicitly bring forward **subjective accounts** of events and developments and thereby break with traditional journalistic values of impartial and objective reporting. As they regard the concept of objectivity as an attempt to disguise the journalist's and mainstream media's own bias, their alternative is to uncover subjectivities and to make their own biases – e.g., their participation in social movements – explicit. From this approach follow, almost automatically, questions regarding the reliability, credibility, and accuracy of the information disseminated through CS Media. Many CS Media respond by claiming to provide a wide range of sources, involve large numbers of people from different sectors of society in media production, and offering opportunities for public debate on media content.[12] Furthermore, they are often more than happy to raise doubts about media content in general, and advise media users not to believe unquestioningly in the authority of any media but to find out about an issue covered in the media with their own eyes (Hintz 2003).

Collective, open, and participatory media production, combined with a non-profit background, uncovers an understanding of knowledge which differs substantially from the individualistic and property-related model found elsewhere. Interpretations of the knowledge and information sphere as part of a **global commons**, definitions of information infrastructure as a public resource, practices of knowledge sharing, and the use and development of **free and open source software** are all widely spread in the CS Media sector. Campaigns against intellectual property rights and for CS Media often go hand in hand.[13]

Opening spaces for participatory communication, CS Media react to the perceived enclosure of information and communication channels by commercial and state media. They create fractures in the domination of, and reclaim public space from, these global organisations. While the mainstream media are operating in increasingly concentrated structures (see below), CS Media are usually organised as decentralised networks of local groups, based on values of **diversity, autonomy, decentralisation** and **horizontality**. They challenge the vision of a single all-inclusive 'global village', suggesting instead a diversity of smaller 'villages' (Dowmunt 1993). In the rapidly changing global political, economic, and cultural landscape, they thus represent a counterpart to forces of centralisation and homogenisation (Notes from Nowhere 2003). Many of them define themselves as integral parts of social movements, others sympathise with such movements while keeping an independent stance and retaining some of traditional journalism's distance.[14]

---

12 E.g., public screenings by video makers and public readings by CS news sheets, which are sometimes followed by debates on the content; or the comment function by which Indymedia allows the readers to comment on the validity of an article.

13 For example, the CRIS campaign (Communication Rights in the Information Society), which is supported by a large number of major NGOs and activist groups working in the field of media and communication, connects both fields.

14 The question of explicit alignment not only separates different CS Media from each other but poses an issue of debate within many organisations. Even a network like Indymedia, which states that it is "part of the worldwide resistance against capitalist globalisation"

The approaches of CS Media display links with several philosophical and political ideas. For example, ecological social theory advocates a decentralisation of power and an embedding of politics and economics in local community life (Helleiner 1996). Direct democracy (as opposed to representative democracy) emphasizes high levels of public participation in collaborative production and decision-making (Costanza-Chock 2005). The public sphere is one of the key concepts to which CS Media refer and which they seek to cultivate as a democratic and plural space (Kidd et al. 2005). The African moral philosophy of Ubuntuism, equally, emphasizes sharing, collectivity, and participation in collective life, with 'community' as the main social category. Placing high value on the active involvement of the journalist, rather than on detachment and attempted objectivity, and regarding media as mediator, participant, and negotiator, rather than as informant, observer, and gatekeeper, it embraces many of CS Media's characteristics (Fourie 2006).

CS Media – examples and practices

Supported by the relatively cheap availability of media technologies, such as desktop publishing, video and the Internet, attempts to "by-pass the mainstream media"[15] can now be found across the whole technological spectrum. Let us look at a few examples of CS Media and how the characteristics outlined above are put into practice.

Printed and photocopied publications represent the most widespread way of grassroots information sharing – practically all oppositional activities, from local environmental initiatives to revolutionary movements, have been accompanied by leaflets, flyers, brochures, or newsletters in order to raise awareness for specific concerns and to mobilise the public. A variety of regular publications include activist newsletters, such as the British *Schnews,* and professional magazines, such as the *New Internationalist* or the Italian *Carta.*

Video activist groups like the German *Kanal B* or the British *Undercurrents* produce alternative news videos showing "the news you don't see on the news" (http://www.undercurrents.org), as well as documentaries on social

---

(Mission statement of Indymedia Germany http://de.indymedia.org/static/ms.shtml, translation by the author) tries not to align too closely with one particular struggle but to stay open for a wider audience, and incorporates both members who see themselves primarily as 'reporters' and those who regard themselves as 'social activists'. Repeatedly there have been heated debates within the network on whether Indymedia volunteers should be seen as reporters or as activists, including the question on whether they should use press cards and other items identifying them as reporters and thereby separating them from other activists.

15 slogan by the Indymedia network

justice resistance or on issues of civil society concern. Video groups often screen their documentaries in public places and invite the audience to discuss the topics addressed in the videos instead of just consuming them (Mader 1993). They have also experimented with terrestrial TV distribution of video programmes (for example, the Italian street TV experience *Telestreet*). In some countries, public access slots in public service TV programmes offer civil society groups the possibility to broadcast TV programmes to a mass audience. Groups like the New York TV collective *Paper Tiger* and the *Deep Dish* project gather contributions of grassroots video producers, compile them as a TV programme and screen them via public access slots, using satellite transmission for distribution.

Radio remains a crucial media platform due to its wide-spread availability, its recognition of oral cultures and illiteracy, and the fact that it does not require vast technical or financial resources. In the Global South, particularly, it serves as an important channel for local content, as well as content on educational issues, health, agriculture and environmental issues. The specific combination of offering relevant local content and taking media production into one's own hands is also the guiding principle of citizens' and 'free' radios and of 'open channels' in the Global North, as it is the background to many pirate radio stations in the world's metropolitan centres. These radio practices highlight the use of media technology to expand public communication spaces and to intervene into privatised zones. The German group *Ligna* has used (legal) radio frequencies for its 'radio ballet' which subverts implicit or explicit rules of behaviour, creates an experience of collectivity and reclaims spaces from the embrace by forces of privatisation and commercialisation.

The Internet has become a major platform for both civil society-based content and participatory media production. Organisations such as *OneWorld*, networks such as the *Association for Progressive Communication (APC)*, and web-based magazines such as *ZMag* have pioneered the use of the technology by providing alternative accounts of global developments and offering a wealth of news and analysis. The Internet also makes alternative real-time reporting possible, without having to rely on resource-consuming satellite broadcasting, and thus without requiring the financial and structural background of large media organisations. On June 18th 1999, media activists, for the first time, used a combination of text-based and audiovisual media platforms and a variety of affordable media technology to provide 'near-live' web-based reporting of the anti-capitalist protests taking place around the globe on that day (www.j18.org). A few months later, the first *Indymedia* website reported live from the anti-WTO protests in Seattle and successfully counter-acted corporate media misinformation about the event. Since then, more than 150 Indymedia nodes have cropped up around the world. Web-based reporting has included web-TV streams, for example about the anti-war protests in 2003, proving that a few committed people are able to provide high-quality TV coverage without the support and background of a media corporation. Most significantly, all these efforts have put the interactive character of the Internet to best use by empowering web-users to publish their own reports through open-publishing mechanisms.

On a more institutionalised scale, alternative news agencies have been distributing information on marginalised communities and neglected issues to the mainstream media. Regarding their organisational structure, they may operate very differently from activist networks such as Indymedia, but in terms of content and general objectives, there are important similarities. Such news agencies include indigenous and regional operations, such as the Maori news organisation *Mana Maori Ltd.* in New Zealand (Fox 1993) and the Latin American radio news exchange agency *Pulsar*, to the worldwide network of the *Inter Press Service (IPS)*. As the largest purveyor of information about the Global South and a major news source for issues related to poverty, human rights, environmental degradation, amongst others, IPS is certainly one of the 'big agencies', and occasionally its content is used by mainstream media on the same level as that of Reuters et al.[16] However, its emphasis on content that goes relatively uncovered in the media, its direct links to civil society actors, and its position as a non-profit, non-governmental organisation identify it as an alternative provider.

Blogs and citizen journalism

The beginning of the 21st century has seen a substantial re-definition of the borders between media producers and consumers. "Citizen journalism" has become a mass movement, triggered particularly by the exploding numbers of blogs and podcasts. Celebrated as "the most originally democratic media" (Speck 2005: 60; translation by the author) and as "mediatic realization of the idea of the polis" (ibid.), blogs empower everyone who has access to an Internet connection and basic technical know-how to start an online publication. Extensive inter-linkages and interactive publishing options (such as the possibility to comment on articles) establish communicative nets between blogs. Podcasts have transferred the blog idea to audio platforms and constitute individually-created and downloadable radio programmes. Websites such as *flickr.com* and *youtube.com* allow people to easily create photo and video diaries, documentaries and fiction.

---

16 Studies about the amount of reporting on UN processes have revealed that in some cases IPS reports have been a more important source for the mainstream press than, for example, Reuters (Giffard 1998).

Blogs have become particularly influential as "watchdogs for the watch-dogs" (Bock 2005), thus as critical observers of media coverage.[17] Subject-specific blogs such as the German *Netzpolitik.org* are now amongst the most important publications on their respective issue areas. However, while some bloggers have conducted high-quality investigative journalism, the vast majority continues to reflect exclusively on their lives and past-times.[18] Moreover, the 'watchdog' bloggers from the political right are at least as active as their counterparts from a rather left-wing civil society perspective.[19] 'Milblogs', on which army members praise the 'war on terror', have spread widely, and in 2005 eight of the ten mostly-linked blogs in the US were right-wing or conservative (Massing 2005). Business entities, too, have increasingly discovered blogs as a means for marketing and PR, and 'corporate bloggers' are busy trying to develop a positive image for their companies (Eck 2005), while seemingly 'authentic' video diaries on websites such as Youtube are being uncovered as guerrilla marketing operations (Patalong 2006).

With the rise of 'citizen journalism', the open publishing principle of Indymedia has seemingly arrived in the mainstream. Two thirds of the articles of the Korean Online Publication *OhmyNews* are written by so-called "Citizen Reporters". An increasing number of news websites operate special sections for articles submitted by the readers, tabloids invite their readers to submit pictures taken on mobile phones and digital cameras and to have them published in the newspaper. From iReport (CNN) to YouWitness (Reuters), 'citizen journalists' are called upon to contribute pictures, films and reports to major news operations.

Big media have been opening doors towards interactivity and participation – yet only within a framework pre-structured and enclosed by the respective media organisation. The knowledge and the resources of 'citizen reporters', as well as their availability at news-worthy events around the globe, are put to use for the particular newspaper or website, but these reporters usually

---

17 Amongst the most-visited blogs have been *Bildblog.de* and *Newshounds.us* which serve to analyze the reports of the German tabloid Bild-Zeitung and the US TV news channel Fox News. The activities of PR- and lobby-organizations are scrutinised on *Spinwatch.org* and *Lobbycontrol.de.* Lovink/Rossiter (2005) have criticised this media focus as reductionist: "At a discursive level the blog was operating internally to mainstream media. In a genealogical sense the blog was part of the news industry."

18 According to a study by the Pew Internet and American Life Project, only around 10 per cent of blogs deals with political issues and related news (Pew/Internet 2006).

19 Campaigns by right-wing blogs against critical government-related media reports forced, for example, the chief news executive of CNN, Eason Jordan, to resign after he had criticised the US army (Rosen 2005).

have little say over the structure of the organisation or the thematic framework within which their reports are selected. The vast majority of reports concern the entertainment genre and merely add 'colour' to the mainstream media product. The cooptation of 'citizen journalism' by established mainstream media is thus in full swing, and so is the integration of 'citizen journalism' platforms into established media empires. In 2005 Murdoch's News Corporation acquired the community web platform MySpace, in 2006 Bertelsmann announced the development its own citizen webspace and Google bought Youtube for the astronomical sum of 1.65 billion dollar.[20]

Qualifications and limitations

The case of 'citizen journalism' highlights the need to qualify the concept of CS Media. Certainly, the possibility to upload pictures and texts does not transform a major media business into a civil society organisation, but the boundaries are seemingly being blurred. On which grounds should certain media actors be included into the concept and others excluded? As we have seen above, straightforward demarcation-lines do not exist, and all actors emphasize certain aspects more than others: Some CS Media focus on facilitating participation in media production, without necessarily transmitting radical oppositional content; others provide counter-information but few possibilities for the public to get involved. Even amongst fairly similar media actors, adherence to the criteria varies: While some community radios operate as open platforms, others have strict editorial guidelines and frequently reject programme proposals, and in some cases (e.g., feminist media) unlimited openness would be highly questionable. Does that exclude the latter from the realm of CS Media?

No media project is likely to fulfil all of the criteria laid out above. These criteria offer a set of guidelines for assessing whether or not a media organisation qualifies as CS Media, but they need to be weighed and their complementary character needs to be acknowledged. Milan's (2004a) comparison of the activities of seven different CS Media organisations at the World Social Forum, ranging from the local pirate radio station Radio Muda to IPS, offers a good example. She recognises vast differences between these media in aspects such as institutionalisation, financial resources, and public participation, with the studied organisations often occupying the full range of a scale from "weak" to "very strong". In many respects, the majority of studied organisations do not live up to their claims of offering a clear alternative to the mainstream sector – e.g., regarding their cultural basis in the industrialised North, or regarding their gender distribution. Yet they all ac-

20 ... and, two weeks later, deleted 30,000 videos from the site because of alleged copyright infringement (http://www.netzeitung.de/internet/447663.html).

knowledge that most of the characteristics mentioned above represent crucial elements of a non-mainstream media sector, and they each strive towards the realisation of several of them.

So, the CS Media model would require that a media project should have more than one type of the above-mentioned characteristics in order to fit under its umbrella. Ownership and control certainly are the most crucial features. There can be no CS Media which is owned or controlled by business or state actors and whose operations are not to a large extent steered by its members/producers/activists in democratic decision-making processes. In addition, a CS Media organisation would strive towards some (but not necessarily all) of the goals laid out in the CS Media model, such as public participation, the rejection of the producer-consumer division, catering for marginalised communities or providing alternative content, and it would agree with basic values such as decentralisation, empowerment and development.

With this instrument, we can assess more easily those actors that form the boundaries of the CS Media model and that do not constitute straightforward cases. For example, while OhmyNews claims to form a true civil society-based media organisation and, indeed, facilitates the inclusion of media non-professionals, it does not adhere to principles of self-organisation and democratic decision-making and may therefore not qualify as CS Media. IPS, on the one hand, is a professional global news agency, offers few possibilities for public participation, shares traditional journalistic values, such as the quest for objectivity, and defines itself as a "public service organisation" (Interview MG). On the other hand, its main characteristics can be seen in a) its structure as a non-governmental/non-profit organisation, b) its focus on issues which are of concern to civil society, c) regular exchanges with civil society groups and participation in civil society events such as the World Social Forum, and d) its original purpose of covering issues which are neglected in the mainstream media. Being firmly embedded in civil society discourses, principles and objectives, IPS would be included in the CS Media realm.

Finally, we need to distinguish the model of CS Media not just from commercial and public service media, but from other non-commercial/non-governmental media which are organised according to different principles or transmit different types of content than the bulk of organisations referred to in this book. Right-wing media may claim to transmit counter-information and to therefore be part of CS Media, but their content is usually repressive and anti-democratic. Media based on what Downing (2001) calls the "Leninist model", i.e. media transmitting a party's elite's priorities and perspectives, are more difficult to dismiss as these media have often played a large role in social and revolutionary movements. However the clear set of characteristics which is at the centre of what constitutes CS Media separates the latter from many of the media just mentioned:

- a structural tendency towards horizontal organisation, non-hierarchical decision-making, and democratic self-governance
- the promotion of participation, empowerment and development
- a content tendency on debate, analysis and reflection, rather than on demagogic slogans and propaganda

Media based on authoritarian or repressive approaches differ fundamentally from these characteristics, whereas CS Media either adopt the latter as basic principles of their work or, at least, share the values and ideas embodied in them.

2.3 The 'Mainstream Model': Aspects of media hegemony

The characterisation of CS Media has already highlighted several aspects of the 'counter-model' – commercial and public service media, which serve as the traditional and dominant (or 'mainstream') forms of media – such as the exclusivity of the journalist profession and the very limited acceptance of public participation, the understanding of media as observers and informants, and the model of one-way information provision from sender to receiver. Many CS Media perceive these aspects as problematic shortcomings and therefore regard them as foundations of the alternative character of their operations – as *raison d'etre* for their existence.

In this final section of chapter 2, I want to look in slightly more detail at further issues which are often criticised and which revolve around the notion of concentration and centralisation. The objective is not to analyze the sector in its entirety but to extract a set of *problematiques* which may enhance the understanding of CS Media and which, furthermore, will re-appear when we approach the World Summit on the Information Society.

Structures and concentration processes

The media industry is one of the most dynamic features of the contemporary world economy. It has been growing rapidly and the restructuring of media companies has been particularly intense, with the sector being subject to accelerating concentration. Newspapers, TV stations, movie producers, book publishers, record companies and other related businesses have merged, have acquired other companies, and have increasingly been concentrated around a small number of global conglomerates. This process has been fed by technological innovations, such as the introduction of cable and satellite delivery in the 1970s and 80s which massively increased the number of TV and radio channels that could be transmitted, as well as by political developments, particularly the world-wide ideological paradigm shift during the same period which questioned state interventions into the economy and led to the liberalisation of media markets. Even in Europe, where national public service broadcasters had enjoyed a virtual monopoly ever since the dawn of broadcasting, private media companies emerged and started to compete with public services. The Italian example shows how quickly waves of new businesses were integrated into existing companies or served as the basis for new corporate empires: Some 600 companies engaged in broadcasting in 1976; three years later, 80 % of advertising revenues were flowing into three private networks, marginalising the remaining channels; another five years later, these networks were owned by just one corporation (Petley/Romano 1993).

Horizontal concentration (i.e., within a particular media sector) has been complemented by vertical integration (i.e. expansion into different levels of media operations to control both content production and distribution channels). Prominent examples have been the Disney take-over of the US network ABC in 1995 and the merger of America Online (AOL) and Time Warner in 2001, but also the failed bid by Comcast, the US' biggest cable company, for Disney, one of the world's largest media corporations, in 2004. At present, six such vertically integrated conglomerates constitute the core of the world-wide media market: AOL Time Warner, Viacom, Disney, News Corporation, NBC-Universal, and Bertelsmann, with other major corporations such as Sony, Vivendi, Comcast ATT, TCI/Liberty and Cox Enterprises following closely.[21] Smaller media firms, such as film studios or national newspapers, are located in networks around the core companies, with which they often enter strategic alliances or joint ventures, tying them to the needs and strategies of the big corporations. Ex-CEO of TCI and 'media mogul' John Malone has been quoted with the statement, that only two or three companies may eventually dominate the media and telecommunications services (Dawson/Foster 1998: 54).

In news production, this has been a reality ever since the agencies Reuters, Havas and Wolff formed a global news cartel in 1859 and carved up the world into exclusive territories of influence (Rantanen 1998). Today the vast majority of news from other parts of the world is provided by the leading agencies Reuters, Associated Press (AP) and Agence France-Press (AFP). Some national agencies, such as Xinhua (China) and DPA (Germany), have

---

21 see, e.g., Herman/McChesney 1997, http://www.mediachannel.org/ownership, http://www.instat.com /abstract.asp?id=39&SKU=IN030689MB

important regional and thematic competencies but do not cover the globe in the way the first tier of global agencies does. Audiovisual news provision is even more concentrated, with AP running APTV and Reuters operating Reuters Television. Some TV news channels, such as CNN and BBC World Service, produce their own material but also subscribe to the agencies. Murdoch's Sky and Fox news networks depend largely on Reuters for international coverage (Boyd-Barrett 1998; Paterson 1997). The Middle Eastern news channels Al-Jazeera and Al-Arabiya have added a new element as they are based in a different cultural background and therefore offer an alternative to the Anglo-Saxon domain of television news. At the same time, however, they also draw from Western news values and don't fundamentally refute the structure of news reporting set out by the traditional networks.

Content: structural biases[22]

Contrary to the Anglo-Saxon tradition of a supposedly impartial and objective 'journalism of information', the choice of what to photograph, with which angle, who to interview and how many seconds to give to each aspect of the story obviously carries the meanings and ideologies familiar to the reporter and are constrained by a media organisation's structures and priorities (Paterson 1998). As an ever greater number of media is being controlled by an ever smaller number of enterprises, and as the latter are exposed to similar sets of constraints which favour certain types of content over others, the production of media information is structured in a way that does not foster diversity of content and may lead to an increasing enclosure of a 'public information sphere'.[23] Pressures of commercialisation and concentration have limited the "intellectual range for political, ideological and other thinking" (Chuck Lewis, executive director of the Centre for Public Integrity, quoted in Gutierrez 2004). Structural constraints that produce content biases may include the following:

1. The cultural background of media producers: Both principal audiovisual news agencies have an Anglo-American background and are based in London. Most foreign news must pass through this bottleneck before being sent

22 The argument put forward in this section is based on the approach of the 'propaganda model' by Herman/Chomsky (1988), which outlines the gates a news item has to pass before being distributed to the viewer or reader, but it considers additional perspectives and aspects.

23 Despite the substantial shortcomings of Habermas' notion of the public sphere (see, for example, Thompson 1995), the general concept of a contrast between a constrained distribution of information, led by hegemonic powers, and an interactive, less constrained communication sphere with zones of critical debate, offers a useful perspective for analysing the media sector. Ironically, the same actors which have, according to Habermas, originally been crucial forces in opening up a public sphere – the mass media – are now helping to reduce it.

to the rest of the world. A small number of culturally homogenous news workers in a few very similar organisations can therefore, consciously or unconsciously, shape the perceptions people have of large parts of the world.

2. The commodification of news: The supposedly factual and objective character of 'spot-news' implicitly assumes the social and political order as fixed and neglects how this order came into being. Structures and relations of power are rendered invisible and prevailing power structures legitimised (Golding 1997).

3. Economic and financial dependencies due to media ownership (Herman/Chomsky 1988). Many media outlets are linked directly or indirectly to the big conglomerates, all of which are transnational corporations, sharing the distinct interests of this sector.[24] Some are linked to non-media companies such as General Electrics, which is involved in arms manufacturing. Critical coverage by media of their owners and related activities is rather unlikely, if not impossible.[25]

4. Most news agencies earn the bulk of their income with financial and economic news services (Palmer et al. 1998).[26] Accurate, reliable and fast information on the latest developments in the financial markets is the basis on which these markets function. News agencies thus operate at the heart of modern international capitalism. Reporting on critical voices concerning neo-liberal globalisation, or putting too much emphasis on the negative impacts of financial markets and of corporate activity has not been in the interest of Reuters et al.

5. Advertising as a "de facto licensing authority" (Herman/Chomsky 1988: 14): Advertisers' choices concerning appropriate media for their messages influence the prosperity and survival of newspapers and TV channels. Alternative frameworks of analysis can be boycotted by advertisers, if they do not appreciate the contents and the environment of the particular paper or

---

24 Several media corporations are connected with conservative think tanks which advocate for neo-liberal economic and conservative social policies – e.g., John C. Malone and Rupert Murdoch are members of the executive board of the Cato Institute, and AOL/Time Warner fund the Manhattan Institute (Becker 2002).

25 For example, Times newspaper columnist Doug Gray resigned in 1998 following the paper's pulling of a column in which he criticised Times owner Rupert Murdoch and stated that it is necessary to "oppose the monopolistic workings of media moguls" (http://www.Undercurrents.org, 1999).

26 This interest in business affairs is not new, as the news cartel of 1859 was in fact preceded by an agreement among the three big agencies concerning the exchange of stockmarket prices in 1856.

channel.[27] Even news programmes are affected, with the press and the broadcast media increasingly conducting surveys to locate the news that would be enjoyed by the affluent market desired by advertisers. News Corporation's Fox News Channel, according to their chairman, "is directed at the needs of advertisers" (quoted in Herman/McChesney 1997: 49).

6. News sources: Media usually rely on the sources they can easily access, as well as on sources that are seen as 'competent' and 'authorised', such as government officials or the police. News from these sources is often accepted as factual information by viewers and readers, eliminating both the need to question the distinct interests and objectives of these 'factual sources' as well as the time-consuming search for alternative voices (Robinson 1995). An estimated 40 per cent of news originate in public relations agencies working for corporate or governmental actors (Becker 2002). In the hierarchy of sources, civil society groups rank far below governmental and corporate institutions, and while the more institutionalised and professionalised NGOs, such as Oxfam and Amnesty, still enjoy some limited access, grassroots activist groups are hardly ever consulted (Manning 2001).

7. The role of the journalists: Their social position and the constraints of the profession often bring about close ties with society's dominant elites, and professional relationships, and daily face-to-face communication often lead to social loyalties. Far from being 'impartial observers of power', top political journalists often share similar lifestyles – and similar opinions – with the government officials and business leaders they 'observe' (Rodriguez 1995). In addition, journalists have to treat government officials, societal leaders, and the institutions they represent with cautious deference if they want to continue to have access to the latest news, be the recipients of a news 'leak', be given regular briefings, or even accompany the troops as an 'embedded' reporter in the next war.

A combination of these factors can lead to a bias in reporting in favour of the interests and opinions of political and economic elites. Some of the best-documented examples of this bias include a media focus on crimes by what their home government would regard as 'enemy states', while failing to report on crimes by 'allies'; a media blackout on their home government's intentions for going to war; and a failure to expose the social effects of international economic agreements from which the media benefit. Extensive documentation on such cases has been gathered by communication scholars

---

27 The US public-television station WNET lost funding of several programmes from a company in 1985 after having broadcast a critical documentary of multinational corporate activity. It was told that this was not an appropriate behaviour "of a friend" of the corporation, and it probably has not done the same 'mistake' again (Herman/Chomsky 1988: 17).

and by organisations such as FAIR (http://www.fair.org). The involvement of Western media in Western military campaigns has increasingly been criticised since the Kosovo war in 1999 (in which, according to Said, the media was "part of the Nato campaign", Said 1999: 2) and, particularly, around the US-led invasion of Iraq in 2003 (see, e.g., Miller 2004).

Transnational social forces

From a North-South perspective, a largely one-way stream of information continues to flow from the industrialised countries to the rest of the world, while most news from the South has to pass the bottle-neck of the Anglo-Saxon news agencies. Yet the state-centric approach of cultural imperialism, as was advocated in the 1970s particularly (see Galtung 1971; Thompson 1995), seems hard to maintain in times of increasing trans-border economic activities. Neither the news agencies, nor the media-cultural industries retain exclusive ties with particular nation-states, which would make them part of deliberate state-led imperialist strategies. Rather than a clear-cut division between North and South, we have been witnessing a transnationalisation of economic, political, and social structures. Concepts of 'core' and 'periphery' increasingly apply within as well as across states. A new type of core comprises groups and alliances of transnational actors. The most visible of these are transnational corporations, business networks such as the World Economic Forum (WEF) and the International Chamber of Commerce (ICC), political associations like the G8, and institutions such as the WTO. The actors who are either involved or sympathising with this transnational concentration of authority have been called "transnational managerial class" (Cox 1981: 147) or "transnational capitalist class" (Sklair 1995: 71; Sklair 2000). Their main objectives can be seen as organising the conditions under which the interests of global capital and the maintenance of a stable system can be furthered within the international, national and local context.

The global media, i.e. those that have links to or even constitute the large media conglomerates, are an integral part of such transnational elite networks. As business operations with a global view, they strive for the expansion of global economic activity as well as enabling governance structures. However they also play a crucial supportive role by providing other transnational actors with the political and economic information needed, and by contributing to the production of values and attitudes favourable for their activities. An increasingly universal world economy requires both information about developments in various parts of the world and a universal ideological and cultural environment, and this is where the media-cultural industries have a role to play. This transnational sphere is not formed by equal contribution by all who are party to it, but is structured according to particular perspectives and interests, specific cultural backgrounds, and related worldviews. It implicitly involves either incorporation, marginalisation, or extinction of cultural practices that are not able or willing to adapt to 'modern lifestyles', industrialisation, urbanisation, and increased implementation of transnational authority (Gill 1995).

While the large global media can be aligned closely to the interests leading to this development, many CS Media as well as their civil society environment perceive the latter as exactly the problem they oppose. Rejecting the dominant development prerogatives of the past decades with their focus on 'modernisation' (and large-scale industrialisation) and the development of a 'cosmopolitan attitude', they share an alternative vision of human and societal development based on local community life, human rights, openness, democracy and autonomy (see chapter 2.1.).[28] This line of conflict runs typically between technocratic planners and managers on the one side, and disempowered and marginalised people on the other, thus between core and periphery – or even between 'inside' and 'outside' – of social, political and economic structures (Luke 1989). Ideological and cultural domination and homogenisation through global news and advertising have been opposed by marginalised communities, such as the Inuit in the Canadian Arctic, indigenous peoples in Brazil or the Maori in New Zealand, but also by dissident political groups and active citizens in the metropolitan centres of the North, producing their own video, radio, television, and websites.

A field of tension in the media sector

If we contrast the characteristic features of CS Media with their counterparts in the mainstream (i.e., commercial and, in some cases, public service) media sector, we can get a clearer idea of the distinctions between both media models. The table on the next page illustrates 'ideal types' of media as two opposing axes. These axes open a 'field of tension' to which media are exposed. Neither of the two opposing categories constitutes homogenous entities. Individual media organisations may differ substantially from the 'ideal' parameters, but all face the challenges and pressures posed by the different axes.

An 'ideal type' media model may not reflect reality in a satisfactory way, but it can point us to crucial characteristics of different media types and to critical issues in the media sphere. It offers a map for analyzing the outcomes of the WSIS process as it gives us a hint on which tendencies, regula-

28 In that, this vision uncovers connections with the increased role of 'identity' and the 'self' in the 'information age', as discussed by Castells (1996). Yet it includes social-political dimensions, and it does not resort to local isolation, but rather advocates dense networks and intensive inter-linkages between autonomous entities.

tions and formulations in the summit documents are likely to favour which type of media.

Mainstream media		**Civil Society Media**
Owned by business/state	↔	Owned by civil society members
Accountable to shareholders or the state	↔	Accountable to a community or civil society
Informant, detached observer	↔	Participant, social purpose
Profit-oriented/corporate	↔	Non-profit approach
Concentration, centralised control	↔	Decentral networks, decentralised control
Hierarchical organisation	↔	Horizontal networks
Universality: 'global village'	↔	Diversity: 'variety of villages'
Exclusivity of professional journalism	↔	Public participation, public access
Objectivity	↔	Subjectivity
Passive consumers	↔	Active audiences
One-way information	↔	Interactive communication
Content focus on elite interests	↔	Content focus on the marginal-ised, counter-information
Professionalisation	↔	Skill-sharing, empowerment
Commodification of information	↔	Global Commons and free knowledge
Links with transnational capi-talist class	↔	Links with civil society and social movements

Table 1 – A field of tension in the media sector

2.4 Conclusion

Beyond the classical media models of commercial and public service media, the media landscape is fragmented. Different terminologies, concepts and traditions co-exist, showing specific features but also significant overlaps with each other. In this chapter, Civil Society Media has been proposed as an umbrella concept to embrace the sector, to accentuate its main characteristics, and to distinguish it from other media actors. Highlighting key features, such as democratic self-organisation, social purpose, participation and decentralisation, and confronting these with typical characteristics of the media 'mainstream', has allowed us to clarify the boundaries of CS Media, to argue against the wholesale inclusion of 'the media' in civil society, and to conceive CS Media as a media space in its own right, rather than a niche and fringe additive to mainstream media. The concept will serve as a tool for understanding the thematic priorities, strategies and challenges of these media at and around WSIS, and for assessing the summit's outcomes for the sector.

3 Global Communication Governance

After chapter 2 introduced the actors which this book focuses on (Civil Society Media), this chapter will highlight the political-institutional and political-historic setting of WSIS as a global policy-making arena. If we define communication policy as the "laws, regulations, and public institutions [that shape] the deployment and use of communication and information systems" (Mueller 2004: 9), and governance as the structure of policy-making, then global communication governance encompasses the structural environment in which communication policy is shaped on a global level.[1]

The chapter will start by outlining recent developments of intensified globalisation and emerging global governance, and it will then focus more closely on the specific issue area of communication, outline the history of communication governance and take a closer look at the debates on a New World Information and Communication Order (NWICO) in the 1970s, which provided a major precedent for the discussions at WSIS.

3.1 Global Governance

Globalisation

In the state-centered world of the past two centuries, international relations were an intergovernmental affair. Sovereign states represented the basic units in the international system, and 'international governance' was based on inter-state diplomacy. However, from the late 1980s an accelerating increase in cross-border flows and global integration has changed the global political landscape. The environmental crisis has shown the unavoidable interconnectedness of the world, as well as the permeability of national borders. The end of the systemic confrontation between East and West opened opportunities for cooperative problem-solving beyond the conflict between major powers. In the economic sphere, international division of labour has deepened, and globally integrated production chains have emerged. Symbolic forms, languages, and cultural patterns are diffusing globally, greatly aided by new information technologies and the expansion of transnational media corporations. Similar forms of (sub-)cultural expressions in different and previously unconnected parts of the world have emerged. As goods and

---

[1] The term *governance* is usually linked with a more recent form of policy-making which goes beyond governmental politics to include new actors and connect different policy levels. This chapter will adopt an understanding of *governance* which recognises the focus on cooperative policy-making implied in many recent references to the term but includes older forms of inter-governmental regulation. It thus distinguishes not between *governance* and *non-governance* (e.g., governmental regulation) but follows Kjaer (2004) in distinguishing between *old* and *new* governance (Kjaer 2004: 10).

messages are floating around the globe, so are people – particularly in the global migration streams that are increasingly overcoming the persistent barriers of national borders.[2]

With 'globalisation' — as these developments have been termed — the world has experienced a "time-space compression" (Held/McGrew 2003: 3). The constraints of distance and time on social organisation and interaction have been eroded, and actions in one locale increasingly have consequences for 'distant others'. Globalisation thus "denotes the expanding scale, growing magnitude, speeding up and deepening impact of interregional flows and patterns of social interaction" (idem: 4). This development, as Scholte notes, "brings an end to what could be called 'territorialism', that is, a situation where social geography is entirely territorial" (Scholte 2000: 46) and instead leads to deterritorialised or "supraterritorial" (ibid.) relations. Globalisation thus requires "an alternative, nonterritorialist cartography of social life" (idem: 57).[3]

Global integration is not necessarily diminishing persistent divides in power, capabilities, and resources, but it is re-configuring patterns of hierarchy and inequality. The traditional core-periphery division between North and South, and thus between homogenous states/regions, is giving way to a puzzle of numerous cores and peripheries which transcend most states and regions.[4] Inside nation-states, there is ongoing segmentation into those who gain and those who lose from economic globalisation.[5] Overall the gap between rich and poor is deepening, and the polarisation in the distribution of income and wealth is increasing (Commission on Global Governance 1995; Castells 1998). Moreover, locality does not become irrelevent.[6] Globalisa-

2 There has been a wide variety of literature on each of these dimensions. For an overview, Scholte (2000) and Held/McGrew (2003) offer a good starting-point.

3 Claims of increasing globalisation, as well as their theoretical implications, have been challenged and refuted, leading to intense debates between proponents and adversaries, which began in the mid-1990s and stretched well into the new millennium (see, e.g., Rosenberg 2001). In this chapter, I will not discuss the arguments of the different sides but focus on the (justified) claims of globalisation as a precondition for global governance.

4 See the description of transnational class structures in chapter 2.3.

5 Hardt/Negri note that "the spatial divisions of the three Worlds (First, Second, Third) have been scrambled so that we continually find the First World in the Third, [and] the Third in the First" (Hardt/Negri 2000: xiii), and Castells recognises the rise of a 'Fourth World', a new underclass of impoverished and over-exploited people, which is "present in literally every country, and every city" (Castells 1998: 164).

6 Scholte, as many others, recognises that the end of a predominant focus on what he calls "territorialism" does not entail the end of territoriality as such, and he observes "many processes of reterritorialization" (Scholte 2000: 60).

tion may transform the scale of human social organisation, particularly linking distant communities and expanding the reach of power relations, but it may also de-link previously bound localities and strengthen separate identities (see, e.g., Castells 1996). The local is not displaced by the global, but it "becomes embedded within more expansive sets of interregional relations and networks of power" (Held/McGrew 2003: 3).

New forms of governance

As "complex interdependence" (Keohane/Nye 1977) is restricting the choices made by states, as the actual control most states possess over their territory becomes limited, and as territory as such becomes a challenged category, the question arises: How to govern the world under the condition of globalisation?

The concept of *global governance* has emerged as a response to this challenge. It differs from a notion of *government* which implies the direct capacity of political leaders to steer society, and focuses instead on systems of rules and interdependent problem-solving by a diversity of actors on a diversity of policy levels. Governance is thus something broader than government, going beyond both state actors and the state level of policy making, but also beyond formal institutions and organisations. Rather, it involves "systems of rule at all levels of humanity (...) in which the pursuit of goals through the exercise of control has transnational repercussions" (Rosenau 1995: 13).

Even though a crucial rationale for the concept is its 'global' approach, global governance does not just transfer policy-making from one level (nation-state) to the next (global), but it involves qualitative changes. An illustration of global governance would encompass self-organising networks and webs of policy-making fora in which capacity for decision-making and implementation is widely distributed and new actors and levels have "transformed sovereignty into the shared exercise of power" (Held/McGrew 2003: 11). The specific characteristics of global governance are:

a) participation of new actors, particularly from business and civil society,

b) re-distribution of spaces and policy layers between local and global, and

c) interaction and cooperation between different actors and layers.

Steps towards global governance

Yet a network policy structure has only been emerging step-by-step and has been accompanied by a continuous struggle around the persistent centrality of nation-states in the global political arena. In 1995 the Commission on Global Governance still regarded states as the main actors and the United Nations (UN) as the "central mechanism" for facing the challenges of the future (Commission on Global Governance 1995: 8). Its main concern was with effective multilateral problem-solving between nation-states within a strengthened UN framework. This somewhat limited degree of innovation has been criticised as an institutional re-redesign of traditional international relations (Messner/Nuscheler 2003: 13).

The world conferences of the 1990s offered a laboratory for going beyond a state focus. They invented a "new dramaturgy of world politics" (Messner/Nuscheler 2003: 4) by putting both the public and the political focus on the global level, and by going beyond the diplomatic exclusivity of states which gradually lost their monopoly of international relations. The UN Conference on Environment and Development (UNCED) in Rio de Janeiro in 1992 set a precedent, particularly by integrating new actors (NGOs and business). A series of summits followed, including (amongst many others) the conference on human rights in Vienna 1993, the womens conference in Beijing 1995, and the Rio plus10 conference in Johannesburg 2002 (Messner/Nuscheler 1996).

Despite representing the most prominent approach to global governance, these summits were still based on state-organised 'inter-national' multilateralism. UN-based summitry thus represents an important point of departure – or a "construction site" (Fues/Hamm 2001) – for global governance but certainly not its end. The role of the state in this emerging system is changing, rather than diminishing. It is transforming from a sovereign ruler to an "interdependency manager" (Messner/Nuscheler 2003: 17) which is increasingly "embedded" (Held/McGrew 2003: 13) in webs of global interconnectedness, supra-national forces, and new emerging players, and whose sovereignty is thus compromised due to both international constraints and the influence of non-state actors. Yet it retains important capacities to negotiate its position within governance networks.

The beginning of the new millennium has shown that the development towards network governance structures – or from "old" to "new" governance (Kjaer 2004) – is not a smooth one and may temporarily be halted or reversed. While the cosmopolitanism of the 1990s had put collaborative problem-solving in areas such as climate change on the global agenda, the new millennium began with new divides as well as the recurrence of old ones. Military conflict has re-intensified, especially after September 11th 2001; there has been a re-nationalisation of foreign and security policies; and the US as the world's greatest military and economic power has undermined multilateral rule on a variety of levels, including the rejection of the International Criminal Court, the Kyoto Protocol, and a weakening of the UN system. Hamelink's observation from the early 1990s is still (or rather: again) valid: "In today's world system the notion of national sovereignty is certainly under siege, but it has not yet surrendered" (Hamelink 1994: 37). What we witness is a) a mixture of cooperative global governance and individual power politics, and b) a mixture of new actors and arenas with the persistent centrality of inter-governmental politics and the UN system.

Normative perspectives

If global governance implies to shape the process of globalisation politically, questions can be asked regarding the direction and the motivation of that process of 'shaping'. For some, global governance represents an alternative to neo-liberalism as a regulatory model, offers leeway for controlling market forces, and may even lead to the establishment of welfare state policies on a global level (Blank 2002; Rodrik 2002). Others claim that the principal actors of current global governance have in fact created the neoliberal policy environment of the present (see, e.g., Dawkins 2003). According to this view, global governance encompasses the activities of the leading governments of the global capitalist economy and of major institutions such as the World Trade Organisation (WTO), the International Monetary Fund (IMF) and the World Bank, supported and pushed forward by the large transnational corporations (TNCs), whose business-friendly privatisation policies have initiated neo-liberal restructuring worldwide. So while for some, global governance is inherently progressive and represents a way to deal pro-actively with a world economy that has gone out of control, for others it equates neo-liberal rule-making by the protagonists of that economy.

While the objective of global governance is to achieve cooperative problem-solving, the definition of these problems and the ways they are 'solved' are established through negotiations between a variety of actors, in which the interests of the most powerful players have the largest influence. Global governance is not per se 'progressive' or 'neoliberal'. The important questions to be asked are, by whom, in whose interests and for what purpose governance is conducted – or more simply: "Who is in charge?" (Dawkins 2003: 15).

Civil Society participation

One of the main challenges of global governance processes is how to achieve legitimacy. In a confined state-centered world, legitimacy was based on elected national parliaments. However, with global multilateral decision-making structures increasing, the corridors of power have wriggled out of the embrace of democratic accountability. The share of decisions taken externally, beyond the space of democratic legitimation and beyond popular scrutiny and participation, is increasing, and so the concept of democratic self-determination is seriously compromised.

As traditional representative democracy is put into question, there have been calls for an increase in public participation in global decision-making – and to thereby develop forms of "global" or "cosmopolitan" democracy (Kjaer 2004; Held 2003). At the centre of these concepts is the recognition of the crucial role of civil society in developing new forms of accountability. The supposed democratic functions of civil society include an increase in transparency, as it makes global decision-making processes public, a watch-dog role of closely scrutinising the activities of decision-makers, and the actual participation in decision-making processes (Messner/Nuscheler 2003). Mobilising civil society is seen as essential for re-gaining legitimacy for the political process. As Cox notes: "Legitimacy is a power that flows from the bottom upwards. It can only come from committed participant citizen action through a multitude of groups and associations that express citizen concern with the various aspects of community life" (Cox 2002: xx). How exactly this is happening will be the subject of chapter 4.

3.2 Communication Governance

As immaterial processes which easily move from space to space and just as easily cross borders, communication flows have generated a particular need for international cooperation and for collaborative regulation. From the beginning of telegraphy, half of the telegrams sent from most places were international (Flichy 1994), and so a universal language and coding for telecommunication was essential; tariffs needed to be calculated and revenues to be distributed between different carriers as well as between senders and receivers. Technical standardisation and compatibility have been crucial for extending both communication systems and economic activity around the globe, the allocation of radio as well as satellite spectrum has represented an important requirement for trans-border information flows, and with economic control being increasingly exerted through intangible assets, the worldwide recognition of intellectual property rights (IPR) has been pursued – particularly by the rich nations. Governments have sought to control cross-border movements of content, to restrict the import of information deemed inappropriate or dangerous for their own power position, and to support the export of information in accordance with their political objectives.

From inter-national regulation to multi-actor governance

Telegraphy was the first area to lead to institutionalised international cooperation: The establishment of the Austro-German Telegraph Union in 1850 was followed by the West European Telegraphic Union in 1855 and finally the International Telegraph Union (ITU) in 1865. The ITU merged with the International Radio-Telegraph Union in 1932 to become the International Telecommunication Union which is still a central actor in communication governance today. The General Postal Union was founded in Berne in 1874 (and was later re-named Universal Postal Union). Copyright and author's rights were debated at the First International Conference on Copyright in Brussels in 1858 and were regulated in the First International Convention on Copyright, adopted in Berne in 1886. Patent legislation was widely standardised at the Congress of Vienna for Patent Reform in 1873, the International Congress on Industrial Property in Paris in 1878, and through the Convention for the Creation of the Union for the Protection of Industrial Property in 1883. The first conference on wireless radio-telegraphy was held in Berlin in 1903 and led to the Berlin Radio Conference in 1906. There the Berlin Radio Convention was adopted to manage and regulate the radio frequency spectrum (Hamelink 1994).

After the creation of the United Nations (UN) in 1945, many of these organisations were integrated into the UN system, and new bodies were created. Amongst the prime players in international information and communication have been the ITU, WIPO (World Intellectual Property Organisation), and UNESCO (UN Educational, Scientific, and Cultural Organisation). Non-UN institutions, particularly the WTO (World Trade Organisation), have recently taken an increasing share in communication policy measures. Yet all these institutions have remained in a model of international, i.e. inter-governmental, 'regulation' and have differed from a multi-actor multi-layer 'governance' model (Kleinsteuber 2004).

However, this 'old' model has been challenged in the past two decades. The emergence of the Internet illustrates the relevant factors: It introduced a new space – cyberspace – which was not defined in geographical terms and therefore existed outside the traditional territorial modes of regulation and it was created largely by civil society, professional groups and commercial actors, without the lead of state bureaucracies – a "grand collaboration of many entities in all sectors" (Cerf 2004: 15). This type of development was supported by the rise of neo-liberal thought amongst Western governments, which emphasized business-led and non-interventionist policies.

The regulatory body for the Internet, which was created in 1998, translated these characteristics into an institutional framework. The Internet Corporation for Assigned Names and Numbers (ICANN) was not based on traditional national representation but on representation of the main groups of actors involved in the development and operation of the Internet: the technical / professional / expert community, the private sector, and civil society. The 'netizens' – the 'inhabitants' of the new non-territorial cyberspace – were involved in the establishment of the institution through online elections. ICANN has chosen a narrow policy agenda, focusing on the maintenance and development of technical interoperability and thus following an approach that deals with 'code' rather than political and social claims (Machill/Ahlert 2001). As ICANN shows, communication governance has been in the front line of innovating governance mechanisms, moving beyond pure inter-governmental logic, experimenting with new constituencies and thereby shaking established power configurations. Global communication governance has spread over a range of spaces and arenas, creating interdependent networks of multiple actors and policy venues (Raboy 2004a).

The private sector and the experts

The prominent role of the private sector, technological experts and professionals constitutes one of the specific characteristics of the sector and its governance. From the invention of the telegraph in the early and mid-19th century, communication engineers were among the first to depart from a state-centered approach and to test the commercial path towards implementing their inventions, and they established some of the most important companies of that time, for example Graham Bell's telephone company in 1876.[7] From its beginning, the ITU recognised the possibility for companies to become a contracting party, and later included them as 'sector members' in the organisation. Early telegraph conferences were attended by private operators, and company delegates were included in US governmental delegations to ITU conferences from the 1930s onwards. Engineers and technicians held their own conferences and they took major decisions in shaping the new technology. Flichy (1994) argues that paradigm changes in telephone technology, such as those from electromagnetic to electronic, towards optical fibre or towards digitalisation, originated in debates and innovations within the technical community, on the one hand, and in economic considerations, on the other. Thus a coalition of technicians and companies essentially shaped the evolution of the medium, taking the lead role in technological evolution out of the hands of the state. Industry self-regulation was accompanied by strong influence in policy-making: At a major (governmen-

[7] By the early 20th century, development and market implementation were mostly done by large corporations. The largely autonomous introduction of electronic television by EMI in the 1930s can serve as an example, see Flichy (1994).

tal) radio conference in Washington in 1927, company representatives drafted large parts of the Radio Convention (Hamelink 1994).

The arrival of personal computers and Internet technology has seen civil society activists take a bigger role in shaping the communications environment. Free and open source software represents the most prominent example for civil society-based development of communications infrastructure. Nowadays, many companies, government administrations and end-users prefer the Linux operating system to Microsoft's Windows. Other examples of civil-society-based experimentation, innovative uses and new developments in communications infrastructure were introduced in chapter 2.2. The open spaces of the Internet, particularly, were first explored by academic institutions, and media activists were among the first to implement web-based live reporting, audio/video streaming, and many other possible applications.

Yet, as we have seen in the previous section, shifts in the loci of power and control are a contested terrain. States do not give up their steering capacity easily, even in a highly technical and expertise-based field such as communication.[8] Unregulated spaces on, for example, the Internet have triggered government attempts to re-gain control over 'lost' territory. Conflicts of that kind between different groups of actors (states, business, civil society) have regularly re-appeared during the history of communication governance, and they played a dominant role at the WSIS, as we will see later.

Paradigm shifts in communication governance

Just as vital for understanding WSIS as the emergence of new actors, new spaces and new technologies are the ideological environment and the political shifts which have accompanied and influenced communication policy. Several authors have divided the history of global communication governance into three phases (Ó Siochrú/Girard 2002; van Cuilenberg/McQuail 2003). During the first phase, roughly from the mid-19th to the early-/mid-20th century, regulation was mostly based on a narrow set of technical and economic considerations as well as state interests. Industry needs, e.g. for common standards, served as the main impetus. Policies for social, political, and cultural objectives did not develop on the international level as they did at the national levels of many countries.

---

[8] Now-familiar conflicts between the private sector and government actors as to the appropriate type of governance and, particularly, the level of 'government interference' and 'government control' appeared already at the above-mentioned radio conference of 1927, see the account by Hamelink (1994).

A second governance period began after the Second World War, as the UN system institutionalised normative concerns regarding development, human rights, and ultimately domination by powerful actors. The Universal Declaration of Human Rights included the freedom of expression, and UNESCO strengthened international cooperation on culture and communication. Media policy was infused with public service values and strengthened requirements of fairness and diversity. Information rights were linked with political, civil, economic and social rights (as well as duties and responsibilities), and information and communication was thus more strongly embedded in social life (Kleinwächter 1989). Following the decolonisation process, the NWICO debates questioned cultural domination and sought equity in international communication flows (see next section for a more detailed overview). Yet dealing with normative issues was hardly a harmonious process, as the East-West confrontation overshadowed multilateral negotiations: "Most of the issues on the political agenda were located in the context of the superpower conflict which made their resolution complex and often unattainable" (Hamelink 1994: 24).

With the defeat of NWICO by the Global North/West in the mid-80s, a third phase of global communication governance has been characterised by a central role of the trade paradigm and trade-/business-institutions, and a shift of regulatory mechanisms towards a market- or industry-dominated model. The world has witnessed the "unobstructed rollout of a neo-liberal model of media development" (Calabrese 2004: 324). Within this paradigm, culture is seen primarily as a commodity for global trade, and communication is usually equated with commercial media, leaving little space for civil society-based media initiatives. The media industry has achieved a global reach, IPR have emerged as main control mechanism in the post-fordist network economy, and GATT/WTO have become the most powerful actors in global media governance, ever since IPR were introduced by Western governments in GATT talks in the mid-80s (Ó Siochrú/Girard 2002). Self- and co-regulatory mechanisms which have been prominent in communication governance and which include, to some extent, new institutions such as ICANN, fit well with the dominant paradigm of this period. They "reflect the thinking of a corporate age in which co-operation between industry and professional associations, rather than the State, is seen as a move away from 'big government' " (Kleinsteuber 2004: 66).

However, after its heyday in the 1990s, serious cracks emerged in the neo-liberal trade paradigm. At the turn of the millennium, a series of major global protests questioned neo-liberal policies on a global scale, anti-capitalist discourses have re-appeared, and the gatherings of social movements and civil society, particularly the World Social Forum, opened spaces for discussing and developing alternative social concepts. In the media sphere, media activists have coordinated amongst each other around global networks such as Indymedia, and community radios, civil society-based Internet service providers and media NGOs have formed networks such as the World Association of Community Radio Broadcasters (AMARC) and the Association for Progressive Communications (APC). The economic breakdowns in East Asia and Latin America between 1997 and 2002 started to delegitimise neo-liberal policies; September 11th 2001, the credit crunch of 2008 and the subsequent global recession quickly revitalised the idea of a 'strong state', both on a security economic level. Thus a vacuum has emerged in which neo-liberalism has been thoroughly demystified, while a new convincing paradigm is not yet visible. Taking place in this ideological and historical environment, a summit like the WSIS had the potential to suffer from lack of orientation but also to develop new visions, create discourses, and set the framework within which future governance can be 'thought'.

3.3 New World Information and Communication Order

History and demands

The most important precedent of a global debate on communication issues was the conflict around a New World Information and Communication Order (NWICO) in the 1970s and 80s. NWICO took place in parallel to a coordinated challenge by many newly decolonised states to develop a New International Economic Order and shake off dependencies in the economic realm. Through NWICO governments of the South confronted the cultural legacy of colonial relations. The space for this challenge was UNESCO whose composition had changed with the entrance of the Soviet Union in the mid-1950s and the newly independent nations from the Global South from the late 1950s. Decolonisation transformed the balance of power, so that by 1980 three quarters of UNESCO member states were from Africa, Asia, the Carribean, Latin America, and the Middle East.

Since its creation in 1945, the 'free flow of ideas' had been a core aspect of UNESCO's mission. The new majority challenged this doctrine as a means of on-going domination by the powerful states from the North/West. It criticised the alleged 'freedom' in information streams as a disguised one-way flow of information from the rich to the poor and thus as a form of cultural imperialism. Control over the means (as well as the content) of communication was seen as essential for progressing on the path of development and independence. Demands centred around a more balanced circulation of news and an equal participation of the South in international information relations, the development of national media to reflect national cultures and realities, and the improvement of the generation of information in the South.

To counter misinformation, a code of conduct to ensure unbiased reporting was proposed (Carlsson 2003).

Elements of this 'new order' were articulated at successive UNESCO conferences. Lines of conflict appeared between defenders of national sovereignty and those of independent media and were underpinned by the ongoing cold war conflict. The West had to accept a certain degree of policy change but succeeded in watering down the various proposals substantially. Documents such as the Mass Media Declaration, which had originally been proposed by the Soviet Union, were adopted, set standards and norms for media operations, called for balance and reciprocity in information flows and allowed for certain extensions of state sovereignty into the area of information (Kleinwächter 1989). Yet they lost their contentious edge, as specific obligations for media, codes of conduct for journalism, and references to state control of the media were deleted (Giffard 1989). The West also had to agree to the appointment of an "International Commission for the Study of Communication Problems", headed by Nobel Peace Price holder Sean McBride, which was to analyse communication issues by giving particular attention to the needs of the South and to the establishment of NWICO. The report of the MacBride Commission was adopted at the 21st UNESCO General Conference in Belgrade in 1980. It contained 82 recommendations which balanced the priorities and objectives of the different sides of the conflict but also included points which clashed with the prime interests of each side. The report affirmed the value of independent media and rejected government control of the media, yet it equally criticised the dominance of major commercial actors in the media sector, it called for laws against media ownership concentration and for limits to the activities of transnational corporations (MacBride et al. 1980: recommendation 58). Amongst the proposed measures to safeguard against the negative implications of such information monopolies was a 'right to communicate'. This right was to complement existing human rights to information and to freedom of expression by adding, for example, a right to privacy, a right to be informed, and a right to participate in public communication (idem: recommendation 54). This new set of rights was to enhance (individual and collective) participation in communication processes and to help transform one-way information flows into interactive communication flows – and thus to strengthen "the concept of dialogue instead of monologue" (ibid.). It implied, as the commission explicitly stated, the democratisation of the media by offering viewers, readers and listeners possibilities for participating in the decision-making processes and the programme activities of the media.

The MacBride report represented an attempt to reconcile divergent perspectives and to open new lines of thought, yet it was unable to bridge the ever-increasing gulf between the three sides in this conflict. The only common approach could be found in the establishment of mechanisms to promote technological assistance for communications development – most notably the International Program for the Development of Communication (IPDC). Those mechanisms helped countries of the South to strengthen local and national media infrastructures, yet they moved the political debate about the global framework of unequal relations to the technical level, on which the core of the demands from the South were impossible to be achieved. In 1984, the US left UNESCO and withdrew their financial contributions, followed a year later by the UK. The NWICO debate continued for a while but was eventually shelved in the late 1980s. The UNESCO general conference in 1989 re-asserted the centrality of the free flow of information, while retaining calls for a wider and better balanced dissemination of information.

NWICO and the media

NWICO touched central aspects of the business operations of Western commercial media. The latter's content was criticised for misrepresenting the South, and Southern governments sought to establish new national media which would become competitors and limit the business opportunities of Western media in foreign markets. The free flow-doctrine, in contrast, favoured those with the largest economic possibilities to actually fill the open spaces of a 'free flow' – the likes of Hollywood and the big news agencies. As a logical extension of the free market economy, it gave opportunities to the strongest actors in the information market and therefore served as a strategy for economic expansion (Kleinwächter 1989). In addition, the state-interventionist implications of many NWICO proposals, particularly those from the Soviet block, ran counter to the dominant Western media ideology which equated media independence with the absence of state regulation and which saw state interventions into the media sector as the prime threat to freedom of expression.

So the "Western media organizations were not detached observers of the debate" (Giffard 1989: 27), and they increasingly contributed to the governmental decision-making process through public interventions and through political campaigns. Regular editorials appeared in major newspapers, most of them condemning the NWICO challenge. 84 percent of editorials in US newspapers were anti-NWICO, anti-UNESCO, or in favour of withdrawal of the US from UNESCO (idem: 181). Often the demands of the South and the communist block were thrown into the same basket and reduced to the simple formula claiming that those challengers sought to establish government control of the media worldwide (idem: 170). In 1976, 33 media organisations, two-thirds of them based in the US, founded the World Press Freedom Committee (WPFC) to represent media interests in the NWICO debate and to, particularly, put pressure on the US and other Western governments to take a stronger position against NWICO. It alerted the US government and congress to the challenges of NWICO at an early stage of the debate, lobbied successfully against references to press controls in UNESCO documents and had a decisive role in the later US decision to withdraw from UNESCO. Giffard (1989) traces this decision back to the advocacy efforts of a very effective de-facto coalition including the WPFC, the commercial media, the US State Department, and conservative think tanks such as the Heritage Foundation. The views of these groups corresponded very closely, and their statements touched on the same themes, with media and think tanks usually setting the tone. In a "symbiotic" relationship, "the government responded to the media's concerns about Unesco and the press in turn supported the government's action" (idem: 272).

Civil Society Media had less capacity to influence the public discourse around NWICO, nor did they have direct access to the policy-making level. Yet the anti-monopoly stance (including both commercial and state monopolies) of the MacBride commission opened inroads for references to their practices. The report stressed the role of "group and local media" (MacBride et al. 1980: 55-57), "alternative communication" (idem: 113) and the crucial need for "horizontal" (idem: 151), "participatory," "decentralized" (idem: 168) and "bottom-up communication" (idem: 149-151; 265-68), in overcoming a model of communication where "the few talk to the many, about the needs and problems of the many, from the standpoint of the few" (idem: 168). The vision expressed there offered concrete starting-points for strengthening the role of CS Media, yet it was eventually crushed between the major powers in the NWICO dispute.

Post-NWICO: civil society and communication rights

After the political approach of NWICO had been buried, the focus applied during the 1990s changed towards technical considerations and business-friendly policies, particularly with regards to digital technology and the Internet. From 1994, several G7 (and later G8) summits brought up issues such as ICT infrastructure development, cyber-security and the digital divide; the G8 summit in Japan in 2000 led to the establishment of the 'Digital Opportunity Task Force'; and one year later, the UN founded the 'UN ICT Task Force' (Kleinwächter 2004; also see chapter 3).

The debate on democratic reform of the global communication system survived outside institutional arenas, as some of the 'new' actors in global governance took up the abandoned discourse. From 1989, civil society activists and communication experts met at regular 'MacBride Round Tables' to monitor world communication and to advocate for changes in its structures.[9] The Istanbul Round Table in 1991, for example, observed "with growing concern the rapidly increasing concentration, homogenization, commercialization, and miniaturization of national and world cultures" as well as "the virtual monopoly of global conglomerates over [...] information". It called for NWICO to be renewed and built by "new peoples' coalitions" including "a broad range of public groups, social movements and organizations" (MacBride Round Table 1991).

International media and communication NGOs, such as the World Association of Christian Communication (WACC), the Association for Progressive Communications (APC), and the World Association of Community Broadcasters (AMARC) particularly picked up the concept of the 'right to communicate' and developed it into a broader agenda of communication rights. They constructed networks such as the Platform on Communication Rights and created the campaign 'Communication Rights in the Information Society' (CRIS). Using the concept of communication rights as a common frame has put the democratisation of media at the centre of their efforts and has positioned them in clear opposition to the NWICO agenda of notably the US government and the US mainstream media, as both had strongly rejected "to accept public participation in the management and operations of private media under the rubric of the 'right to communicate' " (Giffard 1989: 251). However at the same time, these new civil society coalitions have refused to pick up the agenda of the 'other side'. They have not called for restrictions on the freedom of the press, nor for an increased role for governments in regulating the flow of information. The emphasis, rather, has been on empowering individuals and communities. So, as Vincent et al. (1999) reflect in their "update" to the MacBride report:

"What started, historically, with the proposed restructuring of the international information and communication order has grown into an alliance of grassroots organizations, women's groups, ecology networks, social activists, and committed academics. [...] There is a new NWICO in the making which sees itself as a network of networks based in civil society" (Vincent et al. 1999: ix-x).

3.4 Conclusion

World summits have been an integral part of the emergence of global governance – the inclusion and connection of new actors, institutions and policy levels in global political processes. These recent developments have been

---

[9] see http://www2.hawaii.edu/~rvincent/macbride.htm

reflected (and sometimes preceded) in the information and communication realm. The role of business actors and technological experts has been particularly strong there, and the change towards neo-liberal policies particularly fundamental, but a coordinated global forum (a 'summit') which would allow the wider participation of organised civil society has emerged comparably late.

The most extensive global debate on information issues – NWICO – saw interventions by advocates of mainstream media interests, but it largely remained a governmental dialogue between North and South (and between East and West). The focus on state objectives did not provide a favourable environment for CS Media, yet they were recognised in the report of the MacBride commission. Despite NWICO's eventual demise and the resistance against fundamental reform, a catalogue of policy proposals was produced and offered a programme which WSIS could have pursued further.

Since the early 1990s, advocacy and pressure for a change in worldwide communication structures has spread from the institutionalised arena to the (still relatively confined) spaces of NGO discussions and Round Tables, and onwards to a wider set of grassroots activist groups and citizen initiatives. In the next chapter, I will take a closer look at exactly these actors, their strategies and their agendas.

4 Civil society and global governance: Structures, strategies, agendas

Central to the development of 'new' modes of governance has been the entrance of 'new' actors. This chapter will look at the involvement of civil society actors in global governance, highlight the strategies with which they seek to influence policy, and trace agendas. It will introduce different approaches of intervening in governance processes and several theoretical concepts which will be applied in the later analysis of CS Media activities at and around WSIS. Moreover, it will map a number of civil society networks and coalitions which have started to work towards an alternative perspective on global communication governance.

4.1 Intervening from inside and outside

Institutionalised civil society

Parallel to the expansion of economic and political globalisation, civil society actors have expanded campaigns around the globe and have developed their own networks of transnational connections, activities, and infrastructures. Transnational civil society activity is not a new development as such – the campaign for the abolishment of slavery and the transnational labour movement were early examples from the 19th century. Yet the second half of the 20th century has seen dramatic increases (Sikkink/Smith 2002), and their level of professionalism, and the density and complexity of linkages among them has grown substantially (Keck/Sikkink 1998). Since the Rio summit in 1992 when some fifty thousand activists participated in summit proceedings and non-state actors obtained access to discussions and decision-making, civil society has become an integral part of global politics. Major NGOs now have consultative status with the UN through the Economic and Social Council (ECOSOC). Their numbers increased from 41 in 1946, to over 700 in 1992, to over 3,000 in 2008.[1] The roles, rights, and obligations of NGOs have been defined in UN Resolution 1996/31. Their status is usually restricted to one of 'observers' and their rights include the limited right to address the Preparatory Committees (PrepComs) of UN summits as well as the summits themselves. Yet these rules comprise "minimum benchmarks for participation" (Ó Siochrú 2004a: 331) which may vary as their precise interpretation depends ultimately on the governments, secretariats and chairpersons of the respective policy arena.

In addition to their watchdog activities – e.g. the intense monitoring of World Bank policies which triggered the establishment of the World Bank

[1] http://www.un.org/esa/coordination/ngo

Inspection Panel – and agenda-setting, civil society actors have participated in new forms of 'multi-stakeholder' governance – collaborative processes involving all 'stakeholders', usually governments, business, and civil society (Hemmati 2002). However these forms of "neo-corporatism" (Messner/Nuscheler 2003: 16) only involve certain sections of civil society – usually the large professionalised non-governmental organisations (NGOs). Grassroots groups, social movements, fluid networks, and many other civil society associations without hierarchical structure, legal status, and sufficient funding, are left out of the governance equation.

A perspective which only looks at the big (and often politically moderate) civil society actors takes the risk of focusing only on what Kaldor calls "neo-liberal civil society" (Kaldor 2003, see chapter 2.1.) while excluding all the rest, and of integrating civil society together with big business to a set of 'new global players' which take up former state functions and become a quasi "extension of the state" (Zehle 2003). This approach can lead to lumping together corporations and civil society actors under so-called public-private partnerships (PPP) and thus losing any distinction between private sector and civil society (as done by Messner/Nuscheler 2003). 'Civil society participation', in this sense, may not lead to new forms of bottom-up governance, but to a restructuring of top-down mechanisms through the participation of some 'new actors'. Increasingly detached from broader civil society constituencies, these formerly 'new' actors may quickly be integrated into established power structures (Stammers/Eschle 2005). The result would be the continuation of the elite-driven governance processes which more radical parts civil society have rejected increasingly during the past years.

Direct action and protest

An "era of popular unrest" (Dawkins 2003: 97), the end of the 20th and the beginning of the 21st century have seen a very different kind of intervention into global policy processes by civil society actors. Meetings of global institutions and policy elites, such as the G8, the WTO, the IMF, the World Bank, the World Economic Forum (WEF), the European Union (EU), and others, have attracted mass mobilisations and have been seriously obstructed by demonstrations and blockades. Protesters did not come to participate in policy-making but to stop and prevent the 'business-as-usual' of these institutions which have been deemed un-democratic and criticised as contributing to, rather than solving, global problems such as environmental degradation and poverty. Starting with a 'Global Street Party' to coincide with a G8 meeting in May 1998 and a 'global day of action' on the day of the following G8 meeting on June 18th 1999, the more prominent "stages [...] in the process of dissatisfaction with the activities of the institutions of global economic governance" (Wilkinson 2002: 193) were protests against the

WTO in Seattle, November 1999, the IMF in Prague, September 2000, and the G8 in Genoa, July 2001. The protesters contributed to an increased public visibility of these institutions, and to the early ending of several of their conferences. From early 2001, meetings of global governance institutions have increasingly been 'protected' by barbed wire, high fences, tightened anti-protest legislation and paramilitary police operations (Notes from Nowhere 2003).

During the protest events, but also beyond them, civil society activists have met, exchanged perspectives, and created new networks. Influenced by the thinking of anarchism, autonomism, and by do-it-yourself (DIY) culture, they have developed (and experimented with) non-hierarchical organisational forms, decentralised networks and voluntary cooperation, and have focused on direct action (rather than advocacy) and the promotion of self-organised alternatives to the existing order (Day 2005). Characteristic for this approach has been the refusal to work through the state, whether by taking over state power or by addressing the state with sets of policy demands. Rather the objective has been to democratise and change society from below. Nevertheless, policy preferences do exist, including various aspects of sustainable development; a protection of the public sphere and the recognition of global commons; human, social, and labour rights; limits to corporate and state power; freedom of movement; and numerous additional issues. Yet the strategies for achieving these objectives have involved public debate, public pressure, and local self-organising, rather than formulating demands to be addressed to state authorities (Dawkins 2003).

'Inside' and 'outside'

The summit protests "signalled the opening of a legitimation crisis affecting both states and the institutions of global governance" (Cox 2002: xix). To counter dissatisfaction and critique, many global and regional regulatory bodies have entered into communication and exchange with civil society representatives and have offered channels for participation. Some international institutions have embarked on an extensive "process of courtship with civil society" (Wilkinson 2002: 201). Yet only in a very few cases have civil society actors been incorporated into actual decision-making structures. In most organisations, including the IMF, the World Bank and the WTO, civil society is being "kept at arm's length" (idem: 195). These organisations usually invite NGOs on a very selective basis and regard the latter's role primarily in increasing awareness for the organisation's activities. Civil society interaction is thus tightly constrained, and power usually remains firmly with the organisation and its government members. In cases of successful policy influence, the resulting reforms may serve to legitimise the respective institution and reinforce its influence (Nelson 2002). The question thus is: Are civil society actors primarily 'used' for enhancing public reputation and legitimacy, or are they actually able to influence policy processes substantially? What do they give, and what do they get in return?

The answers given to this question by different civil society actors have varied. While many larger NGOs choose to engage with global institutions in an effort to trigger reform and to reduce the damage of harmful policies, many grassroots activists fundamentally oppose the elite-driven policy processes in large unaccountable organisations and prefer to work towards their complete abolition.[2] These differences have repeatedly caused splits between different sections of civil society. For example, while representatives from NGOs such as Greenpeace and Amnesty International accepted invitations to the WEF in 2001, many social movement activists were protesting outside against the forum and had to face police charges and tear gas.[3] Being 'inside' or 'outside' has represented a fundamental dividing line – sometimes only a strategic one, but often one that generates identity and excludes other approaches. This fault line has been the most visible roadblock on the way towards a more coordinated and homogenous civil society 'stakeholder'.

However, traces of such coordination are visible, and occasionally the distinction between more formal and more informal sectors of civil society has been blurred. Looking at the history of US public interest groups in the field of communication policy, Mueller (2004) points to interactions between grassroots social movements and formal advocacy organisations, as the former create political demand for certain policies and sustain the necessary public pressure for having demands considered in a policy process, and the latter translate these demands into specific regulations and act as an "interface between social movement activity and political decision-makers" (Mueller 2004: 7). Accordingly, Banaszak (2005) notes that the successes of the US feminist movement have been assisted by a "state-movement intersection" (Banaszak 2005: 151) which has linked actors inside and outside institutions, as well as institutional and extra-institutional tactics. The separate NGO declarations, which have accompanied many global summits, have represented further traces of a sphere beyond an inside-outside divide. They have shown, on the one hand, a willingness to engage with the global policy level, while, on the other hand, offering a deep critique of the government-business agenda and presenting alternative visions. At UNCED in

---

[2] Naidoo (2005) calls the former an either "Comprehensive Engagement" or "Selective Engagement Approach" and the latter a "Principle Non-Engagement Position".

[3] However, it also needs to be mentioned that most NGO representatives stopped attending WEF meetings in later years.

Rio 1992, civil society actors presented 42 alternative treaties, demonstrating "the growing confidence in the NGO community that it has a legitimate and pertinent claim in the world political arena" (Hamelink 1994: 49).

4.2 The strategies of social movements

Civil society is about "how individuals try to take control of global processes rather than being overwhelmed by them" (Anheier et al. 2004: v) and, essentially, about how citizens and their communities shape globalisation. However, Anheier et al. (2004) note that the ways in which this happens are still "poorly documented and little understood" (ibid.). Here, a look at social movements theory can help us to find out more about the strategies and effects of civil society interventions in global political processes.

Norm change

As we have seen in previous sections, the global political system is increasingly affected by norms – i.e. principled beliefs about appropriate behaviour – and by varying interpretations of interests. Sikkink regards global politics as "a fusion of a particular structure of power and purpose" (Sikkink 2002: 302) in which the two prime sources of regime change are power shifts and norm change. This opens a door for civil society and social movements to put their objectives onto the global policy agenda. Without voting or decision-making power in most institutions, and without financial or economic leverage, they use a mixture of "information politics", "symbolic politics", and "accountability politics" (Keck/Sikkink 1998: 16): generating fast, credible, and politically usable information, creating to symbols and stories that make sense of a situation for an audience, using tactics of persuasion and moral pressure, and holding powerful actors accountable to previously stated policies and principles. They are thereby working simultaneously on different levels of the policy cycle – problem definition, agenda setting, policy formulation, implementation, evaluation and termination (Kingdon 1995) – but play a particular role in the earlier stages: helping to define the issue area, highlighting problems, and prescribing solutions. Global policy discussion fora, such as UN summits, are receptive to these activities, as they represent arenas where actors and interests clash in a "battle for justifications" and where "consensus mobilization" is a prime target (Khagram et al. 2002: 11). In some cases, the effects of civil society's involvement may go beyond narrowly defined policy change and include broader transformations the very nature of international debate and international interactions (Keck/Sikkink 1998).

"(A)ltering the norm structure of global governance" (Sikkink 2002: 302) also influences the understandings of state interests. Norms and discourses do not fundamentally transform the interests of powerful economic and political actors, yet they give guiding-lines for perceptions and interpretations of interests and may therefore open leeway to adapt the given profit or security objectives of dominant players to changing situations. Thus policy agendas favoured by civil society groups (such as debt relief, the reform of financial institutions, or support for free software) may be partially achievable even when they run counter to the interests of powerful actors. Even if the latter's perception of interests does not change substantially, those actors may find themselves in a position in which they cannot afford going against a widely accepted norm. A strong norm may undermine their autonomy in a way that violating the norm by pursuing divergent interests leads to costs that outvalue those interests (Dimitrakopoulos 2005).

Organisation and legitimacy

How civil society groups organise is of crucial importance for their specific perspectives on norm change and for the strategies which they choose to pursue. Norm-building starts inside a group or movement, and the degree to which a group breaks with the constant reproduction of prevailing norms represents a vital component of its philosophy. A thorough change in norms and practices and its reflection in organisational structures may help to socialise members into new norm patterns, to advertise those patterns to outsiders, and to influence wider social practices on a long-term basis. A limited change, on the other hand, which maintains certain forms of prevalent structures and approaches, may correspond more closely with the practices of a target audience, such as a global organisation, and may prove to be more effective for achieving immediate, albeit limited, policy changes.

Mueller (2004: 6) separates "activism" and "social movement activity", on the one side, and "advocacy", on the other. While the former is connected by loosely coordinated communications, meetings, demonstrations, cultural activities, has a "fluid and ephemeral" (ibid.) character, and has a high presence of 'countercultural' and 'identity-oriented' actors (Kriesi 2004) who emphasize the indivisibility of means and ends, the latter is rooted in formal organisations and encompasses citizens groups and similar actors who interact directly with official policy-making institutions and have a more 'instrumental' approach to policy (ibid.).

Khagram et al. (2002: 6-9) propose a typology of four different civil society types:

(1) NGOs: fairly formal and professional non-profit groups with legal status and paid personnel

(2) advocacy networks: informal networks, bound together by shared values, common discourses, and dense information exchange

(3) coalitions: deeper coordination of strategies and tactics, e.g. creating common campaigns, often merging institutional with non-institutional approaches

(4) social movements: networks with a higher level of collective identity, able to generate coordinated and sustained social mobilisation, often including disruptive action and protest

For all these types, the ability to create sufficient *network density*, i.e. a high level of connection between actors, is seen as a crucial precondition for generating and underlining strong policy alternatives. Such connection would optimally lead to the development of shared values, collective beliefs, and ultimately a common identity (Keck/Sikkink 1998).

The legitimatory basis, on which civil society actors seek to influence political processes my include representation, i.e. speaking for affected communities and bringing up marginalised perspectives; a domestic or political constituency; and expertise (Nelson 2002). The latter is particularly relevant in the case of *epistemic communities,* i.e. networks of professionals "with recognised expertise and competence in a particular domain and an authoritative claim to policy-relevant knowledge within that domain or issue-area" (Haas 1992: 3). Members introduce shared beliefs and interests into institutional arenas and provide information and advice to policy-makers. *Critical communities* have similar structural characteristics but they maintain more distance to institutional actors and to the immediate policy process and operate more indirectly, promoting new cultural values, defining new problems, developing new discourses. They "seek acceptance of a new conceptualization of a problem [and] they attempt to influence the conceptual framework used to think about a cluster of issues" (Rochon 1998: 23). Critical communities often challenge the status quo and propose alternative visions, and they operate in connection with social movements which take up their ideas and translate those into action frames. Critical communities can thus be a source of the 'critical discourse' of social movements.

Political opportunity structure and framing

For all these networks and coalitions to achieve successful results on the policy level, a set of preconditions need to be met. First, a favourable *political opportunity structure* requires a relative openness of the institutional setting, strong alliances, weak, or at least vulnerable, enemies, and a motivation for people to engage in contentious politics (Giugni 2004; Tarrow

1998). A crisis, or at least emerging cracks, in a social, political, economic, or ideological system, may lead to a disunity of political elites and may thereby create what economists call a 'window of opportunity', and policy analysts a 'policy window' (Kingdon 1995) – a particular dynamic in which established social orders become receptive to change. In such a situation, *target vulnerability*, i.e. the receptiveness of, for example, a global institution to respond to incentives, sanctions, or pressures on its accountability and legitimacy, would rise. The level of target vulnerability will raise or lower the chances of implementing the objectives of a civil society group (Keck/Sikkink 1998). *Political alliances* are equally crucial for a group's or movement's success. Powerful allies both within and outside the institutional arena may support claims and demands and represent important forces in shifting predominant organisational ideologies as well as public opinion (Giugni 2004).

In addition to material-institutional aspects, political opportunity structures have 'cultural' or 'discursive' dimensions. The discursive environment of a target audience, such as a global organisation or the general public, is likely to have an effect on "what kind of ideas become visible for the public, resonate with public opinion and are held to be 'legitimate' by the audience" (Kriesi 2004: 72). *Issue resonance* (Keck/Sikkink 1998: 26) thus plays a key role as it limits or extends the receptiveness of the target audience to the topics which a civil society group puts on the agenda or to the preferences which it suggests and tries to establish. If those topics and preferences offer linkages with the perspectives of the organisations or social groups which are being addressed, and if demands correlate with wider public opinion, chances for successful intervention rise.

However political opportunities are rarely a given. They only become 'opportunities' "when defined as such by a group of actors sufficiently well organised to act on this shared definition of the situation" (McAdam et al. 1996: 8). So the perceptions, beliefs and interpretations of potential opportunities by those civil society actors who have considerable mobilising capacities are crucial for the subsequent wider mobilisation. Once a particular institution, debate, or historical situation is identified as an 'opportunity', civil society actors can intervene in its formation and development through their repertoire of tools to trigger norm change. So they can influence the political opportunity structure as such by shaping the terms of the debate (Dimitrakopoulos 2005).

The ability to create *conceptual frames* is seen as a particularly valuable key to embark on successful policy interventions and to, particularly, support the development of issue resonance. Frames articulate the characteristics of an issue and the objectives of an actor to policy makers, potential allies and the wider public, and may draw connections with the agendas of those target audiences. If successful, framing an issue makes it comprehensible to an audience, attracts attention and encourages action, and makes it fit with predominant perspectives in an institutional venue (Keck/Sikkink 1998).

A word of caution is necessary regarding the scope of these prescriptions. Although referring to the term 'social movement', most related research focuses on the rather institutionalised sections of civil society and their involvement in government-based policy-making.[4] This reductionist approach has been criticised as it neglects the wide range of movements and activist groups that are not set up formally as organisations. Diani (2003) makes a clear difference between *social movements* and *social movement organisations*, and Stammers/Eschle (2005), accordingly, wonder how *social movements* are actually dropping out of the picture of *social movements theory*. In their view, "a social movement necessarily encompasses informal and non-institutional activism" (Stammers/Eschle 2005: 54).[5] Yet it would be equally reductionist to apply the tactics and strategies proposed by social movements theory only to the work of institutionalised NGOs. Norm change can be achieved through policy interventions as well as through public debate and changing public perceptions of social, political, and economic realities. 'Information politics' can include official statements to governments as well as leaflets distributed in a pedestrian zone.

4.3 Beyond policy: A focus on practices

Characteristics of communication activism

If we take a closer look at civil society activity in the field of information, communication and media, we can identify a set of characteristic features: the centrality of practices, policy-sceptical perspectives, and the complexity of the issue area.

Practices. CS Media and other civil society-based communication initiatives, first and foremost, are autonomous information infrastructures which

[4] e.g., Baumgartner/Mahoney (2005) suggest that the only valuable way to study social movements lies in their connections and interactions with government.

[5] In contrast to the preoccupation of much social movements literature with formal organisations, approaches which focus more on individuals and loose networks offer valuable insights and represent an interesting complement, particularly when looking at CS Media. These approaches allow space for the foggy area between concrete collaboration and occasional cooperation, between formal and informal ties, between individual and collective identity. According to Diani, social movements are "networks of informal interactions, between a plurality of individuals, groups or associations, engaged in a political or cultural conflict, on the basis of a shared collective identity"(Diani 2003: 301).

often constitute alternatives to other ('mainstream' or 'hegemonic') structures and which are "explicit attempts to distance communications practice, as much as possible, from both the state and the market" (Costanza-Chock 2005: 4). Media activism is primarily about the development of alternative information systems as part of a people-based bottom-up information society – and neither about policy advocacy, nor about 'protest'.

Policy-sceptical perspectives. There is wide-spread distrust in established policy processes, based on two schools of thought: the cyber-libertarianism and openness of the Internet pioneers and the anarchism of the global justice movement. The former focuses on developing technical solutions for policy challenges and favours the absence of governmental intervention. The latter adds a strong anti-corporate view and widens the perspective towards a general scepticism of large-scale institutions and power structures.

A policy-sceptical perspective interprets most regulation as 'enclosure' of previously free spaces and regards policy and institutions primarily in the framework of 'threats'. Actors have typically experienced hostile legislation, such as the closure of access to the airwaves or to the Internet, and repressive state measures, such as the seizure of hard-drives, the closure of websites or repression against copyright infringement.[6] They react to policy moves perceived as threats to civil liberties and to the infrastructures and initiatives they have autonomously created.[7]

Complexity of the issue area. Media is all around us, but even though it is very immediate, it often remains abstract. It is largely perceived as a tool, or as information channel, thus as a 'medium' for 'issues' but not as an 'issue' in itself which deserves attention and constitutes an object of mobilisation. In addition, debates on topics such as IPR, spectrum allocation or Internet governance are usually highly specialised and technical, require expert knowledge and are difficult to communicate to a larger non-skilled audi-

---

6 One of the most important cases was the seizure of hard-drives from the global news network Indymedia in October 2004 by the US Federal Bureau of Investigation following a request by Italian police under antiterrorism investigations. See Milan (2004b).

7 This combination of policy scepticism and autonomous practices was exemplified by the call for a gathering of the activist network Peoples Global Action in 2006. On the thematic area of information and communication, the call noted that "Software patents, repression of peer to peer, IP & data retention laws are attacking digital freedom daily" and asked: "How can we collectively face new laws enforcing data retention on the internet, to prevent our communication structures from becoming the weak points in our activism?" These perceived treats were to be tackled by creating robust alternative structures, such as "strong user communities" and "alternative servers". The call can be found at http://stamp.poivron.org/DigitalStruggles

ence.[8] Thus the conditions for the formation of a wider social movement and, particularly, public campaigns are problematic. Clusters of like-minded actors have emerged around the themes of 'media reform' and 'communication rights' (see below), but mostly these have depended on the expertise of a core group of specialists. Epistemic communities and, particularly, critical communities therefore play a lead role and occupy important positions.

Towards a systematic approach

Recent research on media activism and advocacy has developed proposals for integrating these characteristics into conceptual frameworks. Hackett and Carroll (2006) have distinguished different "strands of praxis" of what they call "democratic media activism" into, on the one hand, those that confront existing hegemonic structures and powers, such as the media reform movement, and, on the other, those that build or nurture counter-hegemonic practices. The latter include "building independent, democratic and participatory media [and] opening new channels of communication independent of state and corporate control" (Hackett 2000: 70-71).

Milan (2006b) goes a step further by connecting 'strands of praxis' with a specific strategy towards policy interventions. She identifies three different approaches: 'inside', 'outside' and 'beyond'.[9] While 'inside' actors regard the policy process as an opportunity for change, innovation and potential gains, and as a chance to get themeselves and their issues recognised, 'outside' actors privilege disruptive practices to make their voices heard, putting pressure from the outside and organising counter-summits and direct actions. This rather classical inside-outside division is complemented by a third sphere of actors who operate independently of (and thus 'beyond') policy arenas and define themselves through their practices (see next page).

---

[8] Adilson Cabral describes communication issues as "an oracle – because of its complexity – for people and groups that are not integrated in our discussions". Cabral operates the regular news bulletin "Sete Pontos" which explains current issues in the field of communication and which has the goal "to make the discussions easier" (Interview AC).

[9] Parts of this concept have been developed in conversations between Milan and the author of this book (see, e.g., Hintz/Milan 2006b).

Type of actors and their dimension of engagement		**Repertories of action and strategies towards policy**
INSIDE	Advocacy organisations and coalitions; lobbying groups	Cooperative attitude: active engagement in policy-making; activities are dependent on political process
OUTSIDE	Organised media activist groups, networked activists; joint activists	Confrontational attitude: pressure from outside (counter-summits, campaigns…) and disruptive direct actions; dependent on political process
BEYOND	Practice-oriented actors: Grassroots activists, individuals (software developers, hackers, etc), alternative media, community initiatives	Autonomous attitude: reaction only to perceived threats (repression, enclosure of spaces, etc); bypassing institutions; setting up alternative structures; autonomy from political process

Table 2: Civil society actors 'inside', 'outside' and 'beyond' (table taken from Milan 2006b: 19; with adaptations by the author)

Rather than influencing the policy process, whether through participation inside or protest outside, actors from the 'beyod' sphere focus on setting up self-organised infrastructure and concrete alternatives to mainstream systems. They mostly interact only indirectly with the regulatory environment by developing technical 'by-passes' around regulatory and political obstacles. Technical 'solutions' to such challenges may include self-written software, setting up servers in places which are less prone to state repression, and, generally, self-organised infrastructure.[10] In this way, 'beyond' actors focus on 'by-passing' political regulation, looking for unregulated spaces and expanding them. They directly interact with the political environment only when there are immediate threats to the autonomous spaces and projects which 'beyond' actors have created, or when institutional initiatives outrage their sense of justice.

10 The slogan "By-pass the corporate media" which can be found on stickers and leaflets of Indymedia UK provides a good example for this approach. The 'corporate media' are not to be confronted but simply 'by-passed'.

4.4 An agenda of media democracy and communication rights

The previous chapters have already given us some hints regarding the policy objectives favoured by CS Media. This final section of chapter 4 will outline policy initiatives and identify common objectives. It will thereby construct a reference framework which will allow a more informed analysis of the policy proposals which CS Media have contributed to the WSIS summit.

The World Social Forum

The World Social Forum (WSF), which took place for the first time in January 2001, has become the most prominent space for coordination between civil society groups and social movements, an important arena for civil society to articulate its political demands, and thus a reference point for civil society debates and agendas. Communication became part of the forum agenda in 2003, when a thematic strand was dedicated to discuss media- and culture-related issues. The 2005 forum saw the establishment of a World Forum on Communication and Information (WFCI), a one-day event prior to the WSF, by a transnational network of CS Media and related NGOs. A European Forum on Communication Rights (EFCR) took place alongside the European Social Forum in London in October 2004. Several CS Media organisations, such as Oneworld, the magazines Znet and Le Monde Diplomatique, IPS and AMARC are members of the International Council of the WSF, as are other major NGOs working on communication, such as the Latin American Information Agency *(*ALAI) and APC. Grassroots projects such as Indymedia have been very active in non-official side-events.

The WSF's aggregate agenda on media and communication includes the following (see Hintz/Milan 2006a):

- 'Communication rights', including and transcending Article 19 UDHR
- universal and affordable access to technologies and telecommunication frequencies, with those frequencies to be considered common goods
- the adoption of free software and open source tools
- a redefinition of IPR to allow a free circulation of knowledge
- cultural and linguistic diversity, and the protection of cultural identities

- opposition against the trend of commodifying communication, particularly within the WTO
- opposition against media concentration and media deregulation
- support for media pluralism, and independence of media from powerful economic and political actors
- establish social control over, and accountability of, the media, for example by media monitoring systems
- communication 'from below' by establishing community and alternative media, building public spaces for practicing horizontal and participatory communication and the mutual sharing of know-how and information
- financial support: a tax of 1 percent on advertising revenues of commercial media, a transnational non-profit agency for fundraising for CS Media, and allocation of public resources to the CS Media sector

Media Reform Movement

In 2002 Michael K. Powell, Chairman of the US Federal Communications Comission Commission (FCC), underlined his preference for market-based approaches: "The night after I was sworn in, I waited for a visit from the angel of public interest. I waited all night, but she did not come" (quoted in Tarleton 2002). Shortly afterwards, a crowd of 'angels' descended onto the FCC headquarters, in one of the first demonstrations against media concentration. Singing anti-corporate hymns and wearing white sheets with wings made of cardboard, dozens of media activists protested against the ongoing deregulation of media ownership restrictions and public service obligations. Their action constituted one of the starting points for a recent intensification of campaigns and mobilisations focusing on the media.

A growing range of local groups, connected in broader networks and coalitions, have launched campaigns against the concentration of media ownership and for the decentralisation and democratisation of the media sector. Groups in the US and Canada have been particularly advanced on this endeavour, combining previously sporadic and isolated expressions of dissatisfaction with the mainstream media to a media reform (also called 'media democracy' and 'media justice') movement. This movement is challenging the dominant corporate media, demanding "more equitable access and distribution of resources and technologies, rights and representation", and advocating "a corresponding shift to democratic logics/paradigms" (Kidd et al. 2005: 4). As awareness of media and communication issues is growing, a "movement of movements" (ibid.) around media justice and communications democracy has been emerging.

At the core of this movement is a network of NGOs and activist groups, often combining policy interventions with grassroots activism and protest. Some have been well established, such as the Media Alliance, others, such as Free Press, are fairly new and reflect the recent rise of the movement. They work "to increase informed public participation in crucial media policy debates" (http://www.freepress.net) and to "open up the media system to allow more diversity of opinion to be expressed" (ibid.). Priorities include protecting public service broadcasting, supporting local access to the media, safeguarding net neutrality and opposing commercialisation of the spectrum.

Gatherings and conferences have connected the different parts of the movement and created a common identity. In their declaration "Media Justice: Media for All the People", the organisers of the Media Justice Summit 2004 outline cornerstones[11] for a media reform agenda: accountability of media organisations; the right to communicate; liberation of airwaves, networks and cultural spaces from commercial and corporate control; establishment of community-owned and -controlled media institutions and networks. Mainstream media are criticised as "a willing propaganda machine for corporate interests", and the objective is to "fundamentally change the ownership structure, language usage, and policy discourse around media within the United States and internationally." This will require fundamentally "new policies, systems, and structures that will treat our airwaves and our communities as more than markets for exploitation."

CMFE and AMARC

The Community Media Forum Europe (CMFE) was founded by community radio activists in November 2004 to bring the perspectives of community media to policy processes at the European level. The CMFE seeks to strengthen the "Third Media Sector" which encompasses "non profit-making media serving a local community" (http://www.cmfe.eu), "with specific features such as open access, horizontality, gender equality" (Francesco Diasio, quoted in Milan 2006a: 9), and to "acknowledge the community media sector as part of the mediascape at the national level, alongside with commercial and state-owned media" (ibid).

---

[11] See http://www.reclaimthemedia.org/stories.php?story=03/07/14/1665417, the following quotes are taken from this document.

From that follow a number of other demands: establish funding opportunities for community media within specific EU programmes and create a Community Media Fund; enhance freedom of speech and media pluralism; recognise the radio frequency spectrum as a public resource; give special support to minority media, and draw up a Framework Convention on Community Media in Europe. To prevent a marginalisation of community media, the CMFE claims that 'Third Sector Media' are fulfilling public service duties neglected by national public service broadcasters which are facing increasing commercial pressures. As such, so goes the argument, community media "should get a 'must carry' status on all relevant present and future communication platforms (DAB, etc)" (http://www.cmfe.eu). Thus, like the other examples mentioned here, the CMFE refers to increasing media concentration and the resulting dangers.

The worldwide network of community broadcasters AMARC laid out its policy priorities during its eighth world conference in February 2003 – when the preparation process for the WSIS summit was about to get in full swing. The "Kathmandu Declaration" (AMARC 2003a)[12] outlines some of the issues and proposals that AMARC would later submit as input to the negotiation process. It starts with a dark view on the current situation of the world which "is grievously threatened by rampant militarism, accelerated privatization of our most basic resources, religious fundamentalism, and extreme capitalism." Human rights are seriously threatened by these developments, and poverty is increasing. In the media sphere, consolidation of mass media ownership is accelerating. Yet on the upside, the declaration acknowledges that the community radio movement is rapidly growing. "Community media, particularly community radio, have given communities the means of cultural expression, news and information, and local dialogue" and they help to "bridge across the digital divide between those who have access to the world's information resources and those who do not." So while the "rights of communication" are endangered by many current developments, people are claiming them by practical deeds.

To enhance media and communication policies, AMARC calls for legislation that provides community groups access to media infrastructure, such as the radio frequency spectrum; a recognition of that spectrum as "part of the global commons which should not be privatized"; respect for privacy rights on the Internet and other media platforms and an end to pricacy infringements, "whether corporate or governmental"; full and equal access of all social sectors to the media; a particular focus on enabling access and ownership of all means of communications for women; and the "realization of the

12 The following quotes are taken from this document.

Right to Communicate in its broadest, most inclusive sense." The Strategic Plan 2003-2006 adopted at the Kathmandu conference (AMARC 2003b) includes the establishment of a community media fund.

Communication Rights

The right to communicate, or communication rights, have been a central reference point for many of the groups and networks mentioned on the previous pages and, at the same time, the core connection with the earlier NWICO debates. The role of communication rights in policy discourses has been strengthened by the CRIS (Communication Rights in the Information Society) campaign. CRIS' original purpose was to "ensure that communication rights are central to the information society and to the upcoming World Summit to the Information Society (WSIS)" (http://www.crisinfo.org), but it has diversified its area of activity to, for example, the UNESCO Convention on Cultural Diversity, and it has continued its work after the conclusion of the WSIS process.

Communication rights group together a number of actual or potential human rights which concern the production and sharing of knowledge and ideas, the media, and people's effective participation in communication processes. They are based on, but extend beyond, the right to freedom of expression and include, for example, the right to be properly informed about matters of public interest, the right to practice cultural traditions, the right of minorities and indigenous people to education and to establish their own media, the right to be protected against privacy infringements, the right of protection of common knowledge resources against private appropriation by industries (Hamelink 2002). CRIS has translated these concerns into fours areas of activity:

(1) Media democracy: reverse trends of media concentration; recognise the airwaves as public commons and tax their commercial use for public benefit; promote alternative, independent, and public service media

(2) Intellectual property rights: a full review of copyright; promote alternative systems, such as open source and copyleft

(3) Civil and political rights: oppose excessive data retention and surveillance, established on the pretext of combating 'cyber crime' and 'terrorism'; expand rights to privacy, freedom of expression, communication and association

(4) Equitable and affordable access to information and knowledge, and to ICT and media infrastructure, for all people, specifically the marginalised

such as women, the disabled, indigenous people and the urban and rural poor

Peoples Communication Charter

A further initiative coming out of the MacBride Roundtables, the Peoples Communication Charter was created in 1999 by some of the organisations that later formed CRIS, such as WACC, APC, and AMARC, and additional groups and associations, such as Deep Dish TV and Vidéazimut. The charter was to provide a common framework for an emerging movement concerned with media democratisation, the cultural environment, and the production and distribution of information. It seeks to define "communication rights and responsibilities to be observed in democratic countries and in international law" (People's Communication Charter 1999)[13].

The charter's 18 articles span across many of the issues raised by other networks, and add several elements. Most significantly, they put serious obligations on the media industry. Media are obliged not to "ridicule, stigmatize, or demonize people on the basis of gender, race, class, ethnicity, language, sexual orientation, and physical or mental condition" (Art. 14), and they should avoid "the creation of wasteful, unnecessary, harmful or ecologically damaging needs, wants, products and activities" (Art. 16). People are given "the right to demand that media actively counter incitement to hate, prejudice, violence, and war" (Art. 15) as well as the "right to useful and factual consumer information and to be protected against misleading and distorted information" (Art. 16). Children, specifically, "should be protected from harmful media products and from commercial and other exploitation" (Art. 11). All people should be able to "receive opinions, information and ideas in a language they normally use and understand; to receive a range of cultural products designed for a wide variety of tastes and interests; and to have easy access to facts about ownership of media" (Art. 3). Everyone has "the right of reply and to demand penalties for damage from media misinformation" (Art. 7) and to, generally, "hold media accountable to the general public" (Art. 17).

Beyond the wide range of issues focusing on mainstream media content, the charter includes the right to literacy (which contains computer literacy and "critical media awareness") (Art. 5), the need for "freedom of electronic expression" and for "freedom from electronic surveillance and intrusion" (Art. 12), as well as other privacy rights (Art. 13), and the right to "participate in, contribute to and benefit from the development of self-reliant communication structures" which requires "international assistance to the devel-

[13] The following quotes are taken from this document.

opment of independent media" (Art. 4). Public participation in policy-making is to be extended substantially: "All people have the right to participate in public decision-making about the provision of information; the development and utilization of knowledge; the preservation, protection and development of culture; the choice and application of communication technologies; and the structure and policies of media industries" (Art. 10).

Convergence?

The initiatives which have been mentioned in this section do not operate in an isolated manner. There are connections, collaborations and overlaps, concerns and demands are transported from group to group and diffuse throughout the wider 'network of networks'. Yet these connections still lack a systematic dimension. There is no common platform and no commonly discussed (let alone agreed) agenda which groups and organisations can draw from. The People's Communication Charter offers important building blocks for such a common agenda but has not reached the status of a general reference document for a wider set of media and communication movements. The WSF may have developed into the broadest discussion arena and may therefore be the space where the most far-reaching convergence on policy ideas and governance proposals can take place, yet it has been unable to represent all sections of civil society and social movements and unwilling to generate common agreements and position papers. With the activities of CRIS members at the WSIS summit, at the WSF, but also in local contexts, some authors have greeted the rise of a global movement for communication rights (e.g., Calabrese 2004) and therefore suggest communication rights as the reference theme. Indeed, many of the initiatives mentioned here have started to refer to communication rights, however the discourse has so far remained inside specialised civil society circles, and a wider mobilisation could not yet be achieved.

Within the fuzzy cloud of demands and agenda points, constantly developing, re-shaping, and adapting to new situations, there is no clear common agenda which advocacy initiatives can easily refer to.[14] Yet we can identify issues which re-emerge in various places:

- critique of media structures (concentration) and media content

[14] This finding correlates with the analysis of communication advocacy groups in the US by Mueller (2004). Mueller observes a lack of a general concept, a common label, and sufficient linkages between different actors. The variety of different concepts and demands, according to Mueller, represents a serious problem for progressive communication policy advocacy.

- public participation in media operations, and public accountability of the media
- people's access to communications and media infrastructure
- recognition of, and financial support for, civil society-based media
- rejection of the commercialisation of communication infrastructure, such as the airwaves
- critique of excessive IPR, support for the global commons and the public domain
- communication rights, including freedom of expression, privacy rights, special rights for marginalised communities

4.5 Conclusion

Civil society actors have intervened into global governance processes on several levels: Some have used the growing space for 'new actors' to participate inside institutional settings and to work towards policy reform, while others – particularly those associated with the recent global justice/alter-globalisation movement – have expressed fundamental objections to governance agendas and structures through protest and pressure from outside. Focusing on practices, rather than institutional policy-making, many media and communication activists have chosen a third approach – 'beyond' policy – which focuses on setting up alternative infrastructure and on technical 'by-passes' around regulation.

Attempts to influence policy from 'inside' require a favourable political opportunity structure, strong alliances, weak or fragmented opponents, and the creation of suitable frames for communicating specific objectives to a target audience. With global politics representing a "fusion of a particular structure of power and purpose" (Sikkink 2002: 302), the strategic information and symbolism provided by civil society actors can trigger norm change and thus influence policy. The legitimacy which these actors give to global political processes can be traded into policy gains, yet it can also strengthen those institutions which have been challenged because of democratic deficits. From outside the official political process, indirect and long-term norm change can result from the discourses created by critical communities and from the practices and policy/infrastructure alternatives by 'outside' and 'beyond' groups.

Civil society actors working on media, information and communication, and spreading activities over all different levels, have recently developed vague, yet converging policy programmes calling for public access to media systems, support for civil society-based media and communication rights. This tentative agenda allows us to assess the content discussed at and around the WSIS summit, and it provides the background with which CS Media actors approached the WSIS process.

5 Approaches to information society

Information society is one of the grand narratives that have been proposed to explain and describe current social developments. For some, it is (or has been, for a while) the new framework of perception for contemporary societies. In the (post-)modern world, information is seen as a decisive aspect for human progress, and thus we are inhabiting "societies in which information increasingly is the primary means and product of all processes" (van Dijk 2005: 133). Castells, despite criticising the term 'information society', recognises that "information generation, processing and transmission [have] become the fundamental sources of productivity and power" (Castells 1996: 21) and that core social, economic, political and military processes are being "deeply transformed by the informational paradigm" (ibid.).[1]

However, the theories and discourses that have developed around the recognition of a growing role of information have been criticised because of their tendency to over-enthusiastically suggest dramatic and all-encompassing social re-organisation processes (Webster 2002), and because of their increasing transformation into political rhetoric that displays little connection with the original findings on informational change (Kleinsteuber 1999). The decision (in 1998) to organise a world summit on 'information society' fell into a period in which the 'information society' paradigm experienced its popular re-emergence and its co-optation by political actors as part of political campaigns rather than social reflection, while the wider debate around information and communication (both in academia and civil society) diversified to include a broader set of issues and concerns beyond a techno-economic focus (Kleinsteuber 2003).

In this chapter I will not attempt a broad explanation, nor a comprehensive criticism of information society discourses, but rather identify some aspects – conceptual backgrounds, ideas and issues – which influenced and informed the debates at the WSIS summit and which affected the role of – and the outcomes for – CS Media in this process. These aspects constitute starting-points for understanding the conflicts and tensions at and around the summit.

---

1 Many actors and observers have preferred to talk about a Knowledge Society, in which theoretical knowledge (as opposed to experienced knowledge) is the source of innovation and technology, and in which science has become both foundation and guideline of human activity (see Heinrich-Böll-Stiftung 2006; Stehr 1994). In this chapter I will focus on the 'information society' as the underlying concept of the WSIS summit.

5.1 Elements of the 'new' society

Transformations towards an information society are usually reported in five different areas: technology, economy, labour, space, and culture (Webster 2002). Technology offers the most wide-spread and most obvious explanation. Often referred to as 'information revolution', the emergence of personal computers, cable and satellite television, microelectronics, and eventually the Internet, has changed our lives profoundly. In the economic realm, the value of information activities has increased in comparison with the value of agrarian as well as industrial production. Accordingly, the share of industrial labour has decreased, the share of services has increased, often pictured in a change from 'blue-collar' to 'white-collar' workers, and these so-called knowledge experts, symbol analysts and information workers have become the leading work force.[2] Geographical re-organisation has been made possible by connecting remote locations through communication networks, enabling new social linkages and transcending previously strict borders. Time limitations are being swallowed by real-time information flows. Contemporary culture is filled with information, as we are surrounded by signs and messages. Our immediate environment, including bodies and clothes, carries a multiplicity of symbols, and mediated information occupies a much larger space in our lives than it did in earlier times.

From the 1960s and 70s, scholars such as Fritz Machlup and Marc Uri Porat classified information- and knowledge-related elements of the economy and identified a steep rise.[3] In his theory of the "Post-Industrial Society" Daniel Bell (Bell 1973) pointed to changes in the labour structure: from agricultural to factory (industrial) to service (post-industrial) occupations. Science, research, technology, and administration constitute the defining factors of the post-industrial society, theoretical knowledge (as opposed to experienced knowledge) is the source of innovation, and a country's scientific capacity influences its relative position in the global system far more than its industrial production capacities. The post-industrial society, not least, "is an information society" (idem: 467) in which "there is a greater need for mediation, or journalist translation" and "selection from the vast flow of information" (idem: 468).

'Post-fordist' approaches have offered a further (yet less enthusiastic) view on economic and labour-related changes towards a 'society' in which information plays a larger role (e.g. Lipietz 1987). They have observed how,

---

2 Yet the statistics on which such assertions are made are strongly contested, see Kleinsteuber 1999; Webster 2002.

3 According to Machlup, the size of the workforce in what he called the "knowledge economy" rose by 80 per cent between the years 1940 and 1959 (Mattelart 2003: 64).

from the 1970s, a post-fordist mode of production, encompassing decentralised and networked production processes, flexibility, differentiated specialisation, the universality of market principles and precarious working conditions, has substituted the Fordist-Keynesian economic model which had been based on standardised mass production, industrial labour, class compromises, the nation-state as primary economic space and national elites as primary social actors. The importance of information and symbolism increases with deepening differentiation, and the skills of "symbol analysts" (Reich 1991) – processing, analyzing, and distributing information – have become a key resource. Information-based services are deemed central in facilitating global economic integration and in controlling wide-spread networks. In this "network society" (Castells 1996), economic activities are transformed into nets of autonomous units, leading to the "horizontal corporation" (idem: 166) as a crucial organisational form of "informational capitalism" (idem: 18).[4] Characterised by a multitude of streams and nodes, as well as variable types of interaction, political power structures in networks are sometimes diffused, sometimes concealed. Power appears in a more subtle way than it does in the case of authoritarian global control.

5.2 The hopes and realities of information society

Democratisation through technological innovation

As information and communication technology (ICT) is at the heart of information society discourses, the latter have often been connected with the (explicit or implicit) belief that social transformation will result from technological progress. New technologies have raised hopes of a) enhanced material living conditions, and b) a new age of participatory democracy. The myth of a re-generation of the lost agora of the Attic cities has been a persistent by-product of almost every new cycle of technological innovation in the field of communication. The telegraph represented an early example for the wide gap between high hopes and sober realities and formed an interesting blueprint for further technological cycles. Its invention in the late 18th century, and its promise of enhanced information and unlimited communication, led to the assumption that the result would be, automatically, a more democratic society. The actual implementation of telegraph communication soon destroyed these hopes: the new technology was used primarily by state administrations for purposes of national security and defence. As a means of warfare, the telegraph enabled the immediate nation-wide mobilisation of

[4] Castells adopts Bell's model of three stages of social development, as did Bell, but due to his stronger focus on technology, he refers to Bell's "post-industrial" stage as an "informational mode of development" which is "constituted by the emergence of a new technological paradigm based on information technology" (Castells 1996: 17).

the army, and as an administrative medium it rendered possible the effective control of the state territory. Initially, civil use was heavily restricted or forbidden, and later it focused on the exchange of business news (stock exchange rates, in particular) and thus the expansion of financial markets (Flichy 1994).

Radio was equally celebrated as inherently democratic technology and as a potentially interactive communication media which would allow to by-pass the influential information brokers of the large mass media. Bertolt Brecht demanded to transform the distribution medium into a communication mechanism, and the "listener" into a "speaker" and producer of information (Brecht 1967: 134). Indeed, radio was initially an experimental, civil society-based media, used by large numbers of non-professional activists, not unlike blogs and podcasts are used today. However, it was quickly integrated into traditional media systems and established as receiver for programmes distributed by the very media empires whose position, according to Brecht, it should have undermined. The Internet pushed enthusiasm in media technology to new limits. It was greeted as an "electronic agora" (Castells 1996: 357), as the cornerstone for an "interactive society" (idem: 358) and "a new Athenian Age of Democracy" (Gore 1994) which would be a "more humane and fair" world (Barlow 1996). It was to create new, well-paid jobs, enhance education and health care, and re-invent democratic participation of the citizenry.

As dreams of a more democratic society have been projected into new technologies, so has been an unease with pure economic logic as well as a wish to overcome material needs. Plans for a Japanese computer city in the early 1970s announced that in the new networked and computerised environment, material consumption would loose its central position as a guiding principle in human life and would be replaced by intellectual creativity (Mattelart 2003). Even Bell argued that in the post-industrial society, class problems would be solved and cooperation would replace hierarchical command (Bell 1973); Stehr sees the end of the dominance of large institutions as well as increased power by individual members of society, thanks to a diffusion of knowledge from the centres to the wider population (Stehr 2001); Castells shares with post-fordist approaches a perception that economic reorganisation, based on changes in information infrastructures, leads to human empowerment through an increase in education and in workers' participation in – and control over – the production process (Castells 1996).

Such perspectives, while highlighting important potential gains, tend to neglect the persistent and continuing relations of control that are bound to the fundamental principles of the current economic system. Enhanced participation through flat hierarchies in corporate management only exists within the framework set by the controlling centre, and traditional class divisions have been restructuring but have not vanished in an age of 'informationalised labour' (Webster 2002). Choosing a far more sceptical approach, Hardt/Negri point out that decentred networks and flexible hierarchies can in fact play a core role in command structures and unequal relations of power (Hardt/Negri 2000). Contradicting claims of a socially just and equal information society, Castells recognises that the "rise of informationalism [...] is intertwined with rising inequality and social exclusion throughout the world" (Castells 1998: 70) and observes a "structural trend toward increasing inequality in the network society" (Castells 2003: 435).

Centralisation and decentralisation

The promise of decentralisation of power and control is one of the most prominent normative perspectives that have been attached to information-based social transformation. The history of information technology innovations can be interpreted as a history of decentralisation potentials which were hardly ever fulfilled. As seen in the previous section, both the telegraph and the radio were heralded as decentralising forces, whose potential for interactive communication and for empowering average users to generate content was systematically reduced, while new information monopolies were established. The latest technological wave – the Internet – promised to break this rule by constituting a more robust decentral infrastructure in which data packages diffuse into remote parts of the network. The power of traditional gate-keepers of information seems reduced, if not broken, and Internet users are free to introduce new content.

This quality of the Internet, however, can be attributed primarily to the purpose of its creation – the state-sanctioned objective of developing a decentralised infrastructure – and the lead role of non-commercial and non-governmental actors who shaped the technology according to their needs and interests. It is not necessarily an expression of the assumed intrinsic value of the technology. As lead actors and purposes change, so can the characteristics of the Internet become subject to transformations. Increasingly the web has been conquered by business, commercial web portals offer one-stop shopping malls for e-buyers, and the major media conglomerates have extended their reach to the web, providing the vast majority of news which Internet users come across. The ICT industry has given birth to some of the most far-reaching monopolies which offer a large part of the commonly-used web applications. Furthermore, Internet infrastructure contains heavily centralised elements, such as the root server structure, and with the main Internet governance organisation ICANN (Internet Corporation for

Assigned Names and Numbers) being located in the US, the US government enjoys exclusive rights to influence infrastructure and management issues.[5]

Information society discourses often neglect the persistence of centralised control mechanisms or even connect the positive promise of decentralisation explicitly with traditional concepts of centralised forms of organisation. The plans for the Japanese computer city may, again, serve as an illustrative example. The city was hoped to create a multi-centric society in which citizens' interaction and participation would replace centralised power and hierarchy. Yet the city was to be built around a central "knowledge reservoir" – a single database located in the city centre (Mattelart 2003). Even though this central database would undoubtedly have concentrated power and influence in the hands of those who administer and regulate it, it was believed to be a crucial step towards decentralisation. Moving to the cityscapes of the present reality, the "global city" described by Sassen (Sassen 2001) represents a prime example of information-induced centralisation. It is forming part of a global network of information flows, yet (and exactly due to these flows) it can centralise services and command structures over globally distributed production chains.

Decentralisation is a political project, rather than a technological one, and is based on the initiative and creativity of human beings who seize the opportunities which new technologies bring about and who innovate and develop them according to their specific objectives. A focus on the intrinsic values of ICTs (or, in this respect, information society) will invariably remain inside the nebulous sphere of techno-determinist hopes, whereas an analysis of the actual potential – but also the realistic prospects – of new technology needs to be based on the specific uses as well as the political-economic environment of technology.

Political economy of information and communication

A political-economic approach to technology would thus argue that each technological innovation takes place within a social, geo-political, and political-economic framework, and that this framework influences which technology is being developed and for which purpose it is used. Thus it acknowledges the social embeddedness of technology, the centrality of human agency, and the modes of development and application. Technological developments do not happen in a socially neutral space, outside the sphere of political interests, only to turn towards society after its completion and to ex-post revolutionise social structures. Rather, their functions and applica-

---

[5] ICANN has been criticised for disproportionately considering the interests of big business and marginalising public interests, see Becker (2002).

tions usually correspond with the objectives of certain actors and the dominant perspectives of certain historic periods. Technologically-determined perspectives neglect the existing power relations and cannot answer fundamental questions such as: Who develops the technology, by which means, for which purpose, and for which ends?

Political-economic approaches to information and communication[6] apply these questions to the communication realm and ask how political, economic and social structures and processes constrain and enable the human capacity to communicate. As Keohane/Nye note, "information does not flow in a vacuum but in a political space that is already occupied" (Keohane/Nye 1998: 84). Economic and geo-political motivations, as well as business requirements, have formed the evolution of ICTs.[7] The primary role of many information services has been to extend and to deepen the world market, and the information industry has been an active and integral component of the global expansion of capitalist structures. Accordingly, political economists are sceptical about social transformations which are supposed to happen due to technological innovations, but instead point to the continuity of power structures, resource distributions, value systems, and of the locations of decision-making.

5.3 Ideologies of the information age

Social management

The history of information society, according to Mattelart, is a history of quantification, and data acquisition, based in the "cult of numbers" (Mattelart 2003: 5). With mathematics becoming the hegemonic science model in the 17th century, the belief in rationality, measurability, and utility emerged as the foundation for reason and truth. The purpose of early communication technologies was to rationalise and classify knowledge and to organise it in hierarchical schemes. Statistical methods were developed to measure and to analyze a variety of aspects of social life, leading to the first large population count in Prussia in 1725. The construct of an 'average citizen' was a

---

6 See, e.g., Comor 1994, McChesney 1998, Schiller 1999, Verzola 2004.

7 Early informatics and ICTs were primarily applied for overseas trade and for the geopolitical strategies of imperial powers, and they were paramount for achieving first British and then US hegemony. The telegraph cables spread along the main trading routes and served as crucial means for both extending trade relations and maintaining control over colonial territories. Informationalisation in the 19th and 20th century was triggered in large part by the needs of the industry, as production systems got increasingly complex and required automatisation and electronic data processing, and as consumption patterns needed to be analysed and developed (Becker 2002; Thompson 1995).

precondition for the control of large populations in modern nation-states and represented one of the foundations of modern state bureaucracy. The combination of a functional vision of the world and the new statistical tools formed an understanding of a "society as industry" (Mattelart 2003: 28) which could be led by applying appropriate management techniques.[8] Social management entered the business sector in the form of 'Taylorism' – a rigid system of monitoring all work processes with the objective of minimising production times and costs – and returned to society as 'Fordism' – the management of mass consumption with the help of modern advertising and marketing methods. Opinion management was advocated since the 1920s as an essential mechanism for regulating mass democracies, setting the foundations for modern public relations industries.[9]

The "cult of numbers" thus created the basis for technocratic administration. Accordingly, it may not be a coincidence that the 1990s, the decade of the 'information revolution', was, at the same time, a decade of technocratic policy management by supposedly non-political 'experts', within the context of neo-liberal restructuring (see below).

TINA

Technocratic social management is based on the application of scientific principles which are supposedly factual, ideologically neutral and lead to objective results. Technocracy would thus be the opposite of ideology, and so theories of information society often have a close relation with the rejection of ideology. Not surprisingly, Bell's work on the post-industrial society was preceded by his book "The End of Ideology" (Bell 1962). In a post-ideological environment, the 'right' course of social, political and economic developments is presented as 'reality' which follows a rational and unquestionable logic and which often originates beyond the sphere of human influence. The essence of that logic is the paradigm of TINA – "There Is No Alternative" – which was advocated during the rise of neo-liberal policies in the UK and the US in the early 1980s and which ascended to a hegemonic understanding of the world after the collapse of the state-socialist system, with the "end of history" (Fukuyama 1992) becoming the predominant adaptation of post-ideology in the 1990s. TINA diminishes or totally negates both human agency and the democratic struggle of ideas in the course of

---

[8] Becker (2002) traces the use of information for social management back to the development of writing techniques and pictogrammes 4000 B.C.

[9] Planning and bureaucracy are also crucial elements in Bell's "post-industrial society".

human development. As such, it represents the ideology of a post-ideological world.[10]

With *grand narratives* such as capitalism and Western democracy persisting, the concept of a post-ideological society does not originate outside ideologically-driven spaces. Rather, it is deeply intertwined with the existing ideational realm. Claims of non-ideology can thus be interpreted as a means to conceal the deeply ideological nature of social systems. Declaring such a system as "post-ideological" and describing it as a rational order which transcends and overcomes the struggle of ideas represents a rather crude attempt of legitimising that order.

Neo-liberalism

The field of information and communication was one of the first which attracted experiments with new regulatory approaches beyond the nation-state model. In the early 1980s, AT&T was the first major publicly-owned corporation which was split up into smaller companies. This set the starting-signal for deregulation and privatisation policies to cover the whole communication sector and to spread from the US to an increasing number of countries worldwide. The EU, originally a region with a strong public sector tradition in information and communication, started to issue directives on deregulation in the late 1980s, and the 1994 Bangemann report on "Europe and the Global Information Society" called for wide-spread deregulation and a prominent basis for E-commerce. The G7 summit in 1995 declared that the information society should be created not by public policies but by the private sector, and the "Charter for a Global Information Society", issued by the G8 Digital Opportunity Task Force in 2000, confirmed this view by calling for further deregulation as well as for the worldwide recognition of intellectual property rights (IPR).[11] Since the Uruguay Round of negotiations on the General Agreement on Tariffs and Trade (GATT), information and culture have been included in trade negotiations and have thus been redefined as commodities in a commercial market-place.

Neo-liberal restructuring went hand-in-hand with the development of ICT networks. "Devolving responsibility for the evolution of the Internet from government to the private sector" (Kahn 2004: 18) was of major concern for the founding fathers of the Internet. Calls for the complete privatisation of the electro-magnetic spectrum and, generally, for self-regulation according

---

[10] The term TINA has been used, for example, by critical information society theorist Frank Webster.

[11] http://unpan1.un.org/intradoc/groups/public/documents/apcity/unpan002263.pdf

to supply and demand without any state interference[12] were based on the libertarian-capitalist model in which all services are provided purely by the private sector and expressed a "utopian mercantile vision of information and communication, in which ICTs pave the way for a grand and generous information society, generating wealth and good things for all to consume" (Raboy 2004a: 355). Policy stressed the centrality of individual self-regulation and focused on providing the conditions – the technological, not the social conditions – for every individual to be connected to ICT networks and to thereby have the possibility to, individually, acquire knowledge. Thus the 1990s and early 2000s merged the dreams of an information society with those of a friction-less neo-liberal capitalism in which information society was intrinsically linked to a focus on marketisation and privatisation.

Cyber-libertarianism

The rise of the neo-liberal doctrine was underpinned with the ideas of cyber-libertarianism. The latter added a distinct anti-governmental stance and rejected any interventions by states and other powerful actors into the innovations and the creativity of individual developers, civil society-based creators of information technology and small businesses. Cyber-libertarians have claimed to create a new world – cyberspace – in which different principles of social organisation would prevail. Based on Dave Clark's famous creed from 1992 – "We reject kings, presidents and voting. We believe in rough consensus and running code" – they have demanded that the "Governments of the Industrial World" should "leave us alone. You are not welcome among us. You have no sovereignty where we gather" (Barlow 1996). Not unsimilar to the techno-centric dreams of democratisation presented in chapter 5.2., this new world is presented as "more humane and fair" (ibid.) and would enable everyone to "enter without privilege or prejudice accorded by race, economic power, military force, or station of birth" (ibid.).

Through its rejection of state power, cyber-libertarianism displays some commonalities with the propensity towards anarchism and DIY ("do-it-yourself") culture amongst many CS Media. However, state control remains the strongest object of critique, whereas criticism of the business sector is less developed and the market remains the favoured organising principle.[13] As in neo-liberalism, the emphasis on freedom is essentially translated into the freedom of individuals to compete in a deregulated market.

---

[12] See, e.g., the report "The Telecom Revolution: An American Opportunity" by the Progress & Freedom Foundation, 1995.

[13] Lovink (2003) has called the early cyber-libertarians "a mixture of yuppies and hippies" (idem: 124) with a "childish vision of a fictionless neo-liberal world" (idem: 150) and for whom capitalism was hipp and cool, a "funky business" (idem: 208).

Openness

'Openness' has evolved as a value system which maintains some of the ideas of cyber-libertarianism but reduces the latter's techno-determinism and its belief in markets and goes beyond the focus on cyberspace. The crucial difference is that 'openness' is not based on the assumed inherent values of technological platforms but on the practices and politics of the open source movement.[14] These practices include the openness to participate in processes of technological development, the openness of co-operative work, horizontal collaboration and bottom-up processes, the free dissemination of knowledge, and the freedom to use and further develop the knowledge generated by others. Beyond the realm of technological development, they imply an openness of political processes and suggest a need for "open governance" (Lutterbeck/Ishii 1999).[15] In the knowledge realm, 'openness' expresses deep opposition to a "top down controlled and limited model of knowledge and information deployment" (May 2006: 8). 'Openness' thus provides a counter-model to the proliferation and expansion of intellectual property rights (IPR).

Implementations of the model of 'openness' started with open source software development but have also encompassed open content and open licensing. Copyleft and Creative Commons have challenged licensing (and, generally, business) models that are based on the monopolistic control over the products of creative endeavour. Open access models have been established in, particularly, natural science research. Wikis have evolved as a prime tool for online collaboration, Wikipedia has become a widely-used platform of open knowledge generation, and Indymedia (as well as several 'citizen journalism' platforms) has given rise to open publishing.[16]

---

14 This difference is not always clear-cut, as these practices have, of course, shaped and influenced the technology. Early advocates of 'openness' have indeed talked about the need to translate the "values of cyberspace" into the "real world" (see Lessig 1999; Lutterbeck/Ishii 1999), yet they have regarded this endeavour as a political project which would not automatically evolve in the right technological environment.

15 Later we will see that the openness of the political process was one of the prime discourses around the WSIS summit, and that this openness was particularly developed in the debates about Internet governance.

16 Projects such as Wikipedia and Indymedia have experienced occasional abuses of open publishing models and have developed guidelines and, in some cases, qualifications of 'open' mechanisms, yet the general principle of 'openness' and self-regulation has not been abandoned and continues to serve as default.

5.4 Issues

Privacy, security and surveillance

Social management in modern societies, as we have seen, requires information about the life conditions, habits and activities of the citizenry. New ICTs have greatly enhanced the possibilities to gather and process people's data. Consumption profiles are generated through, e.g., discount (or 'loyalty') cards in supermarkets and the data traces which consumers create on the Internet, and numerous public and private institutions are involved in data mining and data sharing, usually without the control by, and often without the knowledge of, the targeted person. Electronic communication is increasingly subject to state surveillance.[17]

The use of biometrical data has opened new opportunities for identification and control, and CCTV (close circuit television) surveillance of public and work spaces has increased drastically.[18] A growing number of everyday goods and services, such as identification cards, product packaging and tickets for public transport, involve the use of RFID (radio frequency identification) chips which allow the tracking of people's movements and behaviour. Surveillance and data-mining have been crucial techniques for expanding control by states and businesses over their respective areas of interest – security and profits. Civil society groups and initiatives, such as Privacy International or the Big Brother Awards, have criticised the increasing collection of data and have advocated for the privacy rights of consumers and citizens.

Intellectual property

The informationalisation of economic processes has required to adapt the institution of property (and thus the foundation of the capitalist economic model) to immaterial environments. Intellectual property rights (IPR) – encompassing patents, trademarks and copyrights – have evolved as the main mechanism for this transformation and have thus become "the legal form of information society" (May 2006: 6) and the primary means of control over a globalised economy in which the production of tangible goods is

---

[17] Every day the surveillance system Echelon tracks an estimated 3 billion communicative connections, including telephone, email, chats, etc, and up to 90 per cent of Internet-based communication (Becker 2002: 183). Recent legislation on data retention in many countries requires telecommunications providers to track and store the connection data of every customer indiscriminately and make it available to state authorities upon request.

[18] In the past decade, annual increases in the sales volume of surveillance technology sometimes exceeded 50 per cent (Becker 2002: 153).

increasingly moved to poorer countries.[19] Existing IPR have been strengthened, and concepts of intellectual property have been extended "into areas previously unavailable to commodification, where such aspects of knowledge and/or information had previously remained in the 'public domain'" (ibid.).[20] For example, the US Congress extended the terms of copyright eleven times during the past forty years (CRIS 2002), and patents nowadays encompass not only intellectual work but also plant and life forms. However the very nature of IPR is strongly contested, as

- ideas are never entirely the product of a single individual or business entity but are "built upon innumerable layers of accumulated past knowledge" (ibid.) and invariably incorporate concepts developed by others, traditions, collective wisdom and understandings
- information and knowledge are by nature non-rival goods which can be used by many at the same time and do not disappear when they are used, shared, or given away. On the contrary, they increase by reproduction through sharing, and so economic laws of scarcity do not apply (Verzola 2004) – thus scarcity has to be legally constructed and politically enforced (through IPR).

Opposition towards the commodification and privatisation of knowledge through IPR has risen among civil society groups who criticise that IPR have hindered "the public's access to knowledge" and "stifled learning, creativity, innovation" (CRIS 2002). Instead, they advocate for a non-commercial 'public domain' and 'global information commons'.[21]

Information and communication rights

Article 19 of the Universal Declaration of Human Rights, adopted by the United Nations on 10 December 1948, gives everyone "the right to freedom

[19] Verzola (2004) highlights that control over intellectual property is paramount for achieving a hegemonic position in the global order and shows how the US as the main holder of IPR are vigurously pursuing a foreign policy which is directed towards the recognition of IPR by developing countries, whereas the ascent of the US towards hegemony in the 19th century involved large-scale 'piracy' of the works of the previous hegemon, the UK.

[20] May notes that, contrary to assumptions of a retreat of the state in an age of informationalisation and neoliberal policies, the extension of IPR has in fact constituted a "radical widening and institutionalisation of state authority" (May 2006: 6).

[21] Such 'commons' constitute a collective space of open knowledge, not owned or controlled privately, similar to the 'common' land in the middle ages which was collectively cultivated by villagers, or to the environmental 'commons', such as air and water.

of opinion and expression" and "to seek, receive and impart information and ideas through any media and regardless of frontiers"[22], and it is the foundation of people's rights in the information and communication realm. However, questions have been raised regarding its scope in digitalised and commercialised environments.

First, ratings, filters and blockings of websites by the information industry have led to a "privatisation of censorship" (Becker 2002: 89) which circumvents traditional state-oriented anti-censorship policy. Users/consumers/citizens often lack sufficient rights to control their own data as well as a right to anonymity and privacy. Secondly, the right to "receive and impart information" has been criticised as insufficient, as its distinction between 'informing others' and 'being informed' leads to its interpretation as 'press freedom', and thus to a monopoly position of media organisations (Mattelart 2003).[23] Accordingly, Stein (2004) distinguishes into "defensive" and "empowering" interpretations of expression rights. Whereas the 'defensive' argument is limited to the rejection of state intervention and thus regards competitive markets as precondition for freedom of expression, the 'empowering' approach focuses on the opportunities for all individuals to express themselves without coercion by neither governmental nor private actors and envisions "the circulation of the full range of the public's insights, experiences and perspectives" (Stein 2004: 108). Communication and media systems, according to this view, "must act as a means of expression for the broader citizenry" (Stein 2004: 114).

Thirdly, there are social, political and economic obstacles to free communication, as summarised by the CRIS campaign (Communication Rights in the Information Society):

"We live in a society of hugely varying levels of access to power, a society in which most interactions between people are heavily mediated and filtered (...). An exclusive insistence on freedom of expression says too little about the process by which society's means of expression – such as newspapers, television, radio, films, music and educational material - are controlled, and the interests they ultimately uphold. In this context, freedom of expression (...) can do little to prevent the domination of the loudest voices" (CRIS 2005: 21/22).

---

22 http://www.un.org/Overview/rights.html

23 Official statements on freedom of expression, e.g. by the UN Special Rapporteur on the Promotion and Protection of the Right to Freedom of Opinion and Expression, typically refer to "media professionals" and "journalism" rather than the rights of normal people, non-professional citizen journalists, and media activists.

CRIS has proposed to complement the right to freedom of expression with a set of communication rights which expose a multi-faceted picture of obstacles to free communication, concern the conditions of knowledge production and dissemination, such as the roles of media concentration and of IPR, and highlight issues around privacy, surveillance, and cultural diversity.[24] Conceptually, 'communication' has been suggested as a counter-model to 'information'. According to Hamelink, we "do not need 'information societies' – implying a flow of information in one direction – but rather 'communication societies'" (Hamelink 2003) which imply participatory processes of interactive exchange and knowledge sharing. Communication focuses on actors and on the dynamics structuring their interaction, not on the abstract pieces of information which are transmitted between them. Thus it opens a view on the conditions of information exchange – the social and ideological backgrounds of those involved, the particularities of the means of transmission, the obstacles in communication flows, and the social, political and economic environment in which communicative processes take place.

The digital divide

Access to information through new technologies plays a central role in the 'information society', and so the diffusion of ICTs around the globe constitutes a major concern. This diffusion has been strongly unequal and has reflected the differences in the economic and social resources in the global system, as they have developed since colonialisation. In 2005, the Global North had eight times the Internet penetration rate of the South, and four times as many phone lines and mobile phones. Less than 3 out of 100 Africans used the Internet (and the largest part of that fraction lived in South Africa), there were more Internet users in the city of Seoul (Republic of Korea) than in all of sub-Saharan Africa (excluding South Africa), and the small country of Denmark had more than twice the international Internet bandwith than the whole of Latin America and the Caribbean. Around one billion people worldwide lacked connection to any kind of ICT, Internet or otherwise.[25] While the total numbers of Internet users outside Europe and North America, particularly in parts of Asia, are on the rise, unequal distribution of access and resources persists. The same can be observed within countries and societies, where digital divides occur along traditional lines of

---

24 The concept of communication rights goes back to the MacBride Report, endorsed by UNESCO in 1980, which called for a "right to communicate" to extend the traditional understanding of 'information' and to encompass, for example, "the right to privacy" and "the right to participate in public communication" (MacBride et al 1980: Recommendation No. 54). See chapter 3.

25 International Telecommunications Union (ITU), http://www.itu.int/wsis/tunis/newsroom/stats/

social disparities, and research suggests that such gaps are often increasing rather than decreasing (Marr 2004).

The digital divide entered the global political debate in the late 1990s and became a prominent agenda item at the annual meetings of the G8 – the world's leading economic (and political) nations. The 'Okinawa Charter on the Global Information Society'[26], adopted at the G8 summit in Japan in 2000, called for far-reaching measures to close the divide, and support for ICT infrastructure played a large role in the 'Africa Action Plan', adopted at the following G8 summit in 2001.

The concept of the digital divide has paradoxically united the interests of a broad coalition of actors, from political officials and governmental institutions to businesses, civil society groups and academia. As a framework for deploying vast quantities of supposedly beneficial technology to marginalised populations, it has encompassed business opportunities, development agendas, and a rare opportunity for strengthening state activity in the information/communication realm. Meanwhile, the concept has maintained a techno-determinist approach which promises solutions to social problems through the provision of technology, and it reflects the neo-liberal focus on the alleged 'opportunities' of each 'individual'. Interpreting the digital divide as a physical access problem – of having computers and being connected – leads to an information development (or ICT4D – information-and-communication-technologies-for-development) approach which follows the modernisation paradigm and thus risks becoming just the latest in a long series of failed development strategies (Pieterse 2005). However, education, capacity-building, and open access to content are likely to be as significant as technology provision, and while physical access divides may have diminished recently, "skills and usage access divides" (van Dijk 2005: 4) are growing.

Media and 'Soft Power'

Information society discourses are curiously silent as to the content of the information that is spreading through new technological infrastructures, the production modes that influence this content (see chapter 2) and the power aspects that it entails. Concepts of informational and ideological power would include, for example, a separation in "hard" power and "soft" power (Keohane/Nye 1998: 86). Hard power involves coercion as well as coaxing in order to get others to do what they otherwise would not do. Soft power, in contrast, leads to the desired outcomes because others want what you want. It is based on defining norms and ideas and on getting others to agree to

---

26 http://www.dotforce.org/reports/it1.html

them. It involves setting the agenda and thus generating the framework within which others make sense of the world and shape their preferences. Power and authority are conferred on those occupying key decision-making processes in what Susan Strange called a "knowledge structure" (Strange 1994: 119), i.e. those who decide about what knowledge is discovered and how it is communicated, by whom, to whom, and on what terms. Information is thus a meaningful symbolic form that ultimately affects the way we make sense of the world. Power derived from producing and transmitting information has also been called "symbolic power" (Thompson 1995: 17).

The Neo-Gramscian approach applied by Robert Cox (1981) and others contextualises soft and symbolic power within a perspective on social and world orders. What Gramsci called 'hegemonic orders' are based on consent. They require a universal ideology, which is established by bringing the interests of subordinate classes into harmony with the special interests of a hegemonic group or class. This ideology consists of norms and perceptions that lay down rules of behaviour and create expectations consistent with the hegemonic social order.

According to these theoretical approaches, control over and access to symbols, news and interpretations of current developments play a vital role in present world orders. Nevertheless the media have only sporadically been an 'issue' in information society discourses.

5.5 Conclusion

The concept of information society provides a fuzzy and contested framework for the WSIS summit. It is linked to techno-determinist and technocratic perspectives, to the hope that information technology will create a more democratic and more decentralised world, and, more recently, to neoliberal and cyber-libertarian thought. Some aspects offer connections with the practices and preferences of CS Media, particularly the focus on decentralisation and the ideas around 'openness', but at the same time, tendencies towards concentration of control, social management and market-based policies would provide a rather hostile environment for them. Core issues of recent information and communication debates – such as those around privacy, IPR, communication rights and the digital divide – allow for policies that either strengthen or weaken CS Media. An interpretation of information society at and by WSIS that is conducive to CS Media would be sceptical about techno-determinist hopes and technocratic approaches, foster practical (rather than rhetoric) decentralisation as well as interactive communication, criticise the privatisation of knowledge, and recognise unequal power distributions in information provision. However, considering the background of information society discourses and the history of their implementation, it seems reasonable to remain sceptical regarding the likelihood of such an approach.

6 The World Summit on the Information Society (WSIS)

6.1 Structure and history

Origins

The World Summit on the Information Society (WSIS) was the latest in a series of world summits organised within the United Nations framework, which had started with the United Nations Conference on Environment and Development (UNCED) in Rio de Janeiro in 1992. Similar high-level UN conferences had taken place irregularly since the 1970s, but UNCED opened a new stage of conferencing by assembling a wider range of actors around an issue which was of major concern to humanity. A new understanding of global interconnection and interrelation was emerging and suggested that many of the challenges faced by disparate communities were in fact of a global nature and could only be tackled on a global level.[1] The Rio conference was quickly followed by other summits, such as the World Conference on Human Rights (Vienna, 1993), the International Conference on Population and Development (Cairo, 1994), the International Conference on Women (Beijing, 1995) and the "Rio plus10" World Summit on Sustainable Development (WSSD, Johannesburg, 2002). WSSD not only concluded a decade of intense summitry but also made clear that summits were only the starting-points of longer-term follow-up processes.

In 1996 the UNESCO Executive Board started to discuss the idea of a "Conference on Information and Communication for Development". However, the plans never materialised (Ó Siochrú 2004b). Instead, it was the ITU which took the initiative to organise a global summit on information and communication. The ITU was particularly eager to take a lead role as it was in danger of loosing spheres of influence to new regulatory actors such as ICANN and the WTO and thus needed to prove its legitimacy, to expand its area of activity, and to raise its profile in a political arena. Furthermore, it represented the prevalent focus on technical solutions, expertise, and business-led development of the neo-liberal ideological environment and the new-economy-hype of the late 1990s far better than UNESCO which was still connected with the ghosts of NWICO (Ó Siochrú 2004a).[2] The ITU

1 The historical period of UNCED was framed by two major reports – the report of the so-called 'Brundtland Commission', published in 1987, which had established a tentative discourse on global commonalities, and the report "Our Global Neighbourhood" by the Commission on Global Governance, published in 1995, which expressed emerging discourses around 'globalisation' and 'global governance' (see chapter 4).

2 Further explanations given by summit participants and observers include the personal motives of the ITU General Secretary Yoshio Utsumi who was in the middle of his re-

Plenipotentiary Conference in Minneapolis in 1998 accepted Tunisia's proposal to hold the summit and thereby set the starting signal for WSIS. On 21 December 2001 the UN General Assembly endorsed Resolution 56/183 on holding the summit (see UN General Assembly 2002). A High-Level Summit Organizing Committee (HLSOC) and an Executive Secretariat (WSIS-ES) were established.

In addition to its new thematic focus as the first UN summit on information and communication issues, WSIS was equipped with a structural innovation: It was the first summit to be divided into two parts. The first part took place in Geneva on 10-12 December 2003, the second part in Tunis on 16-18 November 2005.

Summit Structure

Prime responsibility for organising the summit lay with the organising committee HLSOC which included representatives of specialised UN agencies and was chaired by ITU Secretary-General Yoshio Utsumi. The Executive Secretariat WSIS-ES assisted with preparations and undertook most administrative tasks. It was separated into four divisions, representing the different groups of actors participating in the summit – governments, UN agencies, private sector and civil society. An Intergovernmental Bureau and a Civil Society Bureau (the latter was created after the initial phase of negotiations) took care of the procedural needs of their respective constituencies in the negotiation process.

Each summit was preceded by a two-year preparation phase, during which the final documents – a political declaration and an action plan – were to be developed and agreed upon, leaving the actual summit as a publicity event for presenting the outcomes and for general debates. Preparation events included (a) meetings of the Preparatory Committee (PrepCom), (b) regional conferences, (c) thematic conferences. While the latter two played a major role in regional and thematic discourses and in bringing together related actors, the PrepCom meetings had by far the largest effect on the summit outcomes. This 'committee' consisted of several delegates from almost every UN member country, as well as a large number of delegates from international institutions, civil society and the private sector. Each of the PrepCom meetings assembled several hundred, often more than a thousand delegates, usually for two full weeks, and thus constituted major con-

---

election campaign, and the wish of the governments of both Switzerland and Tunisia to host a major UN event (Ludwig 2003; Kleinwächter 2004). Common to these legends surrounding the initial summit phase is the view that it was not only guided by historical vision, but also by the personal and institutional motives of the actors involved.

ferences in their own right. The PrepCom was divided into Subcommittees 1 (on Rules of Procedure) and 2 (on Content and Themes), and during the course of negotiations these often split up into intergovernmental working groups dealing with specific conflictive issues.

The PrepCom Chairs, Adama Samassekou (phase 1) and Janis Karklins (phase 2), bore a considerable responsibility for the progress of negotiations. They contributed 'non-papers' as proposals for the WSIS agenda and convened 'Groups of the Friends of the Chair' (GFC) to solve conflicts between different parties and to speed up the negotiation process. In the second phase, the GFC became a quasi-official drafting committee. Two more groups pre-structured the outcomes of the second phase: the Working Group on Internet Governance (WGIG) and the Task Force on Financing Mechanisms (TFFM) were to develop solutions for the two major themes of WSIS2.

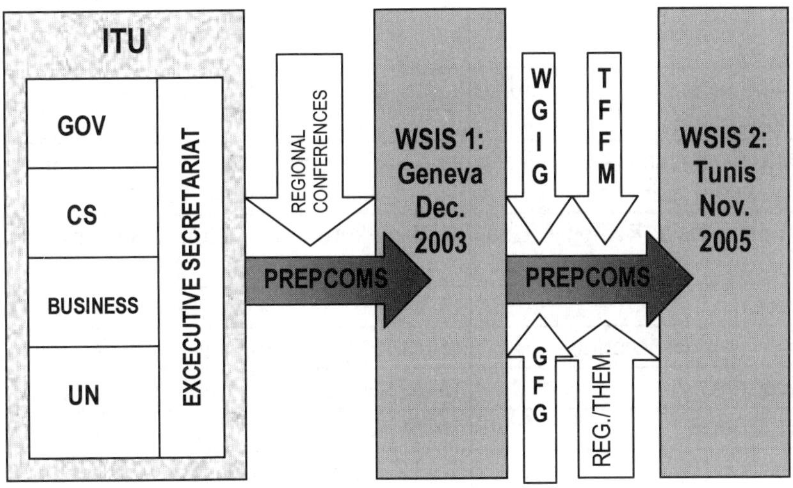

Figure 1: WSIS Structure

Chronology of events

The 'Geneva phase'

Initially, a core structure of three main PrepCom meetings had been envisaged to develop an agenda and reach consensus on it. However, negotiations were slow, and so the plan proved to be insufficient. Several additional meetings became necessary, including an *Informal Meeting on Content and Themes* and an *Intersessional Meeting*, and Prepcom3 had to be re-convened twice (*PrepCom3a+b*).[3] Only on the last day before the official beginning of the summit, agreements on the final texts could be reached. At the summit, heads of state, ministers and other government officials from 175 countries, as well as representatives from international organisations, the private sector, and civil society gave statements on the WSIS texts and on wider issues around the information society. More than 11,000 participants attended the summit and related events.[4]

Main events: WSIS phase 1	**Date**	**Location**
African Regional Conference	25-30 May 2002	Bamako (Mali)
PrepCom1	1-5 July 2002	Geneva (Switzerland)
Informal Meeting on Content and Themes	16-18 Sept. 2002	Geneva (Switzerland)
Pan European Regional Conference	7-9 Nov. 2002	Bucharest (Romania)
Asia-Pacific Regional Conference	13-15 Jan. 2003	Tokyo (Japan)
Latin American and Caribbean Regional Conference	29-31 Jan. 2003	Bávaro (Dominican Republic)
Western Asia Regional Conference	4-6 Feb. 2003	Beirut (Lebanon)
PrepCom2	17-28 Feb. 2003	Geneva (Switzerland)
Intersessional Meeting	15-18 July 2003	Paris (France)
PrepCom3	15-26 Sept. 2003	Geneva (Switzerland)
PrepCom3a	10-14 Nov. 2003	Geneva (Switzerland)
PrepCom3b	5-9 Dec. 2003	Geneva (Switzerland)
WSIS1	10-12 Dec. 2003	Geneva (Switzerland)

Table 3: Chronology of WSIS phase 1

3 The terminology used for the extended or re-convened PrepCom3 sessions was inconsistent. Officially, they were simply called "resumed sessions", some termed them 'Prepcom3bis' and 'PrepCom3bis+', but here I use, for clarity and simplicity, 'PrepCom3a' and PrepCom3b'.

4 See http://www.itu.int/wsis/geneva/index.html

The 'Tunis phase'

Whereas the first phase had chosen a wide and all-encompassing approach, both thematically and procedurally, the second was given a clearer focus by emphasizing the two areas which had been left unresolved: Internet governance and finance. The working groups WGIG and TFFM were to review the current state of their respective issue areas, to structure the debates about them, and to propose ways of resolving them.

Main events: WSIS phase 2	**Date**	**Location**
PrepCom1	24-26 June 2004	Hammamet (Tunisia)
Western Asia Regional Conference	22-23 Nov. 2004	Damascus (Syria)
Africa Regional Conference	2-4 Feb. 2005	Accra (Ghana)
PrepCom2	17-25 Feb. 2005	Geneva (Switzerland)
Asia-Pacific Regional Conference	31 May – 2 June 2005	Tehran (Iran)
Latin American and Caribbean Regional Conference	8-10 June 2005	Rio de Janeiro (Brazil)
PrepCom3	19-30 Sept. 2005	Geneva (Switzerland)
PrepCom3a	13-15 Nov. 2005	Tunis (Tunisia)
WSIS2	16-18 Nov. 2005	Tunis (Tunisia)

GFC	8 meetings between 22 October 2004 and 7 September 2005 (monthly or bi-monthly)
WGIG	4 meetings between November 2004 and June 2005 (bi-monthly), final report submitted on 18 July 2005
TFFM	Launch on 4 October 2004, consultations with stakeholders in November 2004, final report submitted on 22 December 2004

Table 4: Chronology of WSIS phase 2

At the same time, the summit process expanded, as a range of thematic conferences were organised (usually by UN organisations in collaboration with host country governments, and usually for a more specialised audience) to use the momentum of the WSIS in order to deepen the debate on issues beyond the core themes of WSIS2. The following examples are just a small selection from the dozens of thematic conferences and meetings:

Science in the Information Society, 10 November 2004, Berlin (Germany); *Regional Cooperation in ICT for Development*, 16-18 November 2004, Bishkek (Kyrgizstan); *Role and Place of Media in the Information Society in Africa and the Arab States*, 22-24 November, Marrakesh (Morocco);

Economic and Social Implications of ICT, 17-19 January 2005, Antigua (Guatemala); *ICT Applications in Natural Disaster Reduction*, 21 January, Kobe (Japan); *Indigenous People in the Information Society*, 14-18 March 2005, Ottawa (Canada); *Multilingualism for Cultural Diversity and Participation of All in Cyberspace*, 6-7 May 2005, Bamako (Mali); *Forum on ICTs and Gender*, 24-25 June 2005, Seoul (Korea); *Cybersecurity*, 28 June – 1 Junly, Geneva (Switzerland)

6.2 Themes, negotiations and outcomes

Dominant agendas

UN Resolution A/RES/56/183 called for WSIS to "harness the potential of knowledge and technology for promoting the goals of the United Nations Millennium Declaration", to "promote the urgently needed access of all countries to information, knowledge and communication technologies for development", and to "reap the full benefits of the information and communication technologies revolution" (UN General Assembly 2002). The ITU, similarly, identified as main goals "providing access to ICTs for all" and safeguarding "ICTs as a tool for economic and social development".[5] Thus the "common vision and understanding of the information society" (UN General Assembly 2002) which WSIS was to develop, was based on two main pillars: (a) new technologies and (b) development.

The dominant players at WSIS largely shared this perspective. Northern governments were interested in developing ICT applications, infrastructure and security – with the primary aim of enhancing government functions – and welcomed the opportunity to strengthen Northern ICT industries by expanding the latter's operations around the globe. Southern governments hoped to mobilise financial assistance and direct investment to create an ICT infrastructure in their countries. Access to information and knowledge, and safeguarding their cultural heritage, were also amongst their prime objectives. The business sector claimed to provide the services that were requested, hoped for new contracts, and called for a market-based and legally secure environment for investments.

As suggested in chapter 5, the main summit theme of *bridging the digital divide* initially served to combine core interests of all major actors. Differences occurred with regards to the way in which this should be done: through state-led development programmes (as demanded by Southern governments) or by market liberalisation, direct investment and free trade (as favoured by the business sector, supported by the US and other Northern

[5] http://www.itu.int/wsis/newsroom/fact/content_themes_outcome.html

governments). Civil society actors challenged this 'rough consensus' by pointing to the centrality of human rights, particularly freedom of expression and communication rights; education and literacy; linguistic and cultural diversity; gender issues; free software; the knowledge commons and public goods; and expressed scepticism towards both market solutions and top-down government interventions.

The wide-spread wish to hold a *technical* summit on *technical* issues reflected the predominant ideologies of the information age[6] and promised to keep the old NWICO confrontations at bay. In a silent agreement, most actors took pains to circumvent any issue (or language) that may have drawn connections to NWICO debates. Yet despite the efforts of limiting the debate to questions of technocratic management, the course of governmental negotiations soon showed that the deeply political nature of the issues under discussion at WSIS was hard to suppress. WSIS became a conflictive arena for a debate on how fundamental aspects of politics, economy and culture would be re-organised in a globalised and informationalised environment, and on who would control the "core resources of the information age" (Kleinwächter 2004: 2).

Negotiations and conflicts in the Geneva phase

The development of the WSIS documents met the following difficulties:

(1) Debates on procedural issues, particularly with regards to the inclusion of non-governmental actors in the summit process, often overshadowed and side-lined content development (see next section).

(2) Collectively defining a vague concept such as the *information society* proved to be a difficult endeavour, and conflicts persisted regarding the inclusion and exclusion of issues. Certain issues led to particularly hostile confrontations, and consensus between governments was difficult to achieve.

(3) The ITU as a technical organisation was overwhelmed by debates on the social, political and cultural dimensions of information society and had difficulties in organising the negotiation process.

The most conflictive topics were:

---

[6] Sarikakis and Thussu identify as "Internet ideology" a "distinctive worldview predicated on the almost mythical powers of new information and communication technologies" (Sarikakis/Thussu 2006: 3).

- How to finance the development of ICT infrastructure in the South: Southern governments demanded specific assistance programmes and additional funds, while Northern governments were unwilling to pay.

- Internet governance: Southern governments criticised the US-based, business-led ICANN and sought to increase governmental influence, for example through the ITU. The US and other Northern governments rejected this move.

- Control of knowledge, intellectual property rights (IPR), free software: the US expressed the business perspective, emphasizing the need for strict IPR regimes and for proprietary (e.g., Microsoft) software, while Brazil, supported by Southern governments and civil society, advocated for a public domain of knowledge and for free software.

- Human Rights: China rejected prominent references to Article 19 of the Universal Declaration of Human Rights (UDHR) on freedom of expression, while the latter was defended by European delegations. Controversies also occurred on the right to development and the right to communicate.

- Media: Switzerland tried to establish a substantial section on media issues but faced strong resistance from authoritarian governments from Asia and Latin America.

- Security: Russia, initially supported by the US, advocated for strong statements against cyber-crime and cyber-terrorism but triggered questions as to the compatibility with human rights.

Some of these conflicts occurred along a North-South, some along an East-West division. Intergovernmental working groups were created to solve most of these issues, leading to compromise (e.g., between the US and Brazil on IPR and free software), defeat (e.g., of China on the human rights issue), or continued disagreement (e.g., on Internet governance). Yet it took two additional PrepCom sessions, major diplomatic efforts by the WSIS1 host country Switzerland, and the postponement of the two most conflictive issues (Internet governance and financing) to the second phase to break deadlocks and to avoid the imminent failure of the summit.

Outcomes of the Geneva phase

Two documents were finalised for the first summit: the *Declaration of Principles* and the *Plan of Action*. While Swiss President Pascal Couchepin presented them as the "constitution for the information society" (Couchepin 2003), they effectively represented the lowest common denominator between governments, were largely limited to general statements of intent and hardly provided binding regulatory mechanisms. However, their discursive effects should not be underestimated. WSIS constituted a "politics of definition" (Raboy 2004a: 346) – defining issues, identifying problems, outlining possible solutions, and thus providing "a lexicon for speaking about the information society" (idem: 348) rather than deciding on actual regulation. It articulated a common agenda which is likely to be relevant for future policy in the field of information and communication.

The Declaration of Principles (WSIS 2003a)[7] is divided into a "Common Vision" (Art. 1-18) and a set of "Key Principles" which include the following sections:

(1) The role of governments and all stakeholders in the promotion of ICTs for development (Art. 20)

(2) Information and communication infrastructure: an essential foundation for an inclusive information society (Art. 21-23)

(3) Access to information and knowledge (Art. 24-28)

(4) Capacity building (Art. 29-34)

(5) Building confidence and security in the use of ICTs (Art. 35-37)

(6) Enabling environment (Art. 38-50)

(7) ICT applications: benefits in all aspects of life (Art. 51)

(8) Cultural diversity and identity, linguistic diversity and local content (Art. 52-54)

(9) Media (Art. 55)

(10) Ethical dimensions of the information society (Art. 56-59)

(11) International and regional cooperation (Art. 60-64)

---

[7] The following quotes are taken from this document.

The document picks up language proposed by civil society groups and thus adopts a progressive rhetoric. Keywords such as "people-centred", "inclusive" and "sustainable development" all appear in Art. 1, complemented in the following paragraphs by references to "gender equality", a "peaceful, just and prosperous world", the universality "of all human rights and fundamental freedoms", including Art. 19 UDHR (freedom of expression), "communication" as a "fundamental social process", participation of all, and "the special needs of marginalized and vulnerable groups of society". However, beyond this initial "vision", the document primarily promotes the roles of states and business, suggests numerous "public-private-partnerships", adopts a top-down managerial approach and puts emphasis on state security while neglecting user rights, data protection and privacy. The regulative framework outlined for the information society focuses mostly on market-friendly, "pro-competitive" (Art. 39), liberalised environments, yet acknowledges the role of the public sector and reserves certain (albeit limited) space for public services.[8]

The Declaration is infused with the belief that the deployment of new technology will lead to development. The poor results of previous development strategies are to be revolutionised with the help of communications infrastructure, particularly the Internet. This techno-determinist application of the modernisation paradigm is mixed with the enthusiasm of traditional information society discourses: "we are collectively entering a new era of enormous potential, that of the Information Society and expanded human communication. (…) All individuals can soon (…) together build a new Information Society based on shared knowledge and founded on global solidarity and a better understanding between peoples and nations" (Art. 67).

The Action Plan (WSIS 2003b)[9] was to "translate" the principles of the Declaration into "concrete action lines" (Art. 1). The document centres around the theme of "connectivity" and seeks to connect everything and everyone with ICTs until the year 2015: villages, schools, public libraries, hospitals, government departments, etc. However, with most "action lines" based on the words "promote", "encourage" and "should", the programme for achieving these aims is fairly weak and undefined. There is no prospect for mobilising financial resources for infrastructure development, nor for decreasing access barriers to information through, e.g., the relaxation of

[8] The neo-liberal paradigm does not appear in its pure form but with checks and balances. This would confirm the perspective outlined in chapter 4, namely that this paradigm is increasingly being questioned and criticised.

[9] The following quotes are taken from this document.

IPR. The most significant outcomes were the calls for a working group on Internet governance (Art. 13) and for a task force to review and suggest appropriate financing mechanisms (Art. 27). These two groups played a crucial role in the second WSIS phase.

Negotiations and debate in the Tunis phase

The TFFM produced a 125-pages report (TFFM 2004) which provided an overview over recent experiences of financing ICTs but disappointed those who had hoped for an innovative vision for solving future financial challenges. It concluded that market-based approaches had been the most successful mechanisms and that they lacked any viable alternatives.[10] During the ensuing PrepCom debates, Southern government delegations challenged this one-sided perspective and insisted that the crucial role of the public sector in providing necessary infrastructure and services be recognised in the final documents.

WGIG chose a more elaborate approach, with more time for debate, a wider diversity of participants, and a broader range of outputs, including numerous issue papers on individual aspects of Internet governance.[11] It discussed the administration of technical foundations, such as the root zone file system, but also social, political and economic issues such as interconnection costs and spam. Regarding the most conflictive issue – the question of Internet oversight which rested, ultimately, with the US government – WGIG suggested four different options for change, ranging from a model without governmental oversight but with a multi-stakeholder forum as advisory and coordinating body, to transferring oversight to an inter-governmental Global Internet Council (WGIG 2005). The PrepCom debate on this issue saw renewed confrontation between Southern governments,[12] aiming at the internationalisation of Internet control, and the US. Although even the EU departed from its previous support for the US position, proposing compromise models which accepted some sort of internationalisation, the US could not be convinced to give up the status quo in any substantial way.

A third area of debate concerned the follow-up and implementation processes after WSIS2. Here, the extent and the actors of follow-up processes were to be decided. Regarding the former, Southern governments hoped for

---

[10] The issue of financing and the TFFM report will be scrutinised in particular detail in chapter 8.

[11] See http://www.wgig.org

[12] A like-minded group of large Southern countries, including Brazil, India, China, South Africa, Saudi Arabia, and Iran.

rather extensive post-WSIS activities as they had the most to gain from change, whereas their counterparts in the North preferred to maintain the status quo and not commit resources to further deliberations. Regarding the actors, a conflict arose between the option to have UN agencies host and oversee follow-up and implementation processes and the demand by civil society actors to involve non-governmental participants.

Outcomes of the Tunis phase

The Tunis summit, again, led to the adoption of two documents: the *Tunis Commitment* (WSIS 2005a) and the *Tunis Agenda for the Information Society* (WSIS 2005b). Announced as the "summit of solutions" (Annan 2005), and claiming to move "from principles to action" (Tunis Agenda, Art. 1), the Tunis WSIS was to provide substantial regulatory mechanisms to put into practice the commitments agreed at the Geneva summit. Measured by these objectives, results were at least as modest as they had been two years before.

On the issue of finance, it acknowledged the creation of a *Digital Solidarity Fund* (DSF) which the Senegalese delegation had proposed during the Geneva phase and which the North had initially rejected.[13] However, the fund was to be voluntary and thus did not imply any financial commitments (Tunis Agenda, Art. 28).[14] The Tunis Agenda picks up the market bias of the TFFM report, calling for "an enabling and competitive environment for the necessary investment in ICT infrastructure" (Art. 14) and for the "attraction of private-sector investment" (Art. 26), yet it balances this view by pointing to "corporate social responsibility" (Art. 17) and to the necessary "strengthening of international cooperation and solidarity" (Art. 18). A shopping list of tasks that "should" be tackled includes universal access funds (Art. 26) and setting up regional backbone infrastructure as well as infrastructure for remote areas (Art. 23), but a concrete programme for achieving these is lacking.

The conflict on Internet oversight was 'solved' by calling for a process of "enhanced cooperation" (Art. 69) in which "all governments should have an equal role and responsibility" (Art. 68) and which would "maximize the

---

13 The finance negotiations offered some connections with the NWICO conflict. During that earlier debate, countries of the South had already demanded a specific "fund" for developing communication infrastructure, which was rejected by the North and merely led to the possibility of 'voluntary' contributions by governments – not unsimilar to what was finally decided at WSIS (see, e.g., Kleinwächter 2004). However, at WSIS, all actors refrained from openly expressing such links.

14 The following quotes are taken from WSIS (2005b).

participation of developing countries in decisions regarding Internet governance" (Art. 65). In this way, the demands by Southern delegations for change in the power positions in Internet governance could be reconciled with the (temporarily) continued oversight role of the US government.[15] As proposed by WGIG, the Tunis summit established an Internet Governance Forum (IGF) as a "multi-stakeholder policy dialogue" (Art. 72). It also suggested re-establishing the UN Commission on Science and Technology for Development (CSTD) as a main body to oversee follow-up activities (Art. 105). The UN agencies ITU, UNDP and UNESCO were given specific mandates to facilitate implementation activities.

6.3 The "Multi-Stakeholder Approach"

A 'new kind of summit'?

As we have seen, the current series of world summits has changed global governance by integrating new actors in global decision-making processes, particularly the private sector – businesses, corporations, commercial entities – and civil society – usually represented by NGOs and public interest groups. These sectors are conceived to be affected by, and to have a particular interest in, the issues and possible regulations discussed at a summit such as WSIS, and therefore to be 'stakeholders' who deserve to have a say in those discussions. WSIS promised to be innovative by raising the mode of participation of these stakeholders to new levels:

"WSIS, while recommending representation from governments at the highest level, also invites participation of all relevant UN bodies and other international organizations, non-governmental organizations, private sector, civil society, and media to establish a truly multi-stakeholder process".[16]

The *multi-stakeholder approach* became the main buzzword of the WSIS process. A "new kind of summit" was envisaged (Ó Siochrú 2004a: 330), in which private sector and civil society would be 'partners', rather than outside observers, in the summit process. The new discourse not just reverberated through all the official WSIS literature, but re-appeared in civil society analysis and independent accounts. The claim that the multi-stakeholder approach applied at WSIS would constitute a true innovation became a common understanding shared by many summit participants.

---

15 In September 2006, almost one year after the summit, the US government announced that it would phase out its contract with ICANN by 2009 and thus allow it to become an autonomous organisation, without reserving special oversight rights.

16 http://www.itu.int/wsis/participation/index.html

Civil society's "full participation" in summit processes was announced by a senior ITU official in December 2000 (Ó Siochrú 2004a: 333). The exact meaning of "full participation" was not defined, but it seemed to suggest that civil society would be able to participate on equal footing with governments and be included fully in the negotiation process. A first concrete step of putting this claim into practice was the establishment of a tripartite WSIS Secretariat which included three separate divisions, one for each stakeholder group. Underlining its key role, the Civil Society Division (CSD) was the first to take up its work. UNESCO complemented these efforts by holding a series of consultations with civil society actors to develop thematic consensus-building and to formulate proposals for civil society participation. Such proposals included the representation of civil society on the summit Bureau, the establishment of a fund for civil society participation, and the incorporation of civil society statements into the negotiation process. The demands were based on the assumption that civil society actors would be treated "as peers and equals to nation-states and private sector organizations/corporations" (idem: 334).

The struggle over participation

The beginning of the official negotiation process – and thus the entrance of government delegations sceptical towards an increased role of civil society – changed the tone dramatically. Rule 55 of the Rules of Procedure, as agreed by the governments at PrepCom1, noted that "Non-governmental organizations, civil society and business entities … may designate representatives to sit as observers at public meetings of the Preparatory Committee and its subcommittees" (WSIS Executive Secretariat 2002a). Thus the new non-governmental stakeholders were reduced to the status of "observers" who were allowed to attend "public" sessions and given brief slots (at the beginning of these sessions) for contributions and statements, but who were excluded from actual decision-making processes and spaces. These modalities did not represent substantial progress from other recent UN practices.

The prime innovation concerned the private sector. Business had traditionally been represented at summits and other global governance fora through business associations, such as the International Chamber of Commerce (ICC). The WSIS Rules of Procedure changed this practice by allowing individual companies to be accredited at WSIS and participate in summit processes.[17] This provision was based on ITU structures and practices which allow individual companies to become "sector members" and to thereby participate in the activities of one or more of the three main ITU sectors

[17] This decision, in fact, violated ECOSOC rules (Raboy/Landry 2005).

(Radio Communication, Standardization, Development).[18] The result was effectively a double representation of the business sector: individually and through their respective business associations. In addition, the vague self-definition of the civil society sector at WSIS allowed some business actors, for example media corporations and publishers, to be represented in civil society structures, leading effectively to triple representation.[19]

Yet this set-back did not stop civil society actors from claiming broader participation rights throughout the process. In the absence of a detailed framework for advancing the involvement of non-state actors, a struggle emerged between proponents of deeper inclusion – civil society actors, supported by the private sector, the liberal governments of the North/West, and some government delegations from Africa – and the critics – the delegations from Pakistan, China, Iran and Russia being the most vocal, sometimes supported by delegations from Latin America[20] and unofficially supported by others. This *battle of position* continued throughout the whole summit process, dominated large parts of the debate and frequently overshadowed discussions on content and themes. In a permanent one-step-forward, one-step-back movement, rules were sometimes stretched and sometimes restricted, limits were imposed and then lifted again.

The establishment of government-only drafting committees and thematic working groups from PrepCom2 (WSIS1) onwards illustrates this process. These groups served to exclude the 'observers' from the spaces of actual negotiations, yet civil society protests led to openings, such as five-minute speaking slots at the beginning of each session, and in some cases the chairs of meetings allowed observers to attend whole sessions and even contribute substantially to debates. Thus rules were not always applied strictly, depending on the views of the chair and the level of resistance amongst the government delegates present at a particular session. As a form of "constructive ambiguity" (Aizu 2005), such practices occasionally led to cautious progress regarding the inclusion of non-state actors, but without setting hard precedents.

---

[18] see www.itu.int/aboutitu/overview/index.html

[19] In practice, however, the private sector made only limited use of the multiple official channels that were available. Large corporations, such as Microsoft, were absent from most meetings and instead chose to communicate directly with governments and national delegations through established non-official channels.

[20] Members of the Brazilian delegation explained privately that they primarily objected to deeper involvement of the business sector, while they did not object to an inclusion of civil society positions in the negotiation process. Here, the problem of lumping together private sector and civil society in the term "observers" became apparent.

The level of recognition of summit contributions by the 'observers' constituted a similar space of struggle. At PrepCom2 (WSIS1), a proposal by the governmental drafting committee to include statements from private sector and civil society directly in the official draft documents was opposed strongly by some government delegations, resulting in the compromise to only annex them as a separate document, with the explicit agreement "that the proposals by governments would constitute the basis of negotiations" (Heinrich-Böll-Foundation 2003a). While the exclusion of their statements from the official drafts limited non-state actor participation, WSIS nevertheless accepted their contributions as official documents in a UN negotiation process and thereby went beyond the practices of most previous UN summits.

The contradiction between the narrow Rules of Procedure, based on traditional UN practices, and the widely perceived need to enable a far deeper inclusion of non-state actors, surfaced continuously throughout the process.[21] The WSIS process was situated at a strategic crossroads between an old model of an exclusive government sphere of decision-making – with some elementary but strictly limited attendance by non-state actors – and a new model of participatory governance. It did not offer a blueprint for such a new model, but it did put the need to develop new mechanisms clearly visible on the table.[22] Yet the transformation of political processes invariably leads to a new distribution of power between the actors involved. So the struggle over the participation of 'new' actors in the WSIS negotiations reflected an underlying struggle over the new distribution of "agenda-setting and decision-making power in the globalised world of the 21st century" (Kleinwächter 2004: 51; translation by the author).

The *vacuum of universally accepted principles* on non-state actor participation extended to the second WSIS phase and so the two new working groups created after the Geneva summit – WGIG and TFFM – chose different paths. WGIG came very close to a true multi-stakeholder design; with 14 out of 40 members belonging to civil society, half of whom were core

21 This was expressed, amongst many others, by Adama Samassekou, PrepCom President of WSIS phase 1, who emphasized that the issue of non-state actor participation in the summit processes touched on fundamental questions about necessary changes in international cooperation, but that he also expressed he had no idea how to solve them within the WSIS framework (Heinrich-Böll-Foundation 2003b).

22 Observer and participant Wolfgang Kleinwächter put it this way: "The UN is an organisation of the industrial age and WSIS, at least in my eyes, is something like a laboratory for the UN system to investigate where a bridge could be build to reach the information age" (Kleinwächter 2005b).

members of the civil society network at WSIS.[23] The work of WGIG was marked by a cooperative approach in which delegates from different stakeholder groups collaborated on equal footing. The TFFM, in contrast, was convened by the UNDP in a non-transparent manner, hand-picking members, among whom there was only one delegate from a civil society organisation. In the absence of agreed multi-stakeholder guidelines, those responsible for designing the structure of each group had a significant impact on its later working practices. While WGIG-coordinator Markus Kummer chose to include a wide variety of stakeholders, TFFM-convener Mark Malloch-Brown chose a more traditional approach.

The political context of WSIS 'multi-stakeholderism'

To understand the multi-stakeholder approach it is important to look at the context of WSIS. The summit took place at a historic crossroads between two developments. On the one hand, the UN had made significant efforts to expand its cooperation with civil society (and business).[24] On the other hand, a crisis of legitimacy of UN summits, in particular, and of global multilateral regulation, in general, had emerged. Confidence in large summits had been dropping, as they had gained a reputation of over-sized resource-consuming talk-shops, leading to little action in their aftermath. The global political environment was marked by a shift towards unilateralism, and by the growing power of non-UN organisations and associations, such as the WTO and the G8 (Ó Siochrú 2004a). The exploding protests against government summits and meetings of inter-governmental organisations and business associations of that time uncovered a crisis of legitimacy of global institutions which were perceived as undemocratic and elite-driven. The WTO protests in Seattle, 1999, and the G8 protests in Genoa, 2001, represented only the best-known examples of a wave of resistance against prevailing power structures and hegemonic policies. The outcry "Que se vayan todos!" – "They all must go!" – during the Argentinian uprising in December 2001 showed the deep criticism towards political and economic institutions and elites. These more radical perspectives were accompanied with increasing public scrutiny of what actually happened in global policy circles, and with questions regarding legitimacy and accountability. Summits as such did not anymore represent signs of hope for finding solutions to the serious global problems, but were widely regarded with scepticism.

---

23 see http://www.wgig.org/members.html

24 This was, in fact, one of the core objectives during Kofi Annan's term as Secretary-General, as highlighted, for example, in the report *Strengthening of the United Nations: An Agenda for Further Change*, UN document A/57/387.

Just six months before WSIS1, the Geneva region had hosted another global event – the annual G8 meeting – and the city had been the scene of serious confrontations between protesters and the police, in which at least two protesters received nearly lethal injuries. In spring 1998, Geneva had been one of the birthplaces of the global protest movement with the inauguration of the People's Global Action network and a confrontational day of actions against a WTO meeting. A repetition of scenes of street battles, as in Seattle, Genoa, or in Geneva itself, could have become a publicity disaster for WSIS. There was an urgent need for innovation – or at least for a new discourse. So the (alleged) multi-stakeholder approach made a reduction or even elimination of protests possible by claiming to be open for everyone and by integrating potentially critical voices. It served as a response to a crisis of legitimacy on a variety of levels.

Accordingly, the central role of the multi-stakeholder claim was consistently highlighted throughout the summit process. In his opening speech to the very first meeting of the preparatory committee on 1 July 2002, ITU Secretary General Yoshio Utsumi referred to the presence of a variety of stakeholders in his second sentence, before even addressing the themes of the summit (Utsumi 2002). As progress of government negotiations stalled in the run-up to the Geneva summit, WSIS organisers further strengthened the claims of procedural innovation to maintain a positive public perception of the summit and to thereby guarantee its success. The official press statement at the end of PrepCom3 neglected the poor thematic outcomes but instead carried the headline: "Summit Breaks New Ground with Multi-Stakeholder Approach" (ITU 2003).

Civil society had moved from the margins to the very centre of the WSIS process. Even the most cautiously applied criticism by the often effectively excluded and thereby frustrated civil society actors led to sensitive reactions by the WSIS secretariat and many government delegations. When plans for an alternative civil society declaration were made public at PrepCom3 – plans which had the potential to destroy the carefully nurtured impression of broad civil society support to the official WSIS outcomes – PrepCom President Samassekou immediately visited the civil society plenary to promise new mechanisms for including civil society input into the negotiations, but also to warn the plenary of a too critical approach. Such attempts to pacify civil society did not lead to substantial changes in the thematic priorities set out in the summit documents, but they clarified the importance of civil society participation for the success of the summit. As if to underline this point, Samassekou repeatedly approached the civil society *Content & Themes Group* before addressing government delegations to find out which of his thematic proposals would have civil society support. So, even though civil society delegations could not offer any quantifiable trading issues as leverage in the negotiations, their support was perceived as being of fundamental significance. Their negotiation position was based on the necessity of the multi-stakeholder approach.

A new approach?

The analysis of the multi-stakeholder approach by academic observers and participants varies between the recognition of a development towards greater inclusion of non-state actors into governance processes and criticism of the insufficient realities of the WSIS. Padovani acknowledges that "governments have shared the stage" with other actors (Padovani 2004), and she calls the WSIS "a window of opportunity to collectively refine the political agenda for communication" (idem: 188), yet she is sceptical regarding the extent to which WSIS constituted a shift towards a substantially new mode of policy-making. Raboy expresses an emphasis on the positive steps taken at WSIS, which he sees as "the initial steps of a new form of governance" (Raboy 2004a: 355), and notes that WSIS has "transformed" global governance and has shifted its "rules and parameters" (idem: 349) by "sanctifying the place of global civil society as an organized force in this process" (idem: 346). Having "shaken the status quo of global governance", WSIS "should be seen as a laboratory experimenting with a new distribution of power involving emerging as well as established social forces" (idem: 355). However Ó Siochrú, expressing the sceptical perspective, maintains that the outcome of this new distribution is unclear. He even sees a "roll back" of the influence of civil society (Ó Siochrú 2004a: 342): New modalities for civil society participation were not established, and even existing mechanisms were not fully applied. The current international political context, in his view, is rather characterised by a turn against civil society.[25]

6.4 Civil Society structures and agenda

"Civil Society"?

Civil society participants self-defined their sector as encompassing organisations, movements and networks "which are autonomous from the State, are not intergovernmental or do not represent the private sector, and which in principle, are non-profit-making", and which promote "social, economic and cultural interests for mutual benefit".[26] Their understanding was thus in accordance with the definition that was suggested in chapter 2. However,

25 I will analyze the multi-stakeholder practices at WSIS, as well as their possible effects for global governance, in more detail in chapter 9.6.

26 See the description of the main civil society listserve during the WSIS process, http://mailman.greennet.org.uk/mailman/listinfo/plenary

these boundaries were often blurred; as many participants held that civil society should primarily be 'inclusive' and a space for open discussion, rather than a strictly defined sector. Debates on who should legitimately belong to civil society continued throughout the process.

(Self-)Organising

Civil society entities could apply for accreditation for the WSIS process and register representatives. Consistently, several hundred of them attended all PrepCom meetings. A variety of organisations, from universities and foundations to free software associations and community media, took part.[27] A "catalyzing role" (Raboy/Landry 2005: 41) was played by the CRIS campaign which mobilised civil society actors to participate in summit processes, facilitated dialogue among different civil society organisations on thematic objectives for WSIS, and suggested the first steps towards self-organisation at PrepCom1. So CRIS was vital in identifying and developing the 'political opportunity structure' of WSIS.

The structural framework of civil society participants in WSIS was based on three pillars:

(1) Civil society plenary. The plenary of all civil society delegates (CS Plenary) was the collective decision-making body and the ultimate authority on all issues regarding structure and content of civil society participation in the WSIS process. During PrepCom sessions, it was convened every morning or evening. In-between physical meetings, the email listserve plenary@wsis-cs.org constituted a virtual plenary which served as a space to discuss latest developments and all issues related to WSIS and civil society participation.

(2) Families. 21 'families' were created as a 'home' for civil society groups, reflecting their different structural and thematic backgrounds. There were separate families for, e.g., unions, media, youth, indigenous people, creators and actors of culture, think tanks, networks and coalitions, etc. Every family was to send a delegate to the Civil Society Bureau (CSB). This bureau was situated at the heart of WSIS administrative structures and communication channels, as it paralleled the governmental bureau and facilitated the dialogue with governmental delegations. However its remit was strictly limited to procedural questions. Its mandate was to ensure the effective participation

---

[27] Obviously these could not represent civil society in its totality. Many sectors of civil society, particularly those from the Global South and those involved in grassroots activism, were under-represented. I will discuss this problem in chapter 9.6. Keeping these limitations in mind, I will nevertheless refer to those non-state / non-commercial actors that were present in the summit process as *civil society*.

of civil society but did not include questions regarding its thematic objectives and the content of its interventions.

(3) Caucuses. For content debates and lobby interventions, a network of thematic *caucuses* and *working groups* was created, reflecting the different thematic priorities and areas of expertise of civil society groups. There were caucuses on cultural diversity, Internet governance, education, academia and research, health and ICT, human rights, media, gender, patents/copyrights/trademarks, privacy and security, telecentres, etc. These were complemented by regional caucuses including the African, LAC (Latin-American), Asia-Pacific, European, and Western Asia and the Middle East caucuses. The Content & Themes Group compiled and synthesised the thematic objectives of the different caucuses and working groups towards common civil society statements, facilitated agreement on content-related issues, and thereby created a coherent civil society message.

Establishing this structure was not an entirely harmonious process. Particularly the CSB and the family network were controversial within civil society. Even though they represented civil society's formal inclusion in summit structures and thereby constituted a "victory of status" (Raboy/Landry 2005: 51), they were initially established "from on high, top-down" (Frau-Meigs 2006: 82) by the CSD[28] and drew scepticism as to their close proximity to the official WSIS process and the leadership of groups such as the Conference of NGOs in Consultative Relationship with the United Nations (CONGO) which may prioritise the smooth and frictionless running of the process over the substantial influence on summit outcomes and the alternative perspective of civil society. Furthermore, the composition of families revealed a lack of clarity of what was meant by 'civil society', with families such as *local authorities*, *parliamentarians*, and *media* containing actors who go beyond a narrow understanding of the sector as non-state / non-business (Heinrich-Böll-Foundation 2003a).

While the families constituted the channel through which civil society related constructively and as a partner to the government side, the caucuses developed a distinct civil society perspective on information society, which often clashed with the government agenda. They were established in a truly self-organised bottom-up process, and their coordinating body, the Content & Themes group, was led (in the first phase) by members of the CRIS cam-

28 Ó Siochrú criticises the "institutional capture by the Civil Society Division of the Secretariat which could (intentionally or otherwise) impose its visions and priorities" (Ó Siochrú 2004a: 341).

paign[29] who were amongst the more critical and oppositional forces within civil society.

In addition to their organising efforts within the official summit process, civil society actors in some countries established national networks for facilitating information exchange, developing thematic agendas, and lobbying their national governments. Amongst these were the Swiss platform Comunica-ch, CRIS Italy, and the German 'Zivilgesellschaftlicher WSIS Koordinationskreis' (WKK). The German network, for example, met monthly in the capital Berlin during most of the WSIS process from 2002 to 2005 and assembled a variety of actors including, amongst others, academics, Internet activists, librarians, privacy and free software advocates. Members coordinated their interventions into the summit process, conducted occasional meetings with government officials to advocate their perspectives on WSIS-related themes, and developed a common "Charter of Civil Rights for a Sustainable Knowledge Society".[30] Despite its close connection to the WSIS process, the WKK also discussed issues beyond the immediate WSIS negotiations and embraced actors who did not participate in summit proceedings. Thus it used the summit as a political opportunity to establish links between civil society actors working in similar fields.

The Geneva phase: From participation to withdrawal

Civil society interventions into the thematic debates initially achieved positive results. However, as the preparation phase for WSIS1 proceeded, they found a growing number of their positions and thematic preferences removed from the drafts of the WSIS documents. Three months prior to the summit, an analysis by civil society actors of the draft documents queried "Does Input lead to Impact?" and concluded that the vast majority of civil society proposals had been ignored by governments (Global Contract Foundation 2003). Dissatisfaction rose, and civil society participants privately spoke about an "effective break-down of the multi-stakeholder process" (Heinrich-Böll-Foundation 2003c).

At the same time, they developed a critical awareness of their own role as a legitimising force. Whereas previously a majority had seen their principal role in providing expert knowledge to the government delegations, discussions moved to the limits of lobbying and to alternative options, including a public walk-out of the summit process, an alternative civil society summit and a separate civil society declaration. The CS Plenary agreed on a set of

[29] Sally Burch and Bill McIver

[30] Downloadable on http://www.worldsummit2003.de/download_en/Charta-3-0-english.rtf

thematic *non-negotiables* (the "Seven Musts", see Civil Society Working Group on Content and Themes 2003) to serve as a landmark for either supporting or rejecting the WSIS outcomes. The final civil society press statement at PrepCom3 started with the words: "If governments continue to exclude our principles, we will not lend legitimacy to the final official WSIS documents" (Civil Society Plenary 2003a).

Thus civil society strategically used the WSIS multi-stakeholder claims to raise its own negotiation position. Unable to transform the substance of the debate, it eventually decided to stop focusing on lobbying but instead develop a separate civil society declaration. At the end of PrepCom3a, the Civil Society Plenary declared: "We will now stop giving input to the intergovernmental documents" (Civil Society Plenary 2003b).

This did not mean that the summit took place without civil society. A large number of self-organised side-events took place and the civil society declaration was presented. Thus a network of activities between *inside* and *outside* emerged. The civil society summit participants proved that they were not dependent on lobbying, and they raised the bandwidth of possible interventions substantially.

The Tunis phase: GONGOs and fragmentation

The start of the second WSIS phase marked a new attempt by civil society actors to influence the process and claim participation rights. It offered new opportunities, particularly with the WGIG as a truly tripartite forum of debate. However, at PrepCom meetings, the tug-of-war between inclusion and exclusion of civil society continued, and generally conditions for civil society participation degenerated. The Civil Society Division of the WSIS Secretariat was disbanded and key actors, including the coordinators of the Content & Themes Group, left the process or kept a lower profile. While some innovations were achieved – e.g., sophisticated democratic mechanisms regarding the nomination of speakers at government plenaries and of civil society delegates in UN working groups – the civil society network suffered from fragmentation and the lack of a coherent critical discourse which members of the CRIS campaign and the Content & Themes Group had facilitated during the first phase.

The most significant challenge was posed by the host country of WSIS2, Tunisia. Not renowned for their welcoming attitude towards critical civil society actors, the Tunisian authorities sought to disrupt civil society deliberations and interventions from within. A large number of alleged Tunisian 'civil society' representatives entered the process, swamped civil society meetings and interrupted any critique by other civil society actors. According to international civil society activists, their meetings were "hijacked by Tunisian agent provocateurs" (Heinrich-Böll-Foundation 2004). These *GONGOs* (governmental NGOs), as they came to be called within the civil society networks, were officially non-governmental organisations but were suspected to receive orders from the Tunisian authorities and excluded all local oppositional and dissident groups. PrepCom1, which took place in Hammamet, Tunisia, was temporarily suspended as a result of the disruptive acts by Tunisian GONGOs. Ensuing PrepCom meetings were moved back to Geneva, but the continued presence of Tunisian GONGOs made thematic debate and strategising in many caucuses as well as the CS Plenary difficult or impossible. The GONGO strategy partially succeeded, as it contributed to the fragmentation of civil society discourses, structures and strategies – and thus to the weakening of its position.

The Civil Society Declaration

On 8 December 2003, one day before the government documents for WSIS1 were finalised, the CS Plenary unanimously adopted the alternative civil society declaration "Shaping Information Societies for Human Needs" (Civil Society Plenary 2003c). The declaration summarised the perspectives and objectives of the different caucuses and working groups and embedded them in an elaborated social and political vision. In sharp contrast to the cumbersome (and repeatedly stalled) governmental process, the civil society network managed to develop – and agree upon – an extensive set of principles and proposals in just over two months, with restricted resources and in a difficult period of the summit process.

Central to the declaration is the concept of *information and communication societies* which departs from a singular notion of one 'information society'. The concept "expresses the split between two visions of social life and the organization of human relations" (Raboy/Landry 2005: 131) and makes WSIS the "locus of confrontation between opposing paradigms" (idem: 132) – between top-down, technology-focused and managerial "information", and people-centred, diverse and participatory "communication" (Ó Siochrú 2004b). Information and communication societies, according to the declaration, should foster[31] "human knowledge, creativity, cooperation and solidarity", offer everyone "the opportunity to participate in communication processes", enhance cultural and linguistic diversity, and recognise knowledge, information and communication resources "as the common heritage of humankind". Far from automatically generating a techno-utopian paradise, they need to "take into account geo-political and historical injustices", such

[31] The following quotes are taken from CS Plenary (2003c).

as extreme poverty, unequal distribution of resources and human rights violation.

Key areas of concern include poverty eradication; gender justice; basic literacy; the development of community-based, bottom-up ICT solutions; and a wide set of human rights including freedom of expression, the right to privacy, workers rights, the rights of indigenous peoples and the right to participate in public affairs (and thus several parts of the communication rights framework proposed by CRIS). The declaration supports public service and community media, advocates free software, criticizes the privatisation of knowledge through extensive intellectual property regimes and calls for a robust "global knowledge commons" as part of "alternative models for the production and exchange of knowledge and information". The multi-stakeholder approach to Internet governance, which the declaration proposes, comes close to the practices and ideas of the WGIG and the IGF. Finally, far from accepting the back seat as 'awareness-raisers' and 'promoters' assigned by the official documents, the civil society actors proclaim that they "have been key innovators and shapers of the technology, culture and content of information and communication societies".

Besides turning the spotlight on social and communication processes, with a focus on participation and openness, the document provides a view on human nature which leaves notions of individualism and self-interest aside and instead assumes a collaborative perspective which focuses on human practices of cooperation and of exchange with the environment. These practices intersect with "the distributed intelligence of the Internet network" (Frau-Meigs 2006: 87) and an "open source model" (ibid.) of social organisation.

The document presented at WSIS1 was not followed by a second alternative declaration at the Tunis summit. However, the civil society network produced the statement "Much more could have been achieved" (Civil Society Plenary 2005) which analyzes the outcomes of the whole WSIS endeavour and reiterates civil society's fundamental principles and objectives. In a nutshell, the view prevails that[32] "minor achievements in the outcomes from WSIS were offset by major shortcomings, with much remaining to be done". Specifically, WSIS "failed to agree on adequate funding for ICTD" and to develop innovative financing models which go beyond the dominant market-oriented paradigm. Human rights were not adequately addressed, for example the right to privacy was severely compromised by the focus on security. Insufficient attention was paid to gender equality, the persistent need for traditional ICTs such as radio, TV and telephony, media concentration, community media, free software, cultural diversity, and public ser-

[32] The following quotes are taken from CS Plenary (2005).

vices. Civil society reiterates its rejection of the "careless monopolization" of knowledge. However, and despite its harsh criticism during the first phase, it recognises improvements in civil society participation "as a result of constant pressure from Civil Society" and expresses its expectation for these to serve as benchmarks for future governance fora.

6.5 Side-events and counter-activities

The presentation of the outcomes of the preparation process and the speeches by representatives of governments, international institutions, business and civil society occupied just a small part of summit spaces and timetables. By far the largest parts of the Palexpo (Geneva) and Kram (Tunis) exhibitions centres, where the summits took place, housed a) the exhibitions ICT4D (Geneva) and ICT4all (Tunis), and b) a plethora of side- and parallel events.

The exhibitions resembled trade fairs, in which governments, businesses and some civil society organisations presented their products and services, and which were to gather "people acting for a better tomorrow, through a smart use of new technologies" (http://www.expo.ict4all-tunis.org). At ICT4D, 250 exhibitors and numerous presentations and workshops attracted 38,000 visits (http://www.ict-4d.org), while ICT4all claimed 330 exhibitors and 70,000 visits (http://www.expo.ict4all-tunis.org). Between 200 and 300 side-events at each summit included workshops, presentations and conferences, some of them extending over several days, many of them organised by civil society groups. They offered an opportunity to discuss specific aspects of the summit outcomes in more depth and to put issues back on the table which had fallen off the agenda during the negotiation process. Events included, amongst many others, the World Forum on Communication Rights (organised by CRIS), the World Electronic Media Forum (organised by a network of broadcasting unions), a conference on information and development (organised by the World Bank), workshops on community wireless networking (organised by APC) and the conference "Towards a sustainable and inclusive knowledge society" (organised by the Heinrich Böll Foundation).

The major protests which had accompanied previous summits did not occur at WSIS. The multi-stakeholder claims of the summit organisers may account for part of the reason. In addition, the fairly abstract themes, the lack of binding outcomes, the lack of media interest, and (in the case of Tunisia) the likelihood of harsh repression by the authorities discouraged protest activity. However, civil society actors organised alternative events outside the WSIS framework which expressed fundamental criticism of the summit agenda as well as practices. In Geneva, a network of media activists set up a series of events (including a conference, a video stream and a media laboratory) called WSIS?WeSeize!, and in Tunis, civil society summit participants planned a separate Citizens' Summit in protest of the human rights violations in Tunisia and the exclusion of Tunisian human rights activists from summit processes. Whereas WSIS?WeSeize! faced minor trouble from police who temporarily closed the media laboratory, the Citizens' Summit was almost entirely prevented by security forces.

6.6 Conclusion

WSIS was innovative both thematically and structurally: It dealt with current issues around information and communication, and it provided new opportunities for civil society to participate in a global governance forum. At the same time, it illustrated both aspects' highly conflictive nature: Far from constituting technical issues that merely require proper management, information and communication are highly political, and at WSIS, fundamentally different interests clashed and were difficult (and often impossible) to reconcile. Civil society appears to be essential to legitimise policy-making (and to provide expertise on specialised policy issues), yet many of the more traditional governance players are eager to retain the negotiation and decision-making process as an exclusive government domain.

In this environment, civil society actors used openings creatively and applied the centrality of the multi-stakeholder discourse as a leverage for raising their concerns and strengthening their position, but they also encountered serious roadblocks. Returning to the specific sector of CS Media, we will now take a closer look at the details of participation and intervention.

7 Civil Society Media at WSIS

Having developed the frame of the WSIS process, I will now investigate the specific activities of Civil Society (CS) Media with regards to the summit. This chapter will introduce the strategic and tactical approaches chosen by CS Media, their varying degrees of involvement with the official summit, their thematic objectives, the spaces which they created for self-organising and advocacy, and preliminary summaries of their successes and failures.[1] It develops along the spaces which evolved during the WSIS preparation process: the Media Caucus as an advocacy coalition for a wide range of media actors, the Community Media Working Group as a narrower space for CS Media, the alternative spaces set up around the summit, most prominently WSIS?WeSeize!, and the events that took place at the edges between inside and outside, such as the Community Media Forum.

7.1 Media corporations

Before turning towards the spaces in which coalitions of media actors self-organised, we should take a brief look at the involvement of individual media corporations. Direct participation of these corporations had been made possible due to the business-friendly rules of procedure adopted at Prep-Com1 of the Geneva phase. Yet, as was mentioned in the previous chapter, not many business entities chose to take this opportunity. WSIS was met with a relative lack of interest by the business community, and this applied to the large media companies as well as to most other commercial actors. The corporations which were introduced in chapter 2 did not actively participate in the negotiation processes.

However several of the major media corporations, such as Time-Warner, Sony and Vivendi, are members of the International Chamber of Commerce (ICC) which supports the interests of business worldwide and which organised the Coordinating Committee of Business Interlocutors (CCBI) at WSIS, thus being at the forefront of making business demands visible in the WSIS process. The CCBI's interventions into the negotiations focused on the essential role of information technology for social and economic development, and on establishing a business-friendly regulatory framework for creating technical infrastructure. Governments were advised to create competitive market-led environments, alleviate obstacles to investment as well as tax burdens, secure intellectual property rights, and foster cultural changes towards risk-taking and entrepreneurship (CCBI 2002).

---

1 An in-depth discussion of the results of their involvement with follow in chapters 8 and 9.

The contribution of the Asociacion Internacional de Radiodiffusion / International Association of Broadcasting (AIR/IAB), which represents commercial radio and television associations from Europe and the Americas as well as a large number of commercial broadcasters, reads like a translation of this business framework for the media sector (IAB 2002)[2]. According to the AIR, "the existence of free private broadcasting (...) constitutes an essential element for the existence of a free society". Therefore, free access to information through private media must be insured and any restrictions to journalism strictly avoided. Commercial media are portrayed as the guardian of freedom of expression acting in the public interest, and any interference from outside in commercial media operations, including media regulation, ethical standards etc., is rejected and framed as a violation of the right to freedom of expression. The prime source of such interference is seen in state interventions, while corporate or market-led censorship is not addressed as a problem. People are mainly seen as consumers, whose best guarantees for freedom are "natural market processes" and the "free flow of information across national frontiers". Only private and, to a lesser degree, public service broadcasters are recognised, whereas CS Media are ignored.

At the World Electronic Media Forum (WEMF), a side event which took place parallel to the first WSIS summit (see chapter 7.5), the AIR gave further insights into its agenda, particularly its perspectives on two issues which were discussed repeatedly throughout the WSIS process: freedom of expression and media pluralism. As for the first, it introduced the "right to free commercial expression" (WEMF 2004: 132) – thus placing advertising and commercial activity amongst the most fundamental human rights. As for media pluralism, it noted that "[t]his principle must be compatible with the need to foster the growth of radio and television companies" and that therefore "specific legislation that would be discriminatory for private media" (ibid.) should be avoided, whereby it prioritised the right to unrestricted private broadcasting over the need for media pluralism.

The perspective of the AIR, as we will see, was incorporated into the Media Caucus in which the AIR became an influential actor. Yet individual media companies did not give any substantial input to the WSIS process, and the ICC remained silent on specific media issues. The space designated to business actors in the WSIS process did not offer much momentum for strengthening the role of media actors.

2 The following quotes refer to this document.

7.2 The Media Caucus

Formation and composition

Instead, the main body for feeding media interests into the WSIS process emerged within the network of civil society caucuses. A *Media Family* was established during the initial phase of setting up structures for civil society self-organisation – at PrepCom2 of the Geneva phase – as a coordinating body for media actors in the WSIS process. This *Family* set up the *Media Caucus* as its content-related arm, but with the same members and the same meeting schedule. The Family soon ceased to exist as a separate body, and the Media Caucus became effectively the space for coordinating all matters regarding media actors in the WSIS process.

Preparation

The caucus was the result of a longer countdown which had brought together several major media actors in the pre-WSIS phase. The most important of these pre-existing networks was the association of *World Broadcasting Unions* (WBU) which encompassed the big regional radio and television unions – the Asia-Pacific Broadcasting Union (ABU), the Asociacion Internacional de Radiodiffusion / International Association of Broadcasting (AIR/IAB), the Arab States Broadcasting Union (ASBU), the Caribbean Broadcasting Union (CBU), the European Broadcasting Union (EBU), the North American Broadcasters Association (NABA), the Organisacion de la Television Iberoamericana (OTI), and the Union des Radiodiffusions et Televisions Nationales d'Afriques (URTNA). A further pre-existing coalition, the *Coordinating Committee of Press Freedom Organisations*, encompassed the Inter American Press Association (IAPA), the International Press Institute, the World Association of Newspapers (WAN), the World Press Freedom Committee (WPFC), and the two broadcasting unions NABA and AIR. Both networks of media actors had contributed position papers to the constitutional phase of the WSIS, and had thus prepared the work of the Media Caucus both structurally and thematically.

With which of the four stakeholder groups (governments, international organisations, business, and civil society) these coalitions should be aligned was apparently unclear to the WSIS secretariat. The contributions of the broadcasting unions, as well as separate statements by the AIR and by European broadcasters, were put in the section "ITU sector members and accredited business entities" while the contribution of the press freedom coalition (even though it included some of the very same members) was included under "Accredited NGOs and Civil Society Entities".[3] This confu-

---

[3] see http://www.itu.int/wsis/preparatory/prepcom/pc2/index.html

sion reflected the mixture of actors and interests which the groups represented. They brought together public service broadcasters, such as the BBC, RAI and the German ARD and ZDF, commercial networks such as the American CBS, NBC, Fox and Televisa, major newspaper publishers, and journalists. The unions and associations all qualified as non-profit organisations, yet they went far beyond the more narrowly defined understanding of 'civil society' which I introduced in chapter 2 and which was largely adhered to by other caucuses and the WSIS generally.

The dilemma of stakeholder characteristics was 'solved' by the media actors' own choice to create a caucus as part of the civil society network. Some civil society participants who feared that an explicit 'civil society' space was colonised by private sector interests challenged this move and argued for articulating clearer distinctions between civil society and other actors. However the majority opted for 'inclusiveness'.

Caucus composition

Members of the two pre-existing networks emerged as key actors of the newly established caucus. The AIR (representing commercial broadcasters), the EBU (representing public service broadcasters), the WAN (press publishers), and the WPFC sent representatives who actively shaped the work of the caucus. They were complemented by representatives from the World Radio and Television Council (WRTVC, an NGO supporting public service broadcasting), the journalist trade union International Federation of Journalists (IFJ), the Swiss journalist unions Federation Suisse des Journalistes and comedia, the freedom of expression advocacy campaign Article 19, the Media Institute of Southern Africa (MISA), and media researchers from, for example, the International Association for Media and Communication Research (IAMCR).

Some of these actors had already been involved with the NWICO conflict, having supported the US government in its opposition to changes to the dominant Western media systems. The first chair of the Media Caucus, Ronald Koven, represented the WPFC which had been formed in 1976 to explicitly defend the interests of the predominantly US and European corporate media in the NWICO debates (see chapter 4). So the Media Caucus, in its initial phase, was predominantly a lobby and discussion group of the mainstream media establishment.

Representation of Civil Society Media was limited to one delegate of the World Association of Community Broadcasters (AMARC), who sought to increase the Caucus' consideration of community and other civil society media but was unable to prevail against the larger group of representatives from traditional mainstream media organisations. Members of other CS Media organisations, such as the Association for Progressive Communication (APC), chose to engage with different caucuses, such as the regional caucuses (e.g., members of the Korean media organisation MediAct participated in the Asia-Pacific Caucus), the Privacy&Security Caucus, or the Internet Governance Caucus.

However, at subsequent PrepComs the Media Caucus was infused with a stronger presence of AMARC delegates, representatives of NGOs supporting community media, such as the Asociacion Latinoamericana de Educacion Radiofonica (ALER) and the Catholic Media Council (CAMECO), as well as a few activists from Indymedia and other alternative/radical/grassroots media groups. They were not able to transform the caucus into a space specifically for CS Media, but they introduced a CS Media perspective and occasionally challenged the hegemonic mainstream media views. The change in the composition of the caucus was reflected by the election of a new caucus chair at PrepCom3 – Tracey Naughton from MISA – as well as a new vice chair – Victor Van Oeyen from ALER – with Ronald Koven relegated to the position of a further vice chair. The new chair and vice chair were sympathetic to CS Media and supported a bigger role for the latter in the caucus. Yet the domination of mainstream-oriented media actors remained, Ronald Koven effectively co-chaired the caucus and continued to exert a great influence on thematic debates and positions.

Content

Input 1: World Broadcasting Unions

The WBU set the tone for the subsequent position papers by the Media Caucus. It emphasised the importance of content vice versa technology and highlighted the role of the media as major producers and distributors of quality content. In detail, it proposed five statements as priorities for a debate on 'information society' and as pillars for WSIS negotiations (WBU 2003)[4]:

(1) "Communications technology is not an end in itself; it is a vehicle for the provision of information and content"

(2) "Freedom of expression, freedom and pluralism of the media, and cultural diversity should be respected and promoted"

[4] The following quotes are taken from this document.

(3) "The electronic media have a vital role to play in the information society"

(4) "Television and radio are crucial for ensuring social cohesion and development in the digital world"

(5) "Information should remain accessible and affordable to everyone"

These statements uncover a particular understanding of 'media': Media actors engage in "communication to the general public" by "producing, gathering, and distributing quality content" and "selecting and interpreting information and placing it in its proper context". They "need to be strengthened to be able to reach out to everybody". Media are thus seen as informants and gatekeepers, whereas an understanding of media as mediators and participants, as favoured by most CS Media, is not considered.

The particular type of media organisation which the unions have in mind are "independent broadcasting services", with 'independent' referring to a sufficient distance from states and governments. They include commercial media which, amongst other aspects, are said to "ensure a plurality of news sources". "(O)ther forms of legally-established and non-profit media" are recognised, but their role is limited to serving local communities, minority groups, and other specific social sectors.

Input 2: Coordinating Committee of Press Freedom Organisations

The press freedom coalition demanded that Article 19 (freedom of expression) of the Universal Declaration of Human Rights (UDHR) be confirmed by the summit and that press freedom laws and values be applied for the Internet (CCPFO 2002)[5]. It recognised that there may be a need to restrict "pornography, paedophilia, fraud, conspiracy for terrorism, incitement to violence, hate speech, etc" but maintained that existing national legislation was fully sufficient to deal with such matters and rejected any hidden "controls over the free flow of information" justified "on political grounds, regional value systems or national information sovereignty". The press freedom groups explicitly rejected the "now-discredited proposals" for an NWICO. In the preparation to WSIS, they saw "those at work who seek to revive and assert for their own purposes such restrictive proposals in the new guise of countering alleged threats and dangers posed by new communication technologies". They exclaimed: "These proposals must again be successfully resisted, just as they were earlier."

---

5 The following quotes are taken from this document.

Thus the Committee suspected that NWICO would rise again and that governments of the South would seek to restrict the unlimited cross-border operations of transnational media companies. It therefore demanded that "preserving and extending the free flow of news and information [be made] a basic concern of the summit" and it called on all participants to "reject any proposal aimed at restricting news content or media operations". The Committee revealed a decidedly pro-business standpoint by calling for the strengthening and extension of intellectual property rights (IPR) and putting trust in the market to ensure global coverage of communication technologies.

Input 3: IFJ and Article 19

The International Federation of Journalists (IFJ) departed sharply from the uncritical appraisal of the mainstream media sector by the two coalitions (IFJ 2003).[6] While it maintained to a traditional understanding of media and journalism that reserves information production and provision for media workers and limits the public's role to that of a passive recipient, it criticised a market-led approach to regulation which "will drive down employment rights, stifle creativity, lower quality, and reinforce existing divisions within society at large. It will also lead to greater media concentration and undue influence by global media conglomerates, outside the orbit of democratic accountability, on cultural, political and public life." The IFJ noted that the "[q]uality of information is being ravaged by excessive commercialisation"; that media concentration is "damaging to pluralism and freedom of expression"; and that threats to the free flow of information occur through "the establishment of monopolistic positions" by both political and economic forces. It suggested specific concentration and ownership rules for media which differ from usual competition rules for other economic sectors and thereby take into account the specific cultural and democratic value of information; and demanded public funding to assist media that promote the plurality of opinion, including community-based networks. With news and information sources "dominated by northern media conglomerates" and an "increasingly monocultural vision of the world" emerging, it demands: "This imbalance must be rectified." Further recommendations include the establishment of fair and affordable access to a universal service, the preservation of privacy, including limits to the collection and retention of information on citizens and the rejection of monitoring and control of Internet data traffic, and the protection of labour rights for media workers. The IFJ's elaborate position on media concentration and its (self-)critical view on both structures and contents of the media sector offer linkages with the perspec-

---

6 The following quotes are taken from this document.

tives of CS Media. Its roots in a traditional sender-receiver division, however, and its focus on the rights of the senders, including an extension of IPR, reveal substantial differences.

The NGO Article 19 brought up similar concerns. It took note of "the increasing dominance of large media corporations" which may pose a "threat to freedom of expression, along with (...) 'traditional' State threats" (Article19 2003), recognised the need for diverse and pluralistic media, for the right to practice and express one's culture and for privacy rights. Quite different to the AIR's focus on non-interference by the state, it stressed the state's obligations to actively promote pluralism through appropriate legislation and emphasized the necessity to prevent the emergence of both public and private media monopolies through regulatory measures. Subsidy schemes and funding mechanisms were proposed to, for example, encourage community broadcasting, local content production, and access to the media by minority groups. The organisation highlighted the particular role of both public service and community media for creating a pluralistic media environment and ensuring the provision of media content for diverse social groups. Contrary to the other media actors introduced so far in this chapter, it criticised the expansion of IPR as a danger to freedom of expression.

Media Caucus statements in the Geneva phase

The Media Caucus produced a set of demands at PrepCom2 in February 2003 as a foundation for all further advocacy activities by the caucus throughout the whole WSIS process (Media Caucus 2003a)[7]. Priority demands are that Article 19 UDHR is "[t]he guiding principle of WSIS" and to be quoted in full in the WSIS documents, and that the vital role of the media "in producing, gathering and distributing quality content" is highlighted. The list includes 14 points:

(1) Communications technology is not an end in itself; it is a vehicle for the provision and exchange of information and content.

(2) Freedom of expression, freedom and pluralism of the media, and cultural diversity should be respected and promoted.

(3) Media concentration, in all areas including those in the ICTs, should be subject to general anti-monopoly scrutiny and laws.

(4) The electronic media have a vital role to play in the Information Society.

---

[7] The following quotes are taken from this document.

(5) All forms of media can make crucial contributions to social cohesion and development in the digital era.

(6) Information should be accessible and affordable to everyone.

(7) Information access laws should ensure that all people have access to basic information and communication services.

(8) Uniform legal protection of communications privacy is needed to avoid governmental or other interference and official monitoring of Internet traffic and personal communications.

(9) Editorial independence of media professionals and creators must be protected.

(10) Public service values in the Information Society should be encouraged, including genuine public service broadcasting. State-controlled media should be transformed into editorially independent public service organizations.

(11) Information and media development programmes are needed to promote local content services in all regions of the world, as well as access to basic communications technology.

(12) Equitable and pluralistic allocation of broadcasting frequencies should be on the basis of transparent legal frameworks.

(13) Legally established independent and non-profit media operated by local communities can make an important contribution, especially by serving traditionally disadvantaged groups, such as youth, women, indigenous peoples, children and minority groups.

(14) Online media workers should have the same contractual rights and protections as other media workers.

This list represents an attempt at balancing the WSIS' dominant focus on technology by highlighting the role of content. It centres around the rights and freedoms of media organisations and journalists as the primary producers and distributors of content, as well as on freedom of expression. These core agendas of the broadcasting unions and the press freedom groups are complemented with some concerns by other caucus members, including the need for public service values, for the protection of workers' rights, media pluralism, and the recognition of non-profit community media.

However criticism of media concentration is vague, failing to advance specific anti-monopoly laws. Community media are recognised in principle, but they only appear towards the end of the document, require "legally established (...) non-profit" status, and are confined to the edges and niches of the media sphere to serve "traditionally disadvantaged groups". These qualifications marginalise CS Media and shut out all media projects without a legal status (e.g., in regions and states which do not provide laws for the legal operation of community media). The focus of the caucus thus lies on presenting the media as crucial stakeholders in the WSIS process, rather than pointing to their internal weaknesses and suggesting reforms for the sector.

Development of statements during the Geneva phase

Even those few hints at a media reform agenda, which the Media Caucus did incorporate in its initial statement, vanished during its further lobby efforts. The practical course of the WSIS negotiation process required that the Media Caucus focus on a narrow set of 'non-negotiables' to achieve success in some areas. And that focus included two points: freedom of expression (usually in connection with freedom of the media), and reinforcement of the role of media actors in information society (Media Caucus 2003b).

At specific points during the WSIS negotiations, additional aspects were picked out from the initial set of statements. These included ensuring media pluralism and "scrutinizing media ownership concentration"; the need for transforming state-controlled media "into editorially independent public service organizations"; the "important contribution" of "[l]egally established independent and non-commercial media operated by local communities"; and the rights and protections of online media workers (Media Caucus 2003c, 2003d). One caucus document at PrepCom3 even included a call for establishing a Community Media Fund, for opening up broadcast licensing to allow for community broadcasting in every community "and to ensure all of the world's population can access community broadcasting services by 2015" (Media Caucus 2003e). Yet beyond those occasional inroads, the caucus priorities continued to focus on (mainstream) media freedoms. This agenda was complemented at PrepCom3 with a firm position by the caucus on the question of ethical standards: "Formulation of professional and ethical standards in journalism are the responsibility of media professionals themselves" (Media Caucus 2003d).

The thematic focus of the caucus was, in part, a response to government attempts to restrict media freedoms and to weaken references to human rights. This hostile environment strengthened the position of those in the Media Caucus whose principal objective was to prevent state-led interferences in media independence. The more governments rejected media freedoms, the more the caucus insisted on its core objective of safeguarding them – and, as a consequence, neglected other issues. Within this struggle, an expansion of the agenda towards the wider set of issues that community media and the communication rights and media reform movements would favour, and that organisations such as the IFJ and Article 19 would partially support, was difficult to achieve.

Conflicts within the caucus

In an environment characterised by government hostility, key CS Media actors, prominently AMARC, decided not to push for their wider sets of objectives, but rather to "work with other Media Caucus members to put a strong emphasis on freedom of expression" (Buckley 2004a). They thus stayed inside the Media Caucus for strategic reasons. Yet this decision did not change the fact that the caucus marginalised the perspectives of those which it – being a 'civil society' caucus – was to represent. Its thematic vision was at odds with media reform and communication rights agendas which many civil society-based media actors have developed and which include limits to media concentration, public participation in traditional media, accountability of the media, and interactive communication by everyone, as opposed to safeguarding the information monopoly of media organisations and professional journalists (see chapter 4).[8]

Agreeing with the general analysis of the Media Caucus that freedom of expression needed to be saved (almost at all costs), and not wanting to engage in futile battles with the caucus majority, CS Media representatives never forcefully advocated these sets of agenda points. However they did defend the little gains they had made, particularly against attacks by commercial broadcasters. The AIR repeatedly tried to marginalise the role of community media in caucus statements by, e.g., suggesting to limit them to low power transmission and to forbid the creation of community broadcasting networks (Private Broadcasting and Print Working Group 2003). Perhaps unwisely, the AIR did not stop there but also confronted public service media, demanding that "[p]ublic broadcasters will gradually resign their privileges that damage their commercial competitors" (ibid.), thus implying the phasing-out of regulation and financial support which secure the existence of public service media in Europe, particularly. This caused the EBU, representing many large public service broadcasters, to join the community

---

[8] Occasionally, criticism emerged. For example, at PrepCom3 a representative from the CRIS campaign challenged the demand that ethical standards for journalism should be set by journalists themselves. Yet the strategic consensus within the caucus could not be changed by such interventions.

media resistance against the AIR. When AMARC President Steve Buckley interpreted the AIR proposals as "restrictions on freedom of expression", even the press freedom groups, including the WPFC, changed sides.[9] The result of this change in internal Media Caucus alliances (and thus of a power struggle which dominated the largest part of the Media Caucus meetings at PrepCom3) was a rejection of the AIR's proposals, a weakened position by the commercial media in subsequent Media Caucus debates, and a rare victory for CS Media representatives.[10]

Beyond the surface of rough consensus and occasional quarrels, even the agreed parts of Media Caucus statements uncovered deep divides between different media actors. If we compare the characteristics of CS Media, as outlined in chapter 2, with the statements of the caucus, we can identify at least three aspects in which the interpretations of media challenges as well as of the very role of media differ fundamentally.

First, while most commercial and public service media representatives understood 'media pluralism' as the highest-possible number of media outlets and content providers[11], for CS Media the concept usually involves a diversity of content, thus a diversity of opinions as well as of societal groups represented in the media. Secondly, the view of media as 'information providers', as emphasized by the Media Caucus, clashed with the objective of many CS Media to facilitate content *exchange,* participatory information production and interactive distribution, and thus to challenge the traditional sender-receiver division.

Thirdly, mainstream media applied the right to freedom of expression primarily to media organisations, as these were seen as the only viable producers of information and providers of content. Article 19 UDHR was "to be implemented, for the traditional media as well as for media using new in-

---

9 Ronald Koven explicitly stated that he would usually share the side of the commercial media, but that their demands conflicted with freedom of expression and that he therefore had to oppose them.

10 Tracey Naughton, the caucus chair, agreed that "the Latin American lobby can be seen to be monopolising media for commercial gain", "seeks to eradicate community media" and "is espousing unacceptable views", yet she identified the root of the struggle in regional conflicts and in "divisions that were not real" (Interview TN). Other interview partners interpreted the conflict within the framework of a competition between different types of media (commercial, public service, community) and of a very 'real' division of interests which went to the heart of what these media are about. Accordingly, many participants held that "the Media Caucus tries to integrate actors which are separated by fundamental lines of conflict" (MC).

11 E.g.: "we defend the existence of information pluralism, through the broadest offer of radio and television stations in all countries" (WEMF 2004: 131).

formation technologies, such as Internet and Satellite Broadcasting" (Media Caucus 2003b). Thus 'freedom of expression' was interpreted as 'freedom of the media' and as a strategic tool for safeguarding the undisturbed independence of media organisations and professional journalists. In contrast, many CS Media focus on the communication rights of individual persons, both to strengthen their voices in the media and to protect them against misinformation and one-sided coverage by the media (see chapter 4).

Media Caucus statements of the Tunis phase

If the agenda of the Media Caucus was restricted to a limited set of media freedom issues during the first WSIS phase, it became even more so during the second phase. In light of the human rights situation in the WSIS2 host country Tunisia, the battle for worldwide implementation of Article 19 UDHR became the central focus of caucus activity. It was complemented by several fact-finding missions by the International Freedom of Expression eXchange (IFEX) to Tunisia, in which several members of the caucus participated and which revealed gross human rights violations in the WSIS2 host country. The repression against journalists, and the hardly existent press freedoms which the IFEX missions to Tunisia documented, prestructured much of the caucus' debates and activities.

Media Caucus statements of phase 2 reiterated the centrality of Article 19 UDHR, demanded the abolition of legal regulations that prevent free journalism, criticised the targeting of journalists in conflict situations and called for the improvement of their safety. They demanded that neither security concerns nor ethical considerations should be allowed to become "a veiled way to justify censorship" (Media Caucus 2005, 23 February 2005), that 'illegal content' should not be defined by governments but by "laws that derive their legitimacy from universally accepted norms" (ibid.), and that freedom of expression should be fully implemented in cyberspace. The caucus expressed its concern over an increased role of governments in Internet regulation and urged governments not to extend Internet governance to content regulation and censorship. Implicitly, it thereby expressed support for the existing model of private sector-led Internet administration which limited the role of governments and which was supported at WSIS by the US and a few other Western/Northern delegations.

If the second WSIS phase represented, at the same time, a narrowing and a broadening of agendas, activities, and spaces, the same can be said about the Media Caucus. New actors joined the caucus and brought new issues into the debate, in some cases, those new issues were incorporated into summit statements (e.g., journalism in conflict situations), yet in other cases thematic struggles emerged. A large number of participants from Tunisian

GONGOs challenged the caucus' critical view about the human rights situation in their home country as well as its strong position on media freedoms. The caucus (thanks, not least, to its experienced chair) managed to reconcile these very different perspectives on freedom of expression by avoiding to name Tunisia or any other particular country in its criticism of human rights violations. The ordered course of Media Caucus meetings was thus guaranteed and outbreaks of conflict were mostly prevented, but open debate on crucial issues was rendered impossible in this precarious equilibrium between diametrically opposed sides.

In this (mostly suppressed) conflict, community media representatives continued to support the pro-press-freedom perspective of the international media and press freedom groups. They accepted the narrow agenda of the Media Caucus, opting to participate in a strong alliance to advance freedom of expression.

Strategies

The Media Caucus operated on two levels: an *internal* and an *external* one. Internally, the caucus was an attempt to create a common media platform. It was based on the view that media actors had a strong set of common perspectives which outweighed the differences in interests and in media concepts. A large part of its meetings, which usually happened on a daily basis during PrepComs and summits, was consumed by consensus-building processes and by negotiations between different members. The process of arriving at common statements often resembled the inter-governmental negotiations in the WSIS plenary and working groups. Sections were discussed word-by-word, and different camps sought to position their interests in an optimal way. In many instances, only the authority and experience of the chair could ensure that the bargaining and tactical negotiating between the caucus members would lead to eventual agreement. As in inter-governmental debates, the difficulty of producing 'agreed text' in a process of negotiations between divergent (and often diametrically opposed) interests meant that such 'agreed text' would rarely be changed afterwards, so that the caucus produced a stable and but hardly flexible agenda.

Externally, the caucus fed this 'agreed text' into the WSIS negotiation process. For that, it used all the tools that were available to civil society caucuses at WSIS:

(1) Statements in plenary and subcommittee sessions: The caucus chair addressed the WSIS inter-governmental plenary and Subcommittee 2 on several occasions.

(2) Statements in working groups: The chair equally addressed the inter-governmental working group on media issues and made full use of the limited time slots that were provided at the beginning of working group sessions.

(3) Informal lobbying: Caucus members brought up the issues agreed by the caucus (although often focusing on their individual issue of interest) in talks with government delegations, usually those of their respective home-countries.

(4) Collective civil society statements: The caucus provided input to common civil society statements which assembled the priority objectives of the different caucuses.

A particular channel of intervention was opened through the participation of several caucus members in the Swiss civil society platform Comunica-Ch and, furthermore, in the Swiss government delegation. Comunica-Ch had incorporated in its membership a number of media associations and journalist unions, such as the public service media organisation Conseil mondial de la Radio Télévision (CMRTV) and the Swiss journalist and media workers unions. The platform engaged in intensive consultations with the Swiss government delegation and was given several seats in that delegation. As the host country of the first WSIS phase, the Swiss government had a particularly influential position in the WSIS process and thus had some leverage to influence the summit content debates, and it became convinced that supplying WSIS with a strong position on media issues was one of its prime objectives. It developed into the main force on the governmental side for including a media perspective and the most vocal defender of media independence and freedom of expression.

Furthermore, the Media Caucus was able to occupy strategic positions in the inter-governmental working group on media issues which was created during the Geneva phase, even though the working groups had explicitly excluded non-governmental actors from their negotiations. Alain Modoux, former Assistant Director General of UNESCO and President of Orbicom (Network of UNESCO Chairs in Communication) was elected as the chair of the working group; Wolf Ludwig, General Secretary of the journalist union comedia, was assigned as minute taker; Michel Bührer from the Swiss journalist union led the drafting group. All had joined the working group in their role as members of the Swiss government delegation. Even though their role focused on moderation and documentation rather than negotiation, they were occasionally able to support sympathetic considerations of Media Caucus positions.

Successes and failures

In terms of policy outcomes, the Media Caucus was one of the more successful civil society caucuses at WSIS. Its input into the negotiations of the governmental working group on media issues of the first WSIS phase was widely reflected in the debates within that group, and its core demands – particularly a prominent reference to Article 19 UDHR and a reiteration of media independence – appeared in the final summit documents (see chapter 8). Yet these core demands reflected the objectives of certain types of media – the large mainstream media organisations – more than those of CS Media. Demands for increased support for community media and for concrete measures against media concentration rarely made it into the Caucus statements. The Caucus' uncritical mainstream bias ran counter to the agendas of the media reform and communication rights movements.

So, with regards to the internal coordination of media actors and interests, the picture is rather mixed. Gathering such a wide variety of media actors under a common roof and agreeing on certain core demands represented a major achievement. Caucus vice-chair Victor van Oeyen stressed that to "generate a discussion platform about absolutely all items (…) was a unique opportunity for open debate", and that because of "the very real fear about the absence of media in this new information society, it was (…) an absolute sane and wise pact we wanted to seal" (Interview VO). According to caucus chair Tracey Naughton, "[t]here was unilateral agreement to major principles. This can be seen clearly in the succinct statements that emerged from the caucus in the preparatory processes" (Interview TN).

However, the common umbrella could only temporarily cover the vast differences between the various media actors, and the thin ice of consensus often broke up to reveal opposing interests. The regular conflicts between AMARC/community media and AIR/commercial media displayed the most fundamental differences within the media sphere, but divergent perspectives between commercial and public service providers, between representatives of media organisations and those of media workers, and between different variations in the understanding of freedom of expression were equally apparent.

The caucus was held together primarily by its common enemies. The harsh rejection of Article 19 UDHR and of media independence by several governments in the first WSIS phase, and the human rights situation in the host country of the second WSIS phase, created a common line of opposition against the state-led efforts to exercise control over media and to restrict basic rights. The caucus became almost entirely a strategic coalition to counter-act state-led attacks on media independence, rather than a space for thorough reflection on the media itself, and while some CS Media actors accepted this, others left.

Assembling various types of media, the caucus was effectively a multi-stakeholder roundtable, with a dominant position of traditional public service and commercial media. Operating within a civil society framework, the caucus' multi-stakeholder arrangement allowed commercial interests to use designated civil society space to further their agenda. It led to the opportunity for commercial media to a) achieve double-representation through the separate channels of the Media Caucus and the CCBI, and b) blur the efforts of developing common civil society positions by infusing a commercial perspective.

7.3 The Community Media Working Group

Formation

With the Media Caucus being dominated by the interests of bigger, mainstream media, and with CS Media being marginalised in numbers and in content, the latter had to look for other ways to bring their objectives into the WSIS process. A few community media activists thus created a temporary and informal *Community Media Initiative* which developed into the more structured *Community Media Working Group* (CMWG) during the further process. CMWG became one of the official entities through which civil society participated in the WSIS process, with its own mailing list on the civil society platform wsis-cs.org. The listserve represented the main working space of the CMWG inbetween PrepComs and the main possibility for those unable to travel to PrepComs and summits to stay in touch with those meeting physically in Geneva and Tunis and to submit remote input to the discussions. At the end of the WSIS2 process it encompassed 106 members. The list was used far more intensely than the parallel list of the Media Caucus, with thematic discussions and remote participation taking place to a considerable degree. For example, in September 2003, the month of PrepCom3, 104 mails were sent to the list, most of them referring to thematic and strategic discussions. In the same period, 17 mails were sent to the Media Caucus list, most of them distributing statements which had been finalised in face-to-face caucus meetings.

The status of the group – and thus its relation to the Media Caucus – was fluid. Originally it was set up as a "Community Media Caucus" (see Buckley 2003), which emphasized the differences with the mainstream media operating in the Media Caucus and re-asserted the full right of community media to be represented in the WSIS process with their own entity. Yet in the further course of the WSIS process the term 'working group' became the preferred option, suggesting a somewhat limited arrangement compared to a fully-fledged 'caucus'. CMWG practically represented a sub-group to the Media Caucus just as much as it represented a separate entity. Many of its members continued to engage inside the Media Caucus and brought community media issues into the caucus debates and position papers, while at the same time the CMWG had additional separate meetings and produced complementary lobby documents. So, in contrast to most other caucuses, it had a double role and a double objective: strengthening the role of community media within the media sector (as represented by the Media Caucus) as well as in the official WSIS government negotiations. The group gathered a core of five to eight people who regularly and frequently met during PrepComs and summits to develop strategies and contents for community media lobbying. This core group was smaller in numbers than the Media Caucus, but authority and activity were distributed more evenly among members. The CMWG did not formally elect a chair, operating instead on the shared understanding that Steve Buckley, President of AMARC, was acting as a convener.

The group's composition, strategies and thematic preferences relied heavily on the lead role and the policy experience of AMARC and other community media organisations and development NGOs, including ALER, CAMECO, the World Catholic Association for Communication (SIGNIS), and Bread for All. A small but active contingent of members of radical activist media, including the global Indymedia network, the South Korean alternative media centre MediAct and the US grassroots satellite broadcasting network Deep Dish TV, diversified the group but did not change its predominant focus on 'community media' issues.

The advocacy framework of *community media*, rather than, e.g., alternative or citizens media, was used partly for strategic reasons. The term was comparatively widely accepted in previous policy fora,[12] and the WSIS' development-oriented framing of information and communication topics allowed to draw connections with the rich experiences of community media in deprived areas of the Global South and, more generally, with the 'communication for development' frame. Yet the predominance of actors in the CMWG, who were working with 'community media' (as opposed to any other of the CS Media introduced in chapter 2), and more specifically with community radio, represented a further important factor in focusing on issues relevant for this particular type of media.

---

[12] E.g., it is included in the African Charter on Broadcasting, see http://www.misa.org/broadcasting/acb.html

Many of those actors who may have added more strength to the thematic priorities of other CS Media types – alternative, radical, activist or tactical media – were unable (and, in many cases, unwilling) to join. Usually set up as grassroots groups without NGO status, they had difficulties to fulfil the requirements for registering for the summit process and to provide sufficient funding for sending delegates on costly lobbying missions. Favouring 'outside' or 'beyond' approaches (see chapter 4), and thus critical of government-oriented advocacy interventions, many of them were not interested in participating in the WSIS process altogether. Finally, many potentially relevant civil society actors which would have brought in additional perspectives, such as the APC with its focus on Internet communication, chose to participate in other thematic caucuses rather than the CMWG.

A feature which is familiar from the analysis of the Media Caucus was the appearance of a larger number of Tunisian civil society representatives in the second WSIS phase – delegates who were likely to be in close contact with the host country government. They encompassed some of those actors who most strongly rejected any criticism of Tunisian human rights records in other civil society meetings. They were not based in community media and were apparently new to the issues proposed by the CMWG, yet they triggered long and aggressive debates whenever the right to freedom of expression was mentioned and the Tunisian situation was criticised. In this atmosphere of intimidation, the CMWG had difficulties to discuss strategically and make progress. In comparison with the Media Caucus, the informal, horizontal and cooperative working methods of the CMWG made it even easier for those who sought to interrupt procedures to do so. In response, CMWG meetings were increasingly transformed into short presentations on recent developments in the WSIS process, with the actual thematic debate and strategic planning taking place afterwards between the core CMWG people.

Content

Community Media Initiative

The small ad-hoc group that got together at PrepCom2 of the Geneva phase under the name *Community Media Initiative* (CMI) formulated as its prime objective that "Community and Non-Profit Media should be promoted, supported and actively developed" (Community Media Initiative 2003).[13] As a new guiding principle for WSIS it proposed that "[p]riority should be given to community-driven communication initiatives, developed in response to local needs and under community control."

[13] The following quotes are taken from this document.

The group proposed a list of themes which it regarded as essential for an understanding of information society which includes CS Media interests, and it stressed the role of CS Media in all these issue areas:

- ICT systems that are appropriate for local environments, with community radio as an appropriate local technology application
- Cultural diversity is to be enhanced through media based in local communities
- Media pluralism: "Community and non-profit media give voice to many societal groups underrepresented in the traditional media"
- Communication rights, global information commons, and public access to the creation of knowledge: "Community and non-profit media [are] essential channels for the public to contribute knowledge to the public domain."
- Participation and empowerment
- Enabling environment: regulatory frameworks as well as funding mechanisms should consider "the democratic grassroots and non-profit characteristics" of these media.

The CMI combined two different media concepts: community media and non-profit media. Partially these were used together, seemingly synonymously, partially they were used separately, focusing on different aspects. The term community media related primarily to a development orientation, as it was presented, for example, "as a particularly appropriate medium in developing countries for supporting the realization of United Nations Millennium Goals". Its cost-effectiveness and accessibility, particularly for poor rural populations, was emphasized, as well as its responsiveness to local needs. The references to non-profit media, in contrast, brought a contentious and more openly oppositional flavour to the CMI's statements. By giving voice to those underrepresented in the mainstream media and by advancing participation and empowerment, interactive communication and global information commons, they challenged hegemonic media systems, commercialisation, and dominant power structures. By combining the local and the oppositional, the CMI linked two important aspects of CS Media and embraced a wide range of the CS Media characteristics discussed in chapter 2.

AMARC

The community media frame has been popularised in international networking, research and policy by, particularly, AMARC (Lewis 2002). An international organisation of community radio broadcasters with nearly 3,000 members in 110 countries, AMARC has increasingly intervened in global policy fora, including UNESCO and ITU. AMARC has consistently highlighted the social and political characteristics of community radio, such as public participation and empowerment, but it has put a particular focus on the development frame, emphasizing the important roles of community radio for rural, remote, illiterate, and impoverished populations (Buckley 2005).

In a statement to PrepCom2, AMARC stressed that radio "is the most widespread electronic communications device in the world and a unique means of reaching the world's poorest communities" (AMARC 2003c) and that communities can act as "a bridge across the digital divide between those who have access to the world's information resources and those who do not" (ibid.). Therefore, the organisation called for the provision of "sufficient financial resources [for community media] whilst respecting and preserving their independence from government and from commercial media corporations" (ibid.). It suggested the reinvestment of revenues raised by governments from sale of spectrum and telecommunications licensing for community media development.

CMWG: core demands

The CMWG developed an extensive catalogue of positions and demands, taking up some of the previous work done by the CMI and by AMARC, adding new issues and streamlining others. Its priority was to have the WSIS Declaration "include reference to the specific and crucial role of community media" and the Action Plan to

"- strengthen commitment to community broadcasting in country level legislation

- strengthen commitment to spectrum allocation for community broadcasting

- support the establishment of an international Community Media Fund" (CMWG 2003c).

Legal environment. With community media not yet legally recognised in many parts of the world, and their operations severely restricted in many others, the CMWG called for the worldwide legal recognition of community media as an essential part of a three-tier media system encompassing public service, commercial, and community media. Even though this demand did not take centre stage in the day-to-day lobbying efforts of the CMWG, it was implicitly present in the two other core issue areas: securing access to the airwaves and mobilising public funding.

Spectrum. All statements by the CMWG reserved a prominent space for the allocation and management of the radio frequency spectrum. Over the whole WSIS period, references to spectrum outnumbered all other single demands brought forward by the CMWG.[14] The group proposed: "The radio-frequency spectrum should be managed in the public interest through independent and transparent regulatory frameworks to enable the equitable allocation of frequencies among a plurality of media including community media" (CMWG 2003a). Governments were called upon to "establish specific targets for the opening up of broadcast licensing to allow for the operation of community broadcasting services in every community" (CMWG 2003b) to ensure that "all of the world's population can access community broadcasting services by 2015" (CMWG 2003c). Spectrum was to be recognised "as a public resource" and "as a publicly owned asset"[15] (CMWG 2003b), and sufficient capacity was to be reserved for community media "in both the analogue and the digital environment" (ibid.).

Demands on spectrum allocation and management were extended to the orbital paths and satellite capacities which "should be recognised as a public resource and should be allocated to benefit the public interest" (CMWG 2003d). The CMWG demanded to "reserve a fixed percentage of satellite capacity for educational, humanitarian, community and other non-commercial use" (ibid.)

Finance. From the outset, establishing financial mechanisms for community media represented one of the prime objectives of community media advocates. AMARC had originally proposed to reinvest revenues from the sale of spectrum and telecommunications licensing for community media and had demanded that "international investment in information and communi-

---

[14] The issue was of particular importance for AMARC as a network of broadcasters and it gained particular prominence during the AMARC 8 conference in Nepal, parallel to PrepCom2 of phase 1. The headline of the press release which summarised the central themes of that conference read: "Community broadcasters demand right to radio spectrum" (AMARC 2003d). The organisation called "on all nations and governments to create and implement legislation that provides community access and ownership to the airwaves" (ibid.) and it suggested that "the radio spectrum be recognised as part of the global commons" (ibid.).

[15] In another statement, "public resource" was changed to "a natural resource belonging to all humanity" (CMWG 2003c).

cation technologies for development must consistently include support for traditional and community-based media" (AMARC 2003c). The CMWG developed the proposal of a *Community Media Fund,* based on an idea which had circulated within AMARC for a while. It suggested to:

"Establish, by 2006, a Community Media Fund to support new community radio development and community media content including projects that make provision for the poorest communities, for cultural and linguistic diversity and for the equal participation of women and girls. The Fund should also support community projects that combine the use of traditional and new communication technologies. The Fund should be established through a donor - civil society partnership involving leading community media organisations and civil society organisations working in this field" (CMWG 2003d).

This fund became one of the CMWG's major objectives and lobby goals during the further WSIS process, up until the Tunis summit. In her address to the government plenary at PrepCom2 of phase 2, a CMWG representative said that

"a new international fund for Community Media would have immediate and strategic impact in the contribution of communications to the achievement of the Millennium Development goals. (…) We specifically propose, as a first step, the establishment of a Community Radio Fund for Africa. This would be to complement the Digital Solidarity Fund" (CMWG 2005).

Framework and context

Development/Poverty. The CMWG reinforced the focus on development and poverty discourses which the CMI had introduced. WSIS, as the group urged UN Secretary-General Kofi Annan in a public letter, should "give priority to empowerment of the poorest people and communities in the world" (AMARC 2003f). And furthermore: "Much is promised by the information society but the world's poorest communities face the danger of being left out by a vastly unequal access to the global communications environment" (ibid.)

Stating that "the most effective approaches to poverty reduction are community-driven and empowerment-oriented" (CMWG 2003c), the unique role of community media was highlighted: "For large parts of the world population, community media represent the main channel for accessing information. Leaving out any reference to community media ignores the needs and the voices of particularly the most disadvantaged people" (CMWG 2003e). With the help of community media, it would be possible, according to the CMWG, "to bring about a more just and equitable information society that includes the voices of the poor and the marginalised" (CMWG 2003c).

Digital divide/Traditional technology. Traditional and established technologies were characterised as more accessible to large parts of the world population than the 'new' digital technologies on which the summit focused. The CMI led the way by calling for "technology systems which are appropriate to local environments" (Community Media Initiative 2003) and AMARC pointed to community broadcasting as a "bridge across the digital divide" (AMARC 2003c). The CMWG emphasized: "The most widespread and accessible communications technologies remain the traditional media, particularly radio - an oral medium, low cost and receivable by 90 per cent of the world's population" (CMWG 2003c). Addressing the government plenary during the preparation phase for the Tunis summit, a CMWG representative stated:

"When we speak about Communication for Development in the least developed countries, Madam Chairperson, we are not only, or even primarily, speaking about access to the Internet, but also about radio and telephony - oral media, that are more accessible, more widespread and less expensive" (CMWG 2005).

Several times the CMWG expressed its concern that the draft Declaration and Action Plan "give priority to the infrastructure for Internet connectivity whilst failing to address the fundamental barriers of electricity supply, literacy and equipment costs which will exclude the world's poorest people" (AMARC 2003f). The group suggested to foster combinations of traditional media platforms and new ICTs, particularly community radio and the Internet, through community telecentres (CMWG 2003d).

Participation/democracy/empowerment. The CMI had put a strong emphasis on public participation, and it had done so in a very concrete sense that presented CS Media as tools for citizens to actively shape the available body of knowledge and influence the prevalent information streams. It had departed from a traditional media model of information provision from sender to receiver, had focused on "[c]ommunication as a participatory and interactive process" (Community Media Initiative 2003), and had proposed to enable "public participation in the information society through affordable and appropriate ICT applications" including "interactive Web applications" (ibid.). Understood in the context of community and alternative media, such 'interactive applications' would have included activist media such as Indymedia.

The CMWG continued to highlight the importance of public participation but focused more narrowly on local empowerment and on the participation of local communities. With regards to general mechanisms for enhancing participation beyond the local realm, it remained rather vague. It noted the "crucial role" of community media "in ensuring the participation of all in the information society" and demanded that "[t]raditional and new means of communication must be focused on creating opportunities for people and communities to participate in shaping their own destiny" (CMWG 2003c).

Political context. The CMWG called for a "just and equitable information society [which] must be people-centred, inclusive, built on fundamental human rights and focused primarily on the reduction of poverty" (CMWG 2003c). It criticised that "the communication needs of poor people are compromised at the highest levels by a vastly unequal access to the global communications environment" (ibid.) and it noted that "[n]early one third of the world's population still do not have reliable access to electricity. Basic literacy skills are lacking for 20 per cent of the world's population, especially women and girls" (ibid.). Yet CMWG members also recognised other political threats, such as rampant militarism and accelerated privatisation of the world's basic resources (AMARC 2003d).

Community media characteristics. The CMWG focused on "community-driven communication initiatives, developed in response to local needs" (AMARC 2003e), emphasizing that these media are "owned and controlled by communities themselves" (AMARC 2003c). Further characteristics that were deemed important but that were not prioritised for lobbying included their being "driven by social objectives rather than private profit, bottom up rather than top down, empowering people rather than treating them as passive consumers, nurturing local knowledge rather than replacing it with standard solutions" (AMARC 2003c).

Occasionally, the strict focus on the community frame was extended to include references to other forms of CS Media. As we have seen, the CMI referred to "non-profit media" to "give voice to many societal groups underrepresented in the traditional media" (Community Media Initiative 2003). The CMWG noted that "[n]ew forms of community and alternative media are springing up in all continents of the world", providing "an alternative to mainstream public and private media" (CMWG 2003f) and "showing another information society is possible" (ibid.). At the end of the Tunis phase the CMWG expanded its media concept to "grassroots and Civil Society-based media" which "empower people for independent and creative participation in knowledge-building and information-sharing" (Civil Society Plenary 2005).

Complementary issues

Media pluralism. The CMWG demanded "a diverse and pluralist media environment, with public service and community media at its core" (CMWG 2003e). Media pluralism was deemed central to any statement on media issues by the WSIS. The CMI had earlier put forward a more detailed account of media pluralism, emphasising that diversity was needed both in media sources and media output and that the voices of a wider variety of societal groups should be represented in the media.

Knowledge commons. The CMI had originally highlighted the knowledge and information commons as a crucial point of reference and had presented non-profit media as "essential channels for the public to contribute knowledge to the public domain" (Community Media Initiative 2003). During the course of the WSIS process, though, this demand was not explicitly followed up by the CMWG, as other – more practical and more middle-range – objectives gained prominence, and as other caucuses took up the issue.

Cultural diversity. A further concept of reference, cultural diversity was never explicitly demanded, nor a unique understanding of the concept developed, but the crucial role of community media for cultural diversity was highlighted. One of the early proposed additions to the Action Plan stated that "[m]edia that are based in local communities represent the most important channels for creating local content and thus play a vital role in the preservation and development of cultural and linguistic diversity" (Community Media Initiative 2003).

Freedom of expression. With the Media Caucus focusing almost exclusively on safeguarding freedom of expression, press freedoms, and Article 19 UDHR, the CMWG did not make this a core lobbying issue. However, CMWG members were vital proponents of these rights in the caucus and as part of the IFEX missions to Tunisia, and CMWG statements demanded "respect for the provisions of Article 19 of the UDHR" (CMWG 2003c).

Priorities and blind spots

Within the ICT-focused policy environment of WSIS, the CMWG served as a strong advocate for traditional media, such as radio and print. The Community Media Fund, particularly, was designed to highlight the persistent need for 'older' media platforms. The group had less to say, though, about 'new media', even though for many CS Media web-based distribution of content increasingly plays a significant role. Statements on communication governance included demands for the reform of radio and satellite spectrum allocation but neglected Internet governance.

The CMWG's core goals were embedded in a discourse which emphasized poverty eradication and development, and which dominated a possible further focus on participation and interactivity. Highlighting the possibility for media non-professionals to participate in the production of media content, to contribute to the wealth and diversity of global knowledge, and to overcome the one-way information streams of the mainstream media would have emphasized the counter-hegemonic aspects of CS Media, yet the development context of these media was prioritised. Accordingly, CMWG statements were almost as cautious as the Media Caucus with regards to media reform demands. Calls for limiting media concentration or for mechanisms to achieve public accountability of mainstream media were largely missing.

Strategies

As a fairly small and homogenous *policy coalition* (Khagram et al. 2002), the CMWG did not engage in the difficult internal consensus-finding processes which the Media Caucus struggled with. It could focus its entire energies on attempting to influence the day-to-day negotiations and on responding quickly to government agendas. Considering the hardly supportive context of its work – a small number of activists, hostile governments, and a summit agenda focusing on new ICTs – it turned out to be a fairly effective lobbying mechanism.

As the Media Caucus, it applied most of the tactics that were available to a civil society working group at WSIS:

(1) Statements in plenary sessions

(2) Informal lobbying

(3) Input into collective civil society statements

Its particular set-up as a quasi-subgroup in the Media Caucus, and the focus of many of its members on project work and journalism rather than policy intervention, opened additional channels of intervention:

(4) Input into Media Caucus debates: As we saw in chapter 7.2, community media were at the centre of some of the controversies within the caucus. The CMWG did not stage cooperated interventions into the caucus, but some of its members brought in the thematic objectives of the group (e.g., the proposal for the Community Media Fund) and tried to have them adopted as Media Caucus demands.

(5) A multi-lingual radio programme, organised by AMARC and based at the 'African Village' in the ICT4D conference hall and therefore inside the

summit compound, sent impressions from the summit and critical civil society perspectives via an Internet stream around the globe and was picked up and broadcast by community radio stations worldwide

(6) Community Media Forum: Key members of the CMWG organised a Community Media Forum to take place alongside the WSIS1 and WSIS2 summits and to present the experiences and successes of community (and other CS) media (see below).

As noted above, the email list was used consistently, with minutes and statements being circulated in timely fashion, allowing some activists and advocates to participate remotely by, for example, receiving information about current developments and distributing that information onwards. Frieda Werden, a 'remote participant', explained:

"I was able to participate through e-mails, and (…) pulled some items out of them to summarize and distribute to other community/alternative media for their group's endorsements, and also was able to get the community media statement ratified by feminist organizations" (Interview FW).

Targeted lobbying

With some governments being hostile to community media objectives (see chapter 8), the unfocused strategies of plenary statements and general lobby documents, addressed at all delegations, met serious obstacles. The CMWG required committed government allies who would bring its objectives directly into the negotiation process. So, during the final preparation phase for WSIS1, the group changed its approach towards a targeted lobby effort. It created a list of government delegations which were seen as friendly (or, at least, not entirely hostile) towards the cause of community media, as well as of those delegations with which personal channels of communication already existed. The list "Priority countries for community media lobbying" encompassed:

- from Africa: Benin, Burkina Faso, Gambia, Ghana, Mali, Mozambique, Niger, Senegal, South Africa, Tanzania, Uganda
- from Asia/Pacific: Australia, Bangladesh, East Timor, Fiji, Mongolia, Nepal, New Zealand, Japan, Philippines, Thailand
- from Europe: Belgium, Denmark, Finland, France, Germany, Ireland, Italy, Netherlands, Norway, Sweden, Switzerland, United Kingdom

- from Latin America: Argentina, Bolivia, Brazil, Colombia, Dominican Republic, Ecuador, Haiti, Peru, Uruguay, Venezuela
- from North America: Canada, USA
- from Intergovernmental Organisations: FAO, ITU, OAS, UNESCO, UNDP, World Bank

Some of these countries, such as Argentina and Venezuela, had recently adopted community media-friendly policies. With some government delegations, such as Germany and the UK, CMWG members were in regular contact, while to others, such as Canada and Brazil, contacts were secured through other civil society activists. Switzerland and South Africa proved to be particularly valuable allies, because they repeatedly spoke out in favour of community media during negotiations, and because they occupied central positions in the WSIS process – Switzerland as the host country of WSIS1 and the South African delegation as a key negotiator and moderator during phase 1. An important channel for the CMWG into the negotiation was the Colombian delegation, as the Colombian Minister of Communications and head of the Colombian WSIS delegation, Maria Victoria Polanco, had previously been an AMARC activist.

In phase 2 of the WSIS process, the CMWG focused increasingly on these direct contacts to friendly government delegations. Those delegations were provided with ready sentences or paragraphs to include in the draft WSIS documents, and they repeatedly proposed such sentences/paragraphs in the negotiation process.

Strategic discourses and frame-bridging

The CMWG's prime objectives were to have the acknowledgement of community media included in the WSIS documents, and to raise community media's profile among governments, donors and international organisations. In addition, it pressed for a few concrete policy outcomes such as the provision of broadcast licenses and funding. These latter demands had a reflexive character: On the one hand, they represented important potential policy outcomes which would have substantially enhanced the prospects of community media, while on the other hand, they offered strategic options for achieving the primary objective – including reference to community media in the documents. As Steve Buckley said: "If governments agree on a Community Media Fund, they implicitly recognise the existence and the need for community media".[16] So the Fund represented a vehicle for advancing the worldwide legal recognition of community media.

The main reason why the Fund was made a priority of CMWG lobbying, particularly during phase 2, was the conflict around financial mechanisms for bridging the digital divide which led to the establishment of the Digital Solidarity Fund (DSF). Tapping into the controversies around the DSF, the Community Media Fund was presented as a targeted and cost-effective complementary mechanism to help those 'on the other side of the digital divide' with simple, reliable and already successfully tested measures. It thus was a strategic response by the CMWG to the government negotiations on finance issues, which were characterised by a) the demand from the South for a new fund, and b) the unwillingness in the North to contribute vast financial resources to a new structure with a vague mission and unclear beneficiaries. In another discursive environment, other financial mechanisms may have been proposed by the CMWG, or completely different priorities may have been chosen.

More generally, the CMWG's wider thematic focus on development and poverty reduction was – at least in part – a strategic choice. Emphasizing community media's role in development strategies tapped into the predominant discourses at WSIS. Bridging the digital divide, diffusing new ICTs to the Global South, and realising the potential of ICTs to achieve the Millennium Development Goals were central aims of the summit, and the possibilities for strengthening community (and, in fact, other CS) media seemed most promising by taking up a development-oriented argument.

The group thus applied a technique called "frame-bridging" (Khagram et al. 2002), connecting one's frame (here: 'community radio') to accepted international norms and hegemonic discourses to succeed in lobbying. The strategy was to pick up the ex-ante thematic focus of summit organisers and participants – particularly: a) technology and b) development – and redefine it for furthering the group's objectives – here: community media as locally adapted technology to achieve development (Interview CB). Whether the development frame would be less dominating in a different environment remains to be seen. The CMWG's most influential member, AMARC, has used a development frame since the early 1990s to build support for community radio with international organisations (Buckley 2005). An AMARC-led CMWG would probably have tended towards the tried-and-tested development-oriented argumentation in a different environment as well. However the WSIS discourse certainly reinforced and underlined that strategy.

---

[16] Personal conversation, 21 September 2003

CMWG and 'the media'

With regards to the Media Caucus and the mainstream media it represented, the CMWG did not take a confrontational position. Its agenda focused on strengthening community media and leaving other media untouched. There were no calls for new legislation against media concentration or for mechanisms to achieve greater public accountability of the mainstream media. In part, this was due to the governmental threats to curb human rights and media freedoms and to apply media regulation for limiting freedom of expression, particularly of critical and oppositional groups. CS Media increasingly stood united with mainstream media in opposing such repressive measures. The common enemy was temporarily seen as more important than the divisions between different media actors.

At the same time, this common line of defence, which had seemingly been forced upon all media actors, offered a *window of opportunity* for some CS Media – and was nurtured and extended accordingly. Acting in alliance with mainstream media provided a possibility for integrating oneself as a full-scale member in the media sector. It could serve to reduce scepticism on the part of other media actors against the 'activist' CS Media and prove the latter's serious commitment to freedom of expression and other core media values. So, even if governments did not fully recognise community media at the summit, there was a chance that other media actors would acknowledge their role and their existence and would, in the future, not marginalise them in the way they had done in the original Media Caucus statements. The active participation of AMARC in the IFEX missions to Tunisia and in the strong media alliance against governmental attacks on media freedoms further helped to establish community media as an accepted actor in the international media environment.

Successes and failures

The CMWG's practices represented an appropriate response to the dynamics of a global summit. Its strategic interventions into the negotiation process, its timely reactions to newly emerging agenda points, and its active participation in the wider civil society network at WSIS bore some fruits throughout the WSIS process:

- 'Community media' were included in common civil society statements and were highlighted as one of the priority themes which the wider civil society network demanded to have included in the WSIS documents.

- The Media Caucus, after initial scepticism, increasingly respected community media, and AMARC, particularly, strengthened its recognition amongst media actors to become an accepted force in the media sector.

- Several government delegations spoke out in favour of community media during intergovernmental negotiations and supported some of the objectives of the CMWG.

- The final outcomes in the official WSIS documents were poor (see chapter 8) and attempts of frame-bridging largely failed, but awareness of community media was raised substantially amongst many WSIS participants (see chapter 9).

Thematically, the CMWG contributed to the WSIS a much-needed view on traditional media platforms, and by focusing on the community level it offered a grassroots perspective, bringing voices of those for whom WSIS was to speak into the summit process.

Regarding the 'internal' outcomes – i.e., the CMWG's ability to achieve consensus amongst a variety of media actors – the group's narrow focus on 'community media' and on the development frame fell short of creating a voice for a more diverse range of CS Media and thus a broader Civil Society Media sector. Among the marginalised aspects were new ICTs, non-hierarchical production structures, participation by non-professionals, the facilitation of more interactive information exchange, and critical counter-mainstream content.

Equally absent was critique of the mainstream media system. While government hostility towards media freedoms, and particularly the human rights situation in Tunisia, represented a political opportunity for community media delegates to advance their recognition in the wider media sector, this choice of allies had repercussions for the CMWG's other potential alliances and agenda points. The group was far less outspoken and critical towards the media sector as it may have been otherwise, and many potential coalition members, working outside the predominant CMWG frames, chose to engage in other fora, such as other caucuses and the summit side-events (see below).

7.4 Outside WSIS: WSIS?WeSeize! and beyond

WSIS?WeSeize!: Backgrounds and formation

For many grassroots activist media, participation in summit processes was neither a practical possibility, nor a particularly attractive option. Following the process actively required the time to take part in long preparatory meetings, the financial means (or the support from a large organisation) to pay for travel and accommodation, and the patience and particular skills to deal with the complexities of UN diplomacy. It also required the recognition that a global governance arena such as WSIS offered a valuable window of opportunity to affect communications policy in a way that would be conducive to grassroots and alternative media projects. Yet many of those civil society actors identifying themselves as 'media activists' neither had access to the necessary resources for participation, nor did they share the positive recognition of the summit with those civil society groups that formed the network of caucuses and families. With large parts of the global justice movement (see chapter 4), they shared a rejection of global summits and of established international institutions. Participation in the summit process, according to this view, meant to legitimise an otherwise illegitimate process. With technology-focused information workers (see chapter 5), they shared a propensity towards designing and developing their own infrastructure rather than to engage in advocacy efforts.

Discussions on 'intervening without participating' took place in two different camps. The first was an encounter of media, communication, cultural, and political activists with a background in the global network of social movements *People's Global Action* (PGA) at the *Hub* in Florence, Italy, in November 2002. The Hub was a space for workshops, presentations and collaborations alongside the first European Social Forum (ESF). A second thread of discussion involved cultural and media workers and artists who were connected through virtual platforms, such as kein.org and D-A-S-H.org, and who met at gatherings such as the Make World Festival (Munich, October 2001). Characteristic for those actors was a combination of an interest in media technology and in migration. Key participants were active both in media work (such as film-making and Internet experimentation) and in anti-racist campaigns (such as the campaign 'kein mensch ist illegal' and the 'noborder' network). Just as the activists who met at the Hub, many of the protagonists of these networks saw themselves as contributing to a "developing movement of information activism" (Geneva03 2003a), within the social justice movement. Both groups constituted *critical communities* (see chapter 4) who sought to establish critical perspectives on information, communication and media issues amongst their own constituencies and, as a further step, amongst wider civil society.

From April 2003, activists from both strands converged in the loose association *Geneva03.*[17] Its initial membership included *Everyone is an Expert* (a

[17] The name Geneva03 referred to two different events which were to take place in Geneva that year and which both served as targets for interventions by media activists: the G8

German project for media experiments), *Candida TV* (a Rome-based video collective), European *Indymedia* activists, particularly from Indymedias in Switzerland, Italy, and Germany, *Mute* (a London-based cultural/political magazine), and book publisher *Autonomedia*. Members of the CRIS campaign served as a link to the civil society groups inside the WSIS process. The further preparation phase for what came to be called *WSIS?WeSeize!* also saw the participation of the US media project Deep Dish TV.[18] The actual WSIS?WeSeize! events in December 2003 involved further groups and individuals, such as free/open source software advocates from Debian and Oekonux, Samizdat (French autonomous media group), Las Agencias (a Barcelona art/activist network) and Aporrea (a Venezuelan web-based media organisation). The majority of Geneva03 was made up of younger activists from the global North, with interest and skills in 'new technologies', involved in the newer wave of social movements, experienced in practices of non-hierarchical spontaneous association, sceptical towards institutionalised organisation, and influenced by the idea of *openness* (see chapters 4 and 5). Their composition contrasted with the older groups inside the summit, which had been founded in previous waves of movement, with long-standing North-South linkages, and with backgrounds in NGOs and more institutionalised parts of civil society.

Crucial steps for organising the event were taken at meetings during the anti-G8 protests in June 2003, the next5minutes conference[19] in Amsterdam in September 2003, and the MetalloMediaLab which was set up alongside the second ESF in Paris, November 2003. The preparation process met serious obstacles, including logistical difficulties with the envisaged locations for WSIS?WeSeize!, several of which were cancelled on short notice; capacity shortage on the part of the Geneva03 media activists who – in contrast to most of their civil society counterparts inside the WSIS process – had to use their scarce spare-time and their personal financial resources to organise WSIS activities; and differences in approaches and practices amongst members of Geneva03. The network combined actors with very different social and political backgrounds: From anarchist Indymedia activists to established film-makers and academics, members were used to very different types of events, working practices, and degrees of collective organising and decision-making, occasionally leading to conflict and finally to the

---

summit (which actually took place in Evian in neighbouring France, but the protests against it were expected to concentrate on Geneva) in June and the WSIS summit in December.

[18] … and it was DeeDee Halleck from Deep Dish TV who came up with the name WSIS?WeSeize! at a further Geneva03 meeting in September 2003.

[19] A tactical media festival held in Amsterdam every three to four years.

separation of one sub-event – a conference on the links between freedom of expression and freedom of movement – from the rest of WSIS?WeSeize!.[20]

WSIS?WeSeize! took place from 9 to 12 December 2003 in the city centre of Geneva. It encompassed:

- a "strategic conference"
- the live video netcast "High Noon", combining local and worldwide video footage around media activism and community media
- the "Polimedia Lab" as a space for gatherings, meetings, workshops, and collaborative media experiments

Together, these events were to provide "an open platform for interventions in, outside of, counter to and as an alternative to the agendas and organizations of the WSIS" (Geneva03 2003a). They were neither designed for influencing the governmental negotiation process, nor as a counter-summit or as protest event. Geneva03 members felt that even a big protest would have given the summit more credit than it deserved. Rather, their principal objectives were:

- to gather some of those activists who had developed important aspects of information society in self-organised and collaborative working processes and outside the governmental and business realm
- to create an open space for experimentation and collaboration – and thus to establish an environment that was, in Geneva03's view, much more conducive to the development of information society than a government-controlled or a business-led process
- to develop and publicise alternative views to the hegemonic understanding of information society which dominated the WSIS

The events took place outside the summit compound, expressing Geneva03's decision to openly and publicly disassociate itself from WSIS. Furthermore, and in contrast to the summit which was held at the Palexpo convention centre outside the city, Geneva03 sought to be present, visible,

---

[20] For these reasons, not all of the ambitious plans envisioned for WSIS?WeSeize! could be realised by December. Those events that finally were set up relied heavily on the commitment of a few individuals who arrived in Geneva early and solved the manifold logistical problems. These individuals included, particularly, Alan Toner from Autonomedia, Jamie King from Mute Magazine, and Maria from Indymedia Geneva.

and accessible in the Geneva city centre and thus become part of a 'real' inhabited locality.

Content: two challenges

WSIS?WeSeize! launched two sets of challenges onto the summit: a thematic one and a structural one. Thematically it focused on critical issues left out of the WSIS agenda or dealt with at WSIS from the perspectives of government or business interests. The conference programme, related events, and Geneva03 publications included the following topics (Geneva03 2003b):

- intellectual property rights: information control, the privatisation of ideas, intellectual property law, and technical responses such as peer to peer and wireless network communities
- openness as a concept and a practice (countering hegemonic policies of privatisation and control)
- infowar, media misinformation, and propaganda
- hacking and ICT-based activism
- autonomous/civil society-based media infrastructures
- exploitation of immaterial work and informationalised labour
- links between freedom of communication and freedom of movement
- discussions on the advantages and disadvantages of intervening into established information policy structures such as WSIS

Unlike civil society inside the summit process, which questioned the WSIS emphasis on 'new' ICTs, WSIS?WeSeize! took up a technology-focused discourse but approached it from the perspective of those interested in developing and appropriating ICTs for social movements and civil society.

The structural challenge launched by Geneva03 was based on a fundamental critique of the current arrangement of global governance, particularly of global summits and international institutions in which members of the global political and business (and, to some extent, civil society) elite[21] gather to reach decisions with consequences for large parts of the world population but in which this population does not have a say. WSIS?WeSeize! participants rejected the summit as an illegitimate attempt by these actors to regulate (i.e., to control, repress, and appropriate) processes which had been initiated outside their reach. WSIS was regarded as a concerted attempt by the political and business establishment to take over such innovations and to get back into the driving seat of communication processes. Its "rhetoric of inclusion" (Geneva03 2003c) was denounced as a "smokescreen" (ibid.):

"Although it talks about the digital divide, knowledge dissemination, social interaction, political engagement, media, education, and health, this language is used to mystify the continuing use of information to protect and advance the interests of global capital" (ibid.).

Rather than influencing the summit, or protesting against it, WSIS?WeSeize! was to highlight the capacities of activists and 'amateurs', independent from state and business, to develop people-based, bottom-up information and communication environments. Establishing a practical alternative to the grey and sterile trade fair environment of the Palexpo convention centre, WSIS?WeSeize! was to facilitate a culture of non-hierarchical association, non-commercial creativity, and an information society 'from below'.

Strategies

At WSIS?WeSeize!, as we have just seen, the medium was the message. Its attempts of setting up structural alternatives merged thematic objectives with strategic approaches. Influenced both by the cyber-libertarian tendencies of information activists and the DIY culture of recent social movements, its main strategy focused on experimenting with *social alternatives* – non-hierarchical collaboration, training and knowledge sharing – and *technological alternatives* – new activist infrastructure and by-passes around controlled information systems.

WSIS?WeSeize! was designed to trigger 'cultural' transformations. For participants, it was a space to reflect on WSIS-related themes and to experience alternative practices and priorities; for the civil society actors inside the summit compound it was to highlight the value and the possibility of non-institutional practices and to offer a critical interpretation of the WSIS; and

[21] Implicitly, Geneva03 thus referred to the transnational managerial or capitalist class (see chapter 2.3.).

for the Geneva public it offered a perspective on the summit which differed from the glossy advertising campaign launched by the official summit organisers. Geneva03 tried to interact with the latter two groups by, on the one hand, situating its events in the city centre of Geneva and by, on the other hand, inviting NGO delegates from inside the summit to its events outside. To a limited degree, Geneva03 activists also tried to influence the dominant discourse 'inside', especially within the civil society networks – both to keep civil society summit actors questioning their legitimisation of a government- and business-focused process, and to coordinate strategies with them. To these ends, several actors participated significantly inside and out, serving as liaisons, especially between Geneva03, CRIS and the CMWG.

Occasionally, Geneva03's "repertoire of contention" (Tilly/Tarrow 2006) also included slightly more confrontational tactics. On 11 December, half way through the WSIS summit, the side of the building of the World Intellectual Property Organisation (WIPO) served as an impromptu projection screen for *Gimme the mermaid*, a film based on pirated Disney images and spoofing copyright discourses. WIPO had been criticised consistently during the WSIS?WeSeize! conference because of its support for restrictive copyright regimes. According to Geneva03, it "harmonizes intellectual property laws on a US based model that gives corporations full right to decide on intellectual property, (...) doesn't recognise knowledge as a common good, doesn't see information as a cultural expression but as a commercial good, (...) endangers the lives of millions of people while patenting life saving drugs" (Geneva03 2003d). A report on this event on the Geneva03 website uncovers the tactical media characteristics which corresponded with the background of many Geneva03 actors:

"The police initially tried to stop the screening, but were persuaded to go easy when presented with an invitation to the screening, printed (unbeknownst to the police) by the group, which looked like a formal and official invitation from WSIS, inviting people to a reception and screening at the WIPO. Several delegates in suits also showed up, having received the invitation at the summit meetings, where it was widely distributed" (ibid.).

Successes and failures

WSIS?WeSeize's outcomes can be divided into a practical and a symbolic level. Practically, the event offered a fruitful set of workshops, presentations and discussions as well as an experience of an alternative social environment based on values such as free access, horizontality and creativity.[22] It

---

[22] The most outrageous event which has dominated the memories of many participants has been the 'Yomango Dinner' which saw 150 WSIS?WeSeize! participants and guests

clarified a media activist agenda around information and communication issues. The Polimedia Lab provided an example for the values of openness highlighted by Geneva03 – and at the same time unmasked the rhetoric of the official summit: It established the only public and free-of-cost wireless Internet connection that was available at any WSIS or WSIS-related event.

In the WSIS context, however, the event primarily occupied a significant *symbolic* position. WSIS?WeSeize! offered a *reference point* for:

- alternative discourses around information society
- a thematic vision which went beyond the themes laid out in both the official documents and the Civil Society Declaration
- the power of self-organised communication systems
- the feasibility of extra-institutional tactics

One WSIS?WeSeize! member expressed the "utopian element" of the assembled media activists and their agendas:

"They might have the function of some utopian "guiding star", i.e. the star that provides a fix point of navigation for sailors, who use it for orientation without attempting to reach it" (Interview MH).

The significance of this reference point emerged despite its numerous practical shortcomings: The Polimedia Lab took place in a rather uncomfortable environment, the video stream met technical problems, the conference had to be effectively reduced to one day, numbers of participation and interactions with the local population both remained limited, and few of the civil society actors from inside the summit compound could be drawn to Geneva03's events and spaces. The image which had been envisioned – a lively crowded media laboratory, bursting of creativity, with spontaneous experiments taking place in every corner, giving a convincing example of the power of civil society self-organisation and grassroots development, and leading to lasting collaborations and concrete results – did not quite appear.

The reasons were partly internal, partly external. As noted above, internal problems included differences of political practices within the diverse network of Geneva03. External problems were caused by the Geneva police which evicted the Polimedia Lab from its original location, one day before the start of the WSIS summit, and thus left the heart piece of

---

assembled around a long row of tables bursting with enormous quantities of food stolen from surrounding supermarkets.

WSIS?WeSeize! homeless. A substitute location was quickly found, but a crucial day for both the media laboratory and the conference was lost, and the new space never developed the creative atmosphere which participants had hoped for.

While the CMWG inside the summit process was focusing strictly on the community media frame, WSIS?WeSeize! claimed to accommodate a wider range of media concepts. According to Geneva03, the event was to "create autonomous physical and network spaces for diverse tactical, grassroots, activist and community media actions and discussions" (Geneva03 2003c). Media activists and groups identifying themselves as 'independent', 'alternative', 'autonomous', and 'tactical' media all took part. Yet the common features – e.g., a focus on new technologies and distrust in institutionalised forms of politics – created a borderline to other CS Media actors, including most of those working inside the summit process.

Media activists in the Tunis phase

Geneva03 disbanded after WSIS?WeSeize!, and no similar event was set up for the second WSIS summit in Tunis. However, individual participants of WSIS?WeSeize! continued their involvement with WSIS-related issues and activities, and they discussed and partially implemented interventions into the second summit. Here I want to point to three such initiatives.

A loose network of Indymedia activists, led by Indymedia Beirut, discussed a possible WSIS?WeSeize! follow-up event and identified a list of issues that they felt should be at the heart of any debate about 'information society'. Focusing slightly more on the political situation in the WSIS2 host country of Tunisia and in the Arab world, themes included the issues of censorship and freedom of expression, repression of media activists, precarious working conditions and exploitation of information workers, support for locally appropriate technology, and, again, the connection between free communication and free cross-border movement of all people.

For several months, the network discussed the feasibility of setting up alternative events focusing on these thematic priorities around the Tunis summit. Eventually, it shelved the idea. The main reasons for this decision were the repressive political situation in Tunisia which made it unlikely that the authorities would let any contentious event outside the summit take place, and the limited number of committed activists which could afford preparing and participating in an event under such difficult circumstances.

A second initiative – the Spanish/Italian media group EclécticaDV – decided to produce a DVD magazine which was to present a critical understanding of current information society developments as well as the creative experiences of media activists to delegates and observers in Tunis. The group's members, film-makers and Internet activists, had already participated in WSIS?WeSeize!, and the DVD magazine was to pick up many issues discussed there. Under the name "Datafighters", it was to focus on copyleft culture and knowledge commons, grassroots and autonomous media practices, casualised information work, and threats by surveillance and infowar techniques. A preliminary version of the magazine was presented at the civil society side-event "Civil Society Moving Forward: Where to next?" inside the Tunis summit compound, and a 'Datafighters info-point' was set up in the civil society working area where delegates were given information about the project as well as free DVDs.

Finally, a delegation of Media Justice activists from the US held a series of side-events at the Tunis summit presenting cases of mainstream media misinformation as well as their own experiences of autonomous media making. The group of mostly young coloured Americans represented a range of social justice groups from the US, from immigrant rights to youth video making, and was put together by the Media Justice Network that included the media and cultural training and production organisations Third World Majority, Fourth World Rising, Media Tank, and Video Machete (Media Justice Network 2005).

What was significant about the latter two initiatives – EclécticaDV and the Media Justice Delegation – was that they brought issues which had previously been discussed at the extra-institutional space of WSIS?WeSeize! into the centre of the summit. Few government delegates attended their presentations, but a larger number of NGO actors did participate in the events which took place wall-to-wall which government negotiations and used the same gangways, entrances, bars and toilets as the government delegates. The decision by media activists to enter the heart of the summit represented one part of an increasing diffusion of strategies and practices which the Tunis summit triggered.

The Citizens Summit

The other part was played by some of those civil society organisations which had so far been at the core of the lobbying and advocacy efforts inside the summit process – and which now moved some of their activities outside. A coalition of international NGOs and Tunisian civil society groups organised an alternative event to take place outside the summit compound in the city centre of Tunis. Among them were the CRIS campaign, AMARC, APC, the Swiss Civil Society Coalition Comunica-ch, the Human Rights Caucus, and the World Press Freedom Committee. Some of these, such as

AMARC and APC, were likely candidates for applying more confrontational measures as they had been amongst the more radical fraction of the WSIS civil society networks and had been sympathetic to WSIS?WeSeize!. Others, such as the WPFC, had been suspicious to extra-institutional tactics during the first WSIS summit but chose a particularly oppositional stance towards the authoritarian Tunisian government because of the latter's freedom of expression violations.

The lack of meaningful civil society inclusion in the preparatory process for WSIS2 certainly played a role in the NGOs' decision to increase their involvement with outside activities, but the growing suppression of independent voices in the summit host country Tunisia represented the main trigger. The principal force behind the plans was "the alliance of independent Tunisian civil society" (Ludwig/Peyer 2006) which insisted on turning the summit into a "test for the trustworthiness of the host regime" (ibid.). This 'independent civil society' consisted of oppositional groups which were refused accreditation to participate in the official summit proceedings. Planned to take place in the city centre of Tunis, the Citizens Summit on the Information Society (CSIS) was to give access to a wider Tunisian public than the selected actors which the Tunisian government allowed inside the summit compound. The Organising Committee of the CSIS announced as its main objectives "to send a strong message of support and solidarity from international civil society to the local civil society and citizens" and "to address the main issues being debated at the WSIS, from the perspective of citizen groups and the public" (CSIS 2005a).

At the same time, the event was related to previous self-organised NGO events outside UN summits, thus representing "another milestone in the long tradition of UN conferences and Summits being complemented with events organized by citizen groups" (ibid.). Positioning the CSIS in this semi-official and 'respectable' environment, pointing affirmatively to some of the WSIS debates[23], and referring to the accepted concept of 'citizens', the organisers blurred the oppositional and confrontational aspects of the event. They thus chose a different approach than Geneva03 had done two years earlier when it had rejected the official summit entirely. This difference was also reflected in the programme which featured issues discussed inside WSIS – such as privacy, human rights, freedom of expression, Internet governance – with speakers from inside the summit process (CSIS 2005b).

[23] The call notes: "this event will offer an excellent opportunity to promote the Information Society and the basic principles on which it must be based, as articulated in the first phase of the World Summit on the Information, namely: human rights and social justice" (CSIS 2005a).

A major fundraising effort brought together a substantial resource base, and several conference locations were booked. However the Tunisian authorities urged the owners of the reserved spaces to withdraw the booking, and one after the other were cancelled, allegedly due to "unforeseeable renovation works" (Ludwig/Peyer 2006). Two days before the opening of WSIS, a CSIS preparation meeting scheduled to take place in the Goethe Institute, the official cultural institution of Germany, was prevented by Tunisian police. Participants of the meeting were forcefully stopped from entering the building, several of them were insulted and beaten (Heinrich-Böll-Foundation 2005b). Even the head of the German government delegation, rushing to the scene to witness the police blockade, was not allowed to access the Institute. Disturbed by this confrontation, the delegations of the European Union held an emergency meeting and invited the CSIS organisers for consultations at the offices of the EU commission. This show of solidarity temporarily raised the diplomatic pressure on the Tunisian government, yet the latter maintained its determination to prevent any independent meeting of civil society groups outside the summit compound (Heinrich-Böll-Foundation 2005a).

The final option was to hold a press conference on the afternoon of the official WSIS opening at the offices of the Tunisian Human Rights League (LTDH). Originally scheduled to announce the cancellation of the CSIS, this press conference turned into a 'mini-Citizens-Summit', gathering large numbers of civil society activists, international journalists, and government delegates. Amongst the estimated 150 participants were Shirin Ebadi, winner of the Peace Nobel Price in 2003, Manuel Tornare, Mayor of Geneva, and Ambeyi Ligabo, UN special rapporteur of freedom of expression. They, and many civil society speakers, including Steve Buckley and Sidiki Kaba, President of the International League of Human Rights, denounced the repression against civil society activities in Tunisia and expressed support to local human rights groups. For several hours, participants discussed mainly human rights issues and celebrated their partial victory against the authorities, creating an "impressive manifestation of resistance" (Ludwig/Peyer 2006). The heavy presence of international journalists and diplomats prevented the security forces from interrupting. Frédéric Dubois, observing the event for the APC, noted:

"While heads of states' speeches present at the World Summit on the Information Society (WSIS) were pouring in on all TV channels, revolution was just around the corner in another district of Tunis" (quoted in Heinrich-Böll-Foundation 2005c).

The Third Paradise

Only one independent civil society event did take place in the Tunis city centre, undisturbed by police. In contrast to the Citizens Summit, "The Third Paradise" did not openly criticise the Tunisian government, and it did not seek to involve oppositional local civil society groups. A series of discussions, workshops, and exhibitions on art and free knowledge gathered artists, media activists, free software advocates, and a few government delegates. In an Italian-Brazilian co-production, the cultural institution Cittadellarte – Fondazione Pistoletto, under the patronage of the Brazilian Ministry of Culture and the Italian Ministry of Innovation and Technology, curated the event which sought to be part of the "creative tension toward the responsible transformation of society as common source code" (quoted from Heinrich-Böll-Foundation 2005d).

The topics discussed revolved around free software, the global commons, borderless culture, borderless movements. Speakers included Richard Stallman, inventor of the GNU/Linux operating system, and Gilberto Gil, Brazilian Minister of Culture, folk musician, and free software advocate. Yet the event encouraged participatory round-table discussions rather than top-down presentations. The space, a traditional building in the old town of Tunis, offered an open, creative, and relaxed environment, and common meals and spontaneous music sessions were as much part of the agenda as thematic debate. In all that, it resembled the approach taken at WSIS?WeSeize!. However its strong emphasis on harmonious discussion and on finding common ground with some sections of the government side differed from the more confrontational Geneva03 attitude, and the cultural and political base of "Third Paradise" participants in media activism and the global justice movement was less developed.

7.5 Media events between inside and outside

World Electronic Media Forum

As we have seen in chapter 7.2, the Media Caucus participants were gravely concerned about the neglect of traditional media issues in a summit dominated by 'new media' issues and, furthermore, about possible curbs on the rights and freedoms of media organisations due to the control interests of governments. As their intense efforts to strengthen media issues in the WSIS process met resistance by governments, they extended their mission to the outside and organised a major summit side-event. The World Electronic Media Forum (WEMF) started one day before the Geneva WSIS and continued throughout the days of the summit. It took place inside the summit compound as an official but independent and self-organised side-event.

With a large number of organising staff, many high-profile speakers and more than 600 participants, it was the biggest side-event that took place in Geneva. WEMF President Jean Stock, addressing the WSIS Plenary on 12 December 2003, outlined the ambitious objective of positioning the forum as a complementary summit to WSIS. He pointed to the two central aspects of information society, content and technological infrastructure, and claimed: "We, the electronic media, are prepared to provide the content" (Stock 2004: 165).

The Geneva WEMF

The WEMF organising team encompassed the UN Department of Public Information, the Swiss Agency for Development and Cooperation, the Swiss Executive Secretariat for the WSIS, the European Broadcasting Union (EBU), and the Swiss national broadcaster SRG SSR idée Suisse. Executive Director of the World Electronic Media Forum Association was Guillaume Chevenière, Assistant Executive Director was Edouard Markiewicz, both were active participants in the Media Caucus (WEMF 2004: 180). Initiated in response to the disregard of media issues at WSIS, the WEMF may have seemed a more openly confrontational 'counter-event' than WSIS?WeSeize!, yet it was certainly not based in the realm of grassroots media activism. The keynote addresses at the opening ceremony were delivered by UN Secretary General Kofi Annan and Swiss President Pascal Couchepin, and speakers and participants of the various sessions encompassed a wide range of international journalists, director-generals and chairpersons of media organisations, and news anchors, from, amongst others, CNN, BBC, Globo, TV5, ARD, ZDF, RAI, CBS, and Al Jazeera, government ministers and heads of UN organisations. The WEMF gathered the 'who-is-who' in international mainstream (commercial and public service) broadcast journalism.

Contents: Self-assurance and critical spots

As the Media Caucus, WEMF was not the space for self-criticism by the assembled media establishment. Its prime objective was to highlight the achievements by, and the promising developments in, the media sector. In his opening speech, Kofi Annan pointed out that "electronic media are among our most important vehicles of peace, progress and solidarity" (Annan 2004: 11). WEMF plenary sessions highlighted "how editorially independent radio, television and websites have become indispensable tools for the information society" (WEMF 2004: 42) and that broadcasters and media professionals "ensure that quality content is provided to the many diverse publics on all levels" (Cohen 2004: 21). Fritz Pleitgen from the German ARD defined this role as one of a "trusted agent" (Pleitgen 2004: 20) and noted that the knowledge society with its diversity of individualised knowledge niches required that people depend more on such agents "to provide them with (..) information in a reliable and easily understandable way" (ibid.). The major threat to this mission was widely seen in government intervention.[24]

Yet amongst the mainstream perspectives, a few critical tones emerged. Media critics Danny Schechter (Mediachannel.org) and Ignacio Ramonet (Le Monde Diplomatique) questioned self-censorship by journalists and the commodification of information through the media. The outcomes of WEMF sessions included the need for broadcasters to dedicate more space to programmes "analysing reasons for conflict and discussing peace initiatives" (WEMF 2004: 39). Iftekhar Cowdury, Chairman of the UN Committee on Information, pointed to the internal media structures as an important factor for freedom of expression: "Realization of freedom of expression requires [...] a media which is pluralistic and diverse" (Chowdury 2004: 47) and he called for an "end of monopolies of any kind" (ibid.). Kofi Annan noted that "the consolidation of media ownership has sparked concern about lack of media pluralism" (Annan 2004: 11). Even José Roberto Marinho, co-chairman of the Brazilian Globo Organization and thereby of the largest media corporation in the region, criticised "the enormous economic power wielded by the transnational media groups" (Marinho 2004a: 19), stressed that "never before has there been such a great risk of communication becoming so globally concentrated" (ibid.) and warned of a trend towards "cultural uniformity" (Marinho 2004b: 44). Certainly Marinho's outspoken attack primarily addressed those transnational conglomerates that interfere with national and regional media markets – and thus Globo's competitors – rather than commercial media as such.

24 The uncritical approach towards the own profession was exemplified by the appearance of Marcel Granier, representative of Venezuelan commercial media, who challenged governmental use of media space for political causes (having in mind, probably, the regular appearances of Venezuelan President Hugo Chavez on national public television: "This is another form of violence but for political means which is far more dangerous. (…) They use it to promote hatred" (WEMF 2004: 27). He did not mention, however, that the Venezuelan commercial media themselves have very specific political goals, have been part of a national conflict between the country's wealthy elites and the elected government for several years, have conducted a prolonged propaganda campaign against this government, and have supported, in spring 2002, an attempted violent coup d'état (see, e.g., Britto Garcia 2004). While Granier was speaking at the WEMF, activists from the Venezuelan media organisation Aporrea spoke at WSIS?WeSeize! about the propaganda campaigns by the Venezuelan media and about the latter's involvement in the various unlawful attempts to make the democratically elected government fall. By offering a platform for media representatives such as Granier, the WEMF took sides in a social-political conflict, and it exposed its uncritical stance towards the political objectives and activities of media organisations.

CS Media?

WEMF participants also discussed the challenges to mainstream media by new technologies and by participatory approaches to media. Nick Gowing, main programme anchor at BBC World, illustrated the new world of 'citizen journalism': "Increasingly everyone – whether journalists, tourists or ordinary bystanders who happen upon a newsworthy incident – [is] 'doing media' with pocket video cameras and mobile phones" (quoted in WEMF 2004: 70). Furthermore, "these new media actors are transforming the political and social landscape everywhere because individuals are empowered to communicate as never before" (quoted in Heinrich-Böll-Foundation 2003d). According to Gowing, this new form of journalism "is filling an information space not filled by the traditional media" (ibid.).

The perspective towards such developments was positive, yet it focused on the technology rather than on the initiative by people and collectivities to appropriate technology for their own ends, and it promoted a 'citizen journalism' which was seen as complementary to mainstream media programmes and not necessarily as a substantially new form of media (see chapter 2.2.). Only a few speakers called for "the creation of local, rural, community, citizen and independent broadcast media" (Robinson 2004: 105), highlighted the need for local and minority programmes (Smith 2004), and suggested to "provide assistance to create and sustain independent communications" for social movements (WEMF 2004: 112).

The AIR, in contrast, maintained its confrontational stance. Its workshop on 'Private Radio and Television' highlighted the arguments raised in the Media Caucus, namely the demand to eliminate "the multiple privileges public broadcasters enjoy" (WEMF 2004: 132) and to "finish with the endemic phenomenon of illegal stations" (ibid.), with 'illegal' meaning community and alternative media.

The Tunis WEMF

As the second WSIS summit was more thematically condensed than the first one, so was the second coming of the WEMF. For two days – the 15th and 16th of November 2005 – the World Electronic Media Foundation, together with the World Broadcasting Unions (WBU) and the Arab States Broadcasting Union (ASBU), organised a programme of eight sessions that encompassed issues such as development, new ICTs, audiovisual archives and conflict reporting. The specific character of the WEMF as arguably the most elaborate and significant side-event was, again, underlined by an appearance and closing address by Kofi Annan. A session on the Millennium Development Goals featured AMARC Vice-President Lynne Muthoni Wanyeki as one of the panelists.

Whereas the first WEMF had focused on the persistent importance of traditional broadcasting and had thus presented a counter-position to the ICT-focused WSIS, the second forum provided more space for debating the role of ICTs in broadcasting and the connections between traditional media platforms and 'new' technologies. 'Interconnections', 'combinations of traditional and new media', and the pros and cons of 'using ICT' ran as a cross-cutting theme through many WEMF sessions. While the Geneva WEMF had "affirmed the vital importance of radio and television in the information society" (WEMF 2005a), as the WEMF Association noted, "WEMF II built on this affirmation through focused discussions on the role of the electronic media in the digital age" (ibid.). The new agenda issue on the safety of journalists reflected both the increased proximity to the conflict zones of the Middle-East and the emerging debates on this theme in the Media Caucus.

Absent from the agenda, however, was the theme of freedom of expression and state repression. While media actors had been amongst the most outspoken critics of the WSIS2 host government of Tunisia, and the Media Caucus had practically turned into a 'freedom of expression caucus' during the second WSIS phase, the WEMF was silent. Whereas Tunisian President Ben Ali had made a career as principal enemy of free expression and free media in many media statements, he was thanked for his hospitality in the WEMF welcome address by representatives of the ASBU. The leading role of the ASBU, whose headquarters are located in Tunis and which lists amongst its main objectives the "full commitment to Arab national causes" and to "coordinate Arab States positions and back their efforts for the defense of their interests"[25] in organising the second WEMF led to a departure from the severe and consistent criticism of the Tunisian government which media actors had been pursuing throughout the WSIS preparation phase.[26] The WEMF's ambition to establish a particularly high-level conference contributed to the perceived necessity of following diplomatic conventions and scaling down criticism.

As a result of the two-day forum, WEMF participants put together a list of demands which they presented at the concluding session and which were addressed at the governments attending WSIS2. The demands included calls for supportive legislation and funding for editorially independent media; preserving the world's audiovisual heritage and creating appropriate archives; collaborating with broadcasters in addressing development and hu-

---

[25] ASBU Objectives, see www.asbu.net/www/en/doc.asp?mcat=2&mrub=5

[26] Email conversation with Guillaume Chevenière on 1 June 2006. Chevenière, executive director of the first WEMF, openly criticised this change in direction in his address to WSIS2.

manitarian issues; and for the security of journalists in conflict zones" (WEMF 2005b). The statement offered two demands that were potentially useful for CS Media:

"(3) Support the development of technologies, software and open standards for the production of quality low-cost media content oriented to the needs of local populations" (ibid.).

"(7) Foster different forms of media for local communities, including associative radio, to improve dialogue and democratic participation, particularly in rural areas with poor infrastructure" (ibid.).

These demands do not refer to concepts used by CS Media, such as 'community' or 'alternative' media, and they confine those 'low-cost' and 'associative' media to the local and rural niches of the media sphere – as the Media Caucus had done before. Yet these two sections in a very condensed priority list of 10 major issues express a specific recognition of non-mainstream civil society-oriented media.

Community Media Forum

The division which characterised media actors' lobby efforts in the summit process – between the Media Caucus and the CMWG – was reproduced in their side events: In addition to the WEMF, protagonists of the CMWG, including AMARC, ALER, CAMECO, Bread for All and the Swiss Catholic Lenten Fund organised a *Community Media Forum* to showcase the experiences and specific approaches of community media and of civil society-based communication practices which work towards social change. At the Geneva summit, the forum occupied a whole day (12 December 2003, the last day of the official WSIS summit) and was thus one of the biggest civil society side-events. As the WEMF, the Community Media Forum was a self-organised event, separate from the official summit, yet located inside the summit compound and recognised as an official side-event in summit publications. It was therefore situated between the more direct lobby efforts of the CMWG and the oppositional activities of WSIS?WeSeize! – between 'inside' and 'outside'.

Its prime purpose was to raise awareness of community media's practices and objectives amongst summit participants. Activists and specialists from around the globe were to "present their experiences, reflections and proposals" as well as "success stories showing that another information society is possible" (CMWG 2003g). The programme for the Geneva forum was to highlight three main objectives (Community Media Forum 2003)[27]: showing

[27] The following quotes are taken from this source.

"Concrete Examples of Active Community Involvement", presenting "Cost-Effective Means for Connecting the World's Poorest Comunities", and discussing "Steps towards Legal Recognition of Community Media as Equals to Public and Commercial Media". The forum thus linked up with central issues brought forward, and frames used, by the CMWG, including community-based development, poverty reduction and legal recognition. However, and in contrast to the CMWG, it included explicit criticism of mainstream media. The organisers asked: ""Why do the poor apparently not exist in the mainstream media? (…) Why do the media not reflect the cultural and linguistic diversity of peoples? Why do the media often fail to create a space for public discussion and common reflection of all stakeholders in society?" (ibid.).

Three 'roundtable' sessions constituted the core of thematic debate at the Geneva forum. The "Community Media Legislation Roundtable" discussed cases of enabling country-level regulation as well as proposals for enhancing policy, "Community Communication in Africa" focused on positive examples of community media in a region with a particularly highly developed sector, and "Networking and Globalising Community Media" broadened the perspective to other regions, the role of community media in specific thematic areas (such as gender and racism), and other forms of CS Media.

The forum succeeded in bringing together participants from a wide geographic and cultural spectrum, from Brazil to South Korea, and from grassroots media activists to ITU officials. It presented core concerns of CS Media, and it reached a large audience which constituted a counter-point to the neglect which community media faced in the official WSIS negotiations (see chapter 8). In doing so, it greatly contributed to the high profile of CS Media in the events and discussions around the summit (see chapter 9). However the forum reproduced two shortcomings which were already noted for the CMWG (and, in a somewhat different way, for WSIS?WeSeize!):

Predominance of community radio. The latter held a central position in the forum programme, and media platforms other than radio and media concepts other than 'community' were marginalised. The forum diversified beyond this narrow focus, featuring speakers from community television, community newspapers, alternative media and a media activist campaign, but these were mostly relegated to the last session and given minimal speaking time.

Lack of networking and connections. The forum was strategically situated between, on the one hand, the CMWG, its summit-related policy programme and its direct access to the decision-making level, and, on the other hand, WSIS?WeSeize! with its more fundamental criticism of the communications landscape and its alternative practices. However, it failed to establish this connection practically. While the CMWG was closely involved with the forum, the actors, practices and objectives of WSIS?WeSeize! were hardly reflected. The forum did not facilitate information exchanges between, for example, Internet activists from Europe and community radio practitioners from Latin America. To some degree this was due to the forum's focus on presenting the sector and on agenda-setting, rather than on intra-sector debate, but the result was an opportunity lost for intensifying connections between different civil society-based media projects.

With many of the organisers of the Geneva forum having scaled down their activities in the Tunis phase or having left the process altogether, the Tunis forum was planned solely by AMARC and on a much smaller scale. It was, again, supposed to present practices and approaches of community media, this time with a closer focus on freedom of expression as one of the core issues of the second WSIS phase. However, it was exactly the difficult situation around freedom of expression rights in Tunisia that finally prevented it. After Tunisian security forces had stopped the Citizens Summit on 16 November, Tunisian human rights groups asked the international civil society organisations inside the summit compound to suspend their side-events in protest on 17 November (Heinrich-Böll-Foundation 2005b). The Community Media Forum, having been scheduled for that day, followed this request. AMARC representatives issued a statement condemning the acts of the Tunisian authorities and explained why the forum would be cancelled. Even these short statements were interrupted by Tunisian GONGO representatives in the audience while others tried to stop people from entering the room and listening to the organisers' explanations. The Tunis Community Media Forum thus constituted one of the occasions where the influence of the host country was most explicit – proving that the Tunisian authorities tried to prevent civil society activities both outside and inside the summit compound.

World Forum on Communication Rights

A third major side-event on issues relevant to CS Media, the World Forum on Communication Rights (WFCR) took place one day prior to the Geneva Community Media Forum on 11 December 2003. It was primarily organised by the CRIS campaign and thus focused on core themes which the more radical sections of the civil society networks inside the WSIS process had tried to put on the WSIS agenda and which were largely reflected in the Civil Society Declaration. As did the Community Media Forum, it criticised WSIS for having turned "a blind eye to many issues central to an information society that puts people first" (WFCR 2003)[28]. In four main sessions, speakers from NGOs, campaigns and academia linked communication with issues such as poverty, social exclusion, militarism and cultural diversity and thereby developed a practical approach to communication rights.

Several media reformers, practitioners and critical analysts, including Art McGee from the US Media Alliance, Danny Schechter from Mediachannel.org and citizens media advocate and academic Clemencia Rodriguez appeared as speakers, and self-organised civil society-based media were consistently highlighted as a prime strategy to claim and fulfil communication rights. Rather than putting CS Media as such on the agenda, as did the Community Media Forum, the WFCR dealt with the environment in which CS Media operate. It emphasised the importance of free software, rejected extensive intellectual property rights, criticised mainstream journalism and discussed strategies to defend freedom of expression and to overcome poverty. As such, it created a framework for the more specific community media perspective of the following day.

The WFCR connected previously separated campaigns, formulated practical dimensions of communication rights, and thereby strengthened an emerging and converging civil society agenda on communication. On the downside, and in similarity with the Community Media Forum, a format focusing on panel debates and presentations presented crucial perspectives to an audience but left little space for more in-depth discussions, strategising, knowledge-sharing and networking. However, WFCR organisers took a few cautious steps towards connecting with the 'outsiders' at WSIS?WeSeize!. Even though no Geneva03 member or WSIS?WeSeize! invitee was featured in the programme, communication channels and loose linkages between both camps had been established and continued throughout the event. CRIS sympathised with the fellow activists outside, while many of the 'outsiders' saw the WFCR with its debates on issues such as information war and intellectual property rights as their main entrance into the summit.

After WSIS1, connections were consolidated with the planning of a European Forum on Communication Rights (EFCR) to take place alongside the European Social Forum in London in October 2004. Core members of the WFCR organising team, particularly from WACC and Greennet/APC, collaborated with London-based WSIS?WeSeize! participants, particularly from Indymedia UK, resulting in the EFCR as a common project between WSIS 'insiders' and 'outsiders', which combined the policy-oriented approach of CRIS and the practice-oriented approach of Indymedia. This collaborative effort successfully bridged the gap between the political, cultural

[28] The following quotes are taken from this document.

and strategic differences of both camps, yet linkages proved to be fragile and temporary. While communication channels have remained open, intense collaboration was not continued after the EFCR.

The Tunis summit saw a second coming of the WFCR, now with a slightly different face. As a follow-up event, organised again by CRIS, it took place on the final afternoon of the summit under the name "Civil Society Moving Forward: Where to next?" and featured reviews of the successes and failures of civil society interventions, the state of the multi-stakeholder process and priorities for post-WSIS action and collaboration.

Further media events and activities

A number of side- and parallel events at both summits put a focus on media and particularly CS Media. Picking out just a few examples from the Geneva summit, one could find a session by the WHO on 'Broadcasting and Health', UNESCO discussed 'Media Development in Knowledge Societies' and showed special interest in community multimedia centres, and EBU and AIR joined forces for a debate on 'Radio – the New Challenges', including a presentation on 'Ethnic Minorities Broadcasts'. The International Center for Non-Violent Conflict organised the session 'Global Media, Nonviolent Power and Democratic Change' to explore ways in which media can more accurately report on conflicts and how affected groups can make news themselves. Two large fora which paralleled the summit – the 'ICT4D Forum', organised by the Swiss Agency for Development and Cooperation and the Global Knowledge Partnership, and the 'Global Forum on Indigenous Peoples and the Information Society', organised by the UN Permanent Forum on Indigenous Issues, included debates on the use of media for development and on self-organised communication systems.

Providing a different perspective than the WEMF, the event 'Media Liberties in the Information Society', organised by Swiss journalist unions and Amnesty International, put the shortcomings of the mainstream media sector on the agenda. Ignacio Ramonet from the weekly Le Monde Diplomatique and Rita Freire from the Brazilian web platform Ciranda, amongst others, discussed threats to media liberties by state repression, but also focused on the effects of privatisation, commercialisation, and media concentration on media content. At the Tunis summit APC held workshops on community wireless networking, and the Global Knowledge Partnership followed up the Geneva ICT4D Forum with a series of talks on, amongst other themes, 'Local Content' and 'Media for Peace'.

The practices of CS Media were highlighted, particularly, through an AMARC radio stream from the WSIS1 summit. Radio producers from the

Zürich-based Radio Lora set up a broadcasting studio in a small hut at the 'African Village' – a space at the ICT4D fair, presenting local African communication practices and uses of media technologies. During the days of the summit, programmes in a variety of languages (including indigenous languages such the Andean Quechua) were web-streamed from the summit compound and picked up by community radio stations worldwide. The studio was accessible to the public, making the production process a continuous presentation of CS Media practices. The most extensive reporting effort on summit events was pulled by the Inter Press Service (IPS) and its UN summit bulletin Terraviva. Providing "a daily, independent source of news and analysis about the summit, serving as an information and communication resource for participants and observers" (Mirén Gutierrez, IPS chief editor; MG interview), the CS Media outlet Terraviva was the most productive journalist operation at the summits. It appeared in newspaper format at the Geneva summit and as an online magazine at the Tunis summit.

7.6 Conclusion

Media actors self-organised several agenda-setting activities, lobbying efforts and discussion spaces at and around WSIS. They intervened in the summit process from both inside and outside, applying a diversity of strategies and developing substantial catalogues of policy demands. WSIS helped create new connections between different media actors and discuss common agendas. However it also showed that fundamental differences persist between the agendas of mainstream and civil society media, as well as between different types of CS Media with regards to strategies and approaches. Neither did a common 'media agenda' emerge, nor a coordinated CS Media approach to policy-making.

A number of summit side-events and activities established CS Media as a considerable force in the discourses around information society and proved that there was substantial interest in citizen- and civil society-based communication initiatives. In the following chapter I will scrutinise the official WSIS documents and processes to find out whether they reflected this interest.

8 Tracing Civil Society Media in WSIS negotiations and outcomes

After having taken a closer look at the structures of self-organisation, the tactics and strategies, and the thematic objectives of CS Media in the WSIS process, we can now come back to the official WSIS negotiations to find out whether the efforts by CS Media were successful and which of their preferences and priority issues are reflected in the official summit documents. In this chapter, I will consider:

a) Media Caucus objectives, such as freedom of expression and recognition of the role of the media;

b) CMWG objectives, such as development concerns, a focus on socio-economic issues and on the needs of marginalised people, recognition of traditional media, legal and financial support for community-based initiatives, access to the airwaves and other infrastructure;

c) WSIS?WeSeize! priority themes, such as a critique of intellectual property rights (IPR) and of mainstream media, support for free software and for a culture of sharing, recognition of self-organised civil society-based development of information infrastructure and applications, limitation of government and business interference;

d) further CS Media characteristics (as outlined in chapters 2 and 4), such as public participation in information provision, civil society-based contribution to knowledge, interactive and participatory communication, the public domain, media pluralism.

If all or, at least, some of these issues are recognised and supported in the WSIS documents, we can assume that the WSIS outcomes offer support for CS Media and strengthen their role in the media environment and in the wider information society. On the other hand, there are sets of issues which can weaken their position and which may offer obstacles. This is particularly the case with language that strengthens the capacities of governments in areas of security, control, and repression, and with language focusing on commercial and business-led development and, generally, on large-scale projects rather than citizen- and community-based self-organised initiatives. WSIS documents dominated by such language will be likely to represent a defeat for CS Media.

8.1 The Geneva phase

Regional meetings

The regional conferences paralleled the initial WSIS preparation phase and thus played a considerable role in WSIS agenda-setting. The first one, the African Regional Meeting in Bamako, Mali, in May 2002, displayed a considerable connection with the interests of CS Media through an emphasis on local content creation and on free software (Africa Regional Conference 2002).[1] The Bamako Declaration, adopted on 30 May 2002, also referred to "the worldwide public domain" and and called for the "democratisation of access".

The Bucharest Declaration, adopted at the Pan-European Regional Conference[2] in November 2002, put more focus on ICT infrastructure, competitive environments and private sector investment, and less on media and content (Pan-European Conference 2002).[3] It brought the perceived need to "prevent the use of information resources or technologies for criminal or terrorist purposes" into the WSIS debate, as well as the call for a "global culture of cyber-security". Some CS Media goals are implicitly recognised, e.g. the need to "ensure that the knowledge and experience of citizens is [...] the driving force behind the new information society", "sharing of information and genuine participation of all stakeholders", and "the creation of varied information content, which helps to preserve and disseminate local and national culture, language and heritage". "Community-led development" is seen as "a critical element in the strategy for achieving universal access to information and knowledge".

The Asia-Pacific Regional Conference, which took place in Tokyo in January 2003 (Asia-Pacific Regional Conference 2003)[4], put an almost exclusive focus on new ICTs, aiming to "provide connectivity to all". The Tokyo Declaration displays some classic 'information society enthusiasm' as it states that ICT networks and ubiquitous access to information can "promote sustainable economic and social development, improve quality of life for all, alleviate poverty and hunger, and facilitate participatory decision-making processes." The declaration also calls for "local content development", the establishment of "community information and communication centres", and expresses concern over the "imbalance of information flows". Development

1 The following quotes are taken from this document.

2 The "Pan-European" region included the US and Canada.

3 The following quotes are taken from this document.

4 The following quotes are taken from this document.

and deployment of open-source software is encouraged. On the downside, from a CS Media perspective, it picks up the security concerns expressed in the Bucharest Declaration by reiterating the urgency of dealing with "cyber-crime" and even suggesting an "emphasis on preventive approaches". It brings into the debate the notion of "information security" which is not defined further but blurs the boundaries between network and content issues and therefore opens a door for content regulation and censorship.

The Bávaro Declaration, adopted by the Latin America and Caribbean Regional Conference on 31 January 2003 (Latin America and Caribbean Regional Conference 2003)[5], expresses a less technology-focused perspective by defining information society as "an economic and social system where knowledge and information constitute the fundamental sources of well-being and progress" and the digital divide as a reflection of "the differences that exist between and within countries in terms of economic, social and cultural aspects". It focuses on 'national' frameworks, noting that "the transition to the information society shall be led by the Governments". The section on media is stronger than in the other declarations and highlights "independent and free communication media", freedom of expression and the "plurality of information". However it leans strongly towards commercial media, seeks to safeguard their freedom from state intervention but does not recognise CS Media.[6] More interesting for CS Media would be the call for ICTs' "use for public and social purposes", for the "creation and provision of [...] multi-purpose community access points", and for the creation and preservation of indigenous, local and traditional knowledge.

The Beirut Declaration, adopted by the Western Asia Regional Conference on 6 February 2003, has an even stronger focus on governmental activity, to the detriment of civil society and the private sector (Western Asia Regional Conference 2003).[7] Self-organised civil society projects are not considered,

---

5 The following quotes are taken from this document.

6 Particularly references to 'the legal system of each country' serve to exclude CS Media, as many Latin American countries continue to refuse legal licenses for non-commercial/non-state media. With the AIR as the main representative of commercial media in the WSIS process being based in Latin America, and with several Latin American governments holding close relationships with national commercial media, this tendency in the Bávaro declaration is not surprising At the time of declaration and the beginning of the WSIS process, the swing towards left-wing governments in South America was just about to start and was not yet reflected in the negotiations. In the following years, left-leaning governments were elected in countries such as Argentina, Uruguay, Chile and Bolivia, leading to a shift in power relations within those countries, the weakening of traditional conservative elites, and, in some cases, a review of media policy.

7 The following quotes are taken from this document.

nor are media actors and traditional media platforms. Content is discussed under the headline of 'ICT applications' and focuses on the provision of Arab language content. The declaration offers an elaborate position on Internet governance reform, suggesting a stronger role for governments, and giving a first taste of the fierce debates on this issue which accompanied the second WSIS phase. Interestingly, it also refers to the "right to communicate" and thereby offers a connection to one of the priorities of CS Media. However, it does not define it further, referring merely to "the right to access information for citizens and nations".

Overall, the regional conferences recognised numerous issues shared by CS Media – freedom of expression, the role of traditional media, plurality of information, the imbalance of information flows, a focus on marginalised people, community-led development, social progress and people-centred approaches – and there were calls to strengthen community access centres, local content, the public domain, free and open source software. However, the declarations adopted at these conferences do not explicitly refer to CS Media, and they include some disturbing tendencies by over-emphasizing new ICTs, market-based policies, cyber-crime and cyber-security, and the primacy of government interests.

Developing an agenda

Parallel to the regional conferences, PrepCom1 (July 2002) and the Informal Meeting on Content and Themes (September 2002) pre-structured the range of possible issues that would be discussed in the WSIS process. The list included themes such as linguistic diversity, cultural identity, local content, universal and inclusive access, and the "importance of communities and of utilising ICTs for the benefit of disadvantaged groups" (WSIS Executive Secretariat 2002b), but media was not recognised as a priority issue.

The first draft of the Declaration of Principles (WSIS Executive Secretariat 2003b)8, as discussed at PrepCom2, established a section on "Cultural identity and linguistic diversity, local content and media development" (section 8 out of 10), calling for "respect for (…) cultural expression", the "creation of local content", "democratisation of access", multilingualism and cultural diversity, and acknowledging that "traditional media such as broadcasting and print (…) will continue to have an important role in disseminating content". The text picked up the paragraph promoting "independent and free communication media" from the Bávaro Declaration. It also referred to "[t]he right to communicate and the right to access information for citizens" which "should be considered a basic human right".

---

8 The following quotes are taken from this document.

CS Media were not mentioned, neither were issues around media reform. Yet other sections of the draft included references to knowledge sharing, community-led development, participatory decision-making, and for a "people-centred" information society "with citizens and communities at its core". The text explicitly recognised freedom of expression according to Art. 19 UDHR, but exactly the word "create" (in: "the freedom to (…) create, seek, receive and impart information through any media") was put in square brackets[9], reflecting intense conflict over the extent to which the public should be allowed to contribute information.

Looking at the global media environment, the draft suggested to "take into account the imbalance of information flows",[10] and following on from the consensus shaped at the regional conferences, it included the notion of an "adequate balance between intellectual property rights and the needs of the users". The text picked up the security issue established at the Bucharest conference, proposing to establish a "global culture of cyber-security" and to "prevent the use of information resources or technologies for criminal and terrorist purposes". The "enabling environment" for the information society was based largely on promoting competition and investment from the private sector.

The draft Plan of Action (WSIS Executive Secretariat 2003c)[11] was structured according to the sections of the draft Declaration and thus equally included a section 8 on "Cultural identity and linguistic diversity, local content and media development". The latter highlighted "the creation of varied information content", the preservation and dissemination of "local and national culture, language and heritage", the role of "[c]ommunity information and communication centres" for achieving affordable and universal access, and suggested "integrating traditional and new ICTs in order to create alternative forms of access that can help narrow the digital divide".

Media themes enter the stage

Civil society representatives played a key role in reinforcing the emerging recognition of media. Summaries of civil society statements were annexed to – and later partially included in – the official government drafts. A draft version of the Declaration from 21 March 2003 mentioned community me-

---

[9] Square brackets usually mark parts of the text which are heavily contested. They reflect strong views both in favour and against the bracketed text and point to the necessity of intense negotiations in the further course of the process.

[10] This article was later deleted, following a proposal by the EU.

[11] The following quotes are taken from this document.

dia twice, promoted media diversity, and criticised media concentration (WSIS Executive Secretariat 2003d). Furthermore, several government statements in the aftermath of PrepCom2 focused on media issues and argued for a greater role of media themes in the emerging WSIS documents.

Switzerland, having adopted several members from journalist unions, public service media and civil society organisations in its government delegation, proposed a new "key principle 8a: Media" (Swiss delegation 2003)[12] which showed strong overlaps with the Media Caucus agenda, for example in its focus on freedom of expression and its promotion of journalist self regulation, but with a stronger emphasis on the themes prioritised by public service and community media. The Swiss delegation demanded a "generous allocation of frequencies for local radio stations at reasonable prices", "legislation which guarantees the independence and plurality of the media and to transform the State media (radio, TV and other) into public services which enjoy editorial independence", "legal measures limiting the concentration of the media, so as to guarantee diversified, pluralistic information sources", suggested guidelines for the media such as "the separation of editorial content and advertising", strengthened the rights of media workers, suggested partnerships between media professionals in prosperous and disadvantaged regions, and proposed "the development of citizens' associations of listeners/viewers/surfers for conducting a critical dialogue with their media". These proposals were more detailed and more progressive, from a CS Media perspective, than all previous WSIS documents and Media Caucus statements.

A contribution by the Cuban delegation (Cuban delegation 2003)[13] confirmed the critique of "undue concentration of private ownership and control of media", highlighted the "inequalities in the flow of information to and from developing countries", and emphasized the importance of "democratic, responsible, accountable and participatory media". Reference to the latter, in particular, was an interesting further consideration of CS Media, yet the CMWG remained cautious as to Cuba's commitment to freedom of expression and was therefore sceptical about notions such as 'responsibility' in Cuban statements which may allow for repression against oppositional groups.

Tanzania picked up language drafted by the Community Media Initiative at PrepCom2. The delegation proposed to add to the WSIS documents that

12 The following quotes are taken from this document.

13 The following quotes are taken from this document.

"Public participation in the Information Society shall be enabled through affordable and appropriate ICT applications allowing for local content creation such as community media, non-profit media and interactive Web applications. Recognition and support will be given to media based in local communities, thus contributing to creation of local content, preserving and developing cultural and linguistic diversity" (Tanzanian delegation 2003).

The draft Plan of Action discussed at the Intersessional Meeting (WSIS Executive Secretariat 2003e)[14] included all of the points proposed by Switzerland and some of those proposed by Cuba and Tanzania. Art. 43 noted that "recognition and support will be given to media based in local communities" and Art. 44 suggested that "[i]nvestment should be made in regional and community-based media content as well as new technologies". The draft criticised media monopolisation and called for "diversity in the sources of information". Proposals by Mexico and Brazil questioned the ICT focus of the WSIS agenda and highlighted the role of traditional media (Art. 1), and Brazil and Switzerland argued for the promotion of open source software and copyleft licenses (Art. 14).[15]

A separate media article (Art. 51) was created in the draft Declaration but the text was hotly disputed and lost much of its original content during the debate (WSIS Executive Secretariat 2003f). Particular disagreements emerged on the issues of media concentration and freedom of expression. Reference to Art. 19 UDHR was under heavy fire from governments such as China and Iran which sought to blur its strict interpretation. Other articles of the draft proposed to "stimulate participation of stakeholders not only as users but also as providers, creators and generators of contents and innovative applications", included a re-definition of the 'free flow' concept that highlighted the "free flow of a multiplicity of ideas from a diversity of sources", and even the recognition of the right to communicate. However all these proposals were put in square brackets, reflecting serious objections by some governments.

The Media Debate

At PrepCom3 in September 2003, a specific negotiation group was established for solving the controversies over the media issue, complementing the

---

[14] The following quotes are taken from this document.

[15] As a sideline, Art. 42 in the draft Action Plan represents an example for the differences between mainstream and CS Media. It notes: "All citizens should have access to services provided via sound and television broadcasting stations". While the 'provision' of 'services' to consumers may vindicate a mainstream media approach, CS Media would demand the 'contribution' of citizens to, and their participation in, those media.

five other drafting groups that were dealing with conflicts over issues such as security and Internet governance. Media had finally moved to the centre of WSIS debates. As noted earlier, the Swiss government delegation and the Media Caucus managed to occupy key positions in the group: Alain Modoux (former Assistant Director General of UNESCO and President of Orbicom) as the chair, Wolf Ludwig (General Secretary of the journalist union comedia) as minute taker; and Michel Bührer (Swiss journalist union) as convener of the drafting group.[16] In the discussions of the working group, which took place over the full two weeks of the PrepCom, different sets of interests emerged:

(1) **The constructivists**: Switzerland relentlessly proposed new language for the media article, trying to strengthen its substance, with a foundation in freedom of expression, press freedom, and journalist principles, but including emphasis on public service, community media, media diversity, and criticism of media concentration. Norway supported this approach, as did the Media Caucus (whose chair held several statements at the beginning of working group sessions), but the latter emphasized the perspective of the second group:

(2) **The free expressionists**: Delegates from other Western countries, such as the US and the UK, supported the Swiss position particularly on the themes of press freedom, freedom of expression, and the absence of government intervention in media issues.

(3) **The community supporters**: Botswana, Venezuela and Colombia supported the Swiss position, particularly with regards to the inclusion of community media.

(4) **The state controllers**: Delegates from states with more authoritarian political systems forcefully objected to a prominent reference to freedom of expression and Art. 19 UDHR, and to the very notion of media as independent actors. In their view, state sovereignty was to be preserved at all costs and strengthening media as autonomous, un-controllable actors was to be prevented. This group was led by China and supported by Cuba, Russia, Egypt and Saudi-Arabia.

(5) **The corporate legalists**: Several Latin American delegates, with their home governments cultivating close ties with national commercial media, brought across a commercial media agenda which sought to strengthen the latter and weaken their competitors. The delegate from El Salvador was

---

16 The following account of the drafting group proceedings is based partially on my own participation as observer and partially on interviews with Wolf Ludwig.

particularly hostile against any reference to community media and insisted on including the sentence "... in accordance with the legal system of each country", thus shutting out many CS Media. He was regularly briefed by a member of the AIR.

(6) **The telecoms**: A large group of delegates was sitting in the drafting group rather quietly, seemingly un-interested, wondering what the fuss was all about. Coming mostly from national telecommunications regulating bodies, they had little experience with independent media organisations and regarded media primarily as technical channels. Thus they were largely critical of the whole endeavour of a separate media article and tended towards getting rid of it altogether.

Groups 4, 5 and 6 shared a deep scepticism towards the Swiss efforts and created an unofficial alliance against a content-rich media article – in the words of Wolf Ludwig: a "faction of concrete" – which was not willing to make compromise on any of the issues under discussion. This 'faction' was characterised by a "domination of telecom representatives" (Interview WL) with little media competence and no understanding of media needs, a rejection of (or, at least, scepticism towards) media independence and the absence of government control, and, in particularly, of CS Media as potentially oppositional and dissident actors or as competitors of commercial media.

Bit by bit, the language of the article was watered down. References to "independent, pluralistic and free" media[17] and to Art. 19 UDHR were put in square brackets, and the calls to transform state media into editorially independent public service organisations and to protect the labour rights of media workers were deleted. The already weak critique of media ownership concentration was transformed into a merely rhetoric statement asking that "[p]luralism of information and diversity of media ownership should be encouraged". The unwillingness of the 'faction of concrete' to accept media as independent actors was uncovered in several of its interventions:

- The Chinese delegate proposed to change the sentence which was to ensure the media's access to public and governmental information to "media should have access to *available* information", thereby rendering the whole statement absurd and taking away the legitimacy of investigative journalism.

---

[17] Quotes are taken from draft versions of the text which changed day by day and were distributed to participants on paper.

- China and Russia proposed the notion "its TV and its radio" to highlight the connection between governments and broadcast media, particularly the leading and controlling role of the former. Ludwig interpreted this as "panic regarding the possible opening of government-controlled national media towards foreign media" (Interview WL).

- Repeatedly, governments tried to insert the word "technical" as a prefix to "media" in an attempt to exclude consideration of (potentially critical and oppositional) content from the media-related WSIS outcomes.

- Constructive proposals were limited to redundant demands, such as: "Encourage the media – print and broadcast as well as new media – to continue to play an important role in the information society".

The only sections that were not contested encompassed claims that "traditional media have a vital role in the information society" and that media are "central/crucial to any conception of the information society".

The chair of the working group embarked on a variety of attempts to make progress. Contentious references in the paragraph were deleted in the interest of achieving compromise, informal consultations with different delegates took place, and Modoux confronted delegates with the regional WSIS declarations as well as other documents agreed by states unanimously, which recognised 'free, independent and pluralistic media' as well as 'community media'. Yet, "while some representatives were more conciliatory, others stood by previous positions" (Naughton 2003). The solution which finally was achieved was due primarily to Modoux' and the Swiss delegation's tenacity and persistence, and to a few helpers from the diplomatic strategic toolbox – such as holding a very rapid decision-making session one early morning when the Chinese delegate arrived late and when therefore a number of contentious issues could be 'agreed'. Ludwig observed:

"We only succeeded in saving a few sentences of the media section because of the chair of the working group. He consistently highlighted civil society input and never gave in to the blockade by some countries. It could have come much worse. The 'faction of concrete' wanted to prevent the whole media paragraph" (Interview WL, translation by the author).

The reference to community media, though, was deleted. The delegate from El Salvador vetoed it and was unwilling to compromise. The German delegate broke the deadlock by proposing to transfer the reference from the draft

Declaration to the draft Action Plan. This was agreed, yet community media were again moved within the Action Plan, from the section on media to the section on cultural diversity, and were thus thoroughly hidden.

Declaration and Action Plan: The media articles

The final Art. 55 of the Declaration of Principles (WSIS 2003a)[18] on media issues reads as follows:

"55. We reaffirm our commitment to the principles of freedom of the press and freedom of information, as well as those of the independence, pluralism and diversity of media, which are essential to the Information Society. Freedom to seek, receive, impart and use information for the creation, accumulation and dissemination of knowledge are important to the Information Society. We call for the responsible use and treatment of information by the media in accordance with the highest ethical and professional standards. Traditional media in all their forms have an important role in the Information Society and ICTs should play a supportive role in this regard. Diversity of media ownership should be encouraged, in conformity with national law, and taking into account relevant international conventions. We reaffirm the necessity of reducing international imbalances affecting the media, particularly as regards infrastructure, technical resources and the development of human skills."

The paragraph includes the contentious issues of freedom of expression, freedom of the press, media pluralism and media ownership concentration, but it remains largely descriptive and does not propose concrete regulatory measures. Explicit reference to Art. 19 UDH was transferred to the beginning of the Declaration. Media-critical perspectives are included with a call for "responsible use and treatment of information by the media", and they are somewhat reconciled with journalist perspectives by referring to "professional standards". The "international imbalances" in the media environment, as highlighted specifically by Cuba, are reconciled with the diametrically opposed US view, as such "imbalances" refer not to the political issue of unequal information flows between North and South but to "infrastructure, technical resources and the development of human skills".

The article on the regulation of the radio frequency spectrum (Art. 45) notes that "spectrum should be managed in the public interest", which was one of the CMWG objectives, yet it adds that this should be done "in accordance with principle of legality, with full observance of national laws" which serves to shut out many CS Media (see above). Balancing the focus on "na-

---

18 The following quotes are taken from this document.

tional laws" – and thus slightly weakening its effects – the final version adds "relevant international agreements".

Art. 24 of the Plan of Action (WSIS 2003b)[19] includes the following points:

"24. The media—in their various forms and with a diversity of ownership—as an actor, have an essential role in the development of the Information Society and are recognized as an important contributor to freedom of expression and plurality of information.

a) Encourage the media—print and broadcast as well as new media—to continue to play an important role in the Information Society.

b) Encourage the development of domestic legislation that guarantees the independence and plurality of the media.

c) Take appropriate measures—consistent with freedom of expression—to combat illegal and harmful content in media content.

d) Encourage media professionals in developed countries to establish partnerships and networks with the media in developing ones, especially in the field of training.

e) Promote balanced and diverse portrayals of women and men by the media.

f) Reduce international imbalances affecting the media, particularly as regards infrastructure, technical resources and the development of human skills, taking full advantage of ICT tools in this regard.

g) Encourage traditional media to bridge the knowledge divide and to facilitate the flow of cultural content, particularly in rural areas."

The Swiss delegation and the Media Caucus succeeded to include reference to media "as an actor" rather than as a technical transmission channel, to highlight the diversity of media forms and the necessity of diverse ownership structures, a call for legislation to preserve media independence and media pluralism, and North-South relationships amongst media. A new inclusion which CS Media would regard as progressive is the promotion of gender-sensitivity in the media. However, none of these points are developed beyond the realm of vague calls. There is no specific regulatory proposal, let alone a binding agreement, on how to advance media pluralism, freedom of expression, and how to challenge media ownership concentra-

[19] The following quotes are taken from this document.

tion. Most of the 'action points' start with the words 'encourage' and 'promote'. Without any specific obligations for governments or other actors, without new ideas and innovations, and without even references to other international agreements, the document remains in the realm of pure rhetoric. One of two action points which do *not* begin with either 'encourage' or 'promote' and therefore have slightly more authority may actually threaten media, and CS Media in particular: "illegal and harmful content" is to be combated, with the qualification that measures have to be "consistent with freedom of expression", but without any hint of what is "illegal" and "harmful" and what are "appropriate" measures. Such questions are left entirely to the interpretation of national governments, many of which made very clear during the WSIS negotiations that they are hostile towards any critical and dissident content and that they generally prioritise national sovereignty and governmental integrity to freedom of expression.

Community media was transferred to Art. 23 in the section on "Cultural diversity and identity, linguistic diversity and local content":

"j) Give support to media based in local communities and support projects combining the use of traditional media and new technologies for their role in facilitating the use of local languages, for documenting and preserving local heritage, including landscape and biological diversity, and as a means to reach rural and isolated and nomadic communities."

The fact that this reference survived the difficult negotiation processes, both in the media working group and in the wider WSIS plenary, can be celebrated as a success by CS Media. However, the article is vague, does not propose specific support measures, refers only to "media based in local communities" and not to other CS Media, marginalises those media by giving them specific confined tasks and limited areas of operation ("rural and isolated ... communities"), and it was moved out of the original 'media' section and parked in a fairly hidden place, at the end of the cultural diversity section.

Declaration and Action Plan: Related topics

The WSIS Declaration features a number of basic principles which offer a perspective on information society not unsimilar to that favoured by CS Media (WSIS 2003a)[20]. Art.1 calls for the establishment of "a people-centred, inclusive and development-oriented Information Society, where everyone can create, access, utilize and share information and knowledge". Art. 3 reaffirms "the universality, indivisibility, interdependence and interre-

---

[20] The following quotes are taken from this document.

lation of all human rights and fundamental freedoms", and Art. 4 gives special attention to the right to freedom of expression and freedom of opinion according to Art. 19 UDHR, which it proposes "as an essential foundation of the Information Society". Even though there is no explicit reference to communication rights, communication is highlighted as "a fundamental social process, a basic human need and the foundation of all social organization".

Art. 14 and 15 emphasize the need to empower the poor, "particularly those living in remote, rural and marginalized urban areas", who should have the possibility to "use ICTs as a tool to support their efforts to lift themselves out of poverty". Particular attention "must be given to the special situation of indigenous peoples, as well as to the preservation of their heritage and their cultural legacy". Art. 24 reiterates that the "ability for all to access and contribute information, ideas and knowledge is essential in an inclusive Information Society" – and thus highlights one of the priorities of participation-oriented CS Media. Art. 26 calls for a "rich public domain" and strengthens "community-based access points". Art. 32 stresses the important role of content creators, publishers and producers. Art. 52 and 53 seek to "stimulate respect for cultural identity, cultural and linguistic diversity", accord "high priority" to the "creation, dissemination and preservation of content in diverse languages and formats" and emphasize the importance of "local content suited to domestic or regional needs".

The overall focus on new ICTs and on business-friendly regulatory frameworks, however, provide serious difficulties to CS Media which are usually non-profit actors and which often use traditional media platforms. The section on security adds further problems, as the proponents of a strong security article, particularly Russia, managed to retain the language established at the Bucharest conference. Art. 35 calls for "strengthening the trust framework, including information security and network security" and notes that a "global culture of cyber-security needs to be promoted", while Art. 36 stresses the need to "prevent the potential use of ICTs for purposes that are inconsistent with the objectives of maintaining international stability and security" and to "prevent the use of information resources and technologies for criminal and terrorist purposes". The wide definition of negative uses, and the inclusion of the concept of "information security" allow governments considerable freedom to interfere with media and with information exchange.

The Plan of Action, even more than the Declaration, outlines a policy environment which is not conducive to CS Media and which focuses on the needs of states and business (WSIS 2003b)[21]. It calls for "an enabling and competitive environment for the necessary investment in ICT infrastructure and for the development of new services" (Art. 9a), for a "pro-competitive (…) policy, legal and regulatory framework, which provides the appropriate incentives to investment" (Art. 13a), seeks to "foster entrepreneurship" (Art. 13l), and to "prevent, detect and respond to cyber-crime and misuse of ICTs" (Art. 12). Yet, between the building blocks of this mainstream perspective, there are other proposals which support the role of community-oriented, participatory and civil society-based actors. Community access points are highlighted in several articles as prime strategies for enhancing the access of marginalized communities to the Internet, TV and radio. Art. 10d demands that Governments establish such facilities, "providing affordable or free-of-charge access for their citizens to the various communication resources". Art. 11h adds an active component, by committing to "[e]mpower local communities, especially those in rural and underserved areas, in ICT use and promote the production of useful and socially meaningful content for the benefit of all." Art. 23 in the section on cultural diversity demands to

"d) Develop and implement policies that preserve, affirm, respect and promote diversity of cultural expression and indigenous knowledge and traditions through the creation of varied information content"

"i) Nurture the local capacity for the creation and distribution of software in local languages, as well as content that is relevant to different segments of population, including (…) disadvantaged and vulnerable groups"

"k) Enhance the capacity of indigenous peoples to develop content in their own languages"

CS Media seem fit to be included in some of those policies and capacity programmes. Public domain information is to be promoted by developing appropriate policy guidelines (Art. 10a), and the active role of civil society "in creating an equitable Information Society, and in implementing ICT-related initiatives for development" is acknowledged (Art. 3c). Equitable access to the radio-frequency spectrum is demanded in Art. 13r, but this refers only to access by "countries", not by different media actors.

The civil society declaration

The civil society declaration "Shaping Information Societies for Human Needs" was based on a compilation of different inputs by the various cau-

---

21 The following quotes are taken from this document.

cuses and working groups. The first half of the section on media (section 2.3.2.) was drafted by the Media Caucus and contains some of the language developed by the caucus for government lobbying (Civil Society Plenary 2003c).[22] It

- emphasizes the importance of the media, including traditional radio and TV, in the information society
- identifies the role of the media as "producing, gathering and distributing diverse content", thus focusing on the 'provider' approach of the mainstream media, yet it softens this line by adding the necessity that "all citizens are included and can actively participate"
- highlights "Freedom of Expression and Freedom of the Media" as well as Art. 19 UDHR as fundamental principles of the information society
- seeks to limit the possible negative effects of security measures by noting that these "should not be allowed to compromise freedom of expression and media freedom"
- highlights media pluralism and diversity which "should be guaranteed through appropriate laws to avoid excessive media concentration"
- calls for the protection of the editorial independence of media creators and of the rights of online media workers
- reiterates the journalist concern that "the formulation of professional and ethical standards in journalism and other media production must be the responsibility of media workers themselves"
- highlights the specific role of public service broadcasting

The second half was drafted by the CMWG. It

- identifies the specific role of community media "in enabling access to and participation for all in information and communication societies, especially the poorest and most marginalized communities" and in "ensuring vulnerable groups access to information and communication"

---

[22] The following quotes are taken from this document.

- mentions the particular "capacities for dialogue" by community media
- demands "equitable allocation of frequencies", sufficient spectrum capacity for community media, and "the opening up of broadcast licenses to allow for the operation of community broadcasting where this is not currently permitted"
- outlines the proposal of a Community Media Fund

The separation of the media section into two parts recognises, on the one hand, the participation of the (multi-stakeholder) Media Caucus in the civil society spaces at WSIS, but it highlights, on the other hand, the specific focus which many of the organisations and individuals active in civil society assign to community media. The Media Caucus was not given the sole right to represent 'media actors' at WSIS, and CMWG concerns were given due space. However, the section includes several issues – such as the characterisation of media as 'information providers' and the ethical independence of journalists from public considerations – which bring across a mainstream media perspective and which would be criticised by civil society actors at venues such as the World Social Forum. The sentence on media concentration is very weak, regarding only "excessive" media concentration as a problem, and thus reflects the concerns of commercial media representatives. The Community Media section complements this mainstream media perspective but does not limit it. Its brief mentioning of "dialogue" is vague, it does not elaborate on the participatory aspects of CS Media, and it generally fails to bring across the perspectives of other civil society-based media, apart from community media.

Media criticism is instead exposed in section 2.1.9. about conflict situations. This section was partially drafted by individuals involved in WSIS?WeSeize!, and it mirrors the security concerns in the official documents – but from a civil society view. It expresses concern over

"the deployment of 'information warfare' technologies and techniques, including the purposeful jamming, blocking, or destruction of civilian communication systems during conflict situations; the use of 'embedded' journalists coupled with the targeting of non-embedded journalists; the use of media and communication systems to promote hatred and genocide".

It suggests an international convention on information warfare and promotes "media and communications for peace".

The Civil Society Declaration includes a plethora of further issues which are at the heart of CS Media concerns. It promotes free software, rejects the commodification, privatisation and marketisation of information and knowledge, criticises the continuous extension of patent regimes and of intellectual property regulation by WIPO and TRIPS as illegitimate monopolisation of knowledge, and calls for the fundamental review of those regulatory instruments. Information and the means of communication are interpreted as public and global commons, and access to them should be "participatory, universal, inclusive and democratic".

As in the official documents, community telecentres play an important role, but the civil society declaration focuses on the active involvement of the community, on self-organised processes, and on community control. Communities should "create and sustain their own solutions using ICTs", and they "must be empowered to develop their own productive forces and control the means of production within information societies". This fits with the active role which is generally assigned to civil society in the document. Civil society is seen as "key innovators and shapers of the technology" and as "decision-makers in shaping frameworks, policies and governing mechanisms". Whereas the media section refers merely to community media and leaves participatory, autonomous media aside, the document later highlights the need for "new open and self-organised publishing models in science and software production and community-based communications" which would be at the heart of "alternative models for the production and exchange of knowledge and information".

A further issue promoted by the CMWG was taken up in the section on infrastructure (2.4.3.). The latter demands that orbital satellite paths be recognised as a public resource and be allocated to benefit the public interest; spectrum planning and regulation "should ensure equitable access among a plurality of media including sufficient satellite capacity reserved for community media"; and a fixed percentage of satellite capacity and radio frequency spectrum "should be reserved for educational, humanitarian, community and other non-commercial use".

Freedom of expression is highlighted as a key concern and it is explicitly connected with the "free circulation of ideas, pluralism of the sources of information and the media", thus preventing the monopolisation of this right by the mainstream media. The underlying concept of "information and communication societies" refers to 'communication' as a participatory and interactive process, rather than to top-down 'information' provision, and it stresses the active and dynamic role of people in creating these societies – in contrast to the static perspective of the official documents, many of whose articles include statements such as: "The Information Society is …". The declaration is framed in a perspective of global justice which is concerned about "the tensions resulting from (…) global economic liberalisation, cultural globalisation, increased militarism, rising fundamentalisms, racism and the suspension and violation of basic human rights", and it calls for "a more equitable distribution of resources".

While the declaration highlights the achievements of civil society, it recognises that there is a role for states and governments and for national and international policy. Repeatedly referring to development and to the role of ICTs in this process, it retains strong connections with an 'ICT for development' approach favoured by larger NGOs and displays important differences to the approach taken by groups involved in WSIS?WeSeize!.

8.2 The Tunis phase

After the first WSIS phase had chosen a wide and all-encompassing approach, WSIS2 focused on the thematic areas of Internet governance and finance and was largely influenced by the two working groups which were to review the current state of debate in each of these issue areas and to propose ways of resolving challenges: the Working Group on Internet Governance (WGIG) and the Task Force on Financing Mechanisms (TFFM). The narrower focus of the second WSIS phase did not help to increase the role of media actors. Neither WGIG nor TFFM listed members of the Media Caucus or the CMWG as participants.

However both groups continued their attempts to influence the debate. While the Media Caucus tried to defend freedom of expression in the discussion on Internet governance, the CMWG continued to advocate its financing proposals. The development focus of the finance debate offered a close link with the development frame used by the CMWG. It allowed CS Media actors to step out of the shadow of larger mainstream media by establishing a separate area of expertise and to thereby move beyond the fragile consensus position with commercial and public service media, which they had attempted to maintain during phase 1.

The Task Force on Financing Mechanisms

The WSIS Plan of Action had requested the Secretary General of the United Nations to create a task force to study the issue of financial mechanisms and to present a report to facilitate the discussions on the subject:

"While all existing financial mechanisms should be fully exploited, a thorough review of their adequacy in meeting the challenges of ICT for development should be completed by the end of December 2004. (...) Based on the conclusion of the review, improvements and innovations of financing mechanisms will be considered including the effectiveness, the feasibility and the creation of a voluntary Digital Solidarity Fund, as mentioned in the Declaration of Principles." (WSIS 2003b: Art. 27 D2f).

The UNDP, as the convenor of the task force, invited only one civil society actor for TFFM discussions: the Association for Progressive Communication (APC). Even though the APC was not a member of any of the CS Media organising spaces at or around WSIS, it was closely aligned with the CMWG through collaborations in the CRIS campaign, it was also interested in, and acting in solidarity with, WSIS?WeSeize!, and many of its members are genuine CS Media actors, following the criteria outlined in chapter 2. Furthermore, the UNDP commissioned a report on "Innovative Technologies and Community Ownership: A new Model of ICT Access for the Rural Poor" by CRIS members Seán Ó Siochrú and Bruce Girard, to serve as input into the TFFM deliberations. Both authors had long experiences in working with CS Media, and Girard was an occasional participant in the CMWG. The TFFM published its 125-pages report in January 2005.

Civil Society approaches to financing

As we have seen in chapter 6, the CMWG submitted a range of policy proposals which focused on, or touched upon, the issue of financing. It proposed the Community Media Fund, demanded that the radio frequency spectrum and the orbital paths should be recognised as public resources and that community media should have access to such resources. Earlier, AMARC had suggested to re-invest revenues raised by governments from sale of spectrum and telecommunications licensing for community media and community access. The CMWG focused on traditional media, such as radio and telephone, as the most accessible, most widespread, and least expensive media platforms, and it envisioned a governance framework which was based on common, non-commercial infrastructure and global public goods.

The concept of *global public goods* was raised, particularly, by the Uruguay-based Third World Institute (an APC member) which issued several research and briefing papers and made the public goods approach a central frame of reference within civil society. A public good is a good which can be enjoyed by all without depletion, and its value may actually rise the more extensively it is used and shared. Traditional economic laws of scarcity thus do not apply (Verzola 2004). Communication constitutes such a 'good': Since there is an overall gain by adding users, a market model of provision, which leaves out those who cannot afford it, is not the model which leads to the best possible results (Ó Siochrú 2005). The public goods approach does not come with a clear instruction regarding the financial sources for its funding, but it implies a large role for the public sector. Accuosto/Johnson (2004) specifically point to international taxation and to user fees as possible funding mechanisms. Generally, the model challenges the dominant market-led approach.

International taxation has increasingly appeared in finance debates, pushed by the Attac network and its advocacy of the Tobin Tax, and has also been taken up by UN reports and by policy debates amongst heads of state. Proposals for global taxes include taxes on international financial transactions, on carbon dioxide, on arms sales, and on the use of the global commons, such as orbital space or the sea. International reports such as the MacBride report, the Maitland Commission report "The Missing Link" and the UNESCO report "Our Cultural Diversity" have featured calls for taxes on the use of electromagnetic spectrum, orbital space, computer traffic and equipment, in order to promote the creation of local content and to support community media. Further taxes have been proposed on email traffic and on commercial Internet names (Peyer 2005b).

The *Open Access* approach offers an important aspect for a public goods strategy in the communication sphere. It is based on a separation of backbone infrastructure from service supplier, thus of a general infrastructure framework with strong public good characteristics (the backbone) from individual service provision. The backbone would either be owned or strictly regulated by a public authority, with the goal to provide access for a variety of 'last-mile' solutions by different service providers (Ó Siochrú 2005). In a market environment, open access systems would typically channel information and communication to a certain region or locality where they are picked up and transmitted to individual users by commercial service providers. However, this latter part can also be implemented by *community-controlled non-profit networks*. Cooperatives and community networks have been established in many parts of the world and often match their commercial competitors (Ó Siochrú/Girard 2005). Beyond the realm of Internet connection, combinations of an open access 'backbone' and a community network exist in, for example, radio broadcasting.

TFFM recommendations on infrastructure

In his analysis, Ó Siochrú (2005) divided the report into a "majority" and a "minority" report. The majority report maintains that "investment financing should continue to come predominantly from the private sector" (TFFM 2004: 30), while public sector investments may be justifiable only for providing access to remote areas or in "emergency situations" (ibid.), thus as a temporary exception to the rule, and only "where and when these will be a catalyst for further private investment and growth" (ibid.). The minority report – a collection of antagonistic views scattered throughout the text – puts forward a market-sceptical perspective which is shared by Task Force participants from civil society and from some developing countries but is limited to specific cases and exceptional circumstances and not allowed to fundamentally challenge the dominant approach.

Public goods, open access and community ownership are all mentioned. The report notes that "many governments do retain a more central role in implementation of telecom and ICT projects, and there are cases where this model continues to function at least as successfully as other approaches (e.g., Uruguay, Costa Rica)" (TFFM 2004: 50). Open access models are highlighted as the report acknowledges the lack of private investment interest in backbones. Yet financing mechanisms for these which go beyond the market rationale are missing. A public service approach only comes into the picture as "addition" (idem: 63) to private sector investment and is interpreted solely within the framework of a competitive environment, with the main role of "stimulating" (ibid.) private investment. Even in areas of market failure, the TFFM looks for "competitively neutral solutions for open market environments" (idem: 54) and presents private sector investment as the "most promising trend" (idem: 69)

Drawing from Ó Siochrú's/Girard's input, the report highlights community ownership and control as a promising complementary approach for building the network's 'first-mile' to poor rural communities which current market incentives and traditional investment sources fail to serve. Cooperatives are mentioned as viable alternatives to for-profit services, and it is even acknowledged that they "can provide better services at lower cost" (idem: 78). Yet the report fails to offer a coherent proposal of how the public good "backbone" and community ownership of the first/last mile could be connected towards a non-commercial alternative provision system. Instead, it recommends an "integrated strategy" of community/public and market-based mechanisms (idem: 77) in which the market plays the lead role.

CS Media in the TFFM report

Initiated as part of the "digital" solidarity agenda of WSIS, the TFFM focused on ICT infrastructure and Internet connectivity. Traditional media were not its main object of interest. Furthermore, the market focus of the report represents a difficult framework for CS Media. Their fundamental characteristics as non-commercial actors require funding opportunities beyond pure private sector investment. The "majority report" of the TFFM thus reduces the space for CS Media significantly. Their existence is neglected in the document. For example, the report calls for the opening of broadcast licenses to commercial operators, but it fails to mention non-profit operators. The spread of community access points, telecentres, etc is acknowledged in the report, but these organisations and projects are conceived almost exclusively as businesses and for-profit operations (TFFM 2004: 48). Community activists and entrepreneurs are lumped into the same category, and both are recycled in the framework of marketisation in which community activities come to "demonstrate the unyielding push of market forces" (idem: 63).

Despite a general focus on Internet connectivity, the section on backbone infrastructure explicitly addresses the wider media environment. The "key backbone communications networks" (idem: 68) mentioned here include radio and television broadcasting stations, and the report even highlights community-based radio stations. Yet the specific role of community and other CS Media is hardly understood. Even though the TFFM notes that it is essential to put the means to communicate and to share information in the hands of individuals and communities, in order to allow "non-hierarchical knowledge diffusion" (idem: 62), it does not offer any strategy to achieve this aim other than the market.

A discursive approach towards a rationale for CS Media is strongest in the chapter on content. The report notes that "information resources are only valuable if they can reach the communities most in need, and can engage people in a manner that connects with their daily lives and individual aspirations" (idem: 78). No longer the exclusive property of privileged gatekeepers, information is to be "the currency and lifeblood of the masses everywhere" (idem: 78). The report recognises that reality is still nowhere near this ideal, as the centres of content production are based overwhelmingly in the Global North and as major content providers, such as Hollywood television and film studios, dominate the production and distribution of international programming. The challenge is to have larger parts of the world population participate in the production and distribution of information and knowledge. The TFFM even links this objective with explicit criticism of commercial mainstream media:

"What is most missing from the limitless worldwide knowledge base is an adequate representation of the vast diversity and richness of knowledge, ideas, experience, and imagination that thrive throughout the developing world, but rarely find their way into the consciousness of the commercially driven, mass media markets" (idem: 79).

The logical consequence one could expect from this analysis would be a call for a reform of mainstream media systems and for the support of CS Media. The TFFM, however, draws different conclusions. Deeply rooted in the idea that only the market can provide reasonable solutions, the key question of the TFFM "is to what extent there is, or can be, a market for information resources that are relevant to, and produced by and for, the populations of developing countries" (idem: 80). What needs to be done, according to the TFFM, is to create "functioning, sustainable business relationships at all levels of the information value chain" (ibid.). The problem is described purely in economic terms, as the low levels of access to media in the developing world "minimize the potential audience (customers) for commercial content, discouraging establishment of domestic production businesses" (ibid.). Non-commercial content only enters the report through the backdoor of development agencies. The latter's development-related information is deemed valuable, but while the report notes that there is very little potential market for this content, it does not offer a perspective on alternative, non-market approaches to its distribution.

Generally, the TFFM did not illustrate an understanding of both the role and the financial needs of civil society initiatives, and it did not provide any concept for their sustained provision with financial resources. In a report which interpreted all financial concepts within the ultimate framework of private sector investment and competition, there was no space for concepts and initiatives which are non-commercial by definition. A model of civil society-based development was neither developed nor recognised. Equally, the TFFM failed to study local technological requirements that include traditional media, as well as appropriate combination models of 'new' and 'old' media.

The Working Group on Internet Governance

In contrast to the TFFM, the WGIG included a larger number of civil society actors who participated "on an equal footing" (WGIG 2005: 2) with government and business actors. There were no participants from either CMWG or WSIS?WeSeize!, nor any explicit CS Media representatives. Yet the group of civil society participants included representatives from APC and the Information Network for the Third Sector, whose constituencies include CS Media and who were likely to advance CS Media objectives inside the working group.

Civil Society approaches to Internet governance

Neither the CMWG, nor WSIS?WeSeize! put forward any explicit demands for the WGIG outcomes. Given their lists of thematic priorities and policy proposals (see chapter 7), both groups would be likely to agree on the centrality of a) the global commons and a public sphere un-compromised by commercial and state interests, and b) freedom of expression. Their different frames and issue focuses would, however, lead to different perspectives with regards to changing or maintaining current governance mechanisms as well as to different thematic priorities. While the CMWG, with its development focus and North-South connections, may be more open to change in the Internet governance system towards an increased participation from the Global South, the WSIS?WeSeize! participants, being influenced by cyber-libertarian values and openness, would favour the status quo as it promised the highest level of liberty, while criticising any interference by governments and business in Internet processes. They would agree with the perspective of the academic think tank 'Internet Governance Project' on Internet policies as "a decentralized network of networks" (WSIS Executive Secretariat 2005: 32), emerging through "collective action by distributed, private actors" (ibid.), and with the view of the Japanese Center for Global Communications (Glocom) that "bottom-up, distributed open mechanisms have so far functioned well" (idem: 33), as well as with Glocom's concerns regarding "excessive regulation and constraints that might hinder the sound and dynamic development of the Internet" (ibid.).

The only member from the civil society working groups on media who commented extensively on WGIG contents and procedures was the World Press Freedom Committee (WPFC). It followed up its neo-liberal interpretation of freedom of expression, noting that "internationalization of Internet governance would provide opportunities for authoritarian governments that have already found effective ways to institute Internet censorship internally" (idem: 6) and objecting even to global standards for privacy and data protection rights as these would provide "endless opportunities for governmentally inspired mischief, restrictions and controls" (idem: 18). Arguing for the status quo of a special role of the US government in Internet oversight, it praised the practices of that government as "lighthanded, benign and non-interventionist" (idem: 6). The prescription went: "If it ain't broke, don't fix it" (ibid.).

A more elaborate perspective on state interventions, criticising 'democratic' as well as 'authoritarian' governments, reconciling privacy with freedom of expression, and thereby aligning with concerns discussed at WSIS?WeSeize!, was brought up by the WSIS Civil Society Privacy and Security Working Group. In its reaction to the WGIG report, it criticised, for example, "efforts underway in several UN member states for mandatory retention of Internet traffic data, regardless of any offences or criminal investigations" (idem: 25). And it exclaimed: "The Internet can only stay an open and public infrastructure if all individuals can use it freely, without having to fear constant observation and monitoring" (ibid.).

The WGIG report

The working definition of Internet governance – which marks the beginning of the WGIG final report – "reinforces the concept of inclusiveness of Governments, the private sector and civil society" (WGIG 2005: 3) by including all these actors in "the development and application" on Internet policy. It thus puts a far stronger emphasis on civil society participation than the TFFM. The "roles and responsibilities of civil society" (idem: 8), as laid out in the report, start with the usual 'soft roles' which may point to a neo-liberal understanding of civil society (see chapter 2.2), such as "[a]wareness-raising and capacity-building" and "[m]obilizing citizens in democratic processes" (ibid.). However, the list also includes "[r]esearch and development of technologies and standards" and "[b]ringing perspectives of marginalized groups, including (…) grassroots activists" (ibid.). By pointing to the role of grassroots activists and, particularly, to independent civil society-based development of technologies, the report displays a deeper and broader understanding of civil society than other WSIS documents and moves beyond a focus on civil society activities as support for state policies. Still, as the WSIS CS Internet Governance Caucus noted, it "could have given greater attention to the contributions of individual users, sometimes referred to as "netizens", to the development of the Internet" (WSIS Executive Secretariat 2005: 33).

The four main public policy issues which the report identifies suggest a significant influence of government and business interests as they highlight security issues and cyber-crime, on the one hand, and IPR, on the other (WGIG 2005: 4). Regarding cyber-crime, the WGIG calls for the closure of legal loopholes while failing to provide a clear definition of what is cyber-crime – and it is thereby in strong conflict with media activists (such as those who gathered at WSIS?WeSeize!) who have experienced the criminalisation of dissident civil society projects and who are eager to maintain non-regulated spaces on the Internet. On the other hand, WGIG demands that "all measures taken in relation to the Internet, in particular those on grounds of security or to fight crime, do not lead to violations of human rights principles" (idem: 17). It also expresses its concern over the "[l]ack of existence or inconsistent application of privacy and data-protection rights" (idem: 6).

Regarding IPR, the report remains comparably open. It states that "there are different views on the precise nature of the balance (…) between the rights of holders and the rights of users" (ibid.) and on "whether the current IPR system is adequate to address the new issues posed by cyberspace" (ibid.). Considering the strong pressure throughout the WSIS process by the information industry, such open formulations suggest heavy criticism of strict

IPR regimes within the WGIG. The report, furthermore, highlights the group's concern about "market oligopolies, the impediments to access and use of digital content and the perceived unbalanced nature of current IPR rules" (ibid.).

With regards to development issues, WGIG criticises the uneven distribution of interconnection costs (idem: 4), and it calls for "donor programmes and other developmental financing mechanisms to take note of the need to provide funding for initiatives that advance connectivity, Internet exchange points (IXPs) and local content for developing countries" (idem: 16). Here, as in the rest of the WSIS process, 'local content' may be a back-door for including CS Media projects, especially community media as defined by the CMWG. In particular detail, the report highlights the difficulties of participation in governance mechanisms for actors from the South and from civil society (idem: 5) and notes that the existing mechanisms of Internet governance "do not sufficiently take into account geographic balance and linguistic diversity" (idem: 9) which makes it difficult "for developing countries to have their voices heard" (ibid.). The report therefore states as one of the "main aims of WGIG" to "foster full participation in Internet governance arrangements by developing countries" (ibid.).

WGIG was created in response to government ambitions for an enhanced role in governance mechanisms, and so all of the models which WGIG proposes for future Internet governance imply a potential increase in government influence. Even the 'lightweight' model of adding a discussion forum to existing governance structures (which was lster adopted by agreeing on the establishment of the Internet Governance Forum) offers an increased policy role for governments and departs from the cyber-libertarian agenda with which many WSIS?WeSeize! participants sympathised. According to WGIG, the forum "should support the information and communication technologies for development (ICT4D) agenda" (idem: 10) which suits the CMWG frame much more than the WSIS?WeSeize! priorities.

Focusing on governance structures, rather than on actors, providers and services, the report does not explicitly refer to community, alternative, activist or citizens' media. The only clear statement on content is the very last sentence of the report: "Governments, the private sector and civil society are encouraged to promote and create more content in local languages to be posted on the Internet" (idem: 18). Yet here, again, the recognition of civil society as content producers and the specific reference to "local languages" may serve as a vindication of CS Media projects.

The Tunis negotiations

The WSIS process in phase 2 focused closely on the issue areas and specific suggestions proposed by the TFFM and WGIG. The debate on financing mechanisms started from the TFFM's 'majority report' with its emphasis on private investment and market solutions. However this perspective was soon challenged by governments from the Global South who pointed to the role of state programmes and, implicitly or explicitly, opened spaces for CS Media concerns. Argentina, Brazil and Algeria stated that "the issue of financing for various forms of content and applications requires new attention" (Chair of the WSIS PrepCom-2 Sub-Committee 2005a: 4), the South African delegation proposed "Community based and co-operative programmes and projects" (idem: 9) as priorities for funding, and the Argentinian delegation called for financial support for, amongst others, "community radio broadcasts" (idem: 13). Burkina Faso suggested a new article on "Supporting the local production of content" (Chair of the WSIS PrepCom-2 Sub-Committee 2005b: 7), Switzerland on "Promoting the use of traditional and new media in order to foster universal access to information, culture and digital knowledge for all people, especially vulnerable populations and populations in developing countries" (Swiss delegation 2005), and Cuba sought to "safeguard the use of the radio frequency spectrum in the public interest" (Chair of the WSIS PrepCom-2 Sub-Committee 2005b: 14). A civil society coalition of the organisations and networks CRIS, APC, ITeM, Bread for All, Digital Divide Data and IT for Change consistently advocated the promotion of "community-owned and –driven networks" and of "public investments for (…) local and relevant content" (e.g., Art. 6d and 6e bis).

Support for a particular CMWG proposal such as the Community Media Fund was impossible to attain from government delegations. Furthermore, the determination of many influential delegations to strictly limit the number of topics to be negotiated meant that issues deemed as peripheral and not representing vital interests of major delegations did not have much chance to enter the documents and remain there until the summit – and CS Media was definitely such an 'issue'. However, a few of the additions proposed by governments survived all deletions and made it through to the final documents (see below).

As in the first WSIS phase, Switzerland, with support from Norway and the US, made particular efforts to strengthen freedom of expression and the role of the media. Predictably, such initiatives met objections by countries such as China and Saudi Arabia. Cuba elaborated that "the exercise of the right to freedom of opinion and expression carries with it special duties and responsibilities, and it may therefore be subject to certain restrictions provided by law for respect of the rights or reputations of others and for the protection of national security or of public order, or of public health or morals" (idem: 3). The delegation thus highlighted the need for "countering propaganda which are designed or likely to provoke or encourage any threat to the peace (…) or act of aggression", a "call for responsible use and treatment of information by the media", "regulations to impede undue concentration of ownership of the media in the private sector", the need for "a new, more just and more effective world information and communication order", the declaration of "knowledge as a common heritage of humankind", and the removal of "any obstacle limiting the access of everyone and every nation to knowledge and to the enjoyment of the benefits of scientific progress" (idem: 7).

The Cuban input was significant as it represented one of the rare occasions in the WSIS process for discussing the inadequacies of the media system. Some of the Cuban statements would have resonated strongly with CS Media actors, yet, as during the first phase, the Cuban government's restrictive position on freedom of expression and on autonomous civil society-based activities, both in the WSIS negotiations and in Cuba itself, excluded it from the list of allies. Having experienced the repressive attitudes of many government delegations in the first WSIS phase, and approaching a summit in a particularly authoritarian state, the CMWG was firmly on the side of mainstream media and conservative press freedom organisations in prioritising freedom of expression and press freedom over other concerns (such as media ownership concentration and inadequate mainstream media content).

The newly emerging conflict over media and press freedom issues transformed into a deadlock which let neither side strengthen its position substantially. Shortly before the summit started, a last-minute compromise emphasised freedom of expression without the 'restrictions' favoured by Cuba but dropped some of the more substantive Swiss proposals, such as reference to editorially independent media.

The Tunis Commitment

The only explicit reference to 'media' in the final Tunis Commitment is in Art. 9 which lists the priority themes of the Geneva Declaration (WSIS 2005a)[23] and reaffirms the governments' resolution to "recognize the role of the media". The difficult compromise on the freedom of expression debate is laid out in Art. 4 (in connection with Art. 2 and 3) which circumvents the mined territory of divergent perspectives on the topic by simply pointing to the agreed text of the Geneva Declaration. It reaffirms the latter's paragraphs 4 (on freedom of expression), 5 (on Article 29 UDHR and the duties

---

[23] The following quotes are taken from this document.

of everyone to the community), and 55 (on the media). In addition, it highlights freedom of expression and "the free flow of information, ideas, and knowledge" as "essential for the Information Society and beneficial to development". Art. 3 reaffirms "the universality, indivisibility, interdependence and interrelation of all human rights and fundamental freedoms", yet highlighting in particular the right to development and thereby attempting to strike a balance with the right to freedom of expression. Art. 2 offers supportive language for media, and specifically CS Media, reaffirming "our desire and commitment to build a people-centred, inclusive and development-oriented Information Society (…), so that people everywhere can create, access, utilize and share information and knowledge".

References to the types of content provided by CS Media appear in several articles. Art. 14 notes that "in addition to building ICT infrastructure, there should be adequate emphasis on developing human capacity and creating ICT applications and digital content in local language". Art. 26 recognises "the importance of creative content and applications to overcome the digital divide", and Art. 20 adds the necessity to "pay particular attention to the special needs of marginalized and vulnerable groups of society including migrants, internally displaced persons and refugees, unemployed and underprivileged people, minorities and nomadic people". As the Geneva Declaration and the WGIG report, the Tunis Commitment explicitly highlights the need to "prevent the abuse of information resources and technologies for criminal and terrorist purposes" (Art. 15). On a more positive note, it stresses the importance of "open or interoperable standards that are affordable and accessible to all, available anywhere and anytime, to anyone and on any device" (Art. 28) as well as "the need to encourage and foster collaborative development, interoperative platforms and free and open-source software" (Art. 29).

The Tunis Agenda for Action

The section of the Tunis Agenda (the 'Action Plan' of the WSIS2 summit) which deals with finance issues (WSIS 2005b)[24] draws a connection between 'old' and 'new' media by calling upon governments to "give appropriate priority to ICTs, including traditional ICTs such as broadcast radio and TV" (Art. 20). Only two months before the summit, the draft text had still included a call for providing financial support to, amongst others, "media broadcast based in local communities" (Art. 37g; Chair of Sub-Committee B 2005), but with the substantial reduction of that paragraph (which became Art. 27 of the final Tunis Agenda), all proposed recipients of

24 The following quotes are taken from this document, if not otherwise stated.

funding were deleted, and so the only explicit reference to community media fell off.

The role of community-based services and local content, though, is recognised. The proposal by Brazil, Algeria and Argentina (as mentioned above) remained in the documents, forming Art. 15:

"We take note of the challenges for expanding the scope of useful accessible information content in the developing world are numerous, in particular, the issue of financing for various forms of content and applications requires new attention, as this area has often been overlooked by the focus on ICT infrastructure."

Although this statement is a far cry from what the CMWG would have liked to see in the documents, it suggests the need for financing mechanisms such as the Community Media Fund, and it may be helpful in further advocacy efforts for such a fund. Art. 26d, furthermore, encourages "the development of locally relevant information, application and services", and Art. 18 (together with several other articles) qualifies the previous focus on private investment by underlining "that market forces alone cannot guarantee the full participation of developing countries".

Art. 23 lists "initiatives based in local communities that deliver ICT services to communities in areas such as education, health and livelihood support" as an area that is "in need of greater financial resources". Art. 27e recommends "to accelerate the development of domestic financial instruments (…) supporting (…) networking initiatives based on local communities". While such references may be reassuring for community-based projects, they appear only at the end of long lists (as in Art. 23) or amongst a variety of other potential recipients and 'innovators' (as in Art. 27), which raises doubts on the actual effects of the summit outcomes for these projects.

Articles in the section on Internet governance add references on local content development and local services. Art. 53 calls for increased efforts towards multi-lingualisation of the Internet and asks governments to support "local content development, translation and adaptation, digital archives, and diverse forms of digital and traditional media, and recognize that these activities can also strengthen local and indigenous communities."

The far-reaching definition of civil society in the WGIG report was not transferred into the Tunis Agenda. Rather than presenting civil society as active developer and innovator, the text merely notes that "Civil society has also played an important role on Internet matters, especially at community level, and should continue to play such a role" (Art. 35c). Only in a later section, and only in combination with the private sector, civil society is included in the range of those actors that are "the drivers of innovation and private investment in the development of the Internet" (Art. 54). Meanwhile the text recognises "the valuable contribution by the academic and technical communities (…) to the evolution, functioning and development of the Internet" (Art. 36). As WSIS?WeSeize! has illustrated, the border between 'civil society' and 'technical community' is blurred in a sphere of civil society-based 'new media'/technical activists, and the recognition of the active role of a wider set of actors may add significance to their involvement.

The policy-related articles of the Internet governance section reflect the priorities of those governments favouring a security- and business-oriented agenda. Several articles "underline the importance of cybercrime" (Art. 40), "reaffirm the necessity to further promote, develop and implement (…) a global culture of cybersecurity" (Art. 39), and "underline the importance of countering terrorism in all its forms and manifestations on the Internet" (Art. 44). Neither crime, nor terrorism are more closely defined, and the addition "in all its forms and manifestations" leaves room for a wide and arbitrary inclusion of oppositional activities. However, the text does pick up the WGIG's recommendation that security measures "must protect and respect the provisions for privacy and freedom of expression" (Art. 45).

Art. 85 in the section on "Implementation and Follow-up" further weakens the position of civil society actors by stressing "the leading role of governments in partnership with other stakeholders in implementing the WSIS outcomes". Yet at the same time this section offers references from which CS Media may derive support for their activities. Art. 90 expresses the commitment of governments for, amongst others:

"f) promoting public policies aimed at providing affordable access at all levels, including community-level, to hardware as well as software and connectivity through an increasingly converging technological environment, capacity building and local content."

"l) enhancing the capacity of communities in all regions to develop content in local and/or indigenous languages."

"n) promoting the use of traditional and new media in order to foster universal access to information, culture and knowledge for all people, especially vulnerable populations and populations in developing countries and using, inter alia, radio and television as educational and learning tools."

"o) reaffirming the independence, pluralism and diversity of media"

The civil society statement

The civil society statement "Much more could have been achieved" which was published after the end of the Tunis process provided an evaluation of the successes and the shortcomings of the official WSIS process, looking specifically at the issues most relevant for the civil society groups at WSIS (Civil Society Plenary 2005).[25] Media is, again, amongst those issues. This time, the media section of the document was drafted by key members of the Media Caucus and the CMWG collectively.[26] It expresses satisfaction with the recognition of freedom of expression, Art. 19 UDHR, and the place of the media in information society.

The main criticism regarding the substance of WSIS outcomes includes three points:

(1) It criticises the lack of concrete measures for developing media diversity and for "avoiding a growing concentration and uniformity of content";

(2) it notes that the WSIS documents neglect "Community media, telecenters, grassroots and Civil Society-based media" which "empower people for independent and creative participation in knowledge-building and information-sharing" and "should be an integral part of the public policy implementation of the goals of the Geneva Declaration";

(3) it criticises the market focus of the WSIS documents, highlights the public resource character of information infrastructure, such as airwaves and orbital paths, and adds: "These should be managed in the public interest as publicly owned assets through transparent and accountable regulatory frameworks to enable the equitable allocation of resources and infrastructure among a plurality of media including community media."

Thus the media section focuses strongly on CS Media concerns, criticises the mainstream media and general commercialisation, and refers to a wider set of "grassroots and Civil Society-based media" in addition to community media. The fact that agreement on these points was possible with the mainstream-oriented vice-chair of the Media Caucus was a significant success for the representatives of the CMWG.

---

[25] The following quotes are taken from this document, pp. 11-12.

[26] including Ronald Koven, Steve Buckley and DeeDee Halleck

8.3 Further conferences and outcomes

At the fringes of the official WSIS process, further conferences, meetings and declarations put media issues on the agenda. Many of the topics discussed there – and adopted in common statements – offer useful references for CS Media. Here I will take a brief look at two documents which were adopted in the run-up to the Geneva summit – the Bangkok Declaration and the Bellagio Statement on Media, Freedom and Poverty – and two conferences which were part of the official preparation process for the Tunis summit – the Marrakech conference and the Asian Media Summit.

The Bangkok Declaration

The first *Conference of the Ministers in Information and Broadcasting in Asia and the Pacific region* took place on 27-28 May 2003 in Bangkok and adopted the Bangkok Declaration which was proposed as input to the WSIS process (AIBD 2003).[27] The declaration does not explicitly name CS Media but it includes their perspectives in several of its articles. The preamble states that "[g]lobalization should be a two-way road" in which cultural diversity and a diversity of perspectives should be promoted. Media should "[b]ecome fora for public dialogue, knowledge sharing, promotion of diversity, mutual understanding and tolerance" (Recommendation 1.2). The document takes a clear position against the commodification of cultural and audiovisual works which, unlike ordinary goods, "do not lend themselves to governance by general rules of free exchange for goods and services" (Rec. 2.1). Authorities are encouraged to "support (…) public and private Radio and Television programmes aimed to promote cultural diversity" (Rec. 2.2) and to "[c]reate a fund to encourage broadcasters, artists, and producers, to produce and broadcast programmes with local contents" (ibid.). While the main concern of the ministers is with international asymmetries of media flows and with the dominance of Western/Northern media organisations and media content, calls for, e.g., "fora for public dialogue" (Rec. 1.2) fit to the practices and priorities of CS Media.

The Bellagio Symposium

A self-organised quasi-internal meeting of media professionals and advocates, the Bellagio Symposium which took place in Northern Italy in early October 2003 was not part of the official and semi-official range of WSIS preparation meetings. However, it was born out of a conflict amongst civil society and media actors during the preparation phase for WSIS1 regarding freedom of expression and communication rights. The CRIS campaign,

[27] The following quotes are taken from this document.

including CS Media organisations such as AMARC, had proposed the right to communicate as a wider set of rights including, but not limited to, freedom of expression, while press freedom organisations, usually supported by the mainstream media, had criticised this approach fiercely and had insisted that the right to freedom of expression according Art. 19 UDHR would be the only rights background necessary for the information society. So the organisation Panos invited protagonists from both sides, including AMARC, the WPFC, Article 19, and several other civil society organisations to find an agreement. The outcome of the symposium – the Bellagio Statement on Media, Freedom and Poverty – is a remarkable document as it outlines very clearly the rationale for a wider approach to communication rights and as it reflects a consensus between all participants (Bellagio Symposium 2003).[28] It goes beyond the vague and mainstream-dominated consensus reached in the Media Caucus in several aspects:

(1) In addition to re-asserting freedom of expression as "a fundamental right which underpins all other human rights", it recognises that threats to freedom of expression come not only from political influence but also from "economic control and pressure", so that there exists "censorship by government, commercial and social interests".

(2) Media often fail to paint an accurate picture of society as "[e]conomic and market pressures (…) are tending to deprioritise journalistic investigation and reporting on issues of social and public concern."

(3) People living in poverty "face particular obstacles to achieving freedom of expression and access to the media" which include economic, social, educational, logistical and political challenges. Therefore, "[r]ealisation of freedom of expression for people living in poverty requires: media pluralism and diversity, including diversity of forms of ownership; more equitable access to communication; support for cultural and linguistic diversity; and promotion of participation in democratic decision-making processes."

(4) These obstacles to freedom of expression "need to be overcome in the interests of society as a whole" – whereby the statement counter-acts the marginalisation which CS Media experienced in the Media Caucus.

(5) The document supports self-organised media initiatives, such as "participatory media".

(6) Community media deserve special attention and support, "including through access to licences and spectrum allocation", with frequencies being

---

[28] The following quotes are taken from this document.

allocated "in a balanced way amongst community, commercial and public service media".

(7) While the document reiterates that professional standards should be defined by the journalists themselves, it qualifies this view in that the "journalistic ethic should include sensitivity to issues of poverty".

The Marrakech Action Plan

In contrast to the Bellagio statement, the Marrakech Action Plan was the outcome of an official preparatory conference for WSIS2. As was noted in chapter 6, a large number of such conferences were held in 2004 and 2005, often having little effect on the final Tunis documents but offering interesting common agreements relevant for further work in the respective thematic fields. The thematic conference on "Role and Place of Media in the Information Society in Africa and the Arab States", hosted by the Government of Morocco and Orbicom and taking place 22-24 November 2004 in Marrakech, attracted several core CMWG members, led to the adoption of an Action Plan, and served as a framework for a declaration on community media. These documents, together with the following statement of the Asia Media Summit (see below) were amongst the most promising and supportive statements for CS Media in the whole WSIS process.

The six chapters of the Action Plan (Marrakech Conference 2004)[29] encompass foci on (1) Media freedom, independence and pluralism, (2) the place of traditional and new media, (3) the digital divide, (4) gender issues in the media profession, (5) culture and multilingualism, and (6) Internet governance. Considering the large number of authoritarian governments in the region, the document is based on a surprisingly strong and elaborate human rights perspective, highlighting freedom of expression, Internet freedoms, and the need to free all prisoners of opinion. Repeatedly it emphasizes the necessity to achieve full editorial independence for all media, calls on governments to allow the creation of journalist unions, and demands that "Internet service providers are independent of public authorities and not found legally responsible for the content of the online media they service." Most significantly for CS Media, the Action Plan implements a number of core CMWG objectives – including the following:

- "Permit independent and community media to exist without prior political conditions" (chapter 1);

---

[29] The following quotes are taken from this document.

- "Allow for independent community broadcasting services where these are currently not permitted and ensure their equitable access to spectrum by getting governments to set targets for opening up broadcasting licensing opportunities" (chapter 2);

- "Promote the establishment, by governments, of independent funding mechanisms to support pluralistic media, including community media" (chapter 2).

As part of the conference, a 'Round Table on Community Media and Sustainable Development' took place on 21 November 2003 and adopted a declaration which includes all core points of the CMWG agenda and adds further proposals (Buckley 2004b).[30] It calls for

- "equitable allocation of frequencies through transparent and accountable mechanisms"

- "targets to be established for the opening up of broadcast licensing to allow for the operation of community broadcasting"

- "sufficient spectrum and channel capacity, and appropriate technical standards, for community media to develop in both the analogue and digital environment"

- "inclusion of a community media element in all ICT investment"

- "establishment of a Development Fund for Community Radio in Africa"

- "encouragement of national level funds for community media support"

- "establish a Task Force on Funding and Resourcing Community Media"

The Asia Media Summit

The Asia Media summit, an official WSIS regional-thematic meeting like the Marrakech conference, took place on 9-11 May 2005 in Kuala Lumpur, Malaysia. It was a follow-up of the Bangkok ministerial conference from May 2003 (see above). However, with a more prominent presence of regional broadcasters and broadcasting unions, it brought across primarily the perspective of established media, yet with the declared objective of reconcil-

---

[30] The following quotes are taken from this document.

ing this view with the needs and interests of the wider public (Asia Media Summit 2005).[31]

Its recommendations to WSIS are divided into 10 sections: Media and Globalization – Cultural Diversity – Human Resource Development – Children – Gender – HIV/AIDS – Disasters – Preservation of radio and television archives – WIPO Broadcasters' Treaty – Copyright and Digital Technology. Community media are consistently included in many of these sections and are recognised as an established media force. The summit pledged to "promote non-profit community broadcasting and to ensure that suitable frequencies are allocated for such services" (idem: 5), and picked up the demand that "[r]egulatory bodies be encouraged to provide equitable allocation of broadcasting frequencies to public, private and community broadcasters and to establish the appropriate legal and regulatory frameworks to encourage community media" (idem: 2). It agreed to "promote the ability of communities to define and meet their own communication needs" (idem: 3).

Authorities are requested to establish "domestic legislation that guarantees the independence and pluralism of the media" (idem: 2), diversity in broadcasting and a diversity of views expressed in the media. The document stresses that independence from both political and economic pressures is important for the media. As most other WSIS documents, it promotes cultural diversity, local content, and the inclusion of marginalised populations in communication processes, yet its strong public service background and its reference to both community media and "other citizen media initiatives" (idem: 1) make this rhetoric more convincing than in similar statements.

8.4 Conclusion

The negotiations and results of the WSIS process display a mixed picture. Civil society media as such were not recognised, the CMWG's core objectives of legal recognition and funding were rejected, and even the most basic foundations of their work, such as the right to freedom of expression, were challenged. On the other hand, some of their concerns, such as the strengthening of local content and development, were shared by the majority of government delegations and received increased attention. I will analyse this multi-faceted outcome in more detail in the following chapter. The media were not conceived to be a contested issue at the beginning of the WSIS process but moved to the very centre of the debate during the preparatory conferences. In that, the media debate disclosed similarities with the conflict around civil society participation (see chapter 6). Like the latter, issues

[31] The following quotes are taken from this document.

around media freedom and, particularly, community media met strong resistance at the core of the WSIS debate but were more easily accepted at less high-profile conferences in the WSIS vicinity. CS Media thus constituted an emerging topic which was broadly recognised but had not yet reached the inter-governmental mainstream.

9 Within and beyond WSIS: Re-thinking Civil Society Media approaches to global governance

In this chapter, I will draw conclusions from the analysis presented in previous chapters and will deduct general findings from the experiences from the WSIS process. The chapter will move from a closely WSIS-related approach to a wider perspective on issues relevant for both CS Media and global communication governance. I will start by summarising in detail the successes and failures of CS Media at WSIS (9.1.) and discuss the challenges that CS Media faced (9.2.). Looking at the strategies they applied (9.3.) and the governance agenda which they developed (9.4.), I will outline dimensions of a strategic and thematic approach by CS Media to policy processes. Section 9.5. will revisit the CS Media model introduced in chapter 2 and question whether WSIS has either confirmed or rejected that conceptual proposal. Section 9.6., finally, will apply the characteristics of CS Media to the debate on multi-stakeholder governance which dominated large parts of the WSIS process, and will discuss how the specific approaches of CS Media may contribute to the development of participatory forms of global governance.

9.1 Interventions into WSIS: Successes and failures

Weak in the centre: CS Media in the WSIS documents

The official WSIS process was a defeat for CS Media. If we compare the objectives and priorities developed by CS Media in the Community Media Working Group (CMWG) and at WSIS?WeSeize! with the final WSIS documents from Geneva and Tunis as well as the official reports from the Task Force on Financing Mechanisms (TFFM) and the Working Group on Internet Governance (WGIG), the outcomes are poor:[1]

(1) **Community Media** were temporarily included in draft versions of the texts but were later evicted almost entirely. Only a vague reference to 'media based in local communities' remains, well hidden in the section on cultural diversity of the Geneva Plan of Action.

(2) References to **other CS Media**, such as alternative, autonomous or citizens media, are absent. Equally, there is no statement of support to, or even

1 This correlates somewhat with the findings by other observers who analysed other issue areas. Dany (2006) concludes that civil society groups had little influence on the summit outcomes regarding Internet governance, IPR and communication rights. Yet, whereas some limited effect in those areas is nevertheless recognisable, the outcomes with regards to CS Media appear to have been particularly poor.

recognition of, the large number of **civil society-based self-organised communication projects** such as community wireless networks and peer-to-peer networks.

(3) Instead, the summit focused on **business and governments** as main providers of services and policies, hence the strong emphasis on public-private partnerships.

(4) There was no call for the **legalisation** of CS Media. On the contrary, the explicit recognition of the status quo of the 'legal system of each country' implied continued exclusion.

(5) No **funding mechanisms** were proposed. The Community Media Fund was not implemented or addressed.

(6) No **access to airwaves and orbital paths** was secured for community and other civil society-based media.

(7) No concrete measures were initiated to safeguard **media pluralism** and the diversity of opinions represented in the media, and no measures against **media ownership concentration** were introduced.

(8) Deeper **media criticism** and calls for a reform of the mainstream media only appeared in the context of general criticism of media independence by national delegations who preferred state control of media content and limits to freedom of expression.

(9) **Community ownership** and community control were not explicitly recognised. Calls for local content creation, for example, were dressed in language which may imply self-organised bottom-up activity, but which may equally give support to media corporations to develop content geared towards the needs of local communities in a top-down fashion.

(10) **Empowerment**, particularly of marginalised communities, was included in the rhetoric and the 'visions' proposed in Geneva and Tunis, but these were hardly followed up with concrete measures. Marginalised communities were largely seen as recipients of services, rather than as actors.

(11) Public **participation** was approached in similar ways. According to the documents, 'participation in the information society' is secured mainly by receiving broadcasting services and having access to an Internet connection to receive web-based information. No specific mechanisms were proposed to foster the **contribution** to knowledge and information by everyone.

(12) The summit retained its focus on **'new' ICTs**, particularly Internet connections. Traditional media platforms were marginal.

(13) There was no elaborate perspective on the **global commons**, the public domain, and global public goods, and few measures were proposed to strengthen them.

(14) There was no review of **intellectual property rights** (IPR) and no discussion on the increasing privatisation of knowledge. While some of the early regional conferences proposed a better 'balance' between IPR and the public interest, this demand was lost during the further process.

(15) WSIS documents include references to **free/open source software** but lack explicit support and present proprietary software as equally valuable.

(16) There was no reference to the wider concept of **openness** and to issues such as open content.

(17) There was no development of a broader set of **communication rights** (even though a number of human rights are highlighted in the documents).

(18) The proposed **regulatory environment** allows some limited spaces for public services and the public domain but is largely **market-based**, competitive, and diminishes the role (and, in fact, the basis of existence) of civil society-based non-profit actors.

(19) Governments put a particularly strong emphasis on state sovereignty, **cyber-security** and the prevention of cyber-crime, with only few checks and balances to guarantee that 'security' concerns not be used against oppositional political groups and critical media. The tendency was to **extend state activity,** such as surveillance and data retention, not to reduce it.

(20) Overall, the documents display a strong belief in **social centralism**, a homogenous public and an overarching information society in which technological solutions fix social problems. They combine a focus on **social management** with neo-liberal tendencies, whereas the bottom-up approach of CS Media only appears as rhetoric.

CS Media gained recognition from several individual government delegations, such as Argentina, Colombia, Tanzania, South Africa and Switzerland, which all spoke up in favour of community media. Generating this support can certainly be regarded as a success and can represent building-blocks for future governance interventions. However, this time, the opponents of CS Media proved to be stronger, and the support in some corners did not create the momentum to fully establish CS Media in the WSIS outcomes.

Views from the interviewed CS Media representatives

Asked about their perspective on the direct results of summit interventions, most interviewees expressed disappointment. There was a strong feeling that "we had very little impact on the outcome. And that little that got into the final papers are mostly token that will probably not be fulfilled – while others such as property rights etc. are a huge threat to the right to communication" (BM). In the official summit debates, "there was almost no discussion about media trends, like the increasing concentration of ownership in the media sector and its impact for the intellectual range of political, ideological and other thinking; the predominance of the markets and the logic of the corporate business; or censorship, either governmental or commercial" (MG). Only one interviewee emphasized that "our presence as a lobbying and articulating body had an impact on the shape of that document and affected the tone of the summit" (FW).

Mainstream media representatives and advocates were slightly happier with the results. Their main worries during the preparatory period for WSIS1 had been the neglect of the role of the media, the insufficient reference to the right to freedom of expression and to Art. 19 UDHR, as well as the governmental security agenda. Just a few months before the Geneva summit, the Media Caucus had expected the summit to become a complete failure on media issues and a serious step back in the struggle for freedom of expression. However, as the intense efforts of the Swiss government, supported by the Media Caucus, bore some fruits in the immediate run-up to the summit, the final picture looked more positive. Although many issues proposed by the Media Caucus as well as the Swiss delegation had been deleted, such as reference to the specific importance of public service media and the transformation of state-controlled media into editorially independent organisations, the separate media section in the WSIS documents – and thus the particular recognition of media – had survived the storm of the 'media debate', and freedom of expression and Art. 19 UDHR were recognised without qualifications and compromises. Expressing the views of many in the Media Caucus, Michael Wagner from the EBU noted:

"the outcome is fairly positive, and certainly much better than could have been expected (…). Notwithstanding the 'losses', the official texts finally adopted still take up many of the proposals made by civil society organizations involved in the preparation of the Summit and, in particular, by the 'media caucus'" (Wagner 2004: 170).

The grey zone: Reference points in the documents

Despite the lack of direct support for CS Media and CS Media-related issues, the analysis of the WSIS documents in the previous chapter has shown that a number of topics discussed at WSIS and adopted in the documents offer connections with the practices and approaches of CS Media. The generally accepted necessity to generate more local content in the media and on the Internet, for example, points to a neglected area in which CS Media play a crucial role. By highlighting such an area of concern, WSIS indirectly strengthened the environment in which these media operate. It thus offered starting-points for them to further underline their value[2] and provided arguments to recognise CS Media in future policy fora. Amongst those indirectly supportive issues are:

(1) **Local content**. WSIS documents consistently demanded the development of more and better local content. From the African Regional Meeting to the Tunis documents, insufficient local content was highlighted as a major area of concern. It was generally left open who exactly should provide it, and self-organised civil society-based initiatives were rarely mentioned in this respect. Yet, as prominent providers of local content, CS Media can draw arguments from this thematic focus for their role and their legitimate need for support.

(2) **Local initiatives**. Again, rarely were these explicitly linked with civil society-based backgrounds. Furthermore, not all CS Media are local. Yet most of them have a local base and might point to the relevant WSIS articles to strengthen their position. **Community-based access points** were largely conceived as tools for *consuming*, rather than *producing*, information, but they may as well serve as bases from which community media operate.

(3) **Disadvantaged groups**, **indigenous people** and **people living in poverty** were repeatedly highlighted as communities which need particular attention. Occasionally, empowerment of these groups was demanded, and the Geneva Declaration proposed to provide "ICTs as a tool to support their efforts to lift themselves out of poverty" (WSIS 2003a: Art. 14). CS Media often work with disempowered, marginalised and minority groups or originate amongst these, and an indigenous self-organised radio may well be an example for the "efforts" which the Geneva Declaration refers to.

---

2 In the words of Willie Currie from the APC: "hooks to be developed creatively by civil society activists" (Currie 2005).

(4) **Cultural diversity**. Commitments to preserve cultural heritage as well as local and traditional knowledge appear in all WSIS documents. Again, an indigenous self-organised radio may do exactly that. The Geneva Plan of Action included the commitment to "promote diversity of cultural expression" (WSIS 2003b: Art. 23d) and thereby opened a door for a wider range of CS Media activities.

(5) **Participation and contribution of knowledge**. As noted in the previous section, the WSIS was very vague on these points and did not back-up rhetoric with concrete measures. Yet the rhetoric was very outspoken in demanding what many CS Media are doing. The Bucharest Declaration, for example, called for integrating "the knowledge and experience of citizens" (Pan-European Conference 2002: 2), and the Geneva Declaration promoted the "ability for all to access and contribute information, ideas and knowledge" (WSIS 2003a: Art. 24).

(6) **Public Domain**. The dominant market-oriented paradigm was occasionally blurred by references to the public domain. These offer a more favourable framework for CS Media than an orthodox neo-liberal environment.

(7) **Information sharing**. One of the main areas of interest at WSIS?WeSeize!, information sharing was not advocated in many of the documents, particularly not as file sharing with its implicit threat to IPR. Yet the notion of information sharing appeared in, for example, the Bucharest Declaration.

(8) **Public financial support**. Even though the Community Media Fund was not considered, the Tunis Agenda stressed the need to provide greater financial resources for content production, particularly with regards to content diversity and community initiatives, thus underlining the rationale for the Fund.

(9) **Combination of ICTs with traditional media**. Many CS Media like to experiment with media technology and are at the forefront of innovation. At WSIS, the Polimedia Lab and the High Noon video stream were just two examples. The promotion of innovative media use by WSIS implicitly supports some of these projects.

(10) **Freedom of expression**. This traditional human right was once more reiterated by the WSIS documents and continues to represent an important basis for CS Media.

Strong at the edges: CS Media around the WSIS

Those documents which did not serve as immediate foundation for the main WSIS declarations and action plans and which were thus positioned below the highest and most exposed UN level offered more space to integrate new ideas and progressive proposals. The Marrakech Action Plan and the recommendations of the Asia Media Summit, in particular, provided thorough recognition of community media, pledged to support community media in various ways, and included proposals which were at the heart of the CMWG list of objectives. The defeat in the official WSIS negotiation process was contrasted even more by the events and public discourses around the WSIS summits. Numerous side-events – including even the mainstream media summit, the World Electronic Media Forum (WEMF) – celebrated the practices of grassroots media and citizen journalism. The important role of community and alternative media was highlighted not just at the Community Media Forum but at many other summit side-events (see chapter 7.5). 'Create your own media – make your own voice heard' was repeated in many summit-related debates as a prime strategy to bridge the information divide. The active role of civil society groups and individuals, and the possibilities of self-organised media initiatives, represented a prime area of interest for those who participated in side-events. Other areas encompassed the critique of IPR (as well as possible alternatives such as Copyleft and Creative Commons) and innovative financial mechanisms which go beyond the dominant market approach. None of these were reflected in the official WSIS outcomes, so that many participants, particularly at the Geneva summit, regarded the side-events as the place where the 'real' debate took place and where new ideas and latest innovations for the information society were presented. So if CS Media failed to leave their mark in the official documents, they raised their profile in the more current discourses around the summit and around information society.

As the interviews with CS Media activists showed (see below), the prominent participation in side-events had a least four potential effects:

- Norm change
- Development of denser networks of civil society activists
- Capacity-building and learning about policy processes
- Increase legitimacy of further policy advocacy efforts

Beyond the WSIS documents

Despite the negative results of lobbying the official process, the majority view amongst the interviewees regarding the advocacy efforts for CS Media at WSIS was positive. They pointed out that participation offered an important possibility to learn about structures, processes, limitations and opportunities of global governance (BM, MJ) and to make new constituencies aware of the perspectives of CS Media. As MC said: "This is the first step in any advocacy—to inform and educate, so I believe this has contributed to the strengthening of the role of community and independent media." Other participants agreed that CS Media's profile was strengthened "because of presence and consistently ensuring that the terminology used be inclusive of this media" (TN). CS Media's involvement meant that "they have become indispensable partners and interlocutors" (MG). After the summits, many media activists went back "renewed in their commitment to organize for communication rights at home" (FW). It was noted that the number of local and regional events on media issues has stepped up, and public understanding of such issues has been enhanced. One participant pointed to the possibility to use parts of the WSIS documents "as a tool for the local struggle", i.e. pressuring local and national governments on policy issues, as "that is anyway where the struggle really takes place" (BM).

Side-events such as the Community Media Forum played a particular role in raising the profile of CS Media. These events were "more interesting than the official agenda" (MG), "put the main contents to the summit" (BM), and gave CS Media a "massive presence" (MG). Overall, the positive impact of these events was widely appreciated.

Critical voices came from the organisers of the Community Media Forum. According to CD, "the debates surrounding the summit are important, and it is good that community media played a large role in them, but they will soon be forgotten. What remains are the summit documents. They are leading the direction for future developments. And as community media are absent from these documents, there is nothing on which we can build." VO summarised: "We made some noise, but it was very hard to hear."

A further – "paradoxical" (FW) – concern was raised, highlighting a negative side of the higher profile which community media received: Governments, international institutions and funders may want to use the positive image of these media without fully respecting their organisational approach and political values. "We did a good job of raising interest in C/A Media [Community/Alternative Media], and now we will see an increase in faked/funder-controlled C/A that may become a problem – e.g., I've heard the World Bank is planning to fund community radio. […] Development media has a reputation as cloaking a government agenda" (FW).

Mainstream media, too, were finally recognised. UN Secretary General Kofi Annan, in his speech at the opening session of the Geneva summit on 10th December 2003, highlighted media as "creators of content and essential watchdogs" (quoted in WEMF 2004: 165) and noted:

"It is vital that they retain their freedom to do so, as spelt out in Article 19 of the Universal Declaration of Human Rights. Indeed, the right to freedom of opinion and expression is fundamental to development, democracy and peace, and must retain a touchstone for our work ahead" (ibid.).

The WEMF was by far the biggest side-event of the summit and thus underlined the ambition of media organisations to occupy a central position in the information society debate. Wagner summarised: "The media, which, at the outset, had been sidelined in the WSIS discussions, had finally taken centre stage" (Wagner 2004: 171).

These developments were partly reversed during the second WSIS phase. While the first phase had strived to develop a constitution for the information society, the second phase focused on two issues – financing and Internet governance – and thus lost sight of the controversies around media. However media actors remained active – and successful. The Media Caucus and IFEX, with participation from CMWG members, highlighted the violations of the right to freedom of expression in Tunisia and managed to make this issue a central point on the agenda of the Tunis summit.

Recognition in the media sector

The 'Tunis situation' and the issue of freedom of expression bring us to a further crucial transformation which took place in the WSIS process. While CS Media had been sidelined in the Media Caucus at the beginning of the Geneva phase and had to form a separate working group which temporarily had the character of a 'counter-caucus', by the end of the Tunis phase they were fully recognised as partners by most of the mainstream media faction, including the conservative World Press Freedom Committee (WPFC). This was an unlikely outcome as CS Media's wide-spread criticism of mainstream media and their advocacy for communication rights would have positioned them on the 'other side' of a divide pre-structured by the NWICO debate. Community and alternative media, and the movements and civil society groups from which they arose, had sympathised with the countries of the South which sought changes in the international communication flows and had criticised the Western mainstream media. New media organisations, such as Inter Press Service, had originated from this conflict as a counter-weight to the dominant Western media, and several civil society groups, including AMARC, later picked up the allegedly pro-NWICO, anti-Western and anti-mainstream media concept of the right to communicate to form the CRIS campaign. Thus, at the outset of the WSIS process, their commitment to media independence and freedom of expression was regarded as highly doubtful by mainstream media representatives.

The WSIS process changed this perception drastically and transformed enemies into allies. This alliance was created by the existence of a common enemy. Governments of countries like China, Russia and Cuba opposed freedom of expression and media independence, and CMWG members decided to take sides with the Media Caucus, and thus the mainstream media, in defending these core values. Not all CMWG members did this with enthusiasm, but the convenor, AMARC President Steve Buckley, argued strongly for this strategic alliance.

Concerns over freedom of expression moved to the centre of civil society debates in WSIS phase 2, and the two IFEX fact-finding missions to Tunisia united the WPFC, AMARC, and other civil society organisations. Buckley became one of the most vocal defenders of Art. 19 UDHR, the most outspoken critic of the human rights situation in Tunisia, and gained respect from those mainstream media representatives and press freedom advocates who had previously been sceptical about his constituency. Community media were increasingly regarded as accepted media actors. The three-sector media environment – public-service, private, and community media – for which the CMWG tried to get governmental recognition in the WSIS documents, saw its practical development through the internal media debates and emerging alliances at WSIS. The sacrifice which the CMWG made to achieve this recognition was to abandon media criticism and to go along with hegemonic interpretations of, particularly, freedom of expression. It remains to be seen whether this new alliance will live beyond the WSIS-specific situation and how it will develop if mainstream media criticism is again expressed with a louder voice.

Dangers of participation

The relationship between CS Media and mainstream media poses the question of the losses – rather than the gains – of participating in a global summit. In chapter 6 I discussed the problematic of the multi-stakeholder approach and its potentially pacifying effects. In a Gramscian sense, WSIS tried to establish hegemony by taking the critics on board. CS Media activists and advocates were amongst the more sceptical forces within the WSIS civil society network concerning the gains and problems of participation. While they welcomed the opportunity to advocate for CS Media concerns, many of them recognised and highlighted potential pitfalls.

CS Media interviewees saw the following problems in participating in the summit process: the "danger of civil society being coopted" (FW) by governmental and commercial interests; legitimising the summit without affecting its outcomes (BM), which would amount to "just a puppet-like work" (PA) and therefore "one of the most dangerous things" (PA); "being drawn in and gaining some reformist improvements but not radical change" (MH) and, in the process, "loose the utopian element" (MH) of CS Media. Worries that "NGOs may easily compromise and give legitimacy because of pressure from governments" (MJ) were not always confirmed. However one participant (BM) pointed out: "It is questionable if we really should participate in such an event that is ruled by other forces on which we have no influence but we help in hiding the real interests that are ruling the WSIS. We have to demask much more these forces and go more openly in opposition to them. (…) Here we definitively failed very badly."

Developing a CS Media agenda

For many civil society actors, the collaborations, discussions, and emerging networks with other civil society groups from all over the world constituted a major area of activity and concern which often matched or even outmatched their interventions into the official summit process. For the first time, such a large number of groups, organisations and individuals working on information and communication issues came together, shared their expertise and their experiences, learnt from each other and discussed varying perspectives. The summit represented a *political opportunity structure* which was used by previously isolated civil society groups to create networks and converge their agendas to a common set of priorities which was expressed in several lobby documents throughout the WSIS process and finally in the Civil Society Declaration at WSIS1 and the common civil society statement at WSIS2.[3] The "great degree of coordination between the entities [of civil society], the development of networks, expertise and common projects, exchange of ideas and particular ways of doing things, as well

[3] This networking process was also criticised as "self-congratulatory", "reflexive" and "closed", leading to the establishment of a civil society policy caste which was increasingly distanced from the grassroots; see Gurstein 2005. I will discuss this criticism in chapter 9.6.

as articulation of an alternative discourse" (Raboy 2004a: 353), with the latter amounting to the "new paradigm" (ibid.) of communication societies, was widely regarded as the main achievement of the summit.

> The interviews conducted with CS Media practitioners and advocates confirmed this view. Asked about the main gains of participating in the summit process, most interviewees named the possibility to "network" (BM, MH, PA, TN, VO) and to "build or strengthen alliances with civil society, and other alternative media providers" (MG). For this purpose, the participation in side- and alternative events was deemed more useful than the actual summit (BM, PA). One participant (PA) explicitly highlighted the emerging connections between those inside the process, such as the CMWG, and those outside, such as WSIS?WeSeize!. Such new networks have helped to "share visions and perspectives" (MJ) and to converge agendas in the field of communication democratisation (AC), to strengthen a civil society position in struggles with hostile governments (PA) and to increase "international solidarity, because in this age of armed globalization, there is no other way to find the solution to the critical social problems than the solidarity of various social movements in all the countries" (MJ).

The CS Media actors inside the WSIS process shared the double priority of external agenda setting and internal agenda development and networking. From the strategic discussions in the CMWG and its policy interventions emerged a common understanding of the policy framework within which CS Media operate, as well as of its possible alternatives. The outlines of a common agenda were developed (see below).

9.2 Challenges: internal and external

Which are the reasons for the poor outcomes for CS Media in the official negotiation processes? One major reason was already highlighted in the previous section and in chapters 6 and 8: The WSIS was an ICT event, focused on technological infrastructure and 'new' media platforms, and carried the techno-determinist ideologies of information society discourses. Organised by the ITU, and gathering government delegates with expertise in telecommunications rather than media and cultural issues, it offered little space for discussing the topics which CS Media prioritised. The institutional and ideological framing was thus hardly supportive for CS Media.

Here I want to highlight additional areas which played a particular role: 1) structural hurdles for participation, 2) the domination of state/business interests, 3) the lack of committed allies, 4) the media alliance, 5) the fragmentation of the CS Media sector, and 6) CS Media's focus on practices. The first three aspects are *external* as they concern the environment in which CS Media intervened, the last two aspects are *internal* as they focus on the characteristics of CS Media as such, and the fourth aspect is somewhat *semi-internal/semi-external* as it refers to the connections of CS Media with other media actors. There is certainly a wide range of further aspects which can have substantial impact on the outcomes of negotiations, including a lack of transparency, dominant power configurations, political forces in particular countries, and animosities amongst particular delegations. However, the following six areas not only account for a significant number of the challenges faced by CS Media, but they also offer insights into possible strategies for improving their performance at a policy forum such as WSIS.

Difficulties of access

The WSIS organisers had invited 'civil society' to attend the summit and engage in 'full participation' in the preparation process. However, to do so, these potential participants had to surmount serious structural and financial obstacles.

(1) **Registration and accreditation**. The requirements for receiving accreditation for the WSIS process were geared towards formal non-governmental organisations but did not consider the very different structural backgrounds of many CS Media which are often organised as loose grassroots groups, non-hierarchical networks and temporary coalitions. To participate in the preparatory process, an organisation either needed to be an entity officially recognised by ECOSOC for participation in UN processes, or it had to prove its credentials as a formally established organisation with a headquarter, a democratically adopted constitution and annual reports. While formal organisations with experience in UN processes, such as AMARC, had no difficulty to receive accreditation, the majority of CS Media projects found themselves excluded. Those who wanted to participate were sometimes 'adopted' by sympathetic accredited NGOs, such as AMARC, APC, the Irish Nexus consultancy or the German Heinrich Böll Foundation, and attended as 'delegates' of these respective organisations. Internal civil society support mechanisms thus managed to by-pass some of the obstacles posed by the WSIS organisers. Yet this could hardly substitute proper accreditation mechanisms for all CS Media. It required prior contacts to accredited NGOs, which most CS Media did not have, and it meant that the wide variety of CS Media was not recognisable in the WSIS process. There was no chance to submit an official Indymedia contribution to the negotiations, or to speak as a video activist in the governmental plenary, or

to show registration badges with the names of a diversity of CS Media projects to governmental delegates. CS Media were invisible.

The summits set up additional hurdles. The registration process involved giving detailed personal information and receiving a badge with an RFID (Radio Frequency Identification) chip which could theoretically be used to track movements and activities across the whole summit compound. Critics of state surveillance and advocates of privacy rights, many CS Media activists found this difficult to accept. Furthermore, as activists in social movements and dissident political groups, many of them are not known for seamless relations with the authorities in their home countries and were cautious about providing personal details. Some participants who did register noticed special treatment as, for example, they had their bags searched every time they entered the summit compound.

Others were not allowed to register altogether. The NGO Reporters Sans Frontiers had lost its ECOSOC accreditation status due to an action which some of its members had carried out prior to the start of the WSIS process. The organisation was not given accreditation for WSIS, and its chairperson was not even allowed to enter Tunisia, the host country of the second WSIS summit. Tunisian civil society groups were equally excluded as the national government did not recognise them as legitimate participants.

In their WSIS evaluation "Much more could have been achieved", civil society participants of the WSIS process expressed the urgent need to develop

"clearer and less bureaucratic rules of recognition for accrediting Civil Society organisations in the UN system, for instance in obtaining ECOSOC status and summit accreditation, and to ensure that national governmental recognition of Civil Society entities is not the basis for official recognition in the UN system" (Civil Society Plenary 2005: 15).

(2) **Repression**. As the experiences of Reporters Sans Frontiers and the Tunisian civil society groups show, seemingly bureaucratic accreditation procedures occasionally blended in with more direct repression by state authorities. Outside the summit compound, civil society actors were repeatedly confronted with openly repressive acts. In Geneva, the Polimedia Lab was temporarily closed by police, a demonstration was stopped and dispersed, and in Tunis, any independent self-organised civil society meeting – including, but not limited to, the Citizens Summit – was prevented by large numbers of secret police. Even inside the Tunis summit compound, Tunisian authorities tried to physically prevent side-events such as the Community Media Forum. At both summits, security staff screened publications

brought by participants into the summit compound and filtered out those that they deemed inappropriate.

(3) **Funding**. A further set of obstacles was the lack of financial resources. Even if a CS Media group had taken the hurdle of accreditation, it would have had difficulties in covering the expenses of participation: the flight ticket to Geneva (where most PrepComs took place), two weeks of hotel accommodation, food and drinks in this expensive Swiss city – not once but two, three or more times a year. Little funding was provided for civil society delegates by the WSIS Secretariat. Again, only larger NGOs which could mobilise sufficient funds, for example through established contacts with potential donors, could cope with this restriction.

In interviews with CS Media activists and advocates, finance was highlighted as "the biggest barrier to broader participation" (FW). One interviewee recalled: "I know many people who would have been great assets to the discussion and were interested but there was no way I could get them there. From the beginning, there was almost no support available for bringing people into the process and keeping them there. (…) I funded my early support out of my own pocket but had to drop out from lack of funds. (…) AMARC was able to do it only because airfares from London to Geneva were stunningly cheap in that period, and our President lives in the UK" (FW).

(4) **Marginalisation of civil society actors**. As other civil society actors, CS Media suffered from the temporary exclusion from – and the permanent marginalisation in – the negotiation process. Contrary to the initial announcement of 'full participation', they had only limited opportunity to speak in plenary during the preparation process and were denied access to many negotiation sessions (see chapter 6). Furthermore, the structures of self-organisation and self-representation, which the civil society network had established, were not fully respected by the summit organisers. Before the Geneva summit, the civil society network had democratically elected civil society representatives to speak at the opening plenary, amongst them Lynne Muthoni Wanyeki from AMARC. These representatives were proposed to the ITU, but the ITU appointed different civil society speakers. As Bendrath/Panganiban (2003) note, this move "denied civil society its right to choose who speaks on its behalf and brings its points across."

The state-business nexus and government control

The model of the *public-private partnership* which was promoted throughout the WSIS documents, expressed very well the regulatory approach which dominated WSIS, as well as its principal actors. In a nutshell, this model requires governments to develop an enabling regulatory framework and business actors to provide goods and services. At WSIS, the specific configurations of such an approach were under debate, but not the approach as such. Several governments, particularly from the South, tried to put more emphasis on the provision of infrastructure and services by public authorities, while the US delegation, usually with the support of the EU, Canada and Australia, argued for a stronger role for business actors and advocated for liberal regulatory environments. Alternative approaches beyond this state-market framework were rarely considered.

The TFFM report provides probably the clearest example (see chapter 8). Pre-occupied with a market-based approach, and interpreting all financial concepts within the ultimate framework of private sector investment and competition, it failed completely to study the feasibility of non-profit and civil society-based solutions. Even the recognition that markets do not always provide the best outcome did not lead to increased consideration of non-market alternatives. At the WSIS PrepComs, governments criticised the market fundamentalism of the report, only to transfer part of the authority from the market back to the state. Overall, the digital divide – as the underlying thematic focus of the WSIS debate – connected the interests of dominant players from governments and business to form a comfortable symbiosis. The particularities were contested, with Southern governments hoping for the mobilisation of new financial resources from the North and the North being reluctsnat to provide those, but the general direction was not.

CS Media had serious difficulties to enter the debate as they are situated outside this state-market nexus. They are by nature non-profit and are thus not easily integrated into business-focused strategies, and they represent an approach to information society which goes beyond large-scale technological infrastructures, be they financed publicly or privately. In contrast, they are based on a bottom-up approach, focusing on self-organised civil society-centred initiatives. Rejecting control through both political and commercial forces, CS Media were also up against an emerging trend: the widened consensus amongst many governments that there should be an increase, rather then relaxation, of government control. This view was fuelled by two developments:

(1) WSIS took place in the aftermath of 9/11 and amidst a violent 'war on terror'. This offered a window of opportunity for implementing security-

related policy and widening state control. Accordingly, the security section was one of the strongest in the WSIS documents, emphasizing the need to fight cyber-crime and cyber-terrorism and largely neglecting civil rights such as privacy.

(2) Much of recent ICT infrastructure, particularly the Internet, had been developed with limited governmental involvement and beyond the sphere of state control. There was a general perception amongst almost all governments that the time was ripe to reclaim opportunities of intervention and bring the Internet back into the realm of public regulation.[4]

These concerns of security and state sovereignty created a 'negative' political opportunity structure, as the political crisis which they signified did not lead to a disunity of political elites and to cracks in the ideological system but, on the contrary, unified those elites and established a dominant discourse which was very difficult to overcome.

Lack of powerful and committed allies

CS Media (or rather 'community media', as this was the term chosen at WSIS) were swimming against the stream of dominant thematic tendencies shared by a large proportion of government actors. Yet they were also up against the particular interests of governmental coalitions which I classified in chapter 8.1.4. The strongest opposition came from the "corporate legalists", led by El Salvador, who rejected community media in principle, and who were supported by the "state controllers" (led by China) and the "telecoms" (the majority of delegations). For these, community media were trouble-makers who challenged the dominant media (be they commercial or state-controlled) in the respective countries and whose independence undermined state authority. This governmental "faction of concrete" (Interview WL) was unwilling to accept compromises.[5]

There were other delegations amongst which the CMWG generated sympathy. The notion of 'community media' was supported by several governments from the South, including South Africa, Botswana, Tanzania, Colom-

---

4 The prime exception was the US government, being the only one that already had considerable influence, but even the EU governments agreed that some change had to come.

5 Several civil society-based WSIS participants stressed that resistance on the government side was often founded in insufficient knowledge of the needs and possible contributions of CS Media. Tracey Naughton notes: "At times adversaries appear ignorant and to lack understanding of the media other than the way they know it and many times, this is due to a genuine lack of knowledge. I appreciate that some governments are simply resistant, but others simply don't have the experiential basis for understanding. This calls for another level of advocacy and awareness" (Interview TN).

bia, Venezuela and Argentina. Even the more influential delegations from the US and the EU agreed with its inclusion in the documents. However these delegations did not establish a sustained defence against the strong opposition from El Salvador and others. Supporting community media did not represent a vital interest, and few delegations were prepared to make compromises on other issues or to engage in major diplomatic struggles to retain community media in the WSIS documents. Through targeting specific sympathetic delegations, the CMWG tried to create a stronger and bigger alliance to defend its concerns, but while this strategy enjoyed some success and caused more delegations to speak out for community media, progress was not quick enough to change power relations substantially.

The potential strength of a strategy of 'targeted lobbying' was underlined by the fruitful exchanges between media actors and the Swiss government delegation. There, two factors came together which had substantial effects on the WSIS negotiations: the specific authority of Switzerland as the host of WSIS1, and the sustained effort of Swiss media to influence the Swiss government agenda and its priorities for the negotiation process. The media sections in the Geneva documents emerged and survived only because of this combination of actors and capacities. Furthermore, as those media actors who actively engaged with the Swiss delegation had a public service background and acknowledged the importance of community media, the Swiss government contributions put a strong emphasis on CS Media concerns.

Marginalisation in the Media Caucus

Opinions on the effects of CS Media involvement in the Media Caucus and in the further alliances with mainstream media during the Tunis phase vary (see chapter 7.2.). On the positive side, the caucus developed common positions, including perspectives of all three media sectors – private, public-service and civil society-based media – and increasingly recognised community media as partners. On the downside, however, this involvement was accompanied with a number of difficulties:

(1) The struggle for recognition, and particularly the conflict with commercial media, consumed a lot of time and energy which could have otherwise been invested in direct lobbying and in working with other civil society actors towards common agendas.

(2) Community media were marginalised in the initial Media Caucus statement and their activity was limited to the edges and niches of the media environment. Despite the growing recognition of community media actors by mainstream media representatives during the WSIS process, this perspec-

tive was never reversed. Community media never became a priority issue in Media Caucus statements, and other concepts of CS Media were completely absent.

(3) Recognition was achieved by sacrificing crucial content. Promoting a media reform and communication rights agenda was neither feasible against the opposition from established journalist and media organisations inside the caucus, nor was it a strategic objective. A media-critical civil society voice was thus missing, and the elaborate media-related demands discussed at the Social Fora and elsewhere were not channelled into the debate.

(4) The caucus, furthermore, allowed non-civil society actors into a designated civil society space. The inclusion of commercial media, in particular, channelled business interests into civil society debates, obstructed the development of common civil society positions, weakened the common identity of the wider civil society network and watered down its statements.

(5) During the intense negotiation phase on media issues in the run-up to WSIS1, the Media Caucus did not always speak with one voice. Caucus members representing commercial media lobbied against the inclusion of community media in the WSIS documents, and those governments with the strongest ties to national media conglomerates were the fiercest critics of such an inclusion.

Allies or adversaries?

Notwithstanding the successes and the strategic rationale of the Media Caucus, the majority of interviewees were convinced that caucus members were "separated by fundamental lines of conflict" (MC) which divide "ideology, mandate and structure" (MC), "interests" (MC, MG), "approaches and objectives" (FW), "production processes" (AC), "material positions" (VO) and core values (MH, VO). From a CS Media perspective, differences included whether "common people (...) have their own medias to express their thoughts and news" (PA) and "will be able to communicate directly through media" (FW), thus opposing the power of established media organisations with people's communication rights (MJ), and whether civil society has a say in how media operate (VO). The interests of established mainstream media, in contrast, were said to defend the media system (VO), maintain profits (MC) and limit competition to their operations (BM). "As at the WSIS the main stake behind the official goals was the distribution of shares in the information economy, for the commercial and public service media it was to get the biggest share and limit other actors, especially those from the community sector" (BM).

Accordingly, most interviewees regarded mainstream media as core opponents of CS Media in the WSIS process. Particularly, this applied to government-controlled and commercial media, which were called "natural" (MC) and "main" (PA) adversaries, respectively. In the WSIS process, "the Latin American commercial lobbies" (VO) sought "to eradicate community media" (TN). The view on public service media was not so clear-cut, but it was noted that they share the structures, perspectives and power positions of commercial media in many respects and therefore cannot be regarded as natural allies (MJ). "Many public service media do not see the need of alternative media, because they pretend to represent civil society, and any alternative media would be the proof that they are not fully doing this" (BM).

So while some participants held that the caucus "was a unique opportunity for open debate" (VO), the dominant position of established mainstream media forces and the participation of commercial actors constituted serious obstacles for furthering the agenda of CS Media.

According to Dany (2006), the less contested an issue is within civil society, the more adjustments towards its demands take place in policy negotiations. The conflictive alliance between CS and mainstream media confirms this finding. It was successful in advocating a small set of common principles, but it weakened, rather than strengthened, the further interventions by CS Media.

Yet the latter's conceptual reduction on *community media* contributed to their marginalisation. The concept had potential strategic value due to its relative acceptance in previous policy fora and due to its greater appeal to potential institutional allies than concepts focusing on alternative and oppositional aspects. However it played into the hands of those (both in the Media Caucus and on the government side) who wanted to transfer CS Media to the margins of society and prevent their recognition as fully legitimate parts of the media system. With the term 'community' evoking the picture of fairly enclosed, and therefore limited, peer groups, it failed to provide arguments as to why such media should be recognised on the same level as the 'real' media that catered for the general public. Framing CS Media as 'community media' cast them as 'small', 'local', and serving only marginal audiences with very specific types of content. Accordingly, the WSIS documents described community communication as complementary services for certain (limited) deprived sections of the population.

Fragmentation amongst CS Media

At and around WSIS, different concepts of CS Media were separated between different spaces. While those actors who identified themselves as, or aligned with, 'community media' were active inside the process, sought to influence negotiations through lobbying, participated in civil society network structures, and organised official side-events, those who identified themselves as 'autonomous', 'tactical' or 'alternative' media participated in WSIS?WeSeize!, covered the summit as journalists, or stayed away completely. This divide between concepts and spaces was complemented by a divide in the themes that each network prioritised. The CMWG focused on the development frame, on the persistent importance of traditional media platforms, and on the needs of disempowered communities, particularly in the Global South, and it put special emphasis on licences and funding for community broadcasting. WSIS?WeSeize!, meanwhile, focused on new ICTs and related subjects such as IPR, had a strong bias towards techno-centric solutions and celebrated the spontaneous and temporary approach of tactical media.

Partially, this *CS Media divide* had strategic reasons – the CMWG responded to the summit's development frame, whereas WSIS?WeSeize! focused on highlighting alternatives to the summit agenda – but partially it had deeper political and ideological roots: The CMWG was primarily composed of representatives of established NGOs with a history of collaborating with institutions, governments and funders, with strong North-South relations and a propensity towards a 'communication for development' approach, whereas WSIS?WeSeize! combined the radical anarchist-inspired politics of the global justice movement with the philosophies of cyber-libertarianism and 'openness' of technological experts and new media activists towards the rejection of institutional involvement and scepticism of established structures and organisations.

Both spaces offered a 'home' for some CS Media actors – and some CS Media themes – but not for others. The CMWG did not sufficiently reflect the wider range of civil society-based media practices and concerns beyond 'community radio', even the Community Media Forum marginalised those experiences and actors, and so neither of them provided an adequate platform for representing the diversity of actors and issues in the CS Media realm. WSIS?WeSeize! was hardly attractive for those interested in sustained organising and in traditional media platforms, and for those outside a specific 'media activist culture'. In Tunis, the Citizens Summit was dominated by the policy issues discussed inside the summit process, with a particular emphasis on human rights; the Third Paradise focused on arts, culture and IPR; and the Media Justice Delegation had a distinct US background. All of these events, spaces and coalitions offered interesting aspects for CS Media, but neither was destined to overcome the CS Media fragmentation. Several actors found their priority issues eclipsed, with no suitable space to raise them. For those, for example, working with new technologies and trying to strengthen Internet-based CS Media inside the summit process, neither the CMWG nor WSIS?WeSeize! were particularly attractive. Activists leaning towards the ideas of autonomous, alternative and participatory media and operating inside the summit process often dispersed to other civil society spaces, participating, for example, in the regional caucuses.

So if scholars of social movements research are right in identifying *network density* as one of the elementary preconditions for social movement and civil society influence, then CS Media had a particularly difficult starting position for achieving much at WSIS. The development of stronger linkages between different sections of CS Media would be fundamental for generating more success in future policy fora.

Policy vs. practices

The AMARC radio stream and the WSIS?WeSeize! video netcast signified a further space where significant fragments of CS Media were to be found: the space of practices. With WSIS as a policy arena, this space was, naturally, very small. As a result, many CS Media activists stayed away.

> Asked about the main obstacles to participation in the summit process, many interviewees noted either that their own organisation was usually not involved in policy interventions and therefore only engaged temporarily with WSIS, or that it had been difficult for them to raise awareness amongst other CS Media because of the latter's lack of interest in (or scepticism towards) policy processes. A focus on practices vice versa policy was stated repeatedly. Organisations and networks as diverse as the anarchist-inspired activist project Indymedia and the Christian organisation CAMECO share a practices-based approach. Their members noted that "we don't focus on policy-making" (MH) and "we normally work with concrete projects – lobbying is not our main competency" (CD). From this may follow a lack of awareness of global policy processes – as MH says: "We use media, but seem to take the basic communication rights for granted" – and a scepticism towards policy processes – "governments do not and will not have the political will to support community media" (MC).

9.3 Strategy: From challenges to opportunities

Divergent approaches inside and outside

The different CS Media actors in their respective places used different sets of strategies to achieve different sets of outcomes.

The CMWG's main objective was to include reference to community media in the official WSIS documents. The recognition of these media by a high-level UN summit such as WSIS would, explicitly or implicitly, have meant the acknowledgement of a three-sector media environment, including community media. From this would have followed the legitimate necessity for the UN system as well as each member state to develop a supportive regulatory environment for community media, including legalisation and access to communication infrastructure, and to provide the necessary financial mechanisms to enable their operations. The recognition of community media, furthermore, could have opened the door for the recognition of other CS Media which approximate the characteristics of community media.

To build bridges with the dominant discourses at WSIS, the CMWG focused on a development frame. It emphasized the important contribution by community media to strategies of poverty eradication and bridging information divides in the Global South. Occasionally, it also sought to utilise governmental confusion and disunity as a window of opportunity to advance its objectives. This was particularly the case during the finance debate, as the CMWG intervened in the governmental deadlock by proposing the Community Media Fund.

Contributing directly to the language of the official documents, trying to influence the regulatory environment for media and communication, strategically providing information, creating policy-related discourses, and placing new issues on the international agenda, the CMWG was an advocacy group with a particular policy aim. According to the classification by Khagram et al. (2002), it formed a transnational advocacy network which was rather informal, bound together by shared values, common discourses, and dense information exchange, but which did not develop further and more long-term campaigns.

Those CS Media appearing at summit side-events, thus in the space between 'inside' and 'outside', shared the objective of gaining recognition for the types of media which they represented, but addressed different target audiences. Groups such as the Media Justice Delegation or eclectica.dv, both participating in side-events around the Tunis summit, tried to raise their profile and mobilise support for their activities amongst other side-event participants – mostly civil society groups and NGOs, some delegates from

UN organisations and international institutions, and a few government delegates – but did not seek to directly influence the official WSIS outcomes.

CS Media operating outside the summits, particularly at WSIS?WeSeize! but also at the Citizens Summit, focused on mobilisation and cultural outcomes, addressing organised civil society groups, media activists and the wider public. Rather than changing particular sections of policy documents and thus achieving limited but immediate gains, they strove for mid- and long-term norm change and for fundamental transformations of governance systems. Their objective was to influence underlying perceptions, shake established 'realities', and weaken the power structures on which current governance systems were based. Creating forms of organisation which differed from those inside the summit was an important part of that strategy. Non-hierarchical principles, for example, were to express new norm patterns which played a central role in an attempt to influence wider social practices.

Furthermore, both WSIS?WeSeize! and the Citizens Summit exerted pressure from outside on the summit. They did not apply physical confrontation – although the Citizens Summit, operating in an environment of state repression, was invariably faced with confrontational acts by police. Rather, their pressure involved creating alternative agendas and pointing publicly to the WSIS' blind spots. They challenged the legitimacy of the summit by withdrawing the support by (part of) civil society to the summit and thereby attacked one of the main concerns of the summit organisers (see chapter 6).

The legitimatory basis of the groups went beyond traditional forms of representation and was grounded, rather, in individual expertise, experience and reputation. The CMWG retained a somewhat representative outline, with most (but not all) members acting as delegates sent by NGOs, but its daily operations were based on the capacities and knowledge of its individual members.

All of these networks and coalitions, from WSIS?WeSeize! to the CMWG, used the WSIS as a 'political opportunity structure' to a) mobilise support for their needs and concerns, b) weave networks of like-minded actors and supporters, and c) trigger norm change on a variety of levels. With the WSIS as a discursive event which defined an issue area rather than agreeing on concrete policy measures, the summit offered a particularly comfortable arena for such interventions. Strategically, the main difference between these spaces and actors concerned their level of involvement or disengagement, respectively, with the official summit process, and thus their respective perceptions towards the question which was posed in chapter 4: Does a policy arena such as WSIS offer opportunities for civil society actors to substantially influence the debate, or is civil society being used to legitimise a government-/business-led process? And furthermore, is a global summit at all able to create an appropriate space for discussing and regulating communication processes?

A multi-level strategy

The answers to these questions differed among CS Media actors, and so the familiar separation between *inside* and *outside* was established. Yet the significant achievement of these various approaches to the WSIS was that the rather predictable divisions were sometimes crossed and constituencies overlapped. Indymedia activists participated in the CMWG, small and radical community radio groups appeared at the NGO-led Community Media Forum, while the Venezuelan media organisation Aporrea participated in WSIS?WeSeize!. Cautious attempts of collaboration and solidarity emerged, usually advanced by individuals who were active in both camps. The founding meeting of Geneva03, the coalition that organised WSIS?WeSeize!, had among its participants a leading activist of the CRIS campaign (Seán Ó Siochrú from Nexus Research) as well as members of the CMWG. So, from the beginning, those who had pushed for civil society participation inside the summit process collaborated with those who rejected such participation and chose to stay outside. As WSIS1 drew closer, members of the Swiss civil society coalition Comunica-ch published a map of 'progressive' summit side-events which included 'inside' events such as the WFCR and the Community Media Forum as well as the 'outside' WSIS?WeSeize!. WSIS?WeSeize! participants drafted and submitted a section (on infowar) for the Civil Society Declaration, and civil society groups inside WSIS issued press statements condemning repression of demonstrations as well as the temporary shutdown of the Polimedia Lab by the Geneva police.

A small but increasing number of participants from both camps, *inside* and *outside*, interpreted the different approaches between, for example, the CMWG and WSIS?WeSeize! not as fundamental ideological dividing lines but as complementary strategies. Bridging the boundaries between media actors with different tactics and thematic focuses, the WSIS offered an opportunity to transcend the "predictable spheres of influence" (Calabrese 2004: 323). It witnessed the embryonic stages of a multi-layered, multi-level strategy connecting *inside* and *outside*.[6] Such a strategy would combine different types of intervention as well as different thematic priorities and

---

[6] Calabrese (2004), similarly, sees the WSIS process as a catalyst for an emerging movement for communication rights which is not entirely policy-driven but connects 'inside' and 'outside' approaches. This movement "operates on multiples fronts, engaging in official forums [..], while also taking the streets, practicing civil disobedience and using the politics of shame to pressure government and global corporations" (Calabrese 2004: 322).

different sets of expertise. So, whereas the CMWG drafted specific proposals for influencing the ongoing government-led negotiation process, WSIS?WeSeize! (could have) organised public pressure in support. While the CMWG focused on traditional media platforms and a development frame, WSIS?WeSeize! (could have) added expertise on new technologies. The following table summarises some of the differences in approaches, which offered potential for a complementary strategy:

CMWG	**WSIS?WeSeize!**
Participation in multi-stakeholder governance	Critical reflection from outside
Interventions in the policy process	Develop bottom-up infrastructure alternatives, raise public pressure
React to the government agenda, short-term gains and reform	Advocate fundamental (mid- and long-term) changes in governance systems
Strategic cooperation with mainstream media	Media critique and media reform/democracy agenda
Focus on traditional media platforms	Focus on new ICTs
Expertise on broadcast licensing and spectrum allocation	Expertise on ICT-related ad broader issues, such as IPR

Table 5: Potentials for a complementary strategic approach

At the first WSIS summit, this combination of approaches and expertise could not yet fully develop. Logistical problems, restricted access to the official summit spaces, physical distance between venues and capacity shortages in each camp were complemented by persistent political and cultural differences. Cross-participation in each other's events and common strategising remained the exception rather than the rule, and media projects which would have benefited from collaboration – such as the AMARC radio stream from inside the summit and the WSIS?WeSeize! video stream from outside – were not connected. Yet the common use of WSIS as a political opportunity structure fostered new coalitions across traditional boundaries and triggered common post-WSIS initiatives such as the European Forum on Communication Rights (EFCR) which took place alongside the European Social Forum in London in October 2004. The forum was collaborative project by media NGOs, such as WACC, APC and AMARC, which had been key players in the WSIS process, and by Indymedia activists who had participated in WSIS?WeSeize!.

By the second WSIS summit, the dividing lines between inside and outside were thoroughly blurred. While an NGO coalition organised the Citizens Summit outside the WSIS compound and faced heavy-handed police operations, media activists, some of whom had participated in WSIS?WeSeize!, attended official side-events inside the summit building. Certainly the particular political situation in Tunisia contributed to these developments, as it, on the one hand, made independent media activist gatherings like WSIS?WeSeize! impossible and, on the other hand, caused many NGOs to take a more confrontational stance against state authorities. However, the collaborations between 'inside' and 'outside' in the first WSIS phase had helped to reduce scepticism towards the respective 'other side' and to adopt a strategic perspective on the use of diverse approaches towards a summit like WSIS.

Collaborative strategies – integrated interventions

None of the interviewees – core participants of the lobbying process as well as of alternative/counter-events – dismissed the activities on the 'other side' in principle. All seemed to have a strategic approach to political intervention and saw a role for different types of activity. For example, FW highlighted the necessity for community media to participate in ITU meetings "because we need to get our perspective into the discussion day by day and week by week", but equally emphasized the need for "out-and-out resistance: file-sharing, pirate radios, wi-fi, and all the things that radical engineers and their friends are capable of". Interviewees called for "a good synergy between inside and outside groups" (MH), for "integrated work (…) on all levels" (VO), for 'outside' events to have "strong ties with inside civil society" (MJ) and for 'inside' advocates to put more effort into complementing their work with extra-institutional campaigns and platforms (MJ). What was perceived as particularly underdeveloped in CS Media approaches to WSIS was the creation and presentation of structural and organisational alternatives (see next section).

'Beyond' policy and towards practices

A distinction purely in *inside* and *outside* approaches may be too limited. As the concepts of the 'beyond' sphere (see chapter 4.3.) has suggested, and as the illustrations of the spaces of CS Media activity around WSIS have confirmed, many CS Media do not focus directly on policy interventions, whether from 'inside' or from 'outside', but on setting up self-organised information infrastructures which constitute alternatives to predominant information systems. The centrality of practices is a major characteristic.

WSIS?WeSeize! explicitly and almost exclusively emphasized this aspect, largely ignoring the official summit and instead aiming at the development of alternative information systems as part of a people-based bottom-up information society. It expressed deep distrust in established policy processes and it focused on developing technological 'by-passes' against obstructive regulation, rather than trying to influence such regulation. The CMWG chose a different path by engaging with the official process, and it adopted a much more positive view towards the possibilities of achieving supportive results through policy interventions, yet with some limits. At WSIS, it emphasized the need to enable CS Media to operate, and to abolish restrictive and repressive regulations, but it was cautious regarding the prospects for a more fundamental re-structuring of the media system through government actions, and it opposed the government agendas on many occasions. Most of its members had a practical background of working day-to-day with CS Media, and thus of setting up the alternatives which they advocated. Several members prioritised organising the Community Media Forum, networking with other civil society groups, and reporting for their home media, to lobbying governmental delegations. Participants in the Community Media Forum largely shared an anti-institutional approach.

If we re-visit Milan's (2006b) model, we can link the CMWG closely with an 'inside' approach and WSIS?WeSeize! with a 'beyond' approach. The Citizens Summit (or rather: its original plan) approximates an 'outside' approach, but does so only in a limited way, due to its close connection with 'inside' actors, the indirect nature of its protest, and its different thematic focus (see next page).

Type of actors and their dimension of engagement		**Repertories of action and strategies towards policy**
INSIDE	CMWG: Advocacy coalition, primarily made of established NGOs	Cooperative attitude: active engagement in the policy process; activities closely depend on the political processes
OUTSIDE	Citizens Summit: Collaboration of international NGOs and dissident Tunisian civil society	Confrontational attitude: "Policy engagement" through pressure from the outside (counter-summit, but no disruptive direct actions)
BEYOND	WSIS?WeSeize!: Grassroots activists, individuals, autonomous media, disperse networks, community initiatives Community Media Forum and Media Justice Delegation also had a "Beyond" tendency	Autonomous attitude: Rejection of the summit; relation to the official political process only as reaction to perceived threats (e.g., enclosure of knowledge through IPR, police raid against Polimedia Lab); bypassing institutions/regulation by setting up alternative media systems; expanding unregulated media spaces

Table 6: Inside, outside and beyond WSIS - adaptation of the table presented in chapter 4.3 on the strategies of media movements

However, as was shown above, the different spaces and strategies interacted and collaborated, and, furthermore, they did not represent distinct approaches, but each was influenced by several of the different dimensions. We can observe "a continuum ranging from active engagement in policy arenas to pressures by disruptive actions from the outside, to those groups reacting only to 'perceived threats' coming from institutions by trying to find a way 'around' them" (Milan 2006b: 5). The experiences of WSIS particularly highlight three aspects:

(1) **Overlaps**. Even though the main CS Media coalitions around WSIS can be integrated into the concept fairly well, division lines cannot be drawn strictly. Many CMWG actors had 'beyond' characteristics and preferences, many Citizens Summit participants connected 'inside' and 'outside' strategies, WSIS?WeSeize! made cautious approaches towards both the 'inside' and 'outside' sphere, and the Community Media Forum connected all three levels.

(2) **Predominance of 'inside' and 'beyond' approaches**. While other recent global summits were met by strong 'outside' activities, CS Media at WSIS were largely distributed between 'inside' and 'beyond' spaces. This points to a relative weakness of 'outside' strategies by CS Media (and, generally, by civil society actors in the field of information and communication) and to a substitution of 'outside' interventions by, particularly, the 'beyond' approach.

(3) **Specific role of 'beyond' ideas**. Most actors, regardless of the strategy they chose, had a background in practices and put a strong emphasis on using the political opportunity structure of the summit to establish civil society networks independent from, and not focused on, the official political process.

The role of 'beyond' approaches for policy

Actors using 'beyond' strategies do not focus on policy-making, do not wish to participate in multi-stakeholder governance, and seek to by-pass regulation. Yet they do not necessarily reject the need for policy as such, and they may not share the most extreme (and most naïve) promises by cyber-libertarians of an imminent government-free world. Understood as strategy rather than as identity, 'beyond' approaches can play a crucial role in complementing 'inside' and 'outside' interventions. They have a particular potential to achieve norm change, both amongst policy-makers and amongst the wider public.

Connections between 'beyond' and policy

Interviewee MH summarised the 'beyond' approach of her Indymedia activism like this: "We don't focus on policy-making. (…) we find our way around limitations by pooling resources." Reflecting on the linkages between a 'beyond' and a policy-oriented approach, she added: "Indymedia, hacklabs and other diy media projects are in the lucky position to define their activities themselves, therefore they can be very utopian, very experimental. They don't have the pressure to present an outcome at the end, and they can afford to be radical in their practice and analysis, without the need to find consensus with more established organisations. As such, they might have the function of some utopian 'guiding star', i.e. the star that provides a fix point of navigation for sailors, who use it for orientation without attempting to reach it."

Presentation of alternative practices

Several of the 'inside' participants highlighted shortcomings in CS Media strategies regarding the creation and presentation of structural and organisational alternatives. TN proposed "more of a practical visual presence" which "would enable the development of knowledge and opportunities to change attitudes and eventually practices." FW suggested a "grassroots engineering technology show" and a variety of exhibits "with training and hands-on activities, where we can share our methods and technologies with each other as well as the rest of the world. I can imagine a few of the corporate engineers browsing through and being blown away by the elegance of grassroots solutions to communication problems they didn't even know existed."

"I had been hoping for something like the NGO forum in Beijing, where there would be a big display of alternative and grassroots technologies and ideas from many countries. (…) There are so many wonderful grassroots communication activities around the world (…). The African Village was the sole example I saw of practical demonstration of local communications technologies. But nobody I saw was demonstrating how easy it is to build a micro FM transmitter you can carry around in a suitcase with the antenna in an umbrella (…). I think we need to do a lot more to show others how much fun and easy communications is – it makes people understand the risk of losing it better" (FW).

So, going back to the emerging traces of a multi-level strategy, we can now identify three different types of activity which such a strategy would need to integrate:

(1) Policy advocacy, lobbying and monitoring of negotiations inside the official process

(2) Public pressure from outside the official process

(3) Development of policy/governance alternatives and of self-organised alternative infrastructure

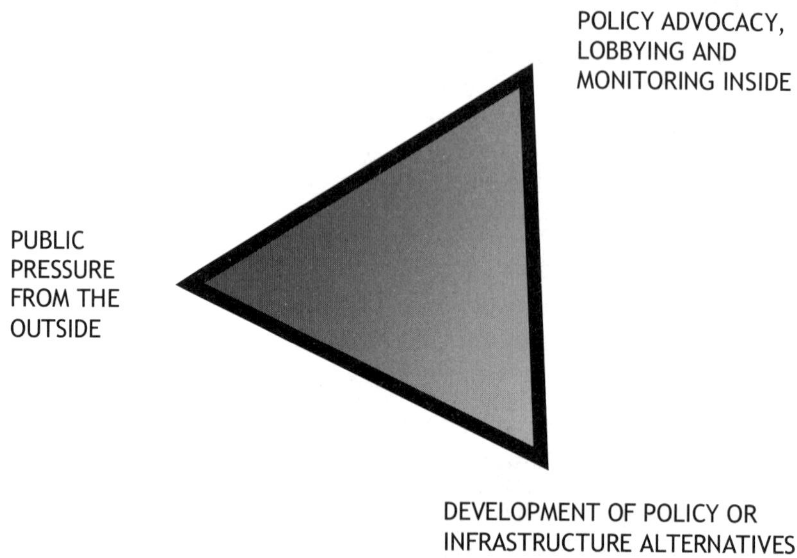

Figure 2: Dimensions of a multi-level strategy to policy intervention

9.4 A governance agenda by CS Media?

The fragmentation of CS Media actors in the WSIS process and the strategic approach of the CMWG affected the development of a coherent common policy agenda. While the civil society declaration "Shaping Information Societies for Human Needs" provided an elaborate framework for the governance of information society, a comparable CS Media document was not achieved. However, the various CMWG lobby documents and the thematic priorities expressed at side- and alternative events constitute building-blocks of an emerging policy programme.

Building-blocks of a CS Media agenda

Legalisation of self-organised communication systems. This was the common demand of most CS Media actors at and around WSIS. The CMWG focused on media controlled by local communities, and WSIS?WeSeize! referred to 'autonomous' media, encompassing a wide range of self-organised media initiatives. Yet only the CMWG laid out specific aspects of an enabling regulatory framework for strengthening the role of these media: a secure legal foundation in every country, an opening of broadcast licensing, and financial assistance. Other CS Media approached the issue from another direction and primarily demanded the absence of police repression and of obstructive state regulation.

Financial support. The CMWG proposed a Community Media Fund. Other funding ideas developed elsewhere have included the reinvestment of revenues raised by governments from sale of spectrum and telecommunications licensing, and a tax on the use of radio frequencies and orbital space by commercial media.

Reform of both the allocation and the governance model of communication channels. The CMWG argued for reserving a fixed percentage of radio frequencies and satellite capacity for community and non-profit broadcasting, and it made the case for airwaves and orbital paths to be recognised as a public resource and to be allocated in the public interest. Spectrum should be publicly owned, governed in a transparent way, and thereby secured as a global commons. This rejection of commercialisation was shared by other CS Media coalitions. An elaborated perspective on Internet governance or other media platforms was missing, yet WSIS?WeSeize! and its successors put a strong emphasis on openness.

Freedom of expression and communication rights. Freedom of expression constituted a crucial and fundamental policy foundation for all CS Media coalitions at and around WSIS, yet many of them pointed to the necessity for a broader set of communication rights and freedoms. Ecléctica DV and Indymedia activists highlighted the rights of information workers and privacy issues, CRIS and the WFCR discussed a wider range of communication rights, and WSIS?WeSeize! advocated for what participants preferred to call communication 'freedoms', linked these with the freedom of movement and thereby expressed their objection to repressive border regimes.

Access to information and knowledge. While the CMWG highlighted the need to spread the means of communication, and thus the material conditions of information divides, WSIS?WeSeize! and its successors (as well as CRIS and the WFCR) added a critique of the privatisation of knowledge through IPR and called for alternatives to restrictive IPR regimes, such as open source models, copyleft licenses, knowledge sharing, and an expansion of the knowledge and information commons.

Media pluralism. Strengthening the diversity of media systems as well as of the views represented in the media was a fundamental concern. However, CS Media were cautious regarding calls for state action to, e.g., limit media ownership concentration and rather focused on positive demands to improve their own role and capacities. Nevertheless, those coalitions that remained outside the immediate negotiation process, such as WSIS?WeSeize! and CRIS, launched heavy criticism of the concentrated structures and the limited content of mainstream media.

Participation. Demands for support, rights and freedoms for civil society-based media initiatives were embedded in a wider perspective on people's participation in the information and knowledge production, community self-organisation, and bottom-up practices – and thus in (explicit or implicit) opposition against the enclosure of civil society activity by state or business interventions.

Development and empowerment. Even though the CMWG's strong focus on the development frame was partially due to strategic considerations and was not shared by other CS Media coalitions, both practices and policy proposals consistently emphasized the empowerment of poor, remote and dissident communities and advocated for positive discrimination in favour of the marginalised.

Shortcomings and inconsistencies

Relations with mainstream media. CS Media will have to develop a clearer position on the level of confrontation or collaboration, respectively, with commercial and public service media and with mainstream journalism. The CMWG sided with other media actors in rejecting interventions into media structures and content from outside the media system and the journalist profession. This approach was grounded in the concern that governments were intent on limiting human rights and expanding censorship. Yet demands for limits on media ownership concentration and for public accountability of the media have been at the heart of civil society requests – expressed, e.g., at the WSF – for an improvement of communication systems (see chapter 4). By neglecting the media reform and communication rights agendas, the CMWG abandoned established civil society positions on media issues.

Media platforms. The CMWG's emphasis on radio largely excluded issues around 'new media'. It coincided with AMARC's broadcasting background, yet it ignored that CS Media have widely adopted Internet distribution of media content, and that alternative Internet Service Providers, Indymedia activists, and bloggers would have had strong views about how further development and regulation of the media landscape (including the Internet) should proceed. Even local community radios have increasingly used the Internet as a platform to exchange and publish programmes and have suggested many innovative ways of combining old and new technologies (Girard 2003). These views were largely absent from the CMWG elaborations and were hardly brought across via other spaces, such as WSIS?WeSeize! and the Community Media Forum.

The details of alternatives. While alternative frameworks and principles, such as community ownership and the global commons, were brought into the debate, their practicalities and administrative design were rarely discussed or presented, so that these concepts remained abstract – for the 'target audience' amongst governments and institutions as well as for many civil society activists.

Conceptual and political questions

Furthermore, several conceptual issues need clarification, in order to a) strengthen linkages between different types of CS Media and b) highlight the specifics of the CS Media approach vice versa a mainstream media approach.

With regards to internal CS Media linkages, political differences include the contrasts 'public vs. open' and 'rights vs. freedoms'. Regarding the former, the CMWG implicitly assigned authority to public regulatory bodies, i.e. governments and state institutions, to manage spectrum, provide financial resources and create a legal framework. WSIS?WeSeize!, in contrast, put more emphasis on openness and deregulation, was sceptical towards any government intervention and trusted in the ability of creative self-organised citizen- and civil society-based projects to prevail in the absence of government interference. The second conceptual difference – 'rights vs. freedoms' – relates closely to this. The communication rights concept advocated by the NGOs and academics collaborating in the CRIS campaign, including some of the main CMWG members, was viewed more critically by WSIS?WeSeize! participants due to its legalist focus, its reference to the government- (and, more recently, business-) dominated UN system, and its character as a particular relation towards institutions. They favoured a focus on the 'freedoms' of each person and each collectivity.

Such conceptual questions uncovered a political and ideological divide, based on two different schools of thought. Whereas the more established and development- or rights-oriented organisations collaborating in the CMWG and other civil society spaces inside the WSIS process tended to prioritise a struggle against neo-liberalism and to regard an increase in state regulation as favourable to the current business-led environment, the media activists at WSIS?WeSeize!, influenced by cyber-libertarianism, openness, and the anarchism of the recent global justice movement, maintained particular scepticism towards state action and rejected any interference by powerful actors, be they states or corporations, into the activities of grassroots civil society groups and individuals. As the analysis of strategies has shown, this political divide was increasingly blurred during the course of the WSIS process, but it was not solved.

Conceptual differences between the CMWG and mainstream media, which were not openly articulated but which boiled under the surface, included the contrasts 'market pluralism vs. content diversity', 'defensive vs. empowering freedom of expression', 'access vs. participation', and ultimately 'information vs. communication'. With regards to the first, CS Media will have to clarify what kind of pluralism and diversity they envision. They will have to differentiate their own perspective from a market approach to diversity which is based on the 'free market place of ideas', focuses on the 'freedom of choice' for consumers, and results in the competition between a multiplicity of media suppliers, without necessarily representing a diversity of social and political perspectives.[7] Media Caucus statements were brief on the question of pluralism and diversity and focused on a diversity of supply channels, rather than a diversity of content, ideas, and social values. CS Media participants did not offer an alternative concept and largely went along with this limited approach.

Equally, they did not question the dominant understanding of freedom of expression. At WSIS, the right to freedom of expression was monopolised by media actors to justify free and un-regulated media operations. Traditionally, CS Media had argued instead for the possibility of all people to generate information and knowledge, and to weaken the information monopoly of the mainstream media, but this line was hardly picked up by CS Media inside the WSIS process.[8] The development of a clearer definition of freedom of expression may use as a starting-point Stein's (2004) distinction of speech rights into "defensive" and "empowering". Whereas 'defensive' interpretations have focused on the absence of obstructive media regulation, an 'empowering' approach would foster the freedoms and the opportunities for all individuals to freely express themselves and circulate their perspectives (see chapter 5). This distinction points to a further conceptual difference – between 'access' and 'participation'. The Media Caucus mixed up the terms by suggesting that broadcasting enables the 'participation' of all in the information society, while it was, in fact, referring to 'access' to the

[7] This discourse of consumer choice gained prominence with the deregulation policies in the 1970s and 80s and has become the dominant mode of analysing pluralism in policy arenas (Karppinen 2005).

[8] Only the Bellagio statement approaches this point, see chapter 8.

reception of information content. CS Media, as we saw in chapter 2, envisage a wider understanding of participation that actually involves "a higher level of public involvement (...) in the production process and also in the management and planning of communication systems" (Servaes 1999: 85). They will need to re-claim the concept of 'participation' according to their own approach.

Ultimately, all these sets of conceptual differences point to the fundamental divide between 'information' and 'communication' – between the provision of informational 'goods' from sender to receiver, on the one side, and a type of communication, on the other, that involves public participation in the production of information and enables interactive exchange. CS Media are usually aligned to the latter (see chapter 2) but at WSIS they often went along with the former. They opposed the most direct attacks by commercial media but failed to question the deeper implications of issues such as media pluralism and freedom of expression.

The lack of a common framework

In their efforts to develop a coherent policy programme, the CMWG and other CS Media actors could draw from lists of demands highlighted previously at other policy fora, discussed at civil society meetings such as the World Social Forum, and developed by experienced actors such as AMARC. However, they could not refer to a generally agreed framework of proposals which would combine the ideas of the diversity of CS Media and provide a common foundation for policy interventions. In the absence of such a framework, the demands brought up in the CMWG often resembled an arbitrary mixture of ideas rather than a defined and complementary system. The life-span of proposals sometimes lasted only for their use in a particular document. The specific knowledge and preferences of those present at meetings often had a significant impact on the set of demands put forward to governments, and so did the decision of individual activists to attend certain meetings and not attend others, as well as the assistance of funding organisations to enable attendance at crucial meetings.

There was a lack of a continuous development of demands and of an interconnection between the diverse proposals. The demands for spectrum regulation may serve as an example: The issue of satellite capacity was included on the initiative of one participant – not because it belonged to a structured set of demands. Proposals on airwave allocation and broadcast licences occupied a central position in the CMWG statements because of the strong presence of the community radio movement. The proposal of a Community Media Fund was barely developed beyond the idea level, and it was not put in relation to the various other financing models which CS Media have developed elsewhere, such as a tax on advertising revenue and on the use of satellite capacity and radio frequency by commercial media.

So, the WSIS interventions by CS Media have shown a clear need for the development of a framework of proposals and demands which can be used by CS Media for future policy advocacy. Such a framework would need to include a coherent and complementary set of regulatory mechanisms which can be advocated by different actors at different policy arenas.

Visions and practices

As we have seen, most CS Media actors do not focus on policy contributions and lobbying, but on creating concrete alternatives to the media environment which they criticise. For most members even of the CMWG, an engagement with policy was linked with an every-day effort in setting up the structures that they advocated. This focus on 'practices' created challenges in a policy environment such as WSIS, but it was also an important asset, as it legitimised CS Media's concerns. The principles which they advocated at WSIS were grounded in the practices of civil society-based communication, and their policy proposals were backed-up with the actual experiences of communication actors. Their characteristics as practitioners and enablers of civil society-based participatory communication positioned them well in the quest for generating policy alternatives.

Interviews with CS Media practitioners and advocates underlined the integrated perspective on policy and practices. Principles and visions for both communication policy and information society were derived directly from fundamental characteristics of CS Media, as discussed in chapter 2. However, as we have seen, the governmental negotiation process provided numerous constraints and led to the focus on some objectives and to the neglect of others. So the priorities expressed in the interviews did not always match the priorities of the CMWG and other coalitions.

An alternative information society

Asked about the most important principles of CS Media which should be strengthened in current policy processes and which, in turn, would provide a supportive framework for enhancing the role of CS Media, the activists and advocates who participated in the interviews were fairly consistent in highlighting a small set of core themes. Five interviewees emphasized 'participation' as a core value – the right of people to participate in the production and dissemination of information, in the media sector, and in wider social and political processes (AC, BM, FW, MG, VO). With similar aspects in mind, five mentioned 'communication rights' or a 'right to communicate' (BM, MG, MH, MG, VO), interpreted as "not just a right to receive information selected for us by corporations or governments, but also a right to communicate ourselves" (FW). In line with a focus on a plurality of voices in media as well as in society, the same number of interviewees stressed 'cultural diversity' as a dimension which CS Media work towards and which should therefore be enhanced (BM, MG, PA, MJ, VO). Further themes included 'development' and the MDGs (CD, VO), 'gender equity' and 'women's liberation' (FW, BM), 'non-hierarchical (horizontal) forms of organisation' (FW), "access to information that is useful to urban and rural poor communities including indigenous communities; information that that they can relate to, that has meaning in their context and realities" (MC), "enhancing local knowledge and the free sharing and exchange of that knowledge" (MC).

Accordingly, the information society which the CS Media activists and advocates envision is to be founded on a set of similar core principles. It is to enable "the participation of people and groups all over the world" (AC) and the representation "of all voices" (VO), allowing for a "diversity of perspectives" (MG). Information flows "must be vice versa not just top down" (BM), "building a multi-directional flow of information that enhances citizen participation" (TN). New technologies as well as older media platforms need to be kept "accessible for non-commercial use" (FW) to create the necessary conditions for enabling people to put into practice fundamental principles such as freedom of expression, press freedom, communication rights and the plurality of opinion (MC, PA). Furthermore, cultural diversity needs to be strengthened (AC, MG), information should be recognised as a public good (MG) and an environment needs to be created "where popular forms of media and local knowledge are encouraged to flourish" (MC). There is a perceived need for commonly accessible communications infrastructure ("free wireless hubs everywhere!", MH), and production processes should be adapted to the practices of open source and free software production (MH).

9.5 The CS Media model revisited

The previous sections on strategies and content of CS Media interventions at WSIS have illustrated potentials but also difficulties of these activities and have uncovered divisions between CS Media actors. It is now time to take a step back and ask whether the CS Media model, as proposed in chapter 2, can be maintained.

Blurred division lines

The WSIS process did not lead to the clear division between mainstream and civil society media that was initially suggested. Instead, we have seen two major developments:

(1) The alliance between community media and established mainstream media. Community media actors remained involved with the Media Caucus throughout the whole WSIS process and collaborated closely with mainstream journalist groups. The Media Caucus assembled actors from a variety of media sectors, including community media, and developed common statements which included perspectives of all these groups.

(2) The fragmentation of CS Media. Different types of CS Media were divided across different spaces, fought for different objectives, rarely collaborated, failed to develop a common agenda, and exposed different political, cultural and ideological tendencies.

The structural and strategic differences between the actors which I have identified here as CS Media can be illustrated by referring to the instruments of social movement research, as outlined in chapter 4. The first WSIS phase, in particular, confirmed a distinction in *activism/social movement activity* and *advocacy*. WSIS?WeSeize!, representing the former, was characterised by a "fluid and ephemeral" (Mueller 2004: 6) approach and had a strong presence of 'countercultural' and 'identity-oriented' actors (Kriesi 2004) who emphasize the indivisibility of means and ends. The CMWG, on the other hand, was rooted in formal organisations which interacted directly with official policy-making institutions.

From this we might conclude that the CS Media model is hard to maintain and that the Media Caucus expressed a common 'media interest'. Within the 'non-mainstream' sector, the diversity of forms of mobilisation, repertories of action and thematic objectives, as well as the distinction in institutional and non-institutional contention, would cast doubts on claims of a common identity.

Confirmation of the model

However, taking a closer look at the processes inside the caucuses and working groups as well as the objectives and conceptual approaches of media actors, a different picture emerges. As was illustrated in chapters 7.2 and 9.2, the veil of a common media perspective was repeatedly broken, uncovering deep divides. The Media Caucus was not a harmonious coalition of like-minded colleagues but was constantly shaken by differences in perspectives. The process of developing common statements was often on the brink of failure and was characterised by tough and long negotiations between actors with opposing objectives. Conflicts were (temporarily) resolved only through the experience and the stamina of the caucus chair; the emergence of authoritarian states hostile towards the right to freedom of expression, which united the caucus against a common enemy; and the strategic decision by CS Media not to insist on objectives such as the establishment of communication rights and public participation in media production

At the same time, we have seen that the fragmentation of CS Media into different spaces was increasingly overcome and that many of the objectives brought forward by the CMI and the CMWG displayed a considerable connection with the issues discussed at WSIS?WeSeize!. As the analysis of strategies has shown, the fragmented arena of non-state/non-commercial media actors has been weaving the first ties of a loose network by developing communication channels, testing collaboration, discussing objectives and strategies, and thus approaching a common discourse. Different perspectives on policy issues have slowly converged. To form a sustained network and a deeper coalition, the different types of CS Media would need to develop denser information exchanges and a greater level of coordination of strategies, and to tackle the political, ideological and conceptual differences discussed in previous chapters.[9] With linkages remaining weak, this would be a task for the future, yet a common base has been established.

Commonalities and differences in the media sector: Results from interviews

A major part of the interviews I conducted with CS Media activists, advocates and practitioners focused on the question whether there can be a common agenda between media actors of all kinds. Interviewees were asked about the common goals as well as the differences between all media actors in a policy process and about their perspectives on the collaborations of media actors, particularly in the Media Caucus.

Four out of ten interviewees rejected the very possibility that there be common interests or values between CS Media and other media, particularly commercial media. Most other respondents named thematic areas where there may potentially be common interests but were convinced that, overall, differences exceeded commonalities. Such (potential) common goals would include a focus on content vice versa technological infrastructure (AC); en-

[9] This corresponds with the criteria suggested by Khagram et al. (2002): information exchange, practical coordination, a sense of shared values, and eventually a collective identity.

suring "that the universality of the principle of freedom of expression including the independence and pluralism in all forms of media are central in any discussion on the Information Society" (MC, also PA, MJ, TN); and "the notion that the people have a right to know how global processes affect them, and that they are not just powerless observers" (MG). One participant (MJ) pointed to possible alliances between CS and public service media "concerning the critical perspective on market driven media policies", while another participant (MG) was doubtful about this connection, noting that "public service media behaves often as commercial media, competing for ads and audience with commercial media while reliant on public funds." One interviewee (TN) highlighted "editorial integrity", independence, and the strengthening of fundamental journalist principles as the main common interest but was contradicted by a fellow Media Caucus member (VO) who questioned the "status of journalists as 'only' competent people to define standards" and pointed to the necessary participation of civil society in defining media ethics. Accordingly, MJ noted that the goals of CS Media would necessarily imply a "loss of the power of the existing media system".

Further differences highlighted by interviewees included a far stronger focus by CS Media on cultural diversity (AC); social and political diversity (AC); communication rights (AC, VO, MJ); the direct participation of people in communication processes through CS Media (FW); questions of media ownership and control, which affect interests and purpose of media (MC, PA); differences in motivation, with commercial media primarily interested in accessing new markets (MH) and tending to monopolise the media sector (MC, TN); and differences on whether the main subject which needs to be empowered is the media system or civil society (VO). One interviewee (BM) pointed to the inevitable competition between different media actors regarding appropriate shares in information society and communication governance, and three (MC, PA, MJ) named commercial and government-controlled media as the prime adversaries of CS Media. Expressing the opposition and conflict in the media sector, FW pointed to the need for CS Media to defend "the interests of local people and their communications needs against top-down media incursions" and to "represent the rights of citizens to communicate".

The values and interests of the media actors from different backgrounds, assembled in the Media Caucus, were thus seen as "radically" (AC, FW) or "fundamentally" (MC) differential (also MG, MH, PA), so that most perspectives on the Media Caucus as an attempt to integrate actors divided by such fundamental lines of conflict were sceptical. Only one person (TN) maintained that "in the end the commonalities were and are more significant than the differences."

One participant (MJ) also pointed to differences amongst CS Media, which became visible a) in tensions between those inside and those outside of the official process, and b) in a "different perspective on how to struggle and negotiate" as well as a "certain tendency of hesitation [by those inside the process] to fight, which may eventually weaken the negotiating power of CS [civil society] as a whole".

In accordance with their views on commonalities and contrasts between media actors, most interviewees divided the social and political sphere into three sectors – government, commercial, and civil society – and applied the same distinction to the media sector (explicitly: BM, FW, MJ, PA). Thus, only particular kinds of media were seen as part of civil society (MC). In the words of AC: "Media [as such] is not from civil society, but civil society has its types of communication such as communitary radios and TVs". A key benchmark was seen in "the participation of civil society in programs or administration" (AC) and in whether media "belongs to citizens" (TN). This would exclude commercial media and possibly public service media, although interviewees were unsure about the latter (MJ, TN).

Only one interviewee (VO) held that "private enterprise is part of civil society". Others (MG, MH) noted that, theoretically, all media could be civil society but that, practically, the rise of some media as multinational corporations and the increasing concentration of ownership caused divisions into commercial and civil society actors.

CS Media as analytical and as strategic category

Both the observations of the WSIS process and the interviews point to several conclusions:

(1) As an *analytical* category, the CS Media model has to be qualified. It is not always diametrically opposed to mainstream media, as suggested by the ideal model outlined in chapter 2, and it does not yet form an explicit common network with a common agenda.

(2) Generally, however, and despite the confusing and often contradictory labyrinth of WSIS processes, the model has largely been confirmed by the underlying differences inside the Media Caucus and the thematic and strate-

gic connections between community media inside and autonomous/tactical/alternative media outside WSIS.[10]

(3) As a *strategic* category, the CS Media model may be a helpful tool for overcoming the fragmentation of the sector and to increase network density. A common frame of reference can trigger new linkages between different actors, strengthen those linkages which already exist, and advance the development of a common identity.

In a policy environment such as WSIS, with its strong emphasis on a civil society discourse, the concept of CS Media may facilitate the convergence of a wider range of civil society-based media actors in transnational policy arenas, thus create strong common platforms, open up opportunities for creating broader policy agendas, and advance mobilisation for those agendas. Furthermore, it would create clear distinctions between civil society-based media – i.e. media set up and run by citizens and civil society groups – and those media with close ties to states and governments as well as those set up as commercial enterprises. It would serve to unmask commercial media as non-civil society, thereby supporting the cohesion of the self-organised civil society spaces and possibly also changing the perception of 'the media' in the minds of the wider public.

The term 'CS Media' may not be appropriate in all circumstances. In some cases, 'community media' may continue to offer a helpful frame for lobbying governments and seeking support from donors. In other circumstances, other concepts may be more appropriate. For example, as it became apparent during the WSIS media debate that the term 'community media' would not be accepted by some governments, a substitute term such as 'non-profit media' may have allowed to keep a reference to CS Media inside the Geneva declaration.[11] Outside policy arenas, where the term 'civil society' provides less identification and even triggers criticism (see chapter 2.1), emphasizing the 'participatory' or 'autonomous' character of CS Media may be more appropriate. Different frames may be necessary for different purposes, but their interrelationships need to be considered and developed.

---

[10] This finding correlates with the analysis of the wider set of "democratic media activism" by Carroll/Hackett (2006) who refer to "different groups, organized in somewhat different ways and pursuing distinctive agendas" (Carroll/Hackett 2006: 89) and therefore lack a clear collective identity, yet create networks of collective action and engage in a "politics of connections" (idem: 93).

[11] Wolf Ludwig, member of both the CMWG and the Media Caucus, notes, regarding the objections to the term 'community media' in the government negotiations: "We missed the opportunity to agree informally on a different term and to propose, for example, 'non-profit' media" (Interview WL).

9.6 Towards participatory communication governance

The characteristics of CS Media and the specific challenges which they faced at WSIS point to a number of shortcomings in the current arrangements of global governance, but also suggest steps towards a more inclusive political process. In this final section of this chapter, I will leave the actor-specific level of CS Media, go back to the systemic level of the multi-stakeholder governance process, as discussed in chapter 6, take a more detailed look at its insufficiencies and sketch some preliminary ideas for participatory governance models.

The WSIS multi-stakeholder experience

WSIS was a laboratory for developing and implementing new modes of governance, struggling between the promise of a multi-stakeholder environment, in which all actors can participate equally, and the attempts by many governments to retain a dominant role for the state. It expressed the contest "between a traditional, hierarchical vision of global governance and a process of dynamic integration that is open to new actors participating at different levels" (Raboy 2004a: 354). It sent mixed signals to civil society – sometimes offering unprecedented levels of participation, then again pushing it out of negotiation spaces.

The analysis of both participants and observers mostly distinguishes between the (progressive) general idea of WSIS, pro-actively pushed and shaped by civil society actors, and the (less progressive) details of the multi-stakeholder realities (see chapter 6.3.4.). There is agreement that WSIS has helped to open previously closed spaces of inter-governmental debate to organised groups of citizens and activists. In its WSIS2 statement, the civil society network praised the "innovative rules and practices of participation" (Civil Society Plenary 2005: 7) established in some areas of the WSIS process "as a result of constant pressure from Civil Society" (ibid.), and it highlighted WGIG as a particularly innovative format "where governmental and Civil Society actors worked on an equal footing" (ibid.). The high degree of formalisation of civil society involvement in WSIS as well as the autonomous structures created by civil society participants, as argues Raboy, "form the basis of a new model of representation and legitimation of non-governmental input to global affairs" (Raboy 2004a: 349), and as a result, "the rules and parameters of global governance have shifted" (ibid.).

However, as notes Ó Siochrú, access to the negotiation process "was fragile, was frequently challenged and regularly withdrawn" (Ó Siochrú 2004a: 338). Civil society actors protested strongly against their repeated exclusion from meaningful participation, and their publicly declared withdrawal from the negotiation process in the run-up to WSIS1 was one of the most far-reaching options in their repertoire of contentious action at that time. In some aspects, WSIS even fell behind innovative practices tested in other summit processes.[12] Cammaerts/Carpentier (2006) conclude that WSIS offered 'extended consultations' to civil society actors but certainly not the 'full participation' which had been promised.

The background of the discrepancy between the 'big picture' and the actual implementation of multi-stakeholderism had several dimensions. First, and not surprisingly, it fitted with the general distinction in 'discourse' and 'reality' which was visible, for example, in the summit documents in which progressive declarations on 'inclusivity' and 'participation' were rarely followed by calls for concrete measures. As was shown in chapter 6, the perceived need for an innovative discourse on multi-stakeholderism did not necessarily lead to a commitment by governments to share power. Secondly, it reflected a struggle between different forces in the summit process, some of whom – e.g., PrepCom President Adama Samassekou – agreed with the need for increased civil society inclusion while others – represented by the government delegations of Pakistan and China, but also Brazil – sought to limit participation of non-state actors and to retain decision-making power in the hands of governments. As Raboy/Landry (2005: 110) write, "[n]egotiation is an activity that rests on relative positions of strength and governments are not very excited about the idea of giving any ground to organizations that are highly critical of them". Thirdly, the dimension of time may have contributed to a perceived "turn against civil society" (Ó Siochrú 2004a: 342) during the period between the announcement and the conclusion of WSIS. With a return to unilateralism by, particularly, the US administration and a perception amongst some governments that the increased involvement of civil society in global governance had gone too far,[13] WSIS saw several "attempts to roll-back the influence of civil society" (ibid.).

[12] Ó Siochrú (2004a) recounts that, e.g., the preparatory process towards the World Summit on Sustainable Development (WSSD) in Johannesburg in 2002 officially included civil society positions in its records, and at Habitat 2 in 1996, composite text amendments were published as official UN documents. Habitat 2 even allowed civil society actors to take the floor and directly table proposals, which was not possible at WSIS PrepComs.

[13] This perception correlated with a view expressed elsewhere by the business community. At the World Economic Forum 2005, Sir Digby Jones, head of Britain's leading employers' organisation, charged: "The pendulum is swinging too far in favour of the NGOs. The World Economic Forum is caving in to them. Davos has been hijacked by those who want business to apologise for itself" (http://business.guardian.co.uk/story/0,,1402183,00.html).

Who is a 'stakeholder' in 'multi-stakeholderism'?

Even the instances of successful implementation of the multi-stakeholder principle uncovered the need to create mechanisms for the less organised, less resourced and less policy-fluent parts of civil society to participate in governance processes – and the necessity to transform these processes into an attractive environment for such groups. WSIS did not overcome the separation in 'official NGOs' and other parts of civil society, which was outlined in chapter 4. The guidelines for participating in the envisioned 'multi-stakeholder' debate only allowed formal organisations with a traditional hierarchical structure and sufficient funds to take part (see chapter 9.2.). Partially, this was due to the unwillingness of many governments to water down the governmental monopoly in decision-making, but partially it reflected the lack of appropriate concepts for including actors which are not based in traditional and familiar formal structures and organisations.

Many of those who are building information society in their everyday practices were missing: autonomous media practitioners, free software developers, creators of grassroots communication infrastructure, such as citizen-based community wireless networks, etc. Gurstein, a critical observer of WSIS processes, missed "significant participation from those working directly at the grass roots in initiating and implementing ICTs in support of community activities and development" and noted that "while there has been a very considerable degree of 'talking about' ICTs for Development there has been remarkably little 'talking with' those who are actually doing the job on the ground" (Gurstein 2005b). The Community Media Forum at WSIS1 constituted one of the few occasions which brought those to the summit compound who worked exclusively in grassroots media projects and had so far not engaged with the global policy level. However, being there primarily to 'showcase' their experiences, their level of exchange with other civil society actors remained weak, and so their direct influence on the civil society agenda at WSIS was limited.

Not only the official WSIS structures, but also the civil society networks were criticised for such shortcomings. Gurstein, again, described the civil society actors at WSIS as "youngish, brightish, well-groomed and well-educated, clearly the winners in the Information Society sweepstakes" who used the WSIS process to create networks amongst themselves but who failed "to reach out and link to other perhaps less privileged or well-placed networks" – to "those below and beyond" (Gurstein 2005c). If we continue Gurstein's thoughts, this process of "networking the networked" (ibid.) would lead to the creation of a global civil society elite and raise the divides between 'inside' and 'outside'/'beyond'.

Civil society and representation

Inside the WSIS civil society network, both the predominance of Northern NGO actors and the close collaboration with the private sector were criticised. Djilali Benamrane, member of an African NGO network, noted: "The civil society is the image and the reality of the real world society, dominated by the North, by the governments associated to private sector and the IGO including UNO, dominated by english language" (Benamrane 2005). Research by Cammaerts/Carpentier (2006) points to European dominance in civil society participation, which the authors link to the unavailability of funding resources for civil society groups in the Global South. This predominance, according to some participants, was reflected in the thematic priorities which focused on human rights problems in the South rather than those in the North. Park, a member of the Internet Governance Caucus, charged: "WSIS CS is willing to pick up human rights issues of Tunisian government practice but have no guts to talk about collection of finger prints and eye inspection whenever people from other countries enter the USA" (Park 2005).

Views differed on how intense the links with other 'stakeholders' should be woven. While some hailed the "shared responsibility" (de La Chappelle 2005), the move "from competing legitimacies to combining legitimacies" (ibid.), and the "process of concertation" (ibid.) inherent in the multi-stakeholder principle, others pointed to the danger of watering down a distinct civil society perspective and warned that "we are being multistakeholdered to death" (Jordan 2005). Controversies over whether to forge alliances between civil society and the business sector caused some to conclude that "'civil society' exists as a false unity" (McLaughlin 2005), and others expressed the vast differences of interests and approaches within the sector by distinguishing between "jet set" (Fullsack 2005) civil society – the leaders of WSIS of civil society structures and of large NGOs – and "real" (ibid.) civil society, i.e. grassroots organisations "working in the field and near to their people and sharing their concerns" (ibid.).

Whereas the first WSIS phase had established a successful example of a "global civil society" (see chapter 2.1) at work, the second phase led to renewed understanding of the political, ideological and resource-related diversity amongst civil society actors. Whereas pragmatic approaches towards self-organisation and summit interventions had prevailed before, underlying questions of delegation and representation were now put on the table. In the words of Gurstein, "the real issue remains how to provide a meaningful and effective voice for this 'larger civil society' and some useful process of legitimation/accountability for those who are able/willing to become 'representatives' for CS in forums such as the WSIS Prepcoms" (Gurstein 2005a).

Tracey Naughton, chair of the Media Caucus as well as of many civil society plenary sessions, added: "Of concern are the limits to two-way feedback between the elite advocates (not to take anything at all away from this grouping) and the masses" (Interview TN).

Individuals and networks

One particular structural challenge for the mechanisms and procedures of 'representing' civil society interests is the specific role that individuals play in information/communication processes. As was noted in earlier chapters, and exemplified by WSIS?WeSeize!, the skills and the knowledge of individual experts are at the basis of communication activism, and collective entities have often been rather loose and temporary, with deep scepticism towards formal long-term structures. Internet development and online campaigning has often been conducted by individuals who do not correspond to any specific organisation or social movement. Personal reputation has been more relevant than representing the interests of a clearly defined collective. According to Vittorio Bertola, Internet activist and member of the Internet Governance Caucus, "the emergence of informal online movements and individual activism, side by side with traditional NGOs, is a key change that has happened in civil society in the last few years" (Bertola 2005a). From this follows that "we have to find a way to incorporate informal and individual activism in civil society participation to UN processes" (ibid.).

The radical approach, according to Internet activists, would be to do away with organisations altogether and instead have "a free assembly of women and men, each equal to each other" (Bertola 2005b). Former ICANN director Karl Auerbach agrees: "We should allow people to speak for themselves in the forums in which decisions (…) are made and not require that they act through artificial proxies" (Auerbach 2005). As a consequence, the term 'stake-holder' should be abandoned "because it forgets that at the bottom of things, all organizations and groupings are aggregations of individual people each with his/her own point of view" (ibid.).

The problem with this approach is that it is based on the idea of a pure and rational public sphere in which honest men and women come together to discuss openly with the best intentions to make decisions for the common good. It neglects the diversity of capacities and power positions which allow some to underline their interests more than others, and it does not give an answer on how to overcome the hurdles for participation mentioned earlier (funding, particularly). Avri Doria, another member of the Internet Governance Caucus, fears that the sheer volume of statements and positions "would tend to make all our voices disappear into an unmanageable mass" and that therefore "scaling in such a process seems to require that there be ways to combine our voices into the aggregate voice of affinity groups of like minded individuals" (Doria 2005).

A conceptual focus on networks, rather than individuals, takes into account some of the innovative proposals of the individualist approach, as well as some of the concerns brought up against it. As the individualist approach, it challenges "the illusion that the myths of representational democracy might somehow be transferred" (Lovink/Rossiter 2005) to the emerging era of post-territorial forms of human organisation, and it thereby calls "for a new logics of politics" (ibid.) characterised by "non-representational democratic models of decision making" (ibid.). However it retains forms of collectivity which allow for an aggregation of individual interests.[14] Panganiban confirms such an approach as he reflects on the civil society operations at WSIS: "We had the most success when we were able to reflect the diversity of our views, and we had the least success when we had to decide on one statement or one position on behalf of civil society" (Panganiban 2005).

Developing participatory governance

If a policy process is to be fully legitimate, the preferences and issues of various types of civil society groups need to be included into policy agendas. The laboratory of multi-stakeholder governance, which the WSIS constituted, has highlighted a number of challenges that require further thought and action. Fundamental access barriers to global governance arenas need to be lowered; rules for registration and accreditation to consider the specific structural characteristics of grassroots groups and loose networks and allow non-formally-established organisations to participate; funding needs to be provided for these groups and networks, both for participating in negotiations and for presenting practices and projects at the summit. These steps of structural reform would increase the breadth of voices and perspectives represented in policy debate and would thus create a more inclusive governance process.

However, the analysis of civil society's lack of participation has pointed to a deeper set of challenges, including

- The focus that many actors place on practices rather than policy.

[14] As noted in chapter 4, Diani's focus on network approaches to studying contentious politics explicitly combines the role of individuals with a perspective on collectivities. He defines social movement networks as "informal interactions, between a plurality of individuals (…) on the basis of a shared collective identity (Diani 2003: 301) and consisting of "formally independent actors who are embedded in specific local contexts (where 'local' is meant in either a territorial or a social sense)" (ibid.).

- The rejection by many civil society actors of the persistent state/business dominance in global governance.
- The disintegration of traditional forms of formal organisation, and the increased role of individuals and loose networks.
- The crisis of institutions and, generally, representational democracy.

These trends suggest that merely inviting broader sets of actors to existing policy processes and lowering the obstacles towards participation would be insufficient. There is a need towards more profound institutional transformation. The challenge is how to move beyond "closed and inter-locking compacts – however tripartite they may appear" (Gurstein 2005c) towards "the wilder reaches of democracy" (ibid.) and forms of participatory decision-making that allow for a diversity of actors with different political approaches and organisational models to come together.

Network concepts offer interesting starting-points. "Organised networks", according to Lovink/Rossiter (2005), are "clouds of social relationships", "temporary and voluntary forms of collaboration", which link the informality of virtual networks and the formality of institutions. In that, they bear resemblance to the organisational structures of many CS Media (see chapter 2). While allowing for fluidity and flexibility, they provide effective forms of collective organising. As a civil society approach to a policy arena such as WSIS, 'organised networks' could position themselves as overlapping circles in different locations – some closer, some more distant – around that arena. The overlaps would ensure that different civil society entities and approaches, from 'inside' to 'outside' to 'beyond' are connected and that information and policy preferences are flowing from one to the next. The 'embryonic stages of a multi-level strategy' which we saw at WSIS were made possible by such overlapping circles, creating lines of communication and affinity from Geneva03 via CRIS and the Community Media Forum to the civil society caucuses. Yet the overlaps were only marginally developed and certainly require much more attention. At the same time, and as has also been shown, the distinctiveness of each circle/network, each with its specific practices and political approaches, needs to be maintained and cannot automatically be subsumed under the same agenda. The following figure exemplifies a few of the potential connections and overlaps between CS Media and related networks around WSIS.

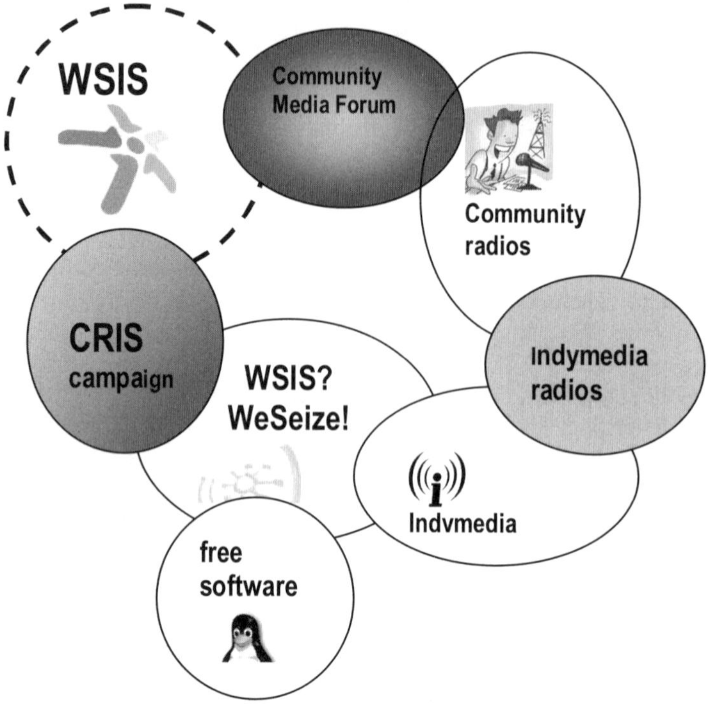

Figure 3: Overlapping network structure – potential connections between CS Media around WSIS

Applying a 'networks' approach to the governance level, one result may be what Kleinwächter has called the "United Constituencies" (Kleinwächter 2005a). He argues that the concept of 'constituencies' has emerged as an important social category which identifies members not according to citizenship and geographical territory, but according to common interest, a common history, and common language. 'Constituencies' thus take note of the "reconfiguration of social space" (Scholte 2000: 46) towards "relative deterritorialization" (idem: 50) and growing "supraterritoriality" (ibid.), and offer a way to move beyond what Scholte called "methodological territorialism" (idem: 56). The 'United Constituencies' may complement traditional national and inter-national structures in a co-regulatory model (Kleinwächter 2005b). However, if territory and nation are being questioned, so may be the concept of unity. The practices of CS Media, the trends of the information age, and the critiques of WSIS?WeSeize! and many other civil society actors challenge centralist approaches and require deep justification for any regulatory measures which may intervene with civil society-based communication systems. From a networks perspective, a united global summit may increasingly look like a dinosaur. Rather than the actual summit with its common (but tooth-less) declarations, the regional and topic-related preparatory conferences, side-events and mobilisations may, in the long run, provide a more appropriate framework for policy debates. They offer more potential for involving a wider variety of actors and more scope for questioning established structures of power, at least if they focus – as did WGIG – on thematic expertise rather than traditional state monopolies in decision-making. Accordingly, not only WGIG delivered better results, from a civil society perspective, than WSIS, but so did the Marrakech conference on the "Role and Place of Media in the Information Society (…)" and many others. A system of interrelated policy clusters, each gathering constituencies from a particular thematic area, may offer more leeway to civil society actors than the attempt of creating unity – even if it is one with a multi-stakeholder face. Moving towards a decentralised and bottom-up approach to policy-making, such a system of clusters may be an important step from 'extended consultations' to participatory governance.

This chapter could only highlight a few of the concerns and ideas which have emerged around the WSIS process and which may provide starting-points for a deeper analysis. A more systematic review of the WSIS multi-stakeholder experience, its challenges and shortcomings, and its further contextualisation in theories of global governance and transnational democracy, may propose ways to think beyond the liberal-institutionalist base of global governance models – as well as of concepts such as cosmopolitan democracy (Held 2003; McGrew 2001) – by including 'networks' (Diani 2003; Lovink/Rossiter 2005), 'affinity groups' (Day 2005) and 'constituencies' (Kleinwächter 2005a) as fundamental categories. Such an endeavour may contribute to the ongoing re-shaping and re-defining of multi-stakeholder processes and to their development into participatory forms of governance.

10 Prospects

Lessons from WSIS

The analysis of the outcomes of CS Media activities at and around WSIS has provided a mixed picture. Whereas the official WSIS negotiations hardly led to positive measurable results for CS Media, the larger WSIS process provided several (more indirect) success stories and raised the profile of CS Media. A platform to discuss the priorities and guiding principles of governance for the 'information society', WSIS was a valuable political opportunity for confronting governments, international institutions and other media actors with the concerns of CS Media and for raising their visibility on the global level.

The translation of their objectives into the official summit documents was inadequate, partially because of the dominant 'new ICT' paradigm embedded in information society discourses and the specific focus on state/security interests and business actors. The openness of the institutional setting was limited; alliances with other media actors were contested and conflictive; government allies either weak or not committed; issue resonance was low; interest configurations were often hostile; and disunity of dominant groups did not occur in a way that opened inroads for CS Media to substantially influence the debate. So, the preconditions for progressive change, from the perspective of CS Media, were difficult. The fact that they were not recognised in the official documents was a step back in their efforts to strengthen a supportive regulatory framework. However, their high profile in side-events, on civil society agendas, and in many of those issue areas which WSIS identified as particular areas of concern represents building blocks for achieving a more central role in future policy processes. The WSIS documents support local content production, cultural diversity, the public domain, freedom of expression, and community ICT centres, amongst others, and they thus vindicate CS Media goals and practices.

The WSIS process has illustrated both the difficulties and the potentials for CS Media on the road towards successful policy influence, and it has provided lessons for future interventions into governance fora. In this chapter, I will briefly re-visit some of these.

Strategies for policy interventions. Responding to the development orientation of the summit, the community media advocates inside the summit process focused on a development frame to communicate their concerns and objectives to their target audience – government delegations. 'Targeted lobbying' raised recognition of CS Media amongst several government delegations and may, over time, build up a counter-weight to those governments who are hostile against these media. CS Media also set up alternative spaces for discussion and collaboration 'outside' and thereby created a reference point for a) alternative agendas, and b) the feasibility of extra-institutional tactics.

Multi-level strategy. WSIS was thus a test case for developing a multi-level strategy between those who lobbied for immediate policy change and those who articulated a broader and more fundamental critique. Such a strategy would consist of:

(1) policy advocacy, lobbying and monitoring of negotiations inside the official process,

(2) public pressure from outside the official process,

(3) development of policy/governance alternatives and of self-organised alternative infrastructure.

The combination of different approaches will need to be extended in order to generate a stronger position in political processes and to benefit from the specific characteristics of the sector. An integrated strategy may constitute a model for civil society approaches to global governance and apply to a wider set of policy agendas beyond the thematic areas of information and communication. Future work may examine the role of integrated strategic approaches in other areas of civil society concern.

'Beyond' policy. Focusing on critical practices and self-organised counter- and complementary media systems is a distinct characteristic of CS Media and is often privileged over direct policy influence. In the context of policy fora such as WSIS, these practices can serve as "guiding stars" (Interview MH) – highlighting problems, offering trajectories and developing future scenarios. Innovative and alternative practices can trigger subtle types of norm change and may need deeper integration with the more directly policy-centred approaches. In this respect, CS Media have a unique opportunity "to serve as both a challenge and an alternative in global communication governance" (Interview MC).

The 'CS Media divide'. Fragmentation within the CS media sector consists of several layers: political-ideological differences between a libertarian emphasis on openness and a focus on development and poverty reduction; different perspectives on global governance between a rejection of global summits and participation; different organisational approaches between loose and temporary activist networks and formal NGOs; conceptual differences between, e.g., an emphasis on either rights or freedoms; and content differences between a focus on new ICTs (and related issues such as IPR) and on traditional media platforms (such as radio). CS Media will need to establish denser information exchanges and develop the positive potential of different but complementary approaches.[1]

A common thematic platform. Individually, the CMWG, WSIS?WeSeize!, and other CS Media coalitions generated elaborate policy agendas for the future evolution of information society and communication governance. From these separate agendas, a common list of concerns can be constructed, which includes the legalisation of self-organised communication systems, the democratic governance of communication infrastructure, public financial support for CS Media, media pluralism, freedom of expression and communication rights, putting a halt to the privatisation and commercialisation of knowledge, and increasing public participation in information production. Yet these objectives were not aggregated to a common agenda, and different CS Media made different claims. While the CMWG chose to emphasize a development frame which excluded other CS media issues, WSIS?WeSeize! created similar boundaries by focusing on 'media activist culture' and new ICTs.

The development of a common policy framework, embracing the thematic priorities and expertise of different types of CS Media, from community radio NGOs to online activists, and encompassing the wide range of objectives discussed at the World Social Fora, brought forward by media reform and communication rights movements, would be an important task to enhance future policy interventions. The WSIS process allowed the development of outlines of such a common agenda. A valuable task for both CS Media activists and sympathetic scholars would be to continue that path towards a clearer policy programme.

Content clarification. Policy objectives will also require clarification and elaboration. CS Media will need to develop and advocate a clearer understanding of concepts such as media pluralism, freedom of expression, participation and communication, and how exactly their specific interpretations of these dimensions differ from those brought forward by other media actors. In the WSIS Media Caucus, the understanding of these terms was largely influenced by the perspectives of commercial media and established

---

[1] WSIS has also shown that there are significant overlaps and that boundaries between different types of CS Media are blurred. AMARC (thus, the more institutional side of CS Media) may serve as an example: One of the dominant strands of discussion at the AMARC9 congress in Amman, 11-17 November 2006, was whether the organisation should be seen as a service provider or a social movement. A large part of participants emphasized the need to strengthen AMARC's social movement characteristics vice versa its service provision.

mainstream journalism, while CS Media did not offer alternative conceptualisations and largely went along with this limited approach.

Framing CS Media. The marginalisation of CS Media in the Media Caucus has shown that a common base and a robust umbrella are vital. This would need to combine different types of community, alternative, autonomous, etc. media under one roof, or generate strong linkages between these concepts. It would need to allow for diversity amongst actors and their specific approaches, while drawing clear boundaries to those media actors – named here as 'mainstream media' – with different characteristics, practices and interests.

I have proposed to use the term Civil Society Media as such an umbrella, as it combines flexibility with the necessary demarcation lines. It relates to the widely-used concept of civil society in UN and other global policy processes, and to the spaces specifically created for civil society as a stakeholder. Just as other terminologies, it may not be applicable to all processes and situations, but it can contribute to clarifying the features, objectives and commonalities within this sector, and it highlights an important claim regarding these media as 'the media of civil society'.[2]

Media alliances. Alliances with other (commercial and public service) media actors were fragile and survived only due to a common enemy who made media actors assemble around a small set of common interests. Beyond this narrow set of common demands, the alliance uncovered deep-rooted divides in values, interests and policy objectives between CS Media and the representatives of other media forms. These observations cast doubts on the prospects of generating a common approach to media policy by different types of media. CS Media will need to agree on clear conditions as well as boundaries for collaboration with other media actors and will need to continuously re-evaluate those efforts.

CS Media and information society. While the coalition of social management objectives and neo-liberal tendencies, which has characterised information society, found its expression at WSIS in the connection between state-security interests and a competitive market environment, CS Media have represented an interpretation of information society as a social framework grounded in openness and bottom-up processes, and based on the crea-

---

2 The concept of 'community media', as used at WSIS, has been recognised at other policy fora but did not reflect a broader set of CS Media concepts and traditions, carried the risk of self-marginalisation, and proved to be a difficult choice for gaining recognition in the WSIS documents. As CMWG member Wolf Ludwig said: "The word 'community' was a 'red rag' for some delegates. We missed the chance to propose, in a timely manner, alternative terms" (Interview WL, translation by the author).

tive acts of civil society initiatives. They constitute an approach of participatory and interactive communication rather than one-way information streams, and their particular perspective on information environments is based on public participation, cultural and social diversity, communication rights and freedoms, public goods, common infrastructure and open knowledge. CS Media constitute one of the forces of decentralisation which have accompanied innovations in the information sphere, yet they largely reject the dreams of techno-centric progress and confirm that decentralisation is a political project, rather than a technological.

Predictably, they did not manage to generate much support for this perspective from those actors representing a very different version of information society, but they influenced the debates which took place around the official summit as well as amongst the civil society networks, and thus proved that there is a continuing struggle between different models of information society – a top-down and a bottom-up model. Rooted in critical practices of setting up alternative information systems, and thus developing 'information society' on an everyday basis, CS Media are well prepared to continue this struggle within as well as beyond global governance fora.

Participatory global governance. Moving from an actor-focused perspective to the systemic environment of policy interventions, the experiences of CS Media highlight significant shortcomings in current global governance mechanisms – even in those with a 'multi-stakeholder' face. They point to the need to include grassroots actors, loose networks and activist groups into global communication governance, to recognise the existing practices and self-organised infrastructure of civil society groups, and to take note of new forms of organisation which emerge beyond territorial and representational models. Further research needs to be conducted on systematising these accounts and conceptualising participatory forms of global governance.[3]

Outlook

WSIS has generated an extensive follow-up process and has triggered the emergence of several related governance fora. The implementation of the agreements of the Geneva Action Plan and the Tunis Agenda is organised according to the main themes of WSIS phase 1, with work on each theme being facilitated by UN agencies, particularly the ITU, UNESCO and the UNDP. UNESCO is the facilitator for the so-called 'action line' on media, and annual meetings serve to discuss progress. The debate on Internet governance is carried forward by the Internet Governance Forum (IGF) which meets on an annual basis (the first meeting took place in Athens in October

[3] For example, see Hintz/Milan 2006b, 2009.

2006); and the Global Alliance for ICT and Development (GAID) was created post-WSIS as a multi-stakeholder forum to address issues around the digital divide and continue the work of the UN ICT Task Force.

The IGF has been the most prominent outcome as it refers to a specific and very conflictive WSIS theme, and because it has continued the particularly open and egalitarian multi-stakeholder approach of the WGIG. The IGF does not replace ICANN as the main regulatory body for the Internet, does not have a decision-making role and cannot negotiate binding agreements, but it can set policy agendas. One innovation has been the establishment of 'Dynamic Coalitions' in which members of all stakeholder groups discuss specific Internet policy sub-themes – such as spam, privacy, freedom of expression, linguistic diversity – and try to find common positions. A large number of NGO representatives have participated in meetings and debates, and so IGF has served to further advance the multi-stakeholder principle. However the obstacles to participation for smaller and informal civil society groups persist (Hintz/Milan 2009).

The large and influential civil society participants from WSIS have continued to be engaged with the follow-up process. APC is an active participant in the IGF, and AMARC convenes a working group on community media in the UNESCO-facilitated media action line, finally bringing CS Media into the core of WSIS debate. However it has been outside the post-WSIS process that CS Media advocates have expanded their activities. In Europe, the Community Media Forum Europe (CMFE) has emerged as the voice of community media in the policy sphere. It has mobilised around the Council of Europe Ministerial Conferences on Mass Media Policy in Kiev 2005 and Reykjavik 2009, it has engaged in consultations with the European Commission and it has achieved observer status with the Group of Specialists on Media Diversity within the Council of Europe. One year after the CMFE, in 2006, the European chapter of AMARC was re-established and has joined the CMFE in regional policy advocacy.

Interest in CS Media amongst policy-makers has increased significantly. In 2007, the European Parliament published a study on "The State of Community Media in the European Union", based on which it adopted a resolution on "Community Media in Europe" one year later. The study highlights community media's contribution to social cohesion, media pluralism, cross-cultural dialogue, local regeneration, local creativity and civic engagement. It calls for legal recognition of community media, access to licences in both analogue and digital environments and financial support for the sector, and it notes that "if society's future relies on the active involvement of informed, media literate citizens community media can play a definitive role in facilitating such a future" (European Parliament, iv). A further report, commissioned by the Council of Europe on "The Role of the media in promoting social cohesion with particular reference to community, local, minority and social media" concluded that community media are an "important factor in social cohesion and citizenship" (Lewis 2008, 5) and urged European policy-makers to create enabling legislation and commit funds to support the sector.

Civil Society Media have thus emerged from the shadows of international policy-making. Their appearance at WSIS was crucial for raising their profile and advancing a discourse around their concerns and policy objectives. They made an impression on the summit debates but did not yet reach the core of mainstream policy interest. There are signs, now, that this is changing. They are increasingly becoming a force that is recognised.

According to Media Caucus chair Tracey Naughton,[4] CS Media "should occupy a position of greater strength". She recommends developing "the vision and the self-legitimacy of being an essential media player":

"This network, as diverse and unwieldy as it is, knows no sovereign boundaries and could be leading the way to a world where there is global governance, where humanity has a chance to influence the sustainability and fairness of the planet and environments (in all senses of the word) that we live in."

[4] The following quotes are taken from the interview with Tracey Naughton (Interview TN).

Tables, figures, acronyms

List of tables and figures

List of acronyms

ABC	American Broadcasting Company
ABU	Asia-Pacific Broadcasting Union
AIBD	Asia-Pacific Institute for Broadcasting Development
AIR	Asociacion Internacional de Radiodiffusion (also: IAB)
ALAI	Latin American Information Agency
ALER	Asociacion Latinoamericana de Educacion Radiofonica
AMARC	Association Mondiale des Radiodiffuseurs Communautaires (World Association of Community Radio Broadcasters)
AP	Associated Press
APC	Association for Progressive Communications
ARD	Arbeitsgemeinschaft der öffentlich-rechtlichen Rundfunkanstalten der Bundesrepublik Deutschland
Art.	Article
ASBU	Arab States Broadcasting Union
ATT, AT&T	American Telephone and Telegraph Company
BBC	British Broadcasting Corporation
BINGO	Business interest non-governmental organisation

CAMECO	Catholic Media Council
CBS	Columbia Broadcasting System
CBU	Caribbean Broadcasting Union
CCBI	Coordinating Committee of Business Interlocutors
CCPFO	Coordinating Committee of Press Freedom Organizations
CCTV	Close circuit television
CEO	chief executive officer
CMFE	Community Media Forum Europe
CMI	Community Media Initiative
CMRTV	Conseil mondial de la Radio Télévision (also: WRTVC)
CMWG	Community Media Working Group
CNN	Cable News Network
CONGO	Conference of NGOs in Consultative Relationship with the United Nations
CRIS	Communication Rights in the Information Society
CS	Civil Society
CS Media	Civil Society Media
CS Plenary	Civil Society Plenary
CSB	Civil Society Bureau
CSD	Civil Society Division
CSIS	Citizens Summit on the Information Society
CSTD	Commission on Science and Technology for Development
DIY	"do it yourself"
DPA	Deutsche Presse-Agentur
DSF	Digital Solidarity Fund
EBU	European Broadcasting Union
ECOSOC	Economic and Social Committee (of the United Nations)
EFCR	European Forum on Communication Rights
ESF	European Social Forum
EU	European Union
FAIR	Fairness and Accuracy in Reporting
FAO	Food and Agriculture Organization of the United Nations
FCC	Federal Communication Commission
G8	Group of Eight (the eight most powerful economies; formerly G7)
GATT	General Agreement on Tariffs and Trade
GFC	Group of the Friends of the Chair

Glocom	Centre for Global Communication
GONGO	Governmental 'non-governmental' organisation
HLSOC	High-Level Summit Organizing Committee
IAB	International Association of Broadcasting (also: AIR)
IAMCR	International Association for Media of Communication Research
IAPA	Inter American Press Association
IBM	International Business Machines Corporation
ICANN	Internet Corporation for Assigned Names and Numbers
ICC	International Chamber of Commerce
ICRA	Internet Content Rating Association
ICT	Information and communication technology
ICTD, ICT4D	Information and communication technology for development
IFEX	International Freedom of Expression eXchange
IFJ	International Federation of Journalists
IGF	Internet Governance Forum
ILO	International Labour Organization
IMF	International Monetary Fund
IPDC	International Program for the Development of Communication
IPE	International Political Economy
IPR	intellectual property rights
IPS	Inter Press Service
ITeM	Instituto del Tercer Mundo (Third World Institute)
ITU	International Telecommunication Union (formerly International Telegraph Union)
IXP	Internet Exchange Point
LAC	Latin American countries
MAI	Multilateral Agreement in Investment
MISA	Media Institute of Southern Africa
NABA	North American Broadcasters Association
NAM	Non-Aligned Movement
NATO	North Atlantic Treaty Organisation
NBC	National Broadcasting Company
NGO	Non-Governmental Organisation
NWICO	New World Information and Communication Order
OECD	Organization for Economic Co-operation and Development

OAS	Organization of American States
OTI	Organisacion de la Television Iberoamericana
PGA	People's Global Action
PrepCom	Preparatory Committee
RAI	Radiotelevisione Italiana
RCA	Radio Corporation of America
RFID	Radio Frequency Identification
SIGNIS	World Catholic Association for Communication
TCI	Tele-Communications Inc.
TFFM	Task Force on Financing Mechanisms
TINA	"there is no alternative"
TNC	transnational corporation
UDHR	Universal Declaration on Human Rights
UDRP	Uniform Dispute Resolution Policy
UN	United Nations
UNCED	UN Conference on Environment and Development
UNCTAD	United Nations Conference on Trade and Development
UNDP	United Nations Development Programme
UNESCO	UN Educational, Scientific and Cultural Organization
UK	United Kingdom
URTNA	Union des Radiodiffusions et Televisions Nationales d'Afriques
US	United States (of America)
WACC	World Association of Christian Communication
WAN	World Association of Newspapers
WBU	World Broadcasting Unions
WEF	World Economic Forum
WEMF	World Electronic Media Forum
WFCI	World Forum on Communication and Information
WFCR	World Forum on Communication Rights
WGIG	Working Group on Internet Governance
WHO	World Health Organization
WIPO	World Intellectual Property Organization
WKK	Zivilgesellschaftlicher WSIS Koordinationskreis (German WSIS Civil Society Coordinating Committee)
WPFC	World Press Freedom Committee
WRTVC	World Radio and Television Council (also: CMRTV)

WSF	World Social Forum
WSIS	World Summit on the Information Society
WSIS-ES	WSIS Executive Secretariat
WSSD	World Summit on Sustainable Development
WTO	World Trade Organisation
ZDF	Zweites Deutsches Fernsehen

Bibliography

This bibliography is divided into four sections:

(1) General and WSIS-related literature
(2) Emails, sent to public listserves established for the WSIS process
(3) WSIS official documents, statements, contributions and speeches
(4) Interview directory

(1) General and WSIS-related literature

Abugre, Charles (2006), 'A leaking ship: The role of debt, aid and trade', *Pambazuka News,* http://www.pambazuka.org/index.php?id=31754

Accuosto, Pablo and Johnson, Niki (2004), *Financing the Information Society in the South: A Global Public Goods Perspective,* Working Paper, Instituto del Tercer Mundo, Montevideo. http://rights.apc.org/documents/financing.pdf

AMARC (2003a), *The Kathmandu Declaration*, Declaration by the World Association of Community Broadcasters at the AMARC 8 congress in Kathmandu, February 2003, http://wiki.amarc.org/index2.php?topic=kathmandu_declaration&lang=EN&style=amarc&site=amarc

AMARC (2003b), *Strategic Plan 2003-2006,* adopted by the World Association of Community Broadcasters at the AMARC 8 congress in Kathmandu, February 2003, http://wiki.amarc.org/index2.php?topic=strategic_planning-03-06&lang=EN&style=amarc&site=amarc

Anheier, Helmut; Glasius, Marlies and Kaldor, Mary (2001), 'Introducing Global Civil Society', in Helmut Anheier, Marlies Glasius and Mary Kaldor (eds.), *Global Civil Society Yearbook 2001,* London: Oxford University Press, pp. 3-22.

Anheier, Helmut; Glasius, Marlies and Kaldor, Mary (2004), 'Mission Statement', in Helmut Anheier, Marlies Glasius and Mary Kaldor (eds.), *Global Civil Society Yearbook 2004/5,* London: Sage, pp. v.

Atton, Chris (2002), *Alternative Media,* London: Sage.

Auerbach, Karl (2005), *Forgotten Principles of Internet Governance*, 22 October 2005, http://www.circleid.com/posts/forgotten_principles_of_internet_governance/

Bailey, Olga; Cammaerts, Bart and Carpentier, Nico (2007), *Understanding Alternative Media, Maidenhead:* Open University Press.

Banaszak, Lee Ann (2005), 'Inside and Outside the State: Movement Insider Status, Tactics, and Public Policy Achievements', in David S. Meyer,

Valerie Jenness, Helen Ingram (eds.), *Routing the Opposition: Social Movements, Public Policy, and Democracy*, Minneapolis: University of Minnesota Press, pp. 149-176.

Barlow, John Perry (1996), *A Declaration of the Independence of Cyberspace*, http://homes.eff.org/~barlow/Declaration-Final.html

Baumgartner, Frank R. and Mahoney, Christine (2005), 'Social Movements, the Rise of New Issues, and the Public Agenda', in David S. Meyer, Valerie Jenness, Helen Ingram (eds.), *Routing the Opposition: Social Movements, Public Policy, and Democracy*, Minneapolis: University of Minnesota Press, pp. 65-86.

Becker, Konrad (2002), *Die Politik der Infosphäre*, Bonn: Bundeszentrale für politische Bildung.

Bell, Daniel (1962), *The End of Ideology: On the Exhaustion of Political Ideas in the Fifties,* New York: Free Press.

Bell, Daniel (1973), *The Coming of Post-Industrial Society: A Venture in Social Forecasting,* Harmondsworth: Penguin.

Bendrath, Ralf and Panganiban, Rick (2003), 'How was the Summit? A helpful list in case your friends (or any reporters) ask you', *worldsummit2003.org,* 16 December 2003, http://www.worldsummit2003.de/en/web/577.htm

Blank, Michael (2002), 'Global Governance', in Christopher Flavin, Brigitte Young, Christoph Scherrer and Klaus Zwickel (eds.), *Global Governance – Gewerkschaften und NGOs – Akteure für Gerechtigkeit und Solidarität,* Hamburg: VSA, pp. 7-10.

Bock, Mary Angela (2005), *Why Blogging's Not Enough: The Case for Sites that Link People to the People's Business*, Paper presented to the Re:activism conference, Budapest, October 2005.

Boyd-Barrett, Oliver (1998), 'Global News Agencies', in Oliver Boyd-Barrett and Terhi Rantanen (eds.), *The Globalization of News*, London: Sage, pp.19-34.

Brecht, Bertolt (1967), *Schriften zur Literatur und Kunst, Teil 1: 1920-1932,* Frankfurt/Main: Suhrkamp.

Britto Garcia, Luis (2004), *Venezuela: Investigación de algunos medios for encima de toda sospecha*, Caracas: Fondo Editorial Question.

Buckley, Steve (2005), 'Community Media and the WSIS', in Daniel Stauffacher and Wolfgang Kleinwächter (eds.), *The World Summit on the Information Society: Moving from the Past into the Future*, UN ICT Task Force, http://www.unicttaskforce.org/perl /documents.pl?id=1544

Calabrese, Andrew (2004), 'The Promise of Civil Society: a Global Movement for Communication Rights', *Continuum: Journal of Media & Cultural Studies,* 18(3), pp. 317-329.

Cammaerts, Bart and Carpentier, Nico (2006), 'The Unbearable Lightness of Full Participation in a Global Context: WSIS and Civil Society Participation', in Jan Servaes and Nico Carpentier (eds.), *Towards a Sustainable Information Society. Deconstructing WSIS,* London: Intellect, pp. 17-50.

Cardoso, Fernando Enrique, et al. (2004), *We the peoples: civil society, the United Nations and global governance. Report of the Panel of Eminent Persons on United Nations-Civil Society Relations,* UN document UN A/58/817, http://www.un.org/reform/a58_817_english.doc

Carlsson, Ulla (2003), 'The Rise and Fall of NWICO', *Nordicom Review,* 24(2).

Carpentier, Nico; Lie, Rico and Servaes, Jan (2003), 'Making Community Media Work', in Jan Servaes (ed.), *Approaches to Development: Studies on Communication for Development,* Paris: UNESCO Communication and Information Sector, pp. 1-44.

Castells, Manuel (1996), *The Rise of the Network Society,* Oxford: Blackwell.

Castells, Manuel (1998), *End of Millennium: Economy, Society and Culture,* Oxford: Blackwell.

Castells, Manuel (2003), 'The Rise of the Fourth World', in David Held and Anthony G. McGrew (eds.), *The Global Transformations Reader,* Cambridge: Polity Press, pp. 430-439.

Cerf, Vinton G. (2004), 'First, Do No Harm', in Don MacLean (ed.), *Internet Governance: A Grand Collaboration,* New York: United Nations ICT Task Force, pp. 13-15.

Chakravartty, Paula, and Zhao, Yuezhi (2008), *Global Communications: Towards a Transcultural Political Economy, Lanham:* Rowman & Littlefield.

Cohen, Benjamin J. (2006), *The Transatlantic Divide: Why are American and British IPE so Different?* Paper for the International Political Economy Society, Princeton, NJ, November 2006.

Commission on Global Governance (1995), *Our Global Neighbourhood,* Oxford: Oxford University Press.

Comor, Edward A. (1994), 'Introduction: The Global Political Economy of Communication and IPE', in Edward A. Comor (ed.), *The Global Political Economy of Communication: Hegemony, Telecommunication and the Information Economy,* Basingstoke: Palgrave MacMillan, pp. 1-18.

Costanza-Chock, Sasha (2005), *Autonomist Tools and Communications Democracy,* Background paper for the programme "Necessary Knowledge for a Democratic Public Sphere" by the Social Science Research Council, http://www.ssrc.org/programs /media/publications/costanza-chock.7.final.doc

Couldry, Nick and Curran, James (2003), *Contesting Media Power. Alternative Media in a Networked World,* Lanham: Rowan&Littlefield.

Cox, Robert W. (1981), Social Forces, States and World Orders: Beyond International Relations Theory', *Millennium: Journal of International Studies,* 10(2), pp. 126-156.

Cox, Robert W. (1983), 'Gramsci, Hegemony and International Relations: An Essay in Method', *Millennium: Journal of International Studies*, 12(2), pp. 162-175.

Cox, Robert W. (2002), *The Political Economy of a Plural World: Critical Reflections on Power, Morals and Civilization,* London: Routledge.

Coyer, Kate; Dowmunt, Tony and Fountain, Alain (eds.) (2007), *The Alternative Media Handbook*, Oxford: Routledge.

CRIS (2002), *Why should intellectual property rights matter to civil society?* CRIS Issue Paper 2, http://www.crisinfo.org/content/view/full/176

CRIS (2005), *Assessing Communication Rights: A Handbook,* http://www.crisinfo.org/pdf/ggpen.pdf

Currie, Willie (2005), 'Creating Spaces for Civil Society in the WSIS', *worldsummit2003.org,* 22 December 2005, http://www.worldsummit2003.de/en/web/848.htm

van Cuilenberg, Jan and McQuail, Dennis (2003), 'Media Policy Paradigm Shifts: Towards a New Communications Policy Paradigm', *European Journal of Communication,* 18(2), pp. 181-207.

Dany, Charlotte (2006), *The Impact of Participation: How Civil Society Organisations contribute to the Democratic Quality of the UN World Summit on the Information Society*, TranState Working Paper 43, Bremen: Collaborative Research Center "Transformations of the State". http://www.state.uni-bremen.de/pages /pubApBeschreibung.php?SPRACHE=en&ID=50

Dawkins, K. (2003), *Global Governance: The battle over planetary power,* New York: Seven Stories Press.

Dawson, Michael and Foster, John Bellamy (1998), 'Virtual Capitalism', in Robert W. McChesney, Ellen Meiskins Wood and John Bellamy Foster (eds.), *Capitalism and the Information Age: The Political Economy of the Global Communication Revolution*, New York: Monthly Review Press, pp.51-68.

Day, Richard J. F. (2005), *Gramsci is Dead: Anarchist Currents in the Newest Social Movements,* London: Pluto Press.

Diani, Mario (2003), 'Networks and Social Movements. A Research Pogramme', in Mario Diani and Doug McAdam (eds.), *Social movements and networks. Relational approaches to collective action,* Oxford: Oxford University Press, pp. 299-319.

van Dijk, Jan A.G.M. (2005), *The Deepening Divide: Inequality in the Information Society,* London: Sage.

Dimitrakopoulos, Dionyssis G. (2005), 'Norms, Interests, and Institutional Change', *Political Studies,* 53(4), pp. 676-693.

Dowmunt, Tony (1993), 'Introduction', in Tony Dowmunt (ed.), *Channels of Resistance: Global Television and Local Empowerment,* London: BFI Publishing, pp. 1-15.

Downing, John D.H. (1984), *Radical Media: The Political Organization of Alternative Communication,* Boston: South End Press.

Downing, John D.H. (2001), *Radical Media: rebellious communication and social movements,* London: Sage.

Eck, Klaus (2005), 'Unternehmen suchen Blogger', in netzwerk recherche (ed.), *nr-Werkstatt: Online-Journalismus*, pp. 103-108.

European Parliament (2007), *The State of Community Media in the European Union,* study prepared by Kern European Affairs for the European Parliament's Committee on Culture and Education, document IP/B/CULT/FWC/2006-169/Lot03/C01

Flichy, Patrice (1994), *Tele: Geschichte der modernen Kommunikation,* Frankfurt/Main: Campus.

Fox, Derek Tini (1993), 'Honouring the Treaty: Indigenous Television in Aotearoa', in Tony Dowmunt (ed.), *Channels of Resistance: Global Television and Local Empowerment,* London: BFI Publishing, pp. 126-137.

Fourie, Pieter J. (2006), *Moral philosophy as a Threat to Freedom of Expression: From Christian-Nationalism to Ubuntuism as a Normative Framework for Media Regulation and Practice in South Africa*, Paper presented to the annual conference of the International Association of Media and Communication Research (IAMCR), Cairo, July 2006.

Frau-Meigs, Divina (2006), 'Civil Society's Involvement in the WSIS Process: Drafting the Alter-Agenda', in Jan Servaes and Nico Carpentier (eds.), *Towards a Sustainable Information Society. Deconstructing WSIS,* London: Intellect, pp. 81-96.

Fukuyama, Francis (1992), *End of History and the Last Man,* New York: Free Press.

Galtung, Johan (1971), 'A Structural Theory of Imperialism', *Journal for Peace Studies,* Vol.8, pp.81-117.

Garcia, David and Lovink, Geert (1999), *The ABC of Tactical Media,* www.sarai.net/events/tml/tml_pdf/abc_tactical.PDF

Giffard, C. Anthony (1989), *Unesco and the Media*, New York: Longham.

Giffard, C. Anthony (1998), 'Alternative News Agencies', in Oliver Boyd-Barrett and Terhi Rantanen (eds.), *The Globalization of News*, London: Sage, pp. 191-201.

Gill, Stephen (1995), 'Globalisation, Market Civilisation, and Disciplinary Neoliberalism', *Millennium: Journal of International Studies*, 24(3), pp. 399-423.

Girard, Bruce (2003), 'Radio and the Internet: Mixing media to bridge the divide', in Bruce Girard (ed.), *The One to Watch: Radio, New ICTs and Interactivity,* Rome: FAO, pp. 1-18.

Giugni, Marco (2004), *Social Protest and Policy Change: Ecology, Antinuclear, and Peace Movements in Comparative Perspective*, Lanham: Rowan&Littlefield.

Global Contract Foundation (2003), 'Does Input lead to Impact? How Governments treated Civil Society Proposals in Drafting the 21 September 2003 Draft Declaration', *worldsummit2003.org,* http://www.worldsummit2003.de/en/web/543.htm

Golding, Peter (1997), 'The Missing Dimensions – News Media and the Management of Social Change', in Tim O'Sullivan and Yvonne Jewkes (eds.), *The Media Studies Reader*, London: Arnold, pp. 250-259.

Gore, Al (1994), 'The global information infrastructure – forging a new Athenian age of democracy. Remarks before the International Telecommunications Union', Buenos Aires, 21 March 1994, http://www.whitehouse.gov/WH/EOP /OVPhtml/telunion.html

Gumucio-Dagron, Alfonso and Tufte, Thomas (2006), *Communication for Social Change Anthology,* New Jersey: Communication for Social Change Consortium.

Gurstein, Michael (2005c), 'Networking the Networked', *worldsummit2003.org,* http://www.worldsummit2003.de/en/web/847.htm

Gutierrez, Miren (2004), 'Fewer Players, Less Freedom', *Inter Press Service,* 19 March 2004, http://www.ipsnews.net

Haas, Peter M. (1992), 'Introduction: Epistemic Communities and International Policy Coordination', *International Organization*, 46(1), pp. 1-35.

Hackett, Robert A. (2000), 'Taking back the media: notes on the potential for a communicative democracy movement', *Studies in Political Economy,* 63 (Autumn), pp. 61-86.

Hackett, Robert A. and William K. Carroll (2006), *Remaking Media: The Struggle to Democratize Public Communication*, London: Routledge.

Hadl, Gabriele (2004), *Civil Society Media Theory: Tools for Decolonizing the Lifeworld,* Paper presented at the annual IAMCR conference, Porto Alegre, July 2004.

Hadl, Gabriele (2006), *Theory for Civil Society Media: Lessons from the World Summit on the Information Society (WSIS),* PhD Dissertation (unpublished), Kyoto: Ritsumeikan University.

Hadl, Gabriele and Hintz, Arne (2009), 'Framing Our Media for Transnational Policy: The World Summit on the Information Society and beyond', in Dorothy Kidd, Clemencia Rodriguez, Laura Stein (eds.), *Making Our Media*, Cresskill, NJ: Hampton Press, forthcoming.

Halperin, Sandra and Laxer, Gordon (2003), 'Effective Resistance to Corporate Globalization', in Sandra Halperin and Gordon Laxer (eds.), *Global Civil Society and its Limits,* New York: Palgrave, pp. 1-21.

Hamelink, Cees (1994), *The Politics of World Communication: A Human Rights Perspective,* London: Sage.

Hamelink, Cees (2003), 'Human Rights for the Information Society', in Seán Ó Siochrú and Bruce Girard (eds.), *Communicating in the Information Society,* Geneva: UNRISD, pp. 121-163.

Hamelink, Cees (2004), 'Did WSIS Achieve Anything At All?', *Gazette: The International Journal for Communication Studies,* 66(3-4), pp. 281-290.

Hardt, Michael and Negri, Antonio (2000), *Empire,* Cambridge: Harvard University Press.

Heinrich-Böll-Foundation (2003a), 'Participation of civil society debated: The proposed Civil Society Bureau receives heavy criticism, but it will be too late to stop it', *worldsummit2003.org,* 18 February 2003, http://www.worldsummit2003.de/en /web/214.htm

Heinrich-Böll-Foundation (2003b), 'PrepCom2 negotiations end: Participation of non-governmental actors as a dividing line', *worldsummit2003.org,* 28 February 2003, http://www.worldsummit2003.de/en/web/242.htm

Heinrich-Böll-Foundation (2003c), 'Divisions between government and civil society positions: Civil society organisations will draft own declaration', *worldsummit2003.org,* 24 September 2003, http://www.worldsummit2003.de/en/web/468.htm

Heinrich-Böll-Foundation (2003d), 'Media Debates at WSIS: World Electronic Media Forum celebrates and reflects – media activists expose "Infowar"', *worldsummit2003.org,* 10 December 2003, http://www.worldsummit2003.de/en/web/559.htm

Heinrich-Böll-Foundation (2004), 'Fight about civil society speaking slots in plenary: Prepcom suspended over human rights dispute, agents provocateurs in Hammamet', *worldsummit2003.org,* 25 June 2004, http://www.worldsummit2003.de/en/web/638

Heinrich-Böll-Foundation (2005a), 'Tunisian government obstructs civil society events: Citizens Summit meeting blocked', *worldsummit2003.org,* 14 November 2005, http://www.worldsummit2003.de/en/web/819.htm

Heinrich-Böll-Foundation (2005b), 'Human rights solidarity action by international civil society organisations: Cancellation of several civil society side events on November 15 2005', *worldsummit2003.org,* 15 November 2005, http://www.worldsummit2003.de/en /web/822.htm

Heinrich-Böll-Foundation (2005c), 'The citizens summit is dead – long live the citizens summit! CSIS press conference becomes major human rights gathering', *worldsummit2003.org,* 16 November 2005, http://www.worldsummit2003.de/en /web/830.htm

Heinrich-Böll-Foundation (2005d), 'Art and Free Knowledge even in Tunis: When Richard Stallman and Gilberto Gil sing a duet…', *worldsummit2003.org,* 17 November 2005, http://www.worldsummit2003.de/en/web/833.htm

Heinrich-Böll-Stiftung (ed.) (2006), *Die Verfasstheit der Wissensgesellschaft*, Münster: Westphälisches Dampfboot.

Held, David and McGrew, Anthony G. (2003), 'The Great Globalization Debate', in David Held, Anthony G. McGrew (eds.), *The Global Transformations Reader,* Cambridge: Polity Press, pp. 1-50.

Held, David (2003), 'Cosmopolitanism: Taming Globalization', in David Held and Anthony G. McGrew (eds.), *The Global Transformations Reader,* Cambridge: Polity Press, pp. 514-529.

Helleiner, Eric (1996), 'International Political Economy and the Greens', *New Political Economy,* 1(1), pp. 59-78.

Hemmatic, Minu (ed.) (2002), *Multi-Stakeholder Processes for Governance and Sustainability: Beyond deadlock and conflict*, London: Earthscan.

Herman, Edward and Chomsky, Noam (1988), *Manufacturing Consent: The Political Economy of the Mass Media*, New York: Pantheon Books.

Herman, Edward and McChesney, Robert W. (1997), *The Global Media: the new missionaries of global capitalism*, London/Washington: Cassel.

Hintz, Arne (2000), 'Global media concentration and the rise of alternative media', in Stefan Brüne (ed.), *Neue Medien und Öffentlichkeiten: Politik und Tele-Kommunikation in Afrika, Asien und Lateinamerika, Band 2,* Hamburg: Deutsches Übersee-Institut, pp. 11-35.

Hintz, Arne (2003), 'Indymedia Germany: A local node of the global network', *Media Development,* XLX(4), pp. 21-25.

Hintz, Arne (2003), *Media Actors at the Dividing Lines of Information Society: Civil Society Media at the World Summit on the Information Society,* Paper presented at the Euricom Colloquium "Information Society Visions and Governance: The World Summit on the Information Society and Beyond", Venice, May 2003.

Hintz, Arne and Milan, Stefania (2006a), 'Towards a new vision for communication governance? Civil Society Media at the World Social Forum and the World Summit on the Information Society', *Communication for Development and Social Change: A Global Journal,* 1(1).

Hintz, Arne and Milan, Stefania (2006b), *Activist networks in communication governance. Potentials and challenges of their involvement in policy processes*, Paper presented at the annual IAMCR conference, Cairo, July 2006.

Hintz, Arne and Milan, Stefania (2009), 'At the margins of Internet governance: Grassroots tech groups and communication policy', *International Journal of Media & Cultural Politics* (forthcoming).

de Jong, Wilma; Shaw, Martin and Stammers, Neil (2005), 'Introduction', in Wilma de Jong, Martin Shaw, Neil Stammers (eds.), *Global Activism, Global Media,* London: Pluto Press, pp. 1-14.

Kahn, Robert E. (2004), 'Working Code and Rough Consensus: The Internet as Social Evolution', in Don MacLean (ed.), *Internet Governance: A Grand Collaboration,* New York: United Nations ICT Task Force, pp. 16-21.

Kaldor, Mary (2003), *Global Civil Society: An Answer to War,* Cambridge: Polity Press.

Kanayama, Tomoko (2006), *Community Ties and Revitalization: the Role of Community FM Radio in Japan*, Paper presented at the annual IAMCR conference, Cairo, July 2006.

Karppinen, Kari (2005), *Diversity and the Politics of Criteria: Diversity Assessment and the Technocratisation of European Media Policy,* Paper presented at the First European Communication Conference, Amsterdam, November 2005.

Keck, Margaret E. and Sikkink, Kathryn (1998), *Activists beyond Borders. Advocacy Networks in International Politics,* Ithaca: Cornell University Press.

Keohane, Robert O. and Nye, Joseph S. (1977), *Power and Independence: World Politics in Transition,* Boston: Little&Brown.

Keohane, Robert O. and Nye, Joseph S. (1998), 'Power and Independence in the Information Age', *Foreign Affairs,* 77(5), pp. 81-94.

Khagram, Sanjeev; Riker, James V. and Sikkink, Kathryn (2002), 'From Santiago to Seattle: Transnational Advocacy Groups Restructuring World Politics', in Sanjeev Khagram, James V. Riker, Kathryn Sikkink (eds.), *Restructuring World Politics: Transnational Social Movements, Networks, and Norms,* Minneapolis: University of Minnesota Press, pp. 3-23.

Kidd, Dorothy; Barker-Plummer, Bernadette and Rodriguez, Clemencia (2005), *Media Democracy from the Ground Up: Mapping Communication Practices in the Counter Public Sphere,* Report to the Social Science Research Council.

Kingdon, John W. (1995), *Agendas, Alternatives, and Public Policies,* New York: HarperCollins.

Kjaer, Anne Mette (2004), *Governance*, Cambridge: Polity Press.

Kleinsteuber, Hans J. (1999), 'Die Informationsgesellschaft – Eine Gesellschaft ohne Information über sich selbst?', in Patrick Donges, Otfried Jarren and Heribert Schatz (eds.), *Globalisierung der Medien? Medienpolitik in der globalen Informationsgesellschaft,* Opladen: Westdeutscher Verlag, pp. 21-38.

Kleinsteuber, Hans J. (2003), 'Abschied vom Konzept Informationsgesellschaft?', in Dieter Klumpp, Herbert Kubicek, Alexander Rossnagel (eds.), *Next Generation Information Society? Notwendigkeit einer Neuorientierung*, Mössingen: Talheimer, pp. 16-24.

Kleinsteuber, Hans J. (2004), 'The Internet between Regulation and Governance', in Representative on Freedom of the Media (OSCE), *The Media Freedom Internet Cookbook,* Vienna: OSCE, pp. 61-75.

Kleinsteuber, Hans J. and Hintz, Arne (2004), 'Von der Politik zur Technik und zurück: WSIS im Spannungsfeld zwischen informationsgesellschaftlicher Beliebigkeit und globaler Kommunikationsregulierung', *Entwicklungspolitik,* No. 5/6(2004), pp. 39-43.

Kleinwächter, Wolfgang (1989), *Weltproblem Information: Massenmedien und Kommunikationstechnologien in den internationalen Beziehungen der Gegenwart,* Berlin: Dietz.

Kleinwächter, Wolfgang (2004), *Macht und Geld im Cyberspace: Wie der Weltgipfel zur Informationsgesellschaft (WSIS) die Weichen für die Zukunft stellt,* Hannover: Heise.

Kleinwächter, Wolfgang (2005a), 'Internet Co-Governance: Towards a Multilayer Multiplayer Mechanism of Consultation and Cooperation (M3C3)', in Petra Ahrweiler and Barbara Thomaß (eds.), *Internationale partizipatorische Kommunikationspolitik: Strukturen und Visionen – Festschrift zum 60. Geburtstag von Hans J. Kleinsteuber,* Münster: Lit, pp. 75-98.

Kriesi, Hanspeter (2004), 'Political context and opportunity', in David A. Snow, Sarah A. Soule and Hanspeter Kriesi (eds.), *The Blackwell companion to social movements*, Oxford: Blackwell, pp. 67-90.

Langlois, Andrea, and Dubois, Frederic (2005), *Autonomous Media: Activating Resistance and Dissent,* Montréal: Cumulus Press.

Lessig, Lawrence (1999), *Code and other Laws of Cyberspace,* New York: Basic Books.

Lewis, Peter (2002), 'Radio Theory and Community Radio', in Nick Jankowsky and Ole Prehn (eds.), *Community Media in the Information Age. Perspectives and Prospects,* Cresskill, NJ: Hampton Press, pp. 31- 46.

Lewis, Peter (2008), *Promoting Social Cohesion: The Role of Community Media,* Report prepared for the Council of Europe's Group of Specialists on media Diversity (MC-C-MD)

Lipschutz, Ronnie D. (2005), 'Networks of knowledge and practice: global civil society and global communications', in Wilma de Jong, Martin Shaw, Neil Stammers (eds.), *Global Activism, Global Media,* London: Pluto Press, pp. 17-33.

Lovink, Geert (2003), *Dark Fiber: Auf den Spuren einer kritischen Internet-kultur*, Bonn: Bundeszentrale für kritische Bildung.

Lovink, Geert, and Rossiter, Ned (2005), 'Dawn of the Organised Network', *fibreculture,* issue 5, http://journal.fibreculture.org/issue5/lovink_rossiter.html

Ludwig, Wolf (2003), 'Genfer UNO-Weltgipfel zur Informationsgesellschaft: Anspruch und Wirklichkeit eines Aushandlungsprozesses', *Widerspruch – Beiträge zu sozialistischer Politik,* No. 45, pp. 93-103.

Ludwig, Wolf and Peyer, Chantal (2006), *Comunica-ch – bilan des activités 2004-2005,* http://www.comunica-ch.net/article.php3?id_article=310

Luke, Timothy W. (1989), *Screens of Power: Ideology, Domination, and Resistance in Informational Society*, Chicago: University of Illinois Press.

Lutterbeck, Bernd and Ishii, Kei (1999), *Open Code and Open Societies,* Presentation at the Wizards of OS conference, July 1999, http://mikro.org/Events/OS/ref-texte/lutterbeck-ishii.html

MacBride, Sean, et al. (1980), *Many Voices, One World. Communication and Society Today and Tomorrow. Towards a new more just and more efficient information and communication order,* Ibandan and Paris: Ibandan University Press and UNESCO Press.

MacBride Round Table (1991), *'Few Voices, Many Worlds' – The Istanbul Statement of the MacBride Round Table on Communication,* 21 June 1991, http://www2.hawaii.edu /~rvincent/mcb3.htm

Machill, Marcel and Ahlert, Christian (2001), 'Wer regiert das Internet? ICANN als Fallbeispiel für neue Formen der Kommunikationsregulierung', *Publizistik,* 46(3), pp. 295-316.

MacLean, Don (ed.) (2004), *Internet Governance: A Grand Collaboration,* New York: United Nations ICT Task Force.

Mader, Roberto (1993), 'Globo Village: Television in Brazil', in Tony Dowmunt (ed.), *Channels of Resistance: Global Television and Local Empowerment,* London: BFI Publishing, pp. 67-89.

Manning, Paul (2001), *News and news sources: a critical introduction,* London: Sage.

Marr, Mirko (2004), 'Wer hat Angst vor der digitalen Spaltung? Zur Haltbarkeit des Bedrohungsszenarios', *Medien und Kommunikationswissenschaft,* 52(1), pp. 76-94.

Massing, Michael (2005), 'The End of News?', *The New York Review of Books*, 52(19), http://www.nybooks.com/articles/18516

Mattelart, Armand (2003), *The Information Society: An Introduction,* London: Sage.

May, Christopher (2006), *A New Democratic 'Technics': 'Openness' in the contemporary global information society*, Keynote speech at the conference "Governing the Knowledge Society", Hamburg, October 2006; http://webapp.rrz.uni-hamburg.de/~swpat /conferences/06knowledgesociety/abstracts/ChristopherMay.pdf

McAdam, Doug; McCarthy, John D. and Zald, Mayer N. (1996), 'Introduction: Opportunities, Mobilizing Structures, and Framing Processes – Toward a Synthesis, Comparative Perspective on Social Movements', in Doug McAdam, John D. McCarthy and Mayer N. Zald (eds.), *Comparative perspectives on social movements: political opportunities, mobilizing structures, and cultural framings*, Cambridge: Cambridge University, pp. 1-20.

McChesney, Robert W. (1998), 'The Political Economy of Global Communication', in Robert W. McChesney, Ellen Meiskins Wood and John Bellamy Foster (eds.), *Capitalism and the Information Age: The Political Economy of the Global Communication Revolution,* New York: Monthly Review Press, pp. 1-26.

McGrew, Anthony (2001), 'Models of Transnational Democracy', in April Carter and Geoffrey Stokes (eds.), *Democratic Theory Today: Challenges for the 21st Century,* Cambridge: Polity Press, pp. 269-294.

Meadows, Michael; Forde, Susan; Ewart, Jacqui and Foxwell, Kerrie (2005), *Shifting Sands: Trends in the community media sector in Australia,* Paper presented at the annual IAMCR conference, Taipei, July 2005.

Messner, Dirk and Nuscheler, Franz (eds.) (1996), *Weltkonferenzen und Weltberichte: Ein Wegweiser durch die internationale Diskussion,* Bonn: Dietz.

Messner, Dirk and Nuscheler, Franz (2003), 'Das Konzept Global Governance: Stand und Perspektiven', *INEF-Report* 67, Duisburg: Institut für Entwicklung und Frieden.

Milan, Stefania (2004a), *Communicating Civil Society: participation as the main benchmark of Civil Society Media. The case of the third World Social Forum*, Paper presented at the annual IAMCR conference, Porto Alegre, July 2004.

Milan, Stefania (2004b), 'Alternative Network's Internet Servers Confiscated', *CommonDreams News Center*, http://www.commondreams.org/headlines04/1010-25.htm

Milan, Stefania (2006a), *Community Media go to Europe. Problem definition and agenda setting at the Council of Europe,* Research paper (unpublished) for the European University Institute, Florence.

Milan, Stefania (2006b), *Transnational Mobilization(s) on Communication and Media Justice: movement formation processes between structures and meanings,* Research paper (unpublished) for the European University Institute, Florence.

Miller, David (2004), *Tell me lies: propaganda and Media Distortion in the Attack on Iraq,* London: Pluto Press.

Mueller, Milton (2004), *Reinventing Media Activism: Public Interest Advocacy in the Making of U.S. Communication-Information Policy, 1960-2002,* Report for the Convergence Center School of Information Studies, Syracuse University, http://dcc.syr.edu/ford/rma /reinventing.pdf

Naidoo, Kumi (2005), *Should civil society engage with governing institutions even when they have deep democratic deficits? Note by the CIVICUS Secretary-General*, http://www.civicus.org/news /content/deskofthesecretarygeneral4.html.

Nelson, P.J. (2002), 'Agendas, Accountability, and Legitimacy among Transnational Networks Lobbying the World Bank', in Sanjeev Khagram, James V. Riker and Kathryn Sikkink (eds.), *Restructuring World Politics: Transnational Social Movements, Networks, and Norms,* Minneapolis: University of Minnesota Press, pp. 131-154.

Notes from Nowhere (2003), *We Are Everywhere: The irresistible rise of global anticapitalism,* London/New York: Verso.

Ó Siochrú, Seán (2004a), 'Civil Society Participation in the WSIS Process. Promises and Reality', *Continuum: Journal of Media & Cultural Studies,* 18(3), pp. 330-344.

Ó Siochrú, Seán (2004b), 'Will the Real WSIS Please Stand Up? The Historic Encounter of the 'Information Society' and the 'Communication Society', *Gazette: The International Journal for Communication Studies,* 66(3-4), pp. 203-224.

Ó Siochrú, Seán (2005), 'Financing Paradigms in the WSIS Process', in Peyer, Chantal (ed.), *Who pays for the Information Society? Challenges and Issues on financing the Information Society,* PPP-Reperes 1/05, Bread for All, pp. 9-24.

Ó Siochrú, Seán and Girard, Bruce (2002), *Global Media Governance,* New York/Oxford: Rowman&Littlefield.

Ó Siochrú, Seán and Girard, Bruce (2005), *Community-based Networks and Innovative Technologies: New models to serve and empower the poor,* Report for the United Nations Development Programme.

Padovani (2004), 'The World Summit on the Information Society: Setting the Communication Agenda for the 21st Century? An Ongoing Exercise', *Gazette: The International Journal for Communication Studies,* 66(3-4), pp. 187-191.

Padovani, Claudia and Tuzzi, Arjuna (2004), 'The WSIS as a World of Words: Building a Common Vision for the Communication Society?', *Continuum: Journal of Media & Cultural Studies,* 18(3), pp. 330-344.

Palmer, Michael; Boyd-Barrett, Oliver and Rantanen, Terhi (1998), 'Global Financial News', in Oliver Boyd-Barrett and Terhi Rantanen (eds.), *The Globalization of News*, London: Sage, pp.61-78.

Patalong, Frank (2006), 'Nur falsch ist wirklich echt', *Spiegel Online*, 11 September 2006, http://www.spiegel.de/netzwelt/netzkutur/0,158,436070,00.html

Paterson, Christopher (1997), 'Global television news services', in Annabelle Sreberny-Mohammadi, Dwayne Winseck, Jim McKenna and Oliver Boyd-Barrett (eds.), *Media in Global Context*, London: Arnold, pp.145-159.

Paterson, Cristopher (1998), 'Global Battlefields', in Oliver Boyd-Barrett and Terhi Rantanen (eds.), *The Globalization of News*, London: Sage, pp.79-102.

People's Communication Charter (1999), *People's Communication Charter text,* http://www.pccharter.net/charteren.html

Petley, Julian and Romano, Gabrielle (1993), 'After the Deluge: Public Service Television in Western Europe', in Tony Dowmunt (ed.), *Channels of Resistance: Global Television and Local Empowerment*, London: BFI Publishing, pp.27-49.

Pew/Internet (2006), *Bloggers: A portrait of the internet's new storytellers,* Report by the Pew Internet & American Life Project, 19 July 2006, http://www.pewinternet.org/pdfs/PiP Bloggers Report July 19 2006.pdf

Peyer, Chantal (ed.) (2005a), *Who pays for the Information Society? Challenges and Issues on financing the Information Society,* PPP-Reperes 1/05, Bread for All.

Peyer, Chantal (2005b), 'Official Development Aid: Illusions about Existing Resources and Opportunities Provided by Global Taxation', in Chantal Peyer (ed.), *Who pays for the Information Society? Challenges and Issues on financing the Information Society,* PPP-Reperes 1/05, Bread for All, pp. 35-43.

Pieterse, Jan Nederveen (2005), 'Digital Capitalism and Development: The Unbearable Lightness of ICT4D', in Geert Lovink and Soenke Zehle (eds.), *incommunicado reader,* Amsterdam: Institute of Network Cultures, pp. 11-29.

Raboy, Marc (2004a), 'The WSIS as a Political Space in Global Media Governance', *Continuum: Journal of Media & Cultural Studies,* 18(3), pp. 345-359.

Raboy, Marc (2004b), 'The World Summit on the Information Society and its Legacy for Global Governance', *Gazette: The International Journal for Communication Studies,* 66(3-4), pp. 225-232.

Raboy, Marc and Landry, Normand (2005), *Civil Society, communication and Global Governance: Issues from the World Summit on the Information Society,* New York: Peter Lang.

Rantanen, Terhi (1998), 'The Struggle for Control of Domestic News Markets', in Oliver Boyd-Barrett and Terhi Rantanen (eds.), *The Globalization of News*, London: Sage, pp.35-48.

Reich, Robert B. (1991), *The Wealth of Nations: Preparing Ourselves for 21st Century Capitalism,* New York: Vintage.

Robinson, Cedric J. (1995), 'Mass Media and the US Presidency', in John Downing, Ali Mohammadi and Annabelle Sreberny-Mohammadi (eds.), *Questioning the Media*, London: Sage, pp. 94-111.

Rochon, Thomas R. (1998), *Culture Moves. Ideas, Activism and Changing Values*, Princeton: Princeton University.

Rodriguez, America (1995), 'Control Mechanisms of National News Making: Britain, Canada, Mexico, and The United States', in John Downing, Ali Mohammadi and Annabelle Sreberny-Mohammadi (eds.), *Questioning the Media*, London: Sage, pp.128-146.

Rodríguez, Clemencia (2001), *Fissures in the Mediascape: An International Study of Citizens' Media,* Cresskill, NJ: Hampton Press.

Rodrik, Dani (2002), 'Ein alternatives Konzept für Global Governance im Handel', in Christopher Flavin, Brigitte Young, Christoph Scherrer and Klaus Zwickel (eds.), *Global Governance – Gewerkschaften und NGOs – Akteure für Gerechtigkeit und Solidarität,* Hamburg: VSA, pp. 11-22.

Rosen, Jay (2005), 'Eason Jordan Resigns', *pressthink,* 11 February 2005, http://journalism.nyu.edu/pubzone/weblogs/pressthink/2005/02/11/esn_res.html

Rosenau, James N. (1995), 'Governance in the Twenty-First Century', *Global Governance, 1(1),* pp. 13-43.

Rosenberg, Justin (2001), *The Follies of Globalization Theory,* London: Verso.

Said, Edward (1999), 'The blind misleading the blind', *Z-mag*, http://www.zmag.org

Sarikakis, Katharine, and Thussu, Daya (2006), 'The Internet as Ideology' in Katherine Sarikakis and Daya Thussu (eds.), *Ideologies of the Internet,* Cresskill: Hampton Press, pp. 1-18.

Sassen, Saskia (2001), *The Global City*, New York: Princeton University Press.

Schiller, Dan (1999), *Digital Capitalism. Networking the Global Market System,* Cambridge, MA: MIT Press.

Scholte, Jan Aart (2000), *Globalization: A Critical Introduction,* London: MacMillan.

Servaes, Jan (1999), *Communication for development. One world, multiple cultures,* Cresskill, NJ: Hampton Press.

Sikkink, Kathryn (2002), 'Restructuring World Politics: The Limits and Asymmetries of Soft Power', in Sanjeev Khagram, James V. Riker, Kathryn Sikkink (eds.), *Restructuring World Politics: Transnational Social Movements, Networks, and Norms,* Minneapolis: University of Minnesota Press, pp. 301-317.

Sikkink, Kathryn and Smith, Jacquie (2002), 'Infrastructures for Change: Transnational Organizations, 1953-93', in Sanjeev Khagram, James V. Riker, Kathryn Sikkink (eds.), *Restructuring World Politics: Transnational Social Movements, Networks, and Norms,* Minneapolis: University of Minnesota Press, pp. 24-45.

Sklair, Leslie (1995), *Sociology of the Global System*, London: Prentice Hall.

Sklair, Leslie (2000), *The Transnational Capitalist Class*, Oxford: Blackwell.

Speck, Ullrich (2005), 'Die offene Gesellschaft, ihre Feinde und das Bloggen', in netzwerk recherche (ed.), *nr-Werkstatt: Online-Journalismus,* pp. 59-62.

Sreberny-Mohammadi, Annabelle (1997), 'Small media and revolutionary change: a new model', in Annabelle Sreberny-Mohammadi, Dwayne Winseck, John McKenna and Oliver Boyd-Barrett (eds.), *Media in Global Context,* London: Arnold, pp. 220-235.

Stammers, Neil and Eschle, Catherine (2005), 'Social movements and global activism', in Wilma de Jong, Martin Shaw, Neil Stammers (eds.), *Global Activism, Global Media,* London: Pluto Press, pp. 50-67.

Stehr, Nico (1994), *Arbeit, Eigentum und Wissen. Zur Theorie von Wissensgesellschaften*, Frankfurt/Main: Suhrkamp.

Stehr, Nico (2001), 'Moderne Wissensgesellschaften', *Aus Politik und Zeitgeschichte*, No. 36 (31 August 2001), pp. 7-14.

Stein, Laura (2004), 'Understanding Speech Rights: Defensive and Empowering Approaches to the First Amendment', *Media, Culture & Society,* 26(1), pp. 103-120.

Strange, Susan (1994), *States and Markets, second edition,* London/Washington: Pinter.

Tarleton, John (2002), 'Public Interest Angels descend on DC', *Indymedia DC*, 24 March 2002, http://dc.indymedia.org/newswire/display/19876

Tarrow, Sidney (1998), *Power in Movement. Social Movements and Contentious Politics*, Cambridge: Cambridge University.

Thomaß, Barbara (2005), 'Die Agenda des Weltgipfels zur Informationsgesellschaft und der öffentliche Rundfunk', in Petra Ahrweiler and Barbara Thomaß (eds.), *Internationale partizipatorische Kommunikationspolitik: Strukturen und Visionen. Festschrift zum 60. Geburtstag von Hans J. Kleinsteuber,* Münster: Lit, pp. 99-116.

Thomaß, Barbara (2006), 'PSB as an Instrument of Implementing WSIS Aims', in Jan Servaes and Nico Carpentier (eds.), *Towards a Sustainable Information Society. Deconstructing WSIS,* London: Intellect, pp. 195-202.

Tilly, Charles and Tarrow, Sidney (2006), *Contentious Politics,* Boulder: Paradigm.

Thompson, John B. (1995), *The Media and Modernity: A Social Theory of the Media,* Cambridge: Polity Press.

Verzola, Roberto (2004), *Towards a Political Economy of Information: Studies on the Information Economy,* Quezon City: Foundation for Nationalist Studies.

Vincent, Richard C.; Nordenstreng, Kaarle and Traber, Michael (eds.) (1999), *Towards Equity in Global Communication. MacBride Update,* Cresskill, NJ: Hampton Press.

Wagner, Michael (2004), 'EBU Report on the first phase of the World Summit on the Information Society', in WEMF (ed.), *Final Report: Radio & TV Fundamental Debates,* pp. 170-171.

Webster, Frank (2002), *Theories of the Information Society, second edition,* London: Routledge.

Wilkinson, Rorden (2002), 'The contours of courtship: The WTO and civil society', in Rorden Wilkinson, Steve Hughes (eds.), *Global Governance: Critical Perspectives*, London: Routledge, pp. 193-211.

Zehle, Soenke (2003), 'Nexus on the eve', *makeworld paper #3*, p. 3.

(2) Emails from WSIS listserves

Aizu, Izumi (2005), "Re: [WSIS CS-Plenary] compilation of comments on Khan's paper on IG online", sent by Izumi Aizu (aizu@anr.org) to plenary@wsis-cs.org on 27 September 2005.

Benamrane, Djilali (2005), "Re: Re: [WSIS CS-Plenary] suite du message coupe ....", sent by Djilali Benamrane (dbenamrane@yahoo.com) to plenary@wsis-cs.org on 5 March 2005.

Bertola, Vittorio (2005a), "Individuals and organizations (was Re: [WSIS CS-Plenary] format for Tunis Summit)", sent by Vittorio Bertola (vb@bertola.eu.org) to plenary@wsis-cs.org on 18 March 2005.

Bertola, Vittorio (2005b), "Re: [WSIS CS-Plenary] Proposed Guidelines for CS Plenary", sent by Vittorio Bertola (vb@bertola.eu.org) to plenary@wsis-cs.org on 27 September 2005.

Buckley, Steve (2003), "WSIS – community media caucus", sent by Steve Buckley (sbuckley@gn.apc.org) to cm@wsis-cs.org on 29 May 2003.

Buckley, Steve (2004a), "[WSIS-CM] Re: (english, espanol) Fwd: Proposal for Formation of CS Working Methods working Group", sent by Steve Buckley (sbuckley@gn.apc.org) to cm@wsis-cs.org on 24 November 2004.

Buckley, Steve (2004b), "[WSIS CS-Plenary] Community Media for Sustainable Development Roundtable issues declaration", sent by Steve Buckley (sbuckley@gn.apc.org) to plenary@wsis-cs.org on 29 November 2004.

Doria, Avri (2005), "Re: [WSIS CS-Plenary] Participations to the Summit by individuals (was Re: from IHT...)", sent by Avri Doria (avri@acm.org) to plenary@wsis-cs.org on 2 Oktober 2005.

Fullsack, Jean-Louis (2005), "Re: [WSIS CS-Plenary] CORRECTED VERSION:CCBI input on Chapters One and Four of Operational Part of WSIS-Tunis documents", sent by Jean-Louis Fullsack (jlfullsack@wanadoo.fr) to plenary@wsis-cs.org on 28 May 2005.

Gurstein, Michael (2005a), "[WSIS CS-Plenary] RE: [WSIS CS-Plenary] Communiqué de Presse de la Société Civile", sent by Michael Gurstein (gurstein@adm.njit.edu) to plenary@wsis-cs.org on 4 March 2005.

Gurstein, Michael (2005b), "[WSIS CS-Plenary] RE: [governance] further comments on Global Alliance", sent by Michael Gurstein (gurstein@adm.njit.edu) to plenary@wsis-cs.org on 14 April 2005.

Jordan, Richard (2005), "Re: [WSIS CS-Plenary] CORRECTED VERSION: CCBI input on Chapters One and Four of Operational Part of WSIS-Tunis documents", sent by Richard Jordan (richardjordan@lycos.com) to plenary@wsis-cs.org on 26 May 2005.

Kleinwächter, Wolfgang (2005b), "AW: Individuals and organizations (was Re: [WSIS CS-Plenary] format for Tunis Summit)", sent by Wolfgang Kleinwächter (wolfgang.kleinwaechter@medienkomm.uni-halle.de) to plenary@wsis-cs.org on 18 March 2005.

de La Chappelle, Bertrand (2005), "[WSIS CS-Plenary] On legitimacy", sent by Bertrand de La Chapelle (bdelachapelle@gmail.com) to plenary@wsis-cs.org on 27 September 2005.

McLaughlin, Lisa (2005), "Re: [WSIS CS-Plenary] YJ's objection and the CS-PS statement", sent by Lisa McLaughlin (mclauglm@po.muohio.edu) to plenary@wsis-cs.org on 25 February 2005.

Naughton, Tracey (2003), "media negotiations in Geneva", sent by Tracey Naughton (t.naughton@iafrica.com) to media@wsis-cs.org on 25 Oct 2003.

Panganiban, Rik (2005), "[WSIS CS-Plenary] Re: [WSIS-CT] 'CS' Press release and CS-Private sector common statement", sent by Rik Panganiban (rikp@earthlink.net) to plenary@wsis-cs.org on 4 March 2005.

Park, YJ (2005), "Re: [WSIS-CT] Background of my objection on final statement of Internet Governance Caucus", sent by YJ Park (yjpark@myepark.com) to plenary@wsis-cs.org on 24 February 2005.

(3) WSIS documents, contributions and statements

Africa Regional Conference (2002), *Bamako, 28-30 May 2002 – Final Declaration,* adopted on 30 May 2002, http://www.itu.int/dms_pub/itu-s/md/03/wsispc2/doc/S03-WSISPC2-DOC-0004!!MSW-E.doc

AIBD (Asia-Pacific Institute for Broadcasting Development) (2003), *Bangkok Declaration: Information & Broadcasting in the Asia-Pacific Region,* adopted on 28 May 2003, http://www.itu.int/dms_pub/itu-s/md/03/wsispc3/c/S03-WSISPC3-C-0148!!MSW-E.doc

AMARC (2003c), *Statement by the World Association of Community Broadcasters to PrepCom2*, 23 February 2003, http://www.worldsummit2003.de/en/web/229.htm

AMARC (2003d), *"Community broadcasters demand right to radio spectrum"*, AMARC Press Release, 11 March 2003.

AMARC (2003e), *Contribution to the WSIS process,* 2 June 2003, http://www.itu.int/dms_pub/itu-s/md/03/wsispc3/c/S03-WSISPC3-C-0107!!PDF-E.pdf

AMARC (2003f), *Community media groups call for empowerment agenda at WSIS,* AMARC Press Release (in cooperation with the CMWG), 26 September 2003.

Annan, Kofi (2004), 'Keynote Address to the World Electronic Media Forum', in WEMF (ed.), *Final Report: Radio & TV Fundamental Debates,* p. 11.

Annan, Kofi (2005), *Statement by H. E. Mr. Kofi Annan, The Secretary–General of the United Nations,* Tunis, 16 November 2005, http://www.itu.int/wsis/tunis/statements/docs/io-un-opening/1.pdf

Article19 (2003), *Statement on the right to communicate by Article 19 global campaign for free expression,* http://www.itu.int/dms_pub/itu-s/md/03/wsispc2/c/S03-WSISPC2-C-0095!!PDF-E.pdf

Asia Media Summit (2005), *Recommendations to the WSIS in Tunis,* adopted 11 May 2005, http://www.itu.int/wsis/docs2/thematic/aidb/recommendations.doc

Asia-Pacific Regional Conference (2003), *The Tokyo Declaration – the Asia-Pacific perspective to the WSIS,* adopted 15 January 2003, http://www.itu.int/dms_pub/itu-s/md/03/wsispc2/doc/S03-WSISPC2-DOC-0006!!MSW-E.doc

Bellagio Symposium (2003), *Statement,* adopted on 5 October 2003, Panos Institute, http://www.panos.org.uk/files/Bellagio statement on media freedom and poverty1.doc

CCBI (Coordinating Committee of Business Interlocutors) (2002), *What are the content and themes that business supports for the summit?,* http://www.itu.int/dms_pub/itu-s/md/03/wsispc2/c/S03-WSISPC2-C-0035!!PDF-E.pdf

CCPFO (Coordinating Committee of Press Freedom Organisations) (2002), *Statement: Press Freedom on the Internet,* http://www.itu.int/ dms_pub/itu-s/md/03/wsispc2/c/S03-WSISPC2-C-0040!!PDF-E.pdf

Chair of the WSIS PrepCom-2 Sub-Committee (2005a), *Compilation of comments on chapter two of the Operational Part (Financial Mechanisms). Part one (Para 12-26),* 19 February 2005, http://www.itu.int/wsis/docs2/pc2/working/dt1-part1.doc

Chair of the WSIS PrepCom-2 Sub-Committee (2005b), *Compilation of comments on chapter one of the Operational Part (Implementation Mechanism),* 5 June 2005, http://www.itu.int/wsis/docs2/pc2/working/dt2rev3.doc

Chair of Sub-Committee B (2005), *Revised chapter two of the Operational Part (Financial Mechanisms),* 8 August 2005, http://www.itu.int/wsis/docs2/ pc3/off7.doc

Chowdury, Iftekhar (2004), 'Statement to Panel1: Media Freedom in General', in WEMF (ed.), *Final Report: Radio & TV Fundamental Debates,* pp. 47-48.

Civil Society Working Group on Content and Themes (2003), *"Seven Musts": Priority Principles Proposed by Civil Society,* 25 February 2003, http://www.worldsummit2003.de/en/web/235.htm

Civil Society Plenary (2003a), *Civil Society Press Release, 26 September 2003,* http://www.worldsummit2003.de/en/web/473.htm

Civil Society Plenary (2003b), *Civil Society Statement at the End of the Preparatory Process for the World Summit on the Information Society,* Geneva, 14 November 2003, http://www.worldsummit2003.de/ download_en/CS-press-statement-14-11-03-final.rtf

Civil Society Plenary (2003c), *"Shaping Information Societies for Human Needs": Civil Society Declaration to the World Summit on the Information Society*, http://www.worldsummit2003.de/download_en/ WSIS-CS-Dec-25-Feb-04-en.pdf

Civil Society Plenary (2005), *"Much more could have been achieved": Civil Society Statement on the World Summit on the Information Society,* http://www.worldsummit2003.de/download_en /WSIS-CS-summit-statement-rev1-23-12-2005-en.pdf

CMWG (Community Media Working Group) (2003a), *Community Media and the WSIS – Statement on the Draft Declaration of Principles and the Draft Action Plan,* 16 July 2003.
CMWG (2003b), *Community Media and the Information Society – Statement on the draft Declaration and Action Plan,* 8 September 2003.
CMWG (2003c), *Community Media and the Information Society – Statement on the Draft Declaration and Action Plan,* 15 September 2003.
CMWG (2003d), *Amendments to the revised Action Plan*, 24 September 2003.
CMWG (2003e), *Statement on community media for civil society press conference*, 25 September 2003.
CMWG (2003f), *Community media demand real "access for all",* Press Release (in cooperation with AMARC), 9 December 2003.
CMWG (2003g), *Invitation to a press point – World Summit on the Information Society: community media demand real "access for all",* 10 December 2003.
CMWG (2005), *Community Radio Fund for Africa,* Civil Society Intervention on Financing, delivered to the WSIS PrepCom by Lettie Longwe, 18 February 2005.
Cohen, Fred (2004), 'Comments on Article 3 (paragraphs 1-2-4) of the WSIS Broadcasters' Declaration, in WEMF (ed.), *Final Report: Radio & TV Fundamental Debates,* p. 21.
Community Media Forum (2003), *Community Media Forum,* programme flyer distributed at the WSIS summit in Geneva, http://www.communicationrights.org/BFA_flyer.pdf
Community Media Initiative (2003), *Contribution by the Community Media Initiative to the Drafting Process,* http://www.worldsummit2003.de/en/web/229.htm
Couchepin, Pascal (2003), *Address by the President of the Swiss Confederation – Closure of the World Summit on the Information Society, Geneva, 12 December 2003,* http://www.itu.int/wsis/geneva/coverage/statement/closing/couchepin.pdf
CSIS (Citizens' Summit on the Information Society) (2005a), *Citizens' Summit on the Information Society (CSIS): First announcement and call for support,* CSIS Press release, 24 October 2005, http://www.worldsummit2003.de/download_en/csis-pr-241005-en.rtf
CSIS (2005b), *CSIS main programme,* http://www.citizens-summit.org/programme.html
Cuban delegation (2003), *Comments and proposals of the Government of the Republic of Cuba on the Draft Declaration of Principles and the Draft Action Plan of the World Summit on the Information Society,* 12 June 2003, http://www.itu.int/dms_pub/itu-s/md/03/wsispc3/c/S03-WSISPC3-C-0104!!MSW-E.doc

Geneva03 (2003a), *About the WSIS?WeSeize! Project,* http://www.geneva03.org/display/about.php
Geneva03 (2003b), *We Seize! Strategic conference programme,* http://www.geneva03.org/sconf/display.php?id=15&lang=en
Geneva03 (2003c), *WSIS?WeSeize! call,* http://www.geneva03.org/display /item_fresh.php?id=1&lang=en
Geneva03 (2003d), *WIPO hit by Little Mermaid,* http://www.geneva03.org /display/item_fresh.php?id=27&lang=en
Hamelink, Cees (2002), 'Keynote at the Opening Session of the Civil Society Sector Meeting at the PrepCom 1 for the World Summit on the Information Society, July 1, 2002, Geneva', *nettime listserve archives* (original source not available anymore), http://www.nettime.org/Lists-Archives/nettime-l-0207/msg00157.htm
IAB (Internatinal Association of Broadcasting) (2002), *Position regarding the World Summit on Information Society,* http://www.itu.int/dms_pub/itu-s/md/03/wsispc2/c/S03-WSISPC2-C-0022!!PDF-E.pdf
IFJ (International Federation of Journalists) (2003), *Quality Journalism for the Information Age – Policy Statement to the United Nations World Summit on the Information Society,* http://www.itu.int/dms_pub/itu-s/md/03/wsispc2/c/S03-WSISPC2-C-0075!!PDF-E.pdf
ITU (2003), *Summit Breaks New Ground with Multi-Stakeholder Approach,* ITU Press Release, 26 September 2003, http://www.itu.int/wsis/ newsroom/press_releases/itu/2003 /prepcom3closure.html
Latin America and Caribbean Regional Conference (2003), *Bávaro Declaration,* adopted on 31 January 2003, http://www.itu.int/dms_pub/itu-s/md/03/wsispc2/doc/S03-WSISPC2-DOC-0007!!MSW-E.doc
Marinho, José Roberto (2004a), 'Comments on Article 2 of the WSIS Broadcasters' Declaration', in WEMF (ed.), *Final Report: Radio & TV Fundamental Debates,* pp. 19-20.
Marinho, José Roberto (2004b), 'Keynote Address to Session 2: Media Freedom and the Information Society', in WEMF (ed.), *Final Report: Radio & TV Fundamental Debates,* pp. 44-45.
Marrakech Conference (2004), *Conference on "Role and Place of Media in the Information Society in Africa and the Arab States": Action Plan,* adopted on 24 November 2004, http://www.itu.int/wsis/docs2/thematic/outcome/morocco-media-plan-action.pdf
Media Caucus (2003a), *Contribution of the Media working group to the PrepCom2,* 20 February 2003, http://www.worldsummit2003.de/en/web/231.htm
Media Caucus (2003b), *Proposal of the Media Caucus for Inclusion in the Final Declaration of PrepCom2*, 24 February 2003.

Media Caucus (2003c), *Unofficial summary of WSIS Media Caucus positions*, 23 July 2003.
Media Caucus (2003d), *PrepCom III – Media Caucus Proposal for Text to be included in the WSIS Declaration*, 16 September 2003.
Media Caucus (2003e), *Media Caucus proposals for changes to the Action Plan,* 18 September 2003.
Media Caucus (2005), *Statement to WSIS II PrepCom 2 on behalf of the Media Caucus*, 23 February 2005.
Media Justice Network (2005), *"Media Justice Now!"*, flyer distributed at the WSIS summit in Tunis, 16-18 November 2005.
Pan-European Conference (2002), *The Bucharest Declaration – Towards an Information Society: principles, Strategy and Priorities for Action,* adopted on 9 November 2002, http://www.itu.int/dms_pub/itu-s/md/03/wsispc2/doc/S03-WSISPC2-DOC-0005!!MSW-E.doc
Pleitgen, Fritz (2004), 'Comments on Article 3 (paragraphs 1-3) of the WSIS Broadcasters' Declaration', in WEMF (ed.), *Final Report: Radio & TV Fundamental Debates,* pp. 20-21.
Private Broadcasting and Print Working group (2003), *Media Caucus Proposals for Changes to the Action Plan*, September 19, 2003
Robinson, Claude (2004), 'Speech delivered to the workshop Public Service Broadcasting Today and Tomorrow', in WEMF (ed.), *Final Report: Radio & TV Fundamental Debates,* pp. 104-105.
Smith, Elizabeth (2004), 'Speech delivered to the workshop Public Service Broadcasting Today and Tomorrow', in WEMF (ed.), *Final Report: Radio & TV Fundamental Debates,* p. 104.
Stock, Jean (2004), 'Statement by Jean Stock, WEMF President, to the WSIS Plenary Session', 12 December 2003, in WEMF (ed.), *Final Report: Radio & TV Fundamental Debates,* pp. 165-166.
Swiss delegation (2003), *Contribution of Switzerland,* 31 May 2003, http://www.itu.int/dms_pub/itu-s/md/03/wsispc3/c/S03-WSISPC3-C-0100!!MSW-E.doc
Swiss delegation (2005), *Submission of the Swiss Delegation,* 20 September 2005, http://www.itu.int/wsis/docs2/pc3/contributions/scb/Swiss.doc
Tanzanian delegation (2003), *Tanzania's contributions to the draft Declaration of Principle and Plan of Action*, 31 May 2003, http://www.itu.int/dms_pub/itu-s/md/03/wsispc3/c/S03-WSISPC3-C-0063!!MSW-E.doc
TFFM (Task Force on Financial Mechanisms) (2004), *Financing ICTD – A review of trends and an analysis of gaps and promising practices. The Report of the Task Force on Financial Mechanisms for ICT for Development,* http://www.itu.int/wsis/tffm/final-report.pdf
UN General Assembly (2002), *Resolution adopted by the General Assembly: 56/183. World Summit on the Information Society,* 31 January 2002 (Resolution adopted 21 December 2001),

http://daccessdds.un.org/doc/UNDOC/GEN/N01/491/83/PDF/N0149183.pdf?OpenElement

Utsumi, Yoshio (2002), WSIS Preparatory Committee Meeting, 1 July 2002, Speech by the Secretary-General of the International Telecommunication Union, http://www.itu.int/wsis/docs/pc1/statements_opening/utsumi.doc

WBU (World Broadcasting Unions) (2003), *Contribution of the World Broadcasting Unions to PrepCom2,* http://www.itu.int/dms_pub/itu-s/md/03/wsispc2/c/S03-WSISPC2-C-0108!!PDF-E.pdf

WEMF (World Electronic Media Forum) (2004), *Final Report: Radio & TV Fundamental Debates,* (downloadable: http://www.wemfmedia.org).

WEMF (2005a), *World Electronic Media Forum II, Tunis 15-16 November 2005,* http://www.wemfmedia.org

WEMF (2005b), *Message of WEMF II to the World Summit on the Information Society (WSIS),* 16 November 2005, http://wemfmedia.org/Message_to_the_WSIS.pdf

Western Asia Regional Conference (2003), *Towards an Information Society in Western Asia: Declaration of Principles (Beirut Declaration),* adopted on 6 February 2003, http://www.itu.int/dms_pub/itu-s/md/03/wsispc2/doc/S03-WSISPC2-DOC-0008!!MSW-E.doc

WFCR (World Forum on Communication Rights) (2003), *World Forum on Communication Rights,* programme leaflet distributed at the WSIS summit in Geneva

WGIG (Working Group on Internet Governance) (2005), *Report from the Working Group on Internet Governance,* http://www.itu.int/wsis/docs2/pc3/off5.pdf

WSIS (2003a), *Declaration of Principles. Building the Information Society: a Global Challenge in the New Millennium,* http://www.itu.int/dms_pub/ itu-s/md/03/wsis/doc/S03/wsis/doc/S03-WSIS-DOC-0004!!PDF-E.pdf

WSIS (2003b), *Plan of Action,* http://www.itu.int/dms_pub/itu-s/md/03/wsis/doc/S03-WSIS-DOC-0005!!PDF-E.pdf

WSIS (2005a), *Tunis Commitment,* http://www.itu.int/wsis/docs2/tunis/off/7.pdf

WSIS (2005b), *Tunis Agenda for the Information Society,* http://www.itu.int/wsis/docs2/tunis/off/6rev1.pdf

WSIS Executive Secretariat (2002a), *Report by the Chairman of Subcommittee 1 on Rules of Procedure*, 4 July 2002, http://www.itu.int/dms_pub/itu-s/md/02/wsispc1/doc/S02-WSISPC1-DOC-0009!!MSW-E.doc

WSIS Executive Secretariat (2002b), *Outcome of the informal meeting of sub-committee 2 of PrepCom 1 of the WSIS*, 18 September 2002, http://www.itu.int/wsis/docs/im/content_themes /non_papers/final_report.doc

WSIS Executive Secretariat (2003a), *Civil Society & NGO Open Ended Bureau: Proposal / 30 January 2003*, http//www.union-network.org/UNIsite/In_Depth/Interna_Relations /WSIS /CivilSocietyNGOBureauProposal.pdf.

WSIS Executive Secretariat (2003b), *Draft Declaration – Based on the Discussions in the Working Group of Sub-Committee 2,* 25 February 2003, http://www.itu.int/dms_pub/itu-s/md/03/wsispc2/td/030217/ S03-WSISPC2-030217-TD-GEN-0002!!MSW-E.doc

WSIS Executive Secretariat (2003c), *Draft Action Plan – Based on Discussions in the Working Group of Sub-Committee 2,* 27 February 2003, http://www.itu.int/dms_pub/itu-s/md/03/wsispc2/td/030217/S03-WSISPC2-030217-TD-GEN-0003!!MSW-E.doc

WSIS Executive Secretariat (2003d), *Draft Declaration of Principles,* 21 March 2003, http://www.itu.int/dms_pub/itu-s/md/03/wsispcip/td/ 030721/S03-WSISPCIP-030721-TD-GEN-0001!!MSW-E.doc

WSIS Executive Secretariat (2003e), *Draft Action Plan,* 20 June 2003, http://www.itu.int/dms_pub/itu-s/md/03/wsispcip/td/030721/ S03WSISPCIP-030721-TD-GEN-0005!!MSW-E.doc

WSIS Executive Secretariat (2003f), *Draft Declaration of Principles (Based on discussions at the WSIS inter-sessional),* 18 July 2003, http://www.itu.int/dms_pub/itu-s/md/03/wsispcip/td/030721/ S03WSISPCIP-030721-TD-GEN-0004!R3!MSW-E.doc

WSIS Executive Secretariat (2005), *Compilation of comments received on the report of the Working Group on Internet Governance (WGIG),* 23 September 2003, http://www.itu.int/wsis/docs2/pc3/working/dt7rev2.pdf

All Internet addresses were accessed and checked in December 2006.

(4) Interviews

Acr.	Name	Organisation	Date of interview	Location
AC	Adilson Cabral	University Rio de Janeiro	21 March 2004	Email
BM	Bianca Miglioretto	Radio Lora	9 April 2004	Email
CD	Christoph Dietz	CAMECO	18 March 2004	Hamburg
FW	Frieda Werden	Wings/AMARC	5 April 2004	Email
MC	Maria Victoria Cabrera	AMARC	26 April 2004	Email
MG	Miren Gutierrez	IPS	19 April 2004	Email
MH	Marion Hamm	Indymedia	13 May 2004	Email
MJ	MJ Kim	MediAct/APC	3 May 2004	Email
PA	PatchA	Jinbonet/APC	9 May 2004	Email
SB	Steve Buckley	AMARC	21 July 2003	London
TN	Tracey Naughton	MISA/Nyaka	23 March 2004	Email
VO	Victor van Oeyen	ALER	28 March 2004	Email
WL	Wolf Ludwig	comedia	25 Sept. 2003	Geneva

Medien & Politik

hrsg. von Hans J. Kleinsteuber in Zusammenarbeit mit der Arbeitsstelle Medien und Politik an der Universität Hamburg

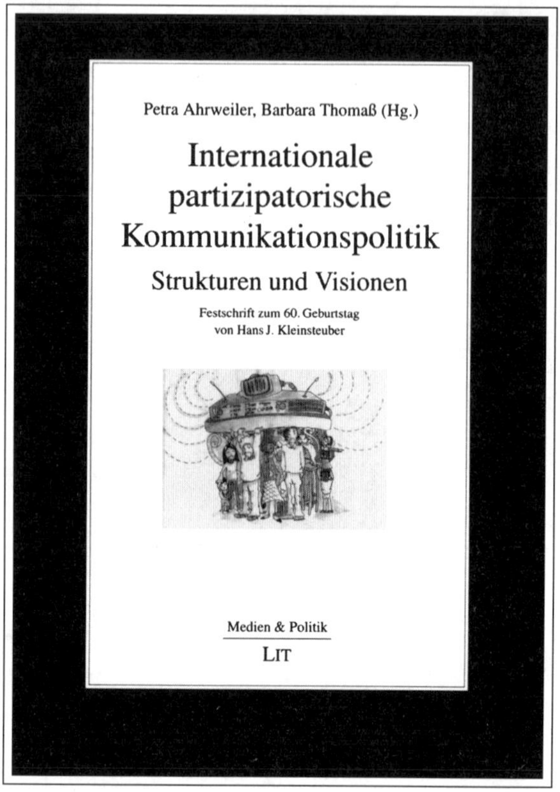

Petra Ahrweiler; Barbara Thomaß (Hg.)
Internationale partizipatorische Kommunikationspolitik
Strukturen und Visionen. Festschrift zum 60. Geburtstag von Hans J. Kleinsteuber

Diese Festschrift zu Ehren von Hans J. Kleinsteubers 60. Geburtstag verbindet zwei zentrale Themenstellungen in der Kommunikationspolitik: die Frage nach dem Potential neuer Kommunikationstechnologien für eine partizipatorische Gestaltung von Gesellschaft und die Frage nach den Möglichkeiten grenzenloser transkultureller Kommunikation. Im Buch wird sowohl eine Bestandsaufnahme geleistet, als auch die Entwicklung begründeter Visionen in Angriff genommen, die das partizipatorische Potential von Medien ausbauen, interkulturelle Kommunikation stärken und Vielfalt – der Angebote, Anbieter und Nutzungsweisen – auch für die weltweite Kommunikation realisieren können.

Bd. 29, 2005, 248 S., 24,90 €, br., ISBN 3-8258-9135-6

LIT Verlag Berlin – Hamburg – London – Münster – Wien – Zürich
Fresnostr. 2 48159 Münster
Tel.: 0251 / 620 32 22 – Fax: 0251 / 922 60 99
e-Mail: vertrieb@lit-verlag.de – http://www.lit-verlag.de

Jens Althoff
Der Faktor Glaubwürdigkeit in Wahlkämpfen
Aufbau, Verlust und Verteidigung durch professionalisierte Kommunikationsstrategien
Glaubwürdigkeit ist eine immer noch unterschätzte Schlüsselkategorie der politischen Kommunikation, deren Bedeutung in der Mediendemokratie wächst. Mit professionalisierten Kommunikationsstrategien müssen zunehmend ungebundene Wähler immer wieder neu gewonnen werden, wobei die Images von Kandidaten und Parteien eine zentrale Rolle spielen. Wirklich überzeugen kann aber nur, wer als vertrauenswürdig wahrgenommen wird und wer glaubwürdig kommuniziert. Ob und wie das den politischen Akteuren im Vergleich gelingt, wird am Beispiel des Bundestagswahlkampfes 2002 untersucht. Insgesamt wird die Funktion des Faktors Glaubwürdigkeit mit einem interdisziplinären Ansatz umfassend aufgearbeitet und geklärt.
Bd. 35, 2008, 320 S., 29,90 €, br., ISBN 978-3-8258-1354-3

LIT Verlag Berlin – Hamburg – London – Münster – Wien – Zürich
Fresnostr. 2 48159 Münster
Tel.: 0251 / 620 32 22 – Fax: 0251 / 922 60 99
e-Mail: vertrieb@lit-verlag.de – http://www.lit-verlag.de

Sebastian Feuß

Die imaginäre Kampagne

Eine Untersuchung der Presseberichterstattung vor und nach der Bundestagswahl 2005

Für Gerhard Schröder war am Abend der Bundestagswahl 2005 in der „Berliner Runde" des ZDF klar: Die Medien hatten ihn und seine rot-grüne Regierung aus dem Amt schreiben wollen. Der Ex-Kanzler witterte eine Kampagne, eine Verschwörung der Medien gegen ihn. Lag der einstmalige Medienkanzler mit seiner Behauptung richtig? Diese Untersuchung der für die Meinungsbildung maßgebenden Printmedien zeigt, dass Schröders pauschaler Vorwurf nicht zutrifft. Es bestanden deutliche Unterschiede zwischen konservativen und progressiven Medien hinsichtlich der Forcierung eines Regierungswechsels.

Bd. 34, 2008, 112 S., 14,90 €, br., ISBN 978-3-8258-1207-2

LIT Verlag Berlin – Hamburg – London – Münster – Wien – Zürich
Fresnostr. 2 48159 Münster
Tel.: 0251 / 620 32 22 – Fax: 0251 / 922 60 99
e-Mail: vertrieb@lit-verlag.de – http://www.lit-verlag.de

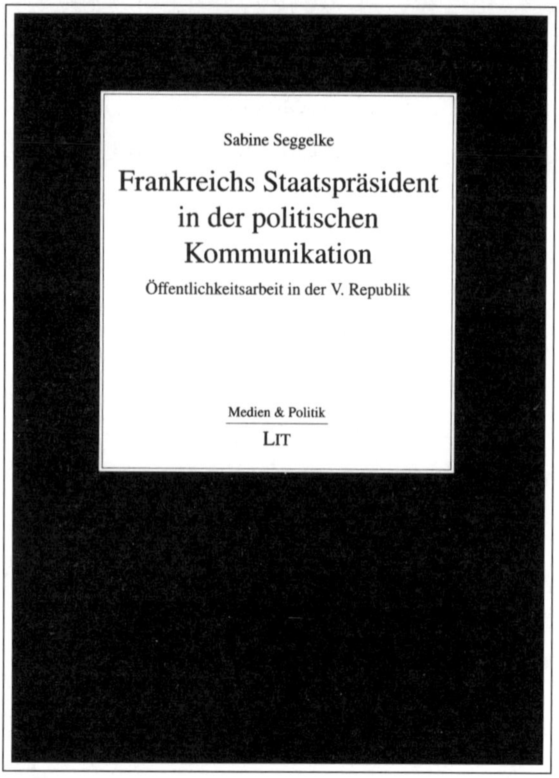

Sabine Seggelke
Frankreichs Staatspräsident in der politischen Kommunikation
Öffentlichkeitsarbeit in der V. Republik

Die Studie leistet einen Beitrag zur Erforschung der politischen Kommunikation in Frankreich. Die Kommunikationsstrategien der französischen Staatspräsidenten werden von den Anfängen der V. Republik bis zum gescheiterten Referendum zum Europäischen Verfassungsvertrag 2005 untersucht. Dabei werden institutionelle Veränderungen, etwa die Amtszeitverkürzung, ebenso analysiert wie die veränderten Erwartungen, die die „Mediengesellschaft" an das Staatsoberhaupt im Elyseepalast heranträgt. Das Spannungsfeld zwischen den Leitideen des Präsidentenamtes und den Anforderungen der Medienlogik verdeutlicht ein integriertes Modell, an dem sich auch die Anforderungen ablesen lassen, die 2007 den nächsten französischen Staatspräsidenten erwarten.

Bd. 33, 2007, 368 S., 34,90 €, br., ISBN 978-3-8258-9975-2

LIT Verlag Berlin – Hamburg – London – Münster – Wien – Zürich
Fresnostr. 2 48159 Münster
Tel.: 0251 / 620 32 22 – Fax: 0251 / 922 60 99
e-Mail: vertrieb@lit-verlag.de – http://www.lit-verlag.de